CW01081303

SHINING PATH

Liverpool Latin American Studies

Liverpool Latin American Studies, New Series 6

Shining Path

Guerrilla War in Peru's Northern Highlands, 1980–1997

Lewis Taylor

LIVERPOOL UNIVERSITY PRESS

First published 2006 by
Liverpool University Press
4 Cambridge Street
Liverpool L69 7ZU

Copyright © 2006 Lewis Taylor

The right of Lewis Taylor to be identified as the author
of this work has been asserted by him in accordance
with the Copyright, Designs and Patents Act, 1988

All rights reserved. No part of this book may be reproduced,
stored in a retrieval system, or transmitted, in any form or
by any means, electronic, mechanical, photocopying, recording,
or otherwise without the prior written permission of the publisher.

British Library Cataloguing-in-Publication data
A British Library CIP record is available

ISBN 1-84631-004-0 cased
1-84631-016-4 limp

ISBN-13 978-1-86431-004-1
ISBN-13 978-1-84631-016-4

Typeset in by XL Publishing Services, Tiverton
Printed and bound in the European Union by MPG Books Ltd, Bodmin

For my mother and in memory of my father

Human appetites are insatiable, for since from nature they have the ability and the wish to desire all things, and from fortune the ability to achieve few of them, there constantly results from this a discontent in human minds and a disgust with the things they possess.

Discourses on Livy
Niccolò Machiavelli

Contents

Preface

During the 1980s and early 1990s Peru suffered one of the bloodiest civil wars in contemporary Latin American history as the state attempted to quell the insurrection launched by the Partido Comunista del Perú–Sendero Luminoso (PCP–SL), commonly known as Sendero Luminoso (Shining Path). According to the Truth and Reconciliation Commission report of August 2003, an estimated 69,280 people lost their lives, of which 79 per cent were inhabitants of rural areas and 56 per cent were peasants. Some 54 per cent of fatalities occurred at the hands of the PCP–SL.[1] Most of the fighting took place in the Andes, with the highland population participating as both passive victims and protagonists who exercised a determining influence on the outcome of the struggle.

Within a situation of generalised violence (by 1992 guerrilla activity was occurring in twenty-one of Peru's twenty-four departments), one important theatre of conflict was the northern highlands. Hostilities here centred on the provinces of San Marcos and Cajabamba in the department of Cajamarca and the neighbouring provinces of Pataz, Julcán, Sánchez Carrión, Otuzco and Santiago de Chuco, located in the *sierra* of the department of La Libertad. As this area housed a considerable rural population in a mountainous terrain well suited to unconventional warfare, the PCP–SL selected it as the nodal point for guerrilla activity on its 'Northern Front'. Despite the fact that this region was allocated a high priority by the PCP–SL (from 1984 until his arrest in June 1988, the insurgency here was directed by Osmán Morote, one of the organisation's leading cadres), developments here remain unresearched. Accordingly, this monograph aims to fill a gap in the literature on the civil war in Peru post-1980. It does not pretend to provide a definitive history of the war in the northern Andes, for many individual experiences remain untold, while alternative interpretations are possible of the events described in the following pages. Hopefully, though, this volume will stimulate further research and debate around these events.

The book opens with a review of the literature on the PCP–SL. The aim in Chapter One is to provide the non-specialist reader with an introduction to the topic and an idea as to how publications on the PCP–SL rebellion have evolved since the early 1980s. Special attention is paid to recent research that focuses on trends in peasant–guerrilla relations during the last ten years. Chapter Two provides a geographical description of the study area, outlines its chief socio-economic characteristics and details some of the main social and political developments that took place in the zone during the period leading up to the onset of guerrilla activity. Chapter Three describes the mechanisms employed by the PCP–SL as it attempted to build up its party structure in the environs of Cajabamba–Huamachuco during the early phase of the insurrection, while Chapter Four analyses why the organisation was able to expand and intensify its level of operations between 1983 and 1992. Chapter Five examines the factors that caused the PCP–SL to enter into a period of retreat in the years after 1992 and details the state of peasant organisation in the zone in the aftermath of civil war. Finally, in the concluding chapter, some points of similarity and contrast are made between the trajectory of the conflict in the northern highlands and those described in recent monographs examining developments in other regions of Peru. The findings are also discussed in relation to more general scholarly work that addresses questions of rural revolt and revolution.

Financial support for this study was generously provided by the Nuffield Foundation. Fieldwork was carried out in March–April 1997, December 1998–January 1999 and March–April 2000, when the findings of the research were discussed with a number of key informants. In many respects, undertaking the fieldwork (which consisted of interviews and the revision of archival documentation) proved more difficult than writing the book. Given the sensitive nature of the research topic, ample scope existed for misinterpreting motives. Careful attention was therefore paid to devising the least risky method of entering the study area and establishing a modus operandi with strategically placed officials (subprefects, mayors, judges, police and army personnel, etc.), whose permission and neutrality was essential if the project was to proceed. No problems were encountered on this front. Indeed, access was gained to confidential intelligence reports and a number of extended interviews were conducted with key players in the events described. Assistance from these sources is gratefully acknowledged, as well as from the friends who facilitated access to these influential individuals. Owing to a tense situation in 1999 and 2000 relating to unsatisfactory prison conditions, it was unfortunately not possible to interview PCP–SL cadres housed in Cajamarca's maximum-security prison. Any future study will need to incorporate their voice.

Having previously been involved in organising peasant federations in the study area, I already possessed a wide network of well-established contacts, who proved invaluable in facilitating access to the rural and urban population under circumstances where a sufficient level of trust existed for frank discussion to take place. Without their collaboration, it would have been impossible to obtain the necessary data. My greatest debt is to these *compañeros*, whose friendship and solidarity has lasted over many years. In order to protect the identity of both official and non-official informants, interviews are numbered and some place names have been altered. Confidential documents and other written sources whose disclosure might jeopardise personal safety have not been referenced fully. Whenever a person is named in the text, her/his involvement in the events described is already in the public domain. Because of its delicate nature, a certain amount of information that backs up the arguments made in the study has had to be excluded on the grounds that it might endanger an individual's security.

The final product has benefited from discussions that arose at seminar presentations at the Institutes of Latin American Studies at the universities of Liverpool, London and Oxford. I am grateful to my colleagues at the Institute of Latin American Studies at Liverpool, who assumed added responsibilities while I was on research leave in order to finish this manuscript. Finally, I owe a special debt to Orin Starn, who passed perceptive comments on the draft manuscript. The usual disclaimers apply.

1. For a summary, see Peru Support Group, *The Findings of Peru's Truth and Reconciliation Commission*. London: Peru Support Group, 2004

List of Tables, Figures and Maps

TABLES

FIGURES

MAPS

List of Abbreviations

ADC/CSJ/CC   Archivo Departamental de Cajamarca/
Corte Superior de Justicia/Causas Criminales

ADC/FDP/SpC   Archivo Departamental de Cajamarca/
Fondo Documental de la Prefectura/
Subprefectura de Cajamarca

ADC/FDP/SpCb   Archivo Departamental de Cajamarca/ Fondo
Documental de la Prefectura/ Subprefectura de
Cajabamba

ADC/FDP/P   Archivo Departamental de Cajamarca/ Fondo
Documental de la Prefectura/ Prefectura

ADC/FDP/Pa   Archivo Departamental de Cajamarca/ Fondo
Documental de la Prefectura/ Particulares

AFA/EACh/C   Archivo del Fuero Agrario/ Correspondencia de la
Empresa Agrícola Chicama/Cochabamba

CHAPTER ONE

Maoism in the Andes

My first contact with the Partido Comunista del Perú–Sendero Luminoso (PCP–SL), popularly known as Sendero Luminoso, occurred in late September 1979 when attending an *escuela campesina* (training workshop) for peasant activists, held outside the town of Cajamarca in Peru's northern highlands. At this event, which had been organised by the country's largest peasant syndicate, the Confederación Campesina del Perú (CCP) – Peruvian Peasants Federation – some fifty participants debated a whole range of rural issues over three days. At the conclusion of the first afternoon's session, approximately ten *campesinos* retired to an adjacent room, where it could be seen through the glass windows that they were engaged in an intense discussion. Upon enquiry, I was told that they were members of a fringe revolutionary group called Sendero Luminoso (Shining Path), which was planning to launch an insurgency aimed at the overthrow of the Peruvian state.

Later that evening, in a surreal scene worthy of Federico Fellini and to the amusement of several observers, the *senderistas* found themselves seated in a bar next to a group of Peruvian army officers from the local garrison. Although one or two of the soldiers cast the occasional suspicious eye over those drinking at the adjoining table, the only communication between the two parties occurred when one of the *campesinos* needed to borrow a match to light his cigarette. Over the following two hours, the soldiers remained blissfully unaware that they would shortly be engaged in mortal combat with the seemingly unassuming peasants sitting nearby. They probably never realised that they had been in a position to detain a number of the PCP–SL's leading rural organisers well before the insurrection in the northern highlands got under way. For their part, the *campesino* revolutionaries – like everyone else living in Peru at the time – most likely failed to comprehend fully the consequences of the course of action upon which they had embarked. Bitter combat with the military who sat alongside them was wholly predictable, as it was with other representatives of the state and easily identifiable class enemies. Perhaps a personal bloody end could be envisaged, but could they have anticipated the many twists and turns their insurrection was to produce? Could the consequences of pitting village against village, family against family and even relative against relative have been foreseen?

In addition to symbolising the violent intimacy that partly characterised the civil war, encapsulated in this vignette are two issues crucial to determining the outcome of any unconventional conflict. The first is the relationship of anti-systemic armed organisations to the civilian population (essentially, their ability to devise an ideological discourse, a political programme and an everyday mode of operation that appeals to subaltern groups, offers them a plausible alternative world view and maintains mass loyalty under difficult circumstances). The second issue is the capacity of the state in the intelligence field and the efficacy of counter-insurgency measures implemented by its civil and military branches.

Accordingly, the aim of this introductory chapter is to anchor the rest of the book by providing an overview of three key bodies of literature on Peru's civil war. First, the origins, ideology, strategy and tactics of the PCP–SL are outlined in some detail, for without a sound appreciation of these it would be difficult to understand the motives behind the organisation's activities in the northern highlands. Second, key texts are reviewed that discuss the wide range of inter-actions that occurred in different areas of rural Peru between PCP–SL 'fish' and the peasant 'river' in which they endeavoured to swim during the 1980s and 1990s. Finally, the chapter provides a summary of publications that detail the efforts of the Peruvian state to quash the insurrection. I have assumed that the reader possesses no prior knowledge of these issues, but through a consid-eration of this literature, the manner in which the civil war in the northern highlands unfolded can be placed in a wider context. This also enables points of comparison and contrast to be made between developments in the northern Andes and events taking place elsewhere in the Peruvian *sierra*.

PCP–SL early development and the road to insurrection

If the soldiers in the bar erred through ignorance, I committed the mistake of minimising what was afoot. Being informed about the PCP–SL's insurrec-tionary agenda failed to impress me. Although most left organisations active in Peru at that time had a programmatic commitment to the need to 'smash the bourgeois state' through armed struggle, in practice, the leadership cliques that dominated these parties were creating, breaking and recreating coalitions with confusing rapidity as they attempted to position themselves advantageously to contest the general elections scheduled for May 1980. I was further under-whelmed by my initial encounter with the PCP–SL when respected friends who had a detailed knowledge of the Peruvian left intimated that 'Sendero' was not a serious outfit. The prevailing view among activists was that a combination of dogmatism, unsophisticated social analysis and adherence to a maximalist programme seemingly divorced from current realities placed the party firmly on the exotic margins of Marxist politics in Peru. Sendero Luminoso was destined, I was reliably informed, to be an insignificant bystander in the approaching political struggles that would accompany Peru's return to elected government after more than a decade of military control.[1] Like many other observers not cognizant of developments unfolding over these months in the south-central highland department of Ayacucho, it therefore came as something of a surprise when the PCP–SL initiated guerrilla activities on 17 May 1980 with the symbolic burning of the electoral list and ballot boxes in the *ayacuchano* village of Chuschi. What road had this organisation travelled along to reach this defining moment in its history?

In all probability, the *senderistas* attending the Cajamarca workshop were being informed of the policies decided at the First National Congress, which had been held during the previous week. Celebrated to the slogan of 'Define and Decide', this event represented the culmination of a process that had been unfolding since the early 1960s, when, along with most of the international communist movement, the Peruvian Communist Party (PCP) divided into pro-Moscow and pro-Beijing factions. A central point of criticism levelled by the dissidents at the incumbent PCP leadership was their failure to take the question of armed struggle seriously; it was argued that they had adopted 'opportunist' and 'conciliatory' positions. On these grounds, a pro-Chinese group led by the lawyer Saturnino Paredes split away shortly after the PCP's Fourth National Conference, which was held in January 1964. They formed a new organisation named the Partido Comunista del Perú–Bandera Roja (PCP–BR), or 'Red Flag', and took with them most of the PCP's youth section and a majority of the members who served on the various regional committees, including those responsible for overseeing party activity in the department of Ayacucho (see Map 1).[2]

One abiding characteristic of the Peruvian left has been a tendency for factionalism and fragmentation, so it came as no surprise that the new organisation did not hold together for long. Accusations were made that Paredes had embezzled funds destined to maintain Bandera Roja's full-time organisers in the countryside, but this aside, dissension centred on the recurrent charge that the PCP–BR Central Committee was not making a serious attempt to construct the military apparatus necessary to wage revolutionary warfare in Peru. The outcome was a split in 1967 headed by the regional committee of the Central Region, whose members edited a newspaper entitled *Patria Roja* ('Red Homeland') and proceeded to form a new Maoist party called the PCP–Patria Roja.

While these events were unfolding, Sendero Luminoso's future general secretary and chief ideologue, Abimael Guzmán, who, as well as being a prominent figure on the Ayacucho regional committee had national responsibilities for agitation and propaganda in Bandera Roja, was biding his time. Although he was an important player in the organisation and already headed a faction opposed to Paredes, it was not until 1970 that Guzmán calculated that the moment was opportune to abandon the PCP–BR and form yet another Maoist organisation, the Partido Comunista del Perú–Sendero Luminoso. Once again, a key point of rupture was the accusation that the PCP–BR leadership was only paying lip service to the need to put the party on a war footing in order to pursue armed struggle.[3]

At the time of its foundation, Sendero Luminoso's membership and influ-

Map 1 *Peru: Departments and Major Cities*

ence were concentrated heavily in the small highland town of Ayacucho and supplemented by a sparse network of members located in Lima and a few other conurbations. Within its heartland, party activity centred on the Universidad Nacional San Cristóbal de Huamanga (UNSCH), where Abimael Guzmán lectured in philosophy. He also occupied the influential position of Director of Personnel, which provided opportunity for hiring and firing, as well as for the creation of patronage ties among teachers and non-academic employees. Another leading cadre, Antonio Díaz Martínez, held the equally strategic post of Director of Student Welfare. This office enabled Díaz to allocate grants and provide access to university accommodation and the subsidised canteen (all matters of crucial importance to students from poor economic backgrounds). Utilising these power bases to maximum effect between 1970 and 1973, the PCP–SL was able to achieve a measure of ascendancy inside the institution. It controlled the students' representative body (the Federación de Estudiantes) and enjoyed a determining presence in the UNSCH's chief decision-making organ, the Executive Council. A predominant position was also established in the local schoolteachers union, which complemented Sendero's most solid base within the university, the Department of Education.[4]

During these early years (1970–72), the PCP–SL dedicated its energies almost exclusively to proselytising within the UNSCH and defining its ideological position. At this stage in its evolution, the leadership stance was that the organisation had first to attain programmatic coherence and acquire the 'correct line'. Once this had been accomplished there was to follow a 'return to the masses', and the task of 'reconstructing the Communist Party' could begin in earnest. To implement the first phase, cadres embarked upon a study of the work of Peru's most important Marxist thinker, José Carlos Mariátegui, with a fervour that would have impressed a Talmudic scholar.[5] This period of introspection was deemed to have been completed by late 1972, and, during a Plenary Session held early in the following year, the PCP–SL Central Committee concluded that the second phase of the organisation's development could commence.

Paradoxically, this initiative occurred at the very time when the party's influence in Ayacucho came under increased challenge and began to wane on a number of fronts. Within the UNSCH, important changes in the composition of students and lecturers (a rise in the number originating from outside the environs of Ayacucho, who tended to have a more 'cosmopolitan' outlook) and growing resentment at Sendero's sectarian and authoritarian behaviour led the organisation to cede control of the Federación de Estudiantes in 1973. This setback was compounded by the loss of its predominant position on the university's Executive Council during the following year. To complicate matters, rival left political parties with larger memberships and a higher national profile, such as the Movimiento de Izquierda Revolucionaria (MIR), or Movement of the Revolutionary Left, and Vanguardia Revolucionaria (VR) – Revolutionary Vanguard – increased their presence in Ayacucho and began to contest the same political terrain as the PCP–SL. In addition to suffering reverses within the

university, Sendero Luminoso found, between 1973 and 1977, that its partici-
pation and influence diminished vis-à-vis other organisations prominent within
Ayacucho's social and political milieu. These included the Federación
Departamental de Comunidades y Campesinos de Ayacucho (FEDCCA), or
Departmental Federation of Communities and Peasants of Ayacucho; the
Federación de Barrios de Ayacucho (FBA) – Federation of Neighbourhoods of
Ayacucho; and the Frente de Defensa del Pueblo de Ayacucho (FDPA), or
Front for the Defence of the People of Ayacucho. The FDPA was an umbrella
organisation that played a decisive role in mobilising a large segment of the rural
and urban population in June 1969 to oppose government attempts to intro-
duce charges for secondary school pupils.[6]

While between 1973 and 1977 the PCP–SL experienced an erosion of its once
hegemonic position inside the UNSCH, lost ground within Ayacucho's popular
organisations and played a peripheral role in the social movements emerging at
the time in Lima and other large urban centres, over these years the Party did
embark upon a process of internal consolidation that was crucial to its future
growth and development. To achieve this, it followed to the letter Lenin's classic
argument that a revolutionary party cannot be built on the quicksand of ideological confusion; it was therefore necessary to 'first divide and then unite'
around a common programme, the guiding principle being: 'Better fewer, but
better'.[7] Once these fundamentals had been accomplished, a revolutionary
organisation could then project itself outwards and insert itself into society
successfully. Copying the Bolshevik model, the PCP–SL first formed study
groups among university students. It later enrolled participants from other
sectors of Ayacucho's urban population, the key texts employed being documents detailing Sendero Luminoso's interpretation of Mariátegui's social
analysis and political thought, along with an assessment of its application to the
current situation in Peru. Pursued in a quietly effective fashion, these activities
yielded positive results, as recruits were indoctrinated and integrated into the
cell structure in a steady flow.

Having built up a layer of militants primarily in the town of Ayacucho and
the neighbouring settlement of Huanta, in April 1977 the leadership decided
that emphasis needed to be given to the 'reconstruction' of the party in the
countryside. Accordingly, 1977 and 1978 witnessed the relocation of activists
to Ayacucho's rural districts. Their implantation in the villages was facilitated
by the peasant roots of many cadres, who came from families that had recently
migrated from the countryside to populate the *pueblos jóvenes* (new neighbourhoods) that were mushrooming around the outskirts of the highland towns. The
fact that UNSCH students from families who still resided in surrounding
villages comprised another important component of PCP–SL membership also
eased the party's task. Both groups possessed strong kinship and friendship ties
with their home communities and, consequently, the suspicion with which
newcomers were viewed initially was less intense.

Hand in hand with the drive to establish a base among the peasantry,
attempts were made through networks of students and schoolteachers who had

graduated from the UNSCH to build up the apparatus in the neighbouring departments of Apurímac, Huancavelica and Junín. Simultaneously, cadres experienced in student politics were sent on recruiting missions to universities in other regions of Peru. Using contacts established through participation in the Frente Estudiantil Revolucionario (FER) – the Revolutionary Student Front, an organisation that linked radical students throughout Peru's university system – PCP–SL cells were formed in Puno, Huancayo, Chiclayo and other provincial capitals. A presence was also established in a number of universities in Lima, particularly the country's leading engineering establishment (the Universidad Nacional de Ingeniería) and the Universidad San Martín de Porres, located in a working-class district close to the city centre. The 'reconstruction' process undertaken between 1978 and 1980 was also assisted by the absorption of a number of small revolutionary sects into the PCP–SL and by independent leftists with no party affiliation. Sendero Luminoso's ranks at this juncture were further supplemented by 'capturing' individual members active in rival revolutionary organisations, who happened to be dissatisfied with the lack of commitment to insurrectionary politics shown by the leaders of the MIR, VR and other groups that had embarked upon an electoral path and were beginning to be absorbed into 'the system'.[8]

The questions of party growth, strategy and the policies that needed to be adopted by the PCP–SL in view of current political circumstances, came under scrutiny at a decisive Plenary Session of the Central Committee, which opened on 17 March 1980. A key item on the agenda involved the leadership in an assessment of the extent to which the accords of the First National Congress of September 1979 had been implemented. After a considerable amount of acrimonious discussion and despite the opposition of a significant bloc on the Central Committee, the Guzmán position prevailed. He argued that the recruitment drive had yielded positive results. Moreover, the policy geared 'to reconstruct the Party to wage war' ('*reconstruir el Partido en función de guerra*'), had been carried through to a point where conditions existed to begin armed struggle. The General Secretary further posited that Peru was living through a developing revolutionary situation. To take full advantage of the favourable circumstances and deepen existing socio-political contradictions, Guzmán maintained that 'the militarisation of the Party through armed actions ... is an immediate task. The groundwork for this has already been laid ... The Party has gone forward and is now able to commence armed struggle'.[9] When this line was approved by the Central Committee, the PCP–SL crossed the Rubicon: in order to promote the 'militarisation of the Party' and create a 'war machine' ('*una máquina de guerra*'), its First Military School was held in early April 1980. Armed actions started during the following month. Few people realised it at the time, but the momentous decisions taken by a handful of leading cadres at this meeting were to affect the lives of millions of Peruvians and set in motion one of the most sanguinary conflicts experienced in the recent history of Latin America.

An important swathe of the PCP–SL's Central Committee (labelled by

Guzmán 'rightist opportunists') remained unconvinced by the General Secretary's brazenly optimistic analysis of the political conjuncture, or by the argument that the Party was equipped to wage guerrilla warfare (given its limited numerical strength, organisational fragility outside the core area of Ayacucho and its lack of military preparation). In fact, the 'reconstruction' of Sendero's apparatus during the 1970s had been accomplished to a far greater degree than the state's intelligence services, the Lima-based political class and even well-informed members of the Peruvian left had imagined. According to one of the most authoritative analysts of this stage in the PCP–SL's evolution:

> While it was true that a number of regional and zonal committees were very weak, each one had a basic structure in place and was functioning. They had all already undertaken some operations. The PCP–SL was far from a small or insignificant organisation when it commenced armed actions. On the contrary, it was a party that plotted every step on the road to war in a meticulous fashion.[10]

When evaluating the operational capacity of the PCP–SL apparatus in 1981, the assessment was that a year after the onset of guerrilla activity:

> Sendero was stronger than assumed. It also possessed greater weaknesses than were suspected. With regard to the former, Sendero was a much larger and more disciplined organisation than almost everyone thought, then or later. It was established over a wider area, with a basic but effective communications system and a centralised command structure, which guaranteed unified control over the party apparatus at all times.
>
> Regarding the weaknesses, the experience that Sendero had of military matters was poor. Its strategic perspective was clearly developed, although at the level of day-to-day tactical operations, a generalised ignorance prevailed. What existed at this time, was an organisation that was competent in general terms, one that possessed committed activists who were nevertheless inexperienced. It also lacked a layer of well-prepared middle-ranking cadres.[11]

Subsequent events confirmed the assessment that by 1980 PCP–SL had managed to establish a cadre structure capable of launching and surviving the crucial opening phase of an unconventional war. Various explanations have been advanced to account for its ability to attract sufficient members in the late 1970s and place the Party in such an unexpected position. One argument propounded frequently concerns the appeal of its political message to a particular strata of the Peruvian population.[12] In view of this, and given that: (i) Sendero's actions cannot be understood fully without a knowledge of its ideology and political strategy; and (ii) an appreciation of how the organisation devised its doctrine and policy provides important insights into the Party's day-to-day mode of operation, it is to a consideration of these issues that we now turn.

The roots of PCP–SL ideology: José Carlos Mariátegui

The fact that Sendero Luminoso derived its name from the Frente Estudiantil Revolucionario por el Sendero Luminoso de Mariátegui (Revolutionary Student Front for the Shining Path of Mariátegui), a student group based in the UNSCH, points to the influence a particular reading of Mariátegui's thought exercised over the organisation. In his seminal work entitled *Seven Interpretive Essays on Peruvian Reality*, José Carlos Mariátegui attempted to 'sketch some of the essential characteristics of the formation and development of the Peruvian economy'.[13] Published in 1928, when historical and social science research on Peru was in its infancy, he argued that since the Spanish Conquest, the economic history of Peru could be divided into four main epochs. During the first epoch, the Inca Empire had been able through socialistic mechanisms to provide a reasonable level of subsistence for the mass of the population, but Inca 'agrarian communism' was destroyed by the Conquest. Spanish rule led to the establishment of a 'feudal' colonial economy, based primarily on extractive mining operations and, secondarily, on the related development of agricultural enterprises geared to supply the mining camps. Both of these activities were dependent on the exploitation of Indian and slave labour.

The second epoch in Peru's development commenced with independence from Spain in the 1820s, when an emerging commercial bourgeoisie managed to throw off the restrictive fetters of Spanish colonialism. Achieving independence, however, was largely a political event: it simply substituted one (peninsular) elite for a different (creole) elite and brought no significant change in social relations or improvements in the living standards of the population. Neither did it usher in meaningful democratic reforms.

This second chapter in Peru's economic evolution was followed by the epoch of the guano and nitrate 'boom', which began in the 1840s and lasted until the onset of the War of the Pacific in 1879. The chief characteristics of this period included an expansion in international trade, greater foreign (especially British) dominance over the Peruvian economy, the birth of a national capitalist class and a shift in economic power from the highlands to the coast. According to Mariátegui, the relative decline of the *sierra* and the growing importance of the coastal region, which gathered pace in Peru over these decades, worked to intensify 'social dualism and conflict, which to this day remain its greatest historical problem'.[14]

For Mariátegui, the latest (and most complex) stage in Peru's post-Conquest economic history ran from the end of the War of the Pacific through to the 1920s. Its defining features embraced the growth of agro-export activities (particularly around sugar, cotton and wool) and greater integration into the world economy (facilitated by the opening of the Panama Canal), which took place hand in hand with tighter foreign domination over the leading sectors of the Peruvian economy by monopoly capitalism, as US companies engaged in the extraction of raw materials displaced British finance and capital. Another key development was the establishment of modern industry, with the parallel creation of an industrial proletariat. These changes signified a further evolution from a feudal social formation to a capitalist economy, with 'a capitalist class no longer dominated by the old aristocracy ... The bourgeoisie has grown stronger'.[15] Progress along this path, however, was far from complete or straight-forward, because in Mariátegui's opinion capitalism's transformative dynamic had, in the case of Peru, been blunted as a result of the traditional cultural mores and retrograde social attitudes prevalent among the elite.

On the basis of these formulations, Mariátegui maintained that in the Peru of the 1920s three different types of economy coexisted: (i) a 'feudal' economy persisted in the *sierra*, structured around great estates (haciendas) that dated back to colonial times; (ii) a communal indigenous peasant economy with pre-Hispanic roots still managed to survive in the highlands; while (iii) on the coast, 'a bourgeois economy is growing in feudal soil', which 'gives every indication of being backward, at least in its mental outlook'.[16] Given such heterogeneity, Mariátegui believed that the situation found in the countryside was particularly complex. Rural society at this juncture remained dominated by a hacienda system that was 'feudal' in the Andes and 'semi-feudal' with regard to the export-orientated coastal sugar and cotton estates. The poverty that afflicted the mass of the indigenous population in the Andes, Mariátegui posited, mainly derived from the usurpation of village land and extra-economic exploitation on the part of local elites and rapacious government functionaries. Highland society was characterised by the concentration of land and power in the hands of a landlord class that remained feudal in outlook and economic behaviour. The large landowners had 'succeeded' in creating a socio-economic system that was less efficient than the 'agrarian communism' of the Inca Empire and possessed little dynamic for modernisation and change. As such, it acted as a brake on national development.

Although different in important respects, the situation on the coast was far from encouraging. Even though a certain number of estates had modernised in terms of technology, were well linked to international markets and employed large numbers of wage labourers, Mariátegui argued that because most coastal labourers were recruited through *enganche* (an indenture system) and share-cropping was widespread, even in this, the most developed sector of Peruvian agriculture, fully-fledged capitalist enterprises were not encountered. Here, the 'survival of feudalism on the coast is reflected in the stagnation and poverty of urban life', while the subservience of the coastal elite to foreign interests restricted Peru's ability to develop.[17] At the political level, the power of tradi-tional landlordism hindered the establishment of a functioning democratic polity, because 'democratic and liberal institutions cannot function and prosper on the back of a semi-feudal economy'.[18]

Mariátegui drew a number of important political conclusions from this analysis. An elite that was weak economically, whose capacity to modernise society was circumscribed by foreign domination over key areas of production, and which retained a 'feudalistic' *Weltanschauung*, remained incapable of undertaking a thoroughgoing national bourgeois revolution on the northern

European model. Given the absence of a 'dynamic bourgeois class' (he claimed the Peruvian elite was 'incompetent'), this task would have to be accomplished by a *'frente único proletario'* ('united proletarian alliance'), with a separate Socialist Party to bring together the most militant activists.[19] To be effective politically, it was essential that 'the Socialist Party adapts its praxis to the concrete circumstances of the country', one consequence of conquest and underdevelopment being that 'the Peruvian masses' were 'four-fifths Indian and peasants'.[20] In view of this situation, Mariátegui maintained that while urban workers (and miners) were at present the most class-conscious and best-organised sector of the forces struggling for social change and that they would, consequently, play a disproportionate role during the first wave of Socialist Party activity, their numerical weakness meant that the large and oppressed component of the population, made up of rural proletarians and peasants, needed to be mobilised in order to abolish Andean 'feudalism' and 'semifeudalism' on the littoral. Although difficult to organise, Mariátegui believed that these social actors were not as docile as was commonly perceived. They possessed revolutionary potential, had in the recent past mounted significant struggles around the issues of land, working conditions and the abuse of power by corrupt authorities, and would therefore be the prime actors in demolishing existing land-tenure structures and *gamonalismo* (political bossism).[21]

To assist this process, he recommended that each group of the rural population (independent smallholders, members of peasant communities, sharecroppers, agricultural labourers, etc.) should be organised in their own nationwide syndicate or federation, in order to pursue trade union-style goals. Involvement in these activities would help raise political consciousness. Isolated rebellions and strikes also needed to be given sharper focus through the dissemination of socialist ideology. This could be spread by sending activists to the countryside: Mariátegui felt that rural people working temporarily in the towns, or miners who migrated from their villages on a seasonal basis, were particularly suited to this task, as they were best placed to surmount cultural and linguistic barriers.

In order to push through the national–bourgeois and the socialist revolutions, it was necessary to construct a worker–peasant alliance around a socialist programme. Since under Peruvian conditions a socialist revolution could not survive solely on the backs of the urban proletariat, he argued that rural workers and peasants would have an equal role to play. While workers and peasants were the pivotal classes in this political project, other groups occupying an important position within Peru's social structure, such as artisans, small traders and non-manual sectors of the petty bourgeoisie (intellectuals, schoolteachers, etc.), also needed to be won over to the revolutionary camp. Although recognising the desirability of attracting support from several classes and occupations, however, Mariátegui was at pains to stress that urban and rural proletarians were central to the project: the middle classes would play second fiddle and no support could be counted on from the 'national bourgeoisie'.[22]

When attempting to devise a revolutionary strategy suited to conditions in one of the most heterogeneous and complex societies in Latin America, Mariátegui's non-dogmatic brand of Marxism led him to adopt a number of unorthodox positions. Indeed, on a number of key issues of strategy, tactics and organisation, he proposed policies that stood in opposition to those advanced by the Moscow-based Communist International, which became increasingly monolithic and 'stalinised' as the 1920s progressed. On the question of strategy, a first point of rupture concerned the 'character' of the revolution in what were labelled 'colonial and semi-colonial' societies. Whereas Comintern resolutions held that the proletariat represented the 'leading' class (the result of eurocentric attitudes and the weight of European concerns within the International), Mariátegui posited that under Peruvian conditions, workers and peasants needed to play an equal role in bringing about the desired transformation of society. Furthermore, Mariátegui argued that certain communal and reciprocal features of Andean peasant society provided 'a basis for a socialist solution to the agrarian question', a position that contrasted sharply with the mistrustful and contemptuous attitude with which many orthodox Marxists viewed the peasantry (and an extremely sensitive one, given that in the winter of 1929 Stalin embarked upon the disastrous policy of wholesale 'dekulakisation' and forced collectivisation).[23]

In addition, Mariátegui did not prioritise class to the exclusion of all else. He regarded the issues of race and ethnicity as of paramount importance in a country such as Peru. They needed to be analysed and appropriate policies incorporated into the Socialist Party programme, even though they represented policy areas that were neglected by the Comintern. Unorthodoxy on the three questions of peasants, race and ethnicity arose from a fundamental difference of approach between Mariátegui and the bureaucrats who administered the International in the late 1920s. Whereas the Peruvian was attempting to devise a strategy based on national reality, the latter tended to view what Bukharin called 'the world countryside' as homogeneous in its essential features and played down the fact of national diversity. In the Latin American context, this supposed 'sameness' meant that once a 'correct' line had been devised, it could be implemented with equal effect in Argentina or Peru, an absurdity that was anathema to Mariátegui's whole approach to politics.

Another policy disagreement vis-à-vis tactics concerned the much-debated question of alliance with the national bourgeoisie. Mariátegui held that the socio-economic and cultural characteristics of this class in Peru rendered such an alliance untenable; it would result in 'tailism' and betrayal. By contrast, at its Fifth Congress, which was held in the summer of 1924, the Comintern (driven by Stalin's foreign-policy interests), approved a policy of collaboration with the national bourgeoisie in 'the rural districts of the world'. At the Sixth Congress (1928) an abrupt volte-face occurred, when Stalin's dizzyingly suicidal 'theory' that social democracy represented 'the moderate wing of fascism' was foisted on the International. This ushered in the ultra-sectarianism of the infamous 'Third Period' (1928–34), with disastrous consequences for the European labour movement, especially in Germany.[24] To compound matters, in December 1928 Stalin called for a policy of breaking with reformist trade unions and the setting up of parallel federations. Again, this ultra-leftist line was at odds with Mariátegui's approach, which laid stress on the need for unity and the establishment of inclusive broad-based working-class organisations. He also advocated a different policy to that adopted at the Fifth Congress of the Comintern, which called for the creation of communist parties throughout the less developed world and their 'bolshevisation' (i.e. organisation along the lines of the Russian party). Instead, Mariátegui maintained that under present circumstances (particularly the weakness of the left and the likelihood of repression by the authoritarian regime headed by Augusto Leguía), conditions in Peru were not propitious to the establishment of a communist party. It was therefore necessary to avoid 'substitutism' and preferable to build up a broader-based Socialist Party that could unite the left and enjoy a wider appeal.[25]

The roots of PCP–SL ideology and strategy: Mao Zedong

Although Mariátegui was immersed in a very different social and political environment from the Chinese leader, a number of interesting similarities exist between the ideas of Mariátegui and those found in contemporaneous writings by Mao Zedong, the second decisive influence on Sendero Luminoso's ideology and strategy. The Communist Party of China (CPC) held that by the late 1920s China had evolved from a 'feudal' into a 'semi-colonial and semi-feudal society'. Its salient features included the maintenance of feudal oppression in the countryside and a weakly developed national capitalism, which had emerged since the turn of the century, along with the more dynamic growth of foreign-controlled ventures. These played a dominant role in light and heavy manufacturing, foreign trade, finance and banking. The overwhelming influence of the foreign powers and the backward-looking nature of the rural elite combined to produce a 'collusion of imperialism with the Chinese feudal forces to arrest the development of Chinese capitalism ... The imperialist powers have made the feudal landlord class as well as the comprador class the main props of their rule in China'.[26]

From this analysis, Mao drew a number of political conclusions that mirrored in important respects those made by Mariátegui for Peru. In his first substantive work, which he penned in 1926 when attempting to discover 'Who are our enemies? Who are our friends?', he posited that in 'economically backward and semi-colonial China the landlord class and the comprador class ... represent the most backward and most reactionary relations of production in China and hinder the development of her productive forces'.[27] These classes ('appendages of the international bourgeoisie, dependent on imperialism for their survival and growth'), comprised 'an extreme counter-revolutionary group'. According to Mao, the 'middle bourgeoisie' (or 'national bourgeoisie'), was 'inconsistent in its attitudes towards the Chinese revolution'. While its members might wish to limit the influence of foreign capital and undermine the feudal landlords, the aspirations of this class to expand their economic power and win control of the state made the national bourgeoisie suspicious of forces from below struggling for social and political change. With regard to the 'petty bourgeoisie' (the owners of viable peasant holdings, master craftsmen, small traders, students, schoolteachers, etc.), the most prosperous layer (those possessing the where-withal to generate a yearly surplus in commodities or money) gravitated towards the national bourgeoisie and remained fearful of revolution; while the 'second section' (those able to meet subsistence requirements) 'hesitate to join it and prefer to be neutral'.[28] The third strata (those who were 'going downhill with every passing year, their debts mounting and their life becoming more and more miserable'; who found themselves 'in great mental distress because there is such a contrast between their past and their present') tended to view the revolutionary movement most favourably. During times of crisis and war, however, the second section (and even elements of the first) may support insurrection.[29]

Among those who fell within the revolutionary camp, Mao identified the largest group as the 'semi-proletariat'. They consisted of various categories of resource-scarce peasants, tenants and sharecroppers working for the landlords, plus poor artisans and street vendors 'who own some simple means of production'. The poorest strata of the peasantry and artisans 'feel the constant pinch of poverty and the dread of unemployment', which made them 'highly receptive to revolutionary propaganda', as were shop assistants, pedlars and individuals in similar occupations possessing 'tiny funds and very small earnings'.[30] For Mao, 'the proletariat' (i.e. the industrial proletariat), although numbering only around two million people because of the nation's backwardness, formed 'the most progressive class in modern China and has become the leading force in the revolutionary movement' given its concentration in a few industrial centres, its capacity for organisation and its 'low economic status'.[31] Other urban workers, who laboured individually or in smaller groups and played 'a less important role in production' (such as coolies, dockers, street cleaners and rickshawmen), represented 'a force meriting attention' but, Mao implied, were secondary to industrial workers in terms of prioritising propaganda and recruitment. As regards the rural proletariat, these were the labourers 'who work the longest hours for the lowest wages, under the worst conditions and with the least security of employment'. Being 'the most hard-pressed people in the villages' they, in conjunction with the poor peasants, played a central role in peasant mobilisations. A final significant group comprised the large numbers of 'lumpen proletarians', 'made up of peasants who have lost their land and handicraftsmen who cannot get work' and 'lead the most precarious existence of all'.[32] Despite their proclivity for joining the Triads and other Mafia-style secret societies, Mao considered them: 'Brave fighters but apt to be destructive, they can become a revolutionary force if given proper guidance'.[33] He concluded with the following assessment:

> The leading force in our revolution is the industrial proletariat. Our closest friends are the entire semi-proletariat and the petty bourgeoisie. As for the vacillating middle bourgeoisie, their right-wing may become our enemy and

their left-wing may become our friend – but we must be constantly on our guard and not let them create confusion within our ranks.[34]

In this and numerous other articles written during the following decade, Mao adhered publicly to the Comintern's interpretation of the 'character' of the Chinese revolution. This was that in its initial 'bourgeois–democratic' stage, when the main targets to be attacked were imperialist tutelage and feudal domination of the countryside, a 'bloc of four classes' was required to establish a revolutionary–democratic regime. The industrial proletariat constituted the principal driving force within this united front, seconded by the peasantry ('the firm ally of the proletariat'), the urban petty bourgeoisie ('a reliable ally'), and finally the national bourgeoisie (which may 'vacillate and defect because of its economic and political flabbiness').[35] Upon completion of its 'national–democratic' tasks (re-establishing national sovereignty in political and economic affairs, the completion of the agrarian revolution against feudalism, etc.), the proletariat, led by the CPC could proceed to the next stage, the socialist revolution.

Forced by the pressure of events, however, between 1926 and 1931 Mao gradually made a number of important alterations to this theoretical schema, while still outwardly acquiescing to Comintern dogma. This intellectual shift was facilitated by his peasant roots, the example given by cadres such as Peng Pai and Fang Zhimin, who were already party-building in the countryside and the geographical isolation of CPC forces. The key innovations concerned: (i) the respective roles allocated to the proletariat and the peasantry in the revolutionary process; (ii) the siting of the fulcrum of revolutionary activity; and (iii) the tactics required to bring the revolution to a successful conclusion. In 1926 the rural poor in Mao's native province of Hunan formed a plethora of peasant associations and engaged in activities that shook the foundations of rural society. When analysing these developments in one of his most famous tracts, the *Report on an Investigation of the Peasant Movement in Hunan*, Mao noted that these organisations had launched a broad attack on 'the local tyrants, the evil gentry and the lawless landlords', during which 'they also hit out against patriarchal ideas and institutions, against the corrupt officials in the cities and against bad practices and customs in the rural areas'.[36] In his opinion, the peasant uprising proved so effective that 'the privileges which the feudal landlords enjoyed for thousands of years are being shattered to pieces'.[37] The extent and depth of these mobilisations meant that an urgent decision had to be made vis-à-vis the peasantry. For Mao, there were:

three alternatives: To march at their head and lead them? To trail behind them gesticulating and criticizing? Or to stand in their way and oppose them? Every Chinese is free to choose, but events will force you to make the choice quickly.[38]

He strongly recommended the first option, in the process making a thinly veiled attack on current CPC policy, which entailed criticism of the peasant associations 'for going too far', accompanied by attempts by party leaders to dampen the unfolding agrarian revolution. This incongruous position was adopted by the Central Committee due to a combination of external pressure from the Comintern and its own ideological mindset, which fostered the assumption that revolution in China would follow a 'European' model, i.e. be based on the proletariat and centred in the towns. Nevertheless, the misguided strategy was soon to produce a calamity of such massive proportions that it spawned a fundamental reassessment of policy and launched the CPC on the road to power.

In May 1925, Stalin advanced the thesis that the Chinese national bourgeoisie had divided into conservative and revolutionary wings, with the Kuomintang (KMT) (Guomindang) headed by Chiang Kai-shek (Jiang Jieshi) being the political expression of the revolutionary faction. Consequently, the argument went, the CPC should enter into an alliance with the KMT. Its cadres were even forced to become individual members of Chiang Kai-shek's party. As landlords comprised one of the main social props underpinning the KMT, CPC cadres found themselves – on the insistence of Comintern representatives in China – in the impossible situation of attempting to put a brake on the peasant movement in 1926–27. To compound matters, they were compelled to stand idly aside when the KMT initiated a bloody campaign of repression in the countryside. The imposition of a policy manufactured in Moscow led to the CPC becoming an appendage of the KMT, with consequent political paralysis and demoralisation among rank-and-file party members. It also terminated in disaster when, in April 1927, Chiang's army launched a counter-revolutionary coup d'état against workers' militias and trade-union organisations based in Shanghai, Canton and other major cities. This action decimated the CPC's working-class base and led to the murder or arrest of a significant proportion of the Central Committee. After six months of 'white terror', the party's urban infrastructure and its political strategy both lay in tatters.[39]

Following this defeat, Mao retreated inland to help consolidate an independent regime on the borders of Hunan and Kiangsi provinces with surviving remnants of the party apparatus. There, encouraged by the 'Autumn Harvest Uprising' (September 1927), and the spread of rural revolt, he gradually turned to peasant revolution. Although lip service continued to be paid to the notion of proletarian hegemony, peasants became henceforth the driving force of the revolution. While Moscow remained suspicious of this 'peasant Bolshevism', isolation meant that the Comintern was ill-informed about developments on the ground. This enabled Mao to consolidate his position and to emerge as effective leader in 1931 (he was elected General Secretary only in 1935 during the Long March).

The changed political circumstances and switch from town to country signified that a new theory of revolutionary warfare had to be devised urgently. This took shape through the hard practicalities of having to counter the various 'encirclement and suppression' campaigns mounted by the KMT against 'Red bases' during the late 1920s and early 1930s. Drawing upon classical Chinese military texts (Sun Tzu, *The Art of War*), lessons taken from the civil war in Russia and, most importantly, learning from costly mistakes committed by the CPC in its ongoing struggle with the KMT, Mao and close associates such as Chu Teh (Zhu De) devised a sophisticated strategy suited to Chinese conditions. At root, its success depended on winning active support from the rural population, which was to be achieved through a deepening of the 'Agrarian Revolutionary War' and the abolition of 'feudalism' in the countryside. This necessitated the eradication of landlordism, a redistribution of land and other assets to the poor peasantry and the landless, putting an end to warlordism and suppressing banditry, hand in hand with imposing sanctions against corrupt officials and replacing them with village-level organs of government staffed by peasants.

Once these popular policies had been implemented in a particular locality, the CPC moved to take advantage of its prestige and authority by building 'support bases' within the community. These groups had the important task of organising production to sustain the guerrilla forces. At the political level, their role was to suppress counter-revolutionary activity, as well as provide a source of cadres to expand the party apparatus. With regard to their military functions, the support bases established village-level militias (called 'peasant self-defence corps' or 'Red Guards'), which policed the locality and received assistance from (and eventually provided recruits for) the full-time troops integrated into the Red Army. Employing a policy of widening the agrarian revolution by 'advancing in a series of waves' when conditions proved favourable, or moving slowly when faced with more difficult circumstances, 'liberated areas' (or 'base areas') were formed, consolidated and expanded gradually until the encircling and capturing of towns became feasible.[40]

With regard to tactics, Mao's theory of guerrilla warfare embraced a number of fundamentals that recur in his main texts on the topic dating from the early civil war period through to the national liberation struggle against the Japanese. These guiding principles included:

(i) the requirement that local commanders 'do some hard thinking', analyse constantly the political–military situation of opponents, and use their intelligence to adapt actions according to changing circumstances;

(ii) the need to choose a terrain favourable for military operations;

(iii) the importance of not committing the 'leftist' error of belittling the enemy while overestimating your own strength, or the 'rightist' error of being too fearful and resorting to 'passive defence';

(iv) the essential need to plan meticulously, engage in a 'gradual advance', lay 'solid foundations' among the populace and resist the temptation to embark on an 'adventurous advance' that entails an attack on various fronts and the dispersal of troops;

(v) while refraining from needless 'flightism', confrontation with stronger forces should be avoided and, if necessary, a 'strategic retreat' undertaken in order to conserve guerrilla strength; 'lure the enemy in deep' and prepare for a counter-offensive when the opposition's 'strong men have worn themselves thin' and their 'thin men have worn themselves to death';

(vi) in order to offset inferiority in numbers and equipment, fighting units should be concentrated to confront and destroy a weaker enemy through 'striking with one "fist" in one direction at one time', under 'conditions favourable to ourselves';

(vii) fixed battle lines and positional warfare should be eschewed in favour of surprise attacks, fluid battle lines and mobility when employing encircling and outflanking operations; and

(viii) ideally, guerrilla units should conduct battles of 'quick decision', concentrating rapidly when the objective is to destroy the enemy, dispersing when the aim is to harass and disrupt.[41]

A clear distinction had to be made between the strategic and tactical aspects of guerrilla war. At the strategic level, through superior political analysis, policies, planning and initiative, it was possible to 'pit one against ten' and 'use the few to defeat the many'; at the tactical level, however, the rule must always be to 'pit ten against one', because in a combat situation 'we use the many to defeat the few'.[42]

Mao calculated that his strategy of 'protracted people's war' would develop through three main stages. During the opening 'strategic defensive' period, guerrilla fighters will find themselves inferior in strength to their opponents. As the conflict develops, the second phase of 'strategic equilibrium' or 'stalemate' arises, brought about by a relative decline in the enemy's position and an 'upgrading' of the insurrectionary forces. This is followed by the third and final phase, that of 'strategic counter-offensive', during which the revolutionaries push the enemy into retreat, expand the base areas and, 'when the time is opportune' gradually enforce the encircling and capture of towns.

Parallel with the move from a position of inferiority to parity and ultimate superiority that occurs over the three stages of the conflict, a different type of warfare predominates during each period. Initially, guerrilla activity is the primary form. In the second 'strategic equilibrium' phase, 'mobile' or 'regular' modes of combat predominate, defined as 'guerrilla warfare raised to a higher level', i.e., more intense armed actions conducted by larger groups over a wider area, involving 'swift advances and withdrawals, swift concentrations and dispersals'.[43] When the 'strategic counter-offensive' phase unfolds, positional warfare becomes the prime form of combat, although 'guerrilla' and 'mobile' military activities will continue where local circumstances dictate.

With regard to the chain of authority, experience taught that a centralised strategic command, responsible for overall planning and direction, combined with decentralised decision-making at the local level was the most efficacious arrangement. It possessed the advantage of permitting concerted action while simultaneously allowing opportunity for grass-roots initiative and rapid response on a day-to-day basis by field commanders. Although decentralisation in matters of detail was to be recommended, it was essential that careful attention be given to the quality of individuals occupying all levels of the party's political–military structures. Those found wanting had to be removed and given additional training in order to improve their performance. Maximum effort and resources should be dedicated to the task of raising the political level and operational capacity of cadres, because to pursue successfully this kind of unconventional war, 'it is people, not things, that are decisive'.[44]

Marrying Mariátegui and Mao: PCP–SL strategy and tactics

Even a cursory reading of the PCP-SL's programme and early policy statements indicates that the organisation's leadership copied, without critical appraisal or any significant reformulation, key ideas developed by Mariátegui and Mao. Much of Sendero's argumentation regarding the nature of Peruvian society in the 1970s, for example, was lifted straight from the analysis undertaken by Mariátegui in the late 1920s. One of the Party's first documents (most likely written by Guzmán), stated that 'Mariátegui laid down the general political line of the Peruvian revolution'. Despite the passage of five decades that had brought massive social changes, including substantial rural–urban migration and a thoroughgoing agrarian reform implemented during the military government of Juan Velasco (1968–75), Peru allegedly remained a 'semi-feudal' country. 'Semi-feudalism' prevailed in the countryside because of the 'persistence' and 'development of new forms' of supposedly non-capitalist socio-economic arrangements and institutions, namely 'unpaid labour, personal obligations, servitude, the maintenance and consolidation of the old haciendas and the continued prevalence of *gamonalismo* in social and political relations.[45]

Following Mariátegui (and Mao), Peru was deemed to be a 'semi-colonial' country characterised by increased dependence on (and domination by) imperialism. The nation had long been ruled by a 'comprador bourgeoisie', incapable of pushing through an 'independent industrialisation' programme, establishing a functioning bourgeois democracy, or pursuing policies for the benefit of the poor majority. While recognising a certain level of capitalist expansion in Peru over recent decades, the Party line held that such change remained of limited impact. Capitalist development had, nevertheless, brought greater state interference in the economy, which led to the related growth of 'bureaucratic capitalism' (a concept taken from Mao), in the shape of nationalised industries and monopoly enterprises linked closely to the state. Indeed, the policies implemented by the reformist military regime that seized power on 3 October 1968 signified a 'third restructuring of the Peruvian state'. This, it was believed, had produced a reordering within the counter-revolutionary camp: now the 'bureaucratic bourgeoisie commanded the feudal landowners and the comprador bourgeoisie', that is, the two classes that had hitherto ruled Peru. According to the PCP-SL, a newly hegemonic 'bureaucratic bourgeoisie' had 'assumed control of the state' in 1968 and was engaged in a 'reactionary corporatist offensive' aimed at achieving the total 'corporativisation of Peruvian society'. While quite prepared to hoodwink workers and peasants via reformist measures, this emergent elite was not afraid to repress them when 'circumstances dictated'. For this reason, Sendero embraced the position that the military presided over a 'fascist government'. However, the argument proceeded, 'deep economic crisis' and popular unrest in the late 1970s signi-fied that the 'stationary revolutionary situation' that Peru had allegedly been living through since 1968 had evolved into a 'developing revolutionary situa-tion'. Conditions existed to launch the 'National Democratic' revolution. Therefore, the Party's present task was to eschew 'parliamentary cretinism' and 'support the struggles of the masses as they move towards the initiation of armed revolt to destroy the old order and construct a state of New Democracy'.[46]

Flowing from these particular interpretations of the character of Peruvian society and the contemporary political conjuncture, PCP–SL documents stated that a 'two stage' revolutionary process was unfolding, the 'national democratic' and the 'socialist'. During the initial 'national democratic' revolution, the main targets were said to be 'semi-feudalism and imperialist domination'. Central political objectives included 'the destruction of the Peruvian state' (point 1 of the PCP–SL's 'General Programme of the Democratic Revolution'); expropri-ation of all foreign assets (point 2); confiscation of property owned by 'bureaucratic capitalism', both private and public (point 3); and a 'liquidation of semi-feudal property' by applying the principle of 'land to the tiller' (point 4). In a recycling of Mao's answer to 'Who are our enemies? Who are our friends?', Sendero ideologues opined that these 'national democratic' tasks would be carried out by an alliance of four classes. This 'united front' should be built around: (i) the proletariat ('the leading class'); (ii) the peasantry ('because it forms the majority and bears the weight of semi-feudalism'); (iii) the petty bourgeoisie; and (iv) 'under certain conditions and circumstances', the 'national bourgeoisie'. The last two classes needed to be subordinate to the former and the whole project to be led by the Party.[47]

Regarding the strategy and tactics to be employed in order to accomplish these goals, since Mariátegui wrote relatively little on these aspects of revolu-tionary politics, the PCP–SL adopted wholesale many ideas developed by Mao. As Peru (supposedly) remained a 'semi-feudal' society and the peasantry (supposedly) formed the largest and most exploited sector of the population, Sendero believed that its 'people's war is a peasant war or it is nothing' – the title of one of the organisation's earliest documents (and filched from Vo Nguyen Giap). During the 'National Democratic' stage, the peasantry was to act as the 'principal motor force' of the revolution, which would be centred in the countryside and advance in accordance with the strategy of encircling and capturing towns. To push forward this 'protracted people's war', a policy of *batir el campo* (churning up the countryside) needed to be pursued. In the words of Guzmán, this entailed:

cleansing the countryside, incendiarising it, removing all the political author-ities and landlords, eliminating all functionaries. The rural areas should be thrown into confusion, the land cleansed before we sow and build up revo-lutionary bases of support.[48]

By creating a political vacuum in those rural areas where it was active,

Sendero hoped to gain influence among the peasantry to recruit new cadres (establish 'bases de apoyo', or 'support bases') and expand the ranks of its Ejército Guerrillero Popular (EGP) – Popular Guerrilla Army, in much the same way as the CPC had done in China from the mid-1920s. Over time, as insurrection gathered momentum in the villages, 'liberated areas' could be established on the Chinese model and a parallel state to that centred on Lima constructed in the interior, i.e. an 'Andean Yenan'. Although the countryside remained 'the principal theatre of armed revolt', with time, the geographical spread and deepening of rural conflict created opportunities for the towns to become 'complementary but necessary' areas of Party development and military activity.

Mao's schema was also taken on board in other important respects. Sendero envisaged that its 'protracted people's war' would pass through three phases ('strategic defensive', 'strategic equilibrium' and 'strategic offensive'). Furthermore, operations needed to be conducted according to 'a centralised strategic plan', with 'tactical decentralisation' occurring at the local level to take account of varied circumstances in different theatres of combat and permit maximum flexibility when carrying out day-to-day actions.[49]

One striking impression given by an examination of PCP–SL publications is the absence of any worthwhile attempt to understand the processes of social change that occurred in Peru during the second half of the twentieth century. No serious class and cultural analysis can be found, nor any indication that Party leaders had done 'some hard thinking' (Mao's phrase) by studying the burgeoning social-science literature on the population's highly complex rural and urban household survival strategies and socio-economic relations. In addition to holding a superficial view of the social context in which the Party hoped to insert itself, Party documents indicate a lack of a subtle consideration of vital questions: the nature of the state, the political potential of the peasantry, the countryside versus the city, the relationship between vanguard party and class, gender, ethnicity, etc. Instead, a perusal of PCP–SL tracts shows that the organisation's leadership took on board uncritically ideas from Mariátegui and Mao; it lacked inquisitiveness and imagination. They were plagiarists rather than innovators. Guzmán and his associates possessed a mechanistic, one-dimensional method of social analysis that was totally alien to the praxis of their chief mentors.[50]

In this sense, the PCP–SL leadership fell into the trap of many revolutionaries: they committed the mistake of attempting to reproduce past successful revolutions (a pitfall flagged by Lenin) and forgot that 'orthodoxy is a matter for the Church' (Fidel Castro).[51] While copying brought the organisation some short-term benefits (for example, its optimistic assessment of the political potential of the peasantry coupled with a romanticised view of Andean peasant life aided the recruitment of urban petty bourgeois radicals), an unimaginative, deterministic approach to politics was to percolate top-down through the Party and ultimately be an important factor in the demise of its revolutionary project. This development was most in evidence with regard to the PCP–SL's increasingly complicated and conflictual relationship with the civilian population between 1985 and 1992.

Early explanations of PCP–SL growth:
'subsistence crisis', 'deindianisation', 'marginalisation'

The failure of left activists to take the PCP–SL seriously, the superficial scrutiny given by the state's intelligence services to the content of its political programme, and efforts to proselytise in the two years prior to the outbreak of insurrection have already been alluded to. Academic researchers and serious journalists also ignored Sendero. Their attention focused understandably on the large-scale social mobilisations that occurred in Peru during the late 1970s, and the complex transition to civilian rule that dominated national politics between 1977 and 1980. One consequence of this neglect, when combined with a logical attempt by PCP–SL leaders to shun publicity during the vital opening phase of their military campaign, was that it took time for serious studies of the party and its political project to emerge.[52] Such difficulties (soon to be compounded by the unleashing of a full-blown 'dirty war', which made research in the countryside extremely dangerous), meant that prior to 1985, lengthier publications on the insurgency typically comprised generalised commentaries of an empirical nature on PCP–SL origins, ideology and strategy. These were supplemented by short journalistic reports detailing particular incidents that occurred as the civil war deepened, which focused invariably on Ayacucho, the department where most armed activity was taking place.[53]

Two articles that attempted to move beyond the purely descriptive and provide a theoretical explanation for the emergence of the PCP–SL were published in 1984 by Henri Favre and Cynthia McClintock. According to McClintock, the PCP–SL had 'gained considerable peasant support in Peru's southern highlands, especially in the Ayacucho area'.[54] When trying to account for this 'widespread support', a range of theories on the roots of peasant protest and rural revolution were reviewed with the conclusion that the 'subsistence crisis' and 'moral economy' arguments of James Scott and ('especially') Eric Wolf 'are supported by the Peruvian experience'.[55] While she maintained that the disruptive impact of capitalism remained marginal to explaining Sendero's appeal in rural Ayacucho (smallholders were supposedly 'relatively unintegrated into the capitalist market economy'), McClintock highlighted the crisis of subsistence as being 'outstandingly important' for explaining why 'the peasants' rage and despair are intense'.[56] A desperate situation had been brought about by a concatenation of factors: demographic increase and concomitant land hunger, the failure of an overwhelming majority of smallholders to benefit from agrarian reform, a succession of environmental disasters (drought) and the pernicious nature of government policy towards agriculture (ineffective rural development; unfavourable rural–urban terms of trade). Furthermore, Ayacucho and its environs represented an inaccessible zone where state authority and repressive capacity were weak. A combination of these factors enabled a 'radical peasant movement', in the shape of the PCP–SL, to emerge and prosper, even though 'some twenty villages in the highest altitudes of Ayacucho, inhabited by a distinct ethnic group called the Iquichanos, have been hostile toward the Senderistas'.[57]

In an equally penetrating essay (on this occasion influenced by Durkheimian concerns about the disruptive effects of social change, a decline in social cohesion and the spread of anomie), Henri Favre attempted to account for contrasting responses to the PCP–SL among the rural populace of the south-central highlands in the early 1980s and to identify which social groups found its revolutionary political message most appealing. After noting that during the initial phase of the insurgency (1980–82), a minimal state presence and an inadequate response to the outbreak of armed revolt allowed the PCP–SL to gain a foothold in the villages of the region and create 'liberated zones' without too much difficulty, Favre argued that 1983 saw the appearance of a number of fractures in guerrilla–peasant relations. These had been caused by the government's more robust response to the rebellion. Forced recruitment of adolescents into PCP–SL military units fuelled peasant resentment and fears about the safety of their offspring – sentiments that intensified when the Party attempted to impose a 'natural economy' on smallholders as part of its strategy of 'starving' the towns.[58]

The villages that proved least receptive to PCP–SL propaganda and were best placed to resist rebel demands on this and other issues were the more 'peasant', more 'Indian' and more geographically isolated communities sited at higher altitudes (in the *puna*, or moorland). These, Favre argued, remained poorly integrated into national life and resented their dependent position vis-à-vis adjacent valley settlements, which housed the local merchant class and representatives of the state.[59] On the other hand, he maintained, the PCP–SL's political message was better received among floating 'semi-peasants' from the valley communities, whose denizens exhibited greater mobility through having to migrate in search of work: 'the rural inhabitant who is depeasantised and deindianised', who was more incorporated into national life, but simultaneously experienced 'marginalisation' and barriers to social advancement because of ethnic discrimination and a lack of employment opportunities, formed the social base of the PCP–SL.[60] Against this backdrop of the economic decline and social decomposition of highland society, Favre posited, the PCP–SL emerged out of an 'explosive' encounter between a provincial 'lumpen intelligentsia' and *cholos* (mestizos, acculturated Indians), who resented their exclusion. The resulting alienation found expression in 'peasant luddism'.[61]

Explaining Sendero: support for a 'benevolent *gamonal*' and 'attacks against the rich'

Although commendably ambitious in scope, the articles by Favre and McClintock possessed common weaknesses: neither was based on a detailed understanding of contemporary developments in the conflict zone acquired through recent fieldwork; in addition, parts of the argumentation relied on the controversial findings of a commission formed to investigate the assassination of eight journalists at the village of Uchuraccay in January 1983.[62] Two works that avoided these flaws were published in 1986 by Carlos Iván Degregori and Ronald Berg. When attempting to explain why the PCP–SL was able to survive and expand between 1980 and 1982, Degregori made the valid points that McClintock's peasant 'subsistence crisis' was insufficient to account for rebel success. Furthermore, Favre's contrast between *puna* (anti-guerrilla) and valley (pro-guerrilla) communities proved simplistic in that he ignored the important differences in access to resources, wealth and levels of commercial activity between villages located in similar ecological zones. Nor could Favre's model account for varying reactions to the PCP–SL encountered among valley communities sited adjacent to Ayacucho (favourable response) and the neighbouring town of Huanta (hostile response).[63]

For Degregori, three factors were fundamental to an explanation of the extent to which the PCP–SL was able to establish itself in a particular locality. First, he made a link between the degree of PCP–SL presence in a given community and the existence of schools, because students and teachers comprised 'the original base of Sendero in Ayacucho'.[64] Second, support for the PCP–SL was facilitated by the political inexperience of the local peasantry and its ambivalent attitude towards the state. The rural population of Ayacucho had not participated in the large-scale land invasions that occurred in other regions of Peru during the 1970s, nor had it been deeply involved in national peasant syndicates such as the Confederación Campesina del Perú, or the Confederación Nacional Agraria (CNA) – National Agrarian Confederation. This situation reflected their 'inward looking' nature and a relatively low density of political interactions with the wider world. Although they possessed 'hardly any traditions of modern organisation', these communities often entered into conflict with the state, as evidenced by anti-tax revolts in the nineteenth century through to more contemporary mobilisations aimed at preventing the establishment of village police posts during the 1960s and 1970s. Given this history, 'it was possible that when in 1981 and 1982 Sendero Luminoso attacked police posts scattered throughout the region, it did so with a degree of peasant approval, or at least neutrality'.[65] However, hostility only extended to the repressive aspects of the state; other facets of state intervention (such as the opening of schools and medical posts, or land-titling) were received favourably. Nor did the peasantry reject the market. The third factor highlighted by Degregori to explain the PCP–SL's ability to gain adherents touched on Andean cultural and political traditions: upon entering a village, the PCP–SL took on the mantle of 'a benevolent new landlord ... who appeared from above to impose a new (or perhaps, not so new) order, more just but not necessarily democratic', through popular sanctions against petty thieves, small-scale landowners and abusive public functionaries.[66] Nevertheless, although the PCP–SL attained a degree of support between 1980–2, Degregori noted that 'the implantation of Sendero

Luminoso in the countryside was fragile in that it was too dependent on students and schoolteachers, and not based enough on the peasantry'.[67]

If late 1982 represented 'the pinnacle of Sendero's utopian authoritarian project', this Achilles' heel was to be ruthlessly exposed during the agricultural year 1982–83. The denouement arose when the insurgents strove to remove established village leaders and replace them with individuals loyal to the Party and to interfere in community civil affairs, religious practices and kinship relations. Guerrilla demands that peasants eschew commodity exchange and reduce plantings, hand in hand with moves to close rural markets and block roads, generated rifts between the rural population and the PCP–SL. Peasant support for Sendero in Ayacucho was eroded further when cadres failed to honour their promise to stay and protect villagers following the armed forces' saturation of the countryside in 1983.[68] The end result, Degregori noted, was an upsurge of inter- and intra-community violence, ruin of the local economy and peasant alienation from the two main protagonists in a rapidly escalating 'dirty war': the armed forces and the PCP–SL.[69]

The line of enquiry embarked upon by Degregori was also pursued by Ronald Berg, who in a valuable article examined the PCP–SL's complex and evolving relationship with the rural population settled in the province of Andahuaylas (department of Apurímac), which borders on Ayacucho. Berg noted that after commencing armed activity in the province (December 1981), the rebels met with little effective state resistance, so that by late 1982 they 'controlled most of rural Andahuaylas' and enjoyed ample capacity to intervene in village affairs.[70] In order to acquire a social base, guerrilla units attacked those members of rural society who had become the focus of peasant hostility, especially merchants with a reputation for sharp business practices, well-to-do peasants who had profited from General Velasco's land reform (1969–76) and leaders of agricultural production cooperatives tainted by accusations of corruption. Having established an effective underground network, PCP–SL activists proved 'remarkably precise in their targeting of unpopular individuals', while their policy of hitting 'the rich' through assassination, the sacking of stores, or the redistribution of land and livestock received widespread approbation. However, Berg proceeded to make the fundamental point that it was necessary to differentiate between:

> active support, passive support, and sympathy. Sympathy means a general or specific agreement with the actions or philosophy of the guerrillas. Passive support refers to a willingness to tolerate the presence of the guerrillas and a disinclination to take any action against them, including informing the police. Active support refers to acts of commission.
>
> The evidence from Andahuaylas suggests that the peasants have a great deal of sympathy for the actions of Shining Path, and this leads to widespread passive support but not a great deal of active support. Active support is limited to attacks on unpopular individuals, usually between villages with historical reasons for mutual antagonism.[71]

Echoing the 'moral economy' argument advanced by James Scott, Berg held that through playing upon 'notions of economic justice in Andahuaylas communities where the core value is reciprocity and there is resentment against those who accumulate wealth, particularly if they do not remain involved in relations of reciprocity', the assassination of kulaks by insurgents received a sympathetic response, as did their attacks against the state and agricultural cooperatives.[72] For the PCP–SL, the key task was to transform 'sympathy' into a deeper commitment and enrol the population into its political and military structures, an objective that the organisation had failed to achieve by the mid-1980s.

Sendero in Puno: intense land conflicts, high politicisation

Around the time Berg was undertaking research in Andahuaylas, attention was increasingly being focused on Puno (sited in the high *puna* that surrounds Lake Titicaca on Peru's southern border with Bolivia). It was widely feared that this department might undergo a process of *ayacuchanización*, i.e. acquire levels of violence similar to that currently occurring in Ayacucho. In the first of what became a clutch of articles on socio-political developments in the department, José María Salcedo described how the PCP–SL had been establishing a presence in Puno since 1982. Salcedo noted that the Party was concentrating its organisational efforts on the Quechua-speaking provinces in the northern half of the department by drafting in cadres from Cusco and Ayacucho to bolster its local apparatus. He posited that the extreme poverty of the rural population potentially made Puno fertile terrain for insurgent recruitment. Guerrilla prospects were also enhanced by the state's complete abandonment of the zone with respect to social and infrastructural improvement. Irrigation and other agricultural development projects aimed at bettering the lot of the peasantry were practically non-existent; health-care facilities remained wholly inadequate; most communities lacked electricity, as well as other basic services; and the communications network was rudimentary. Furthermore, judicial corruption proved systemic, as was unprofessional behaviour among the police, who exhibited a proclivity to exact money and produce from the peasantry, in addition to dishing out unprovoked beatings and making arbitrary arrests with impunity. Such conduct, Salcedo argued, had alienated many *puneños* from key state institutions, to the extent that some sectors of the population were not 'against' the PCP–SL; nor were they 'for' the misnamed 'forces of law and order'.[73]

Opportunities to recruit and expand activities also presented themselves to the rebel organisation as a consequence of the acute land conflicts that beset the department, especially in its northern provinces. The agrarian reform had expropriated enterprises belonging to the old landed elite, but because the state wished to maintain the economies of scale and improved farming practices found on many ex-haciendas (pedigree livestock, modern systems of stock management, etc.), these had been converted into cooperatives entitled Sociedades Agrícolas de Interés Social (SAIS) – Agricultural Societies of Social Interest, or Empresas Rurales de Propiedad Social (ERPS) – Rural Social

Property Enterprises. Expropriation had thus benefited small groups of permanent employees. An overwhelming majority of the rural poor who had settled in peasant communities surrounding the large estates had received nothing. To compound matters, the land-hungry *comuneros* who populated these villages (many of whom worked micro-plots no larger than a quarter of a hectare), possessed historic claims against the ex-haciendas and had expected to benefit from land redistribution. In Salcedo's opinion, such frustrated aspirations opened up possibilities for the PCP–SL to attain a peasant base.[74]

The manner in which agrarian reform had been implemented also gave rise to new conflicts. According to Salcedo, the leadership cliques controlling these recently established cooperatives (often made up of ex-administrators and foremen) behaved like the departed landowner and had been assimilated into reconstituted district-level elites, a state of affairs that fuelled discontent among *comuneros*, as well as fostering resentments among cooperative members.[75] It was further noted that the indigenous peasantry of Puno department had a long history of collective action and rebellion dating back to the colonial period and beyond. Salcedo speculated that this tradition might facilitate PCP–SL goals. Conversely, the fact that the rural population was organised in peasant federations to a far greater extent than in Ayacucho could act to block the advance of the PCP–SL. While Degregori posited that the relative political inexperience of Ayacucho's peasantry assisted guerrilla goals, for Salcedo, the greater degree of politicisation, levels of organisation and participation in (left-wing) nationwide peasant syndicates provided *campesinos* in Puno with the political skills to evolve an alternative project to that advanced by the insurgents. It also made them better able to resist their blandishments.[76]

A number of these issues were also addressed by Raúl González, who noted that since 1982, the PCP–SL had 'grown and advanced in a slow but steady fashion' in Puno, despite having had to overcome a number of military reverses.[77] Party cadres encountered a measure of support in Puno's villages and small rural towns, their proselytising efforts assisted not only by the negative impact of police abuse and corruption, but also by the withdrawal of the Guardia Civil from the countryside. Afraid to confront the guerrillas militarily, they had closed down rural police stations and, in effect, left the peasants to cope with the build-up of Sendero's operations as best they could. Exploiting the resultant freedom for manoeuvre, PCP–SL strategy was to occupy and destroy the cooperatives, distributing land, livestock and other resources with the expectation that grateful peasants would join their ranks. To the same end, PCP–SL activists targeted for recruitment village leaders who enjoyed prestige and legitimacy at the grass roots, a number of whom occupied positions within local peasant federations and belonged to the legal left, Izquierda Unida (IU) – United Left. In contrast to the position adopted by Salcedo, González stressed that Puno's peasant federations were not political parties and so lacked the capacity to block the advance of the PCP–SL. Rather, guerrilla units could win adherents in Puno because:

here, like in Ayacucho, Sendero has not faced any political competition, for nobody stands up to them and competes with them for the population they are trying to win over. Nobody has activists who inform the peasants that there are clear political alternatives to those proposed by Sendero ... The *puneño* peasantry ... needs to believe in something ... They need to not feel abandoned by the politicians, who only visit their villages when votes are needed at election time.[78]

González held that in Puno, as in other areas of highland Peru, the PCP–SL could only be halted 'if together with a serious and decided effort by the state to solve the various structural and conjunctural problems of the peasantry', the political parties strove to work with and organise the rural population in order to offer them political alternatives and 'address their sense of injustice, which at present only Sendero appears to understand'.[79]

The Central Sierra: imposing a Maoist 'moral order'

When attempting to build up its political and military presence in Puno in the mid-1980s, the PCP–SL was simultaneously working to expand its level of operations in Junín. This strategically important department covered Lima's hinterland and provisioned the capital with appreciable amounts of foodstuffs, was the source of its electricity and much of its water supply, and its mines produced sizeable mineral exports, a key component of Peru's foreign-exchange earnings. For these reasons, Nelson Manrique labelled the struggle for supremacy in the Central Sierra 'the decisive battleground' and believed that developments in the region would go a long way to determine whether the state or the PCP–SL emerged victorious in the civil war.[80] Although the Central Sierra had a very different socio-political milieu from that existing in Puno, Manrique homed in on a number of themes highlighted in the literature on Puno: (i) the state's inability to respond effectively to peasant needs and demands; (ii) guerrilla intervention in land conflicts that the agrarian reform of the early 1970s had failed to resolve; and (iii) the PCP–SL's acquisition of a social base among the rural population.

Sendero aimed to exploit the second issue to achieve the third. Manrique noted that two distinct responses to guerrilla activity could be perceived in the zone. Inhabitants of peasant communities located in the Mantaro Valley adjacent to Huancayo (the departmental capital and most important urban commercial centre), who possessed a long history of involvement in labour and commodity markets, repudiated PCP–SL acts of sabotage, to the extent that they were even prepared to take up arms against the insurgents.[81] On the other hand (and in contrast to Favre's claims for Ayacucho), the response of *campesinos* housed in the mainly pastoral communities sited up in the *puna* proved more complex. From 1986, guerrilla activity had intensified in the Canipaco Valley, so that by late 1988 it had become something of a 'liberated zone' following the destruction of various police posts. Insurgent forces moved to gain acceptance and recruits by intervening in the bitter land conflicts troubling the area: shepherds living in the communities reclaimed pastures that had been usurped by neighbouring livestock-rearing haciendas, but found their demands resisted by a Ministry of Agriculture bureaucracy intent on maintaining the SAIS model. Amid widespread discontent with state policy on this matter among both *comuneros* and cooperative members, large-scale invasions of SAIS lands took place. In an effort to resolve the impasse, CCP activists associated with the IU left coalition proposed a 'democratic restructuring' of these enterprises. The policy envisaged that through a process of negotiation and agreement, lands would pass to the communities, and the productive core of the ex-haciendas would be maintained to the benefit of both land groups. Events on the ground, however, were shortly to render this initiative irrelevant. In January 1989 a PCP–SL column attacked the ex-hacienda Laive, one of the most important *anexos* (sections) of the SAIS Cahuide, 'destroying completely the *casa hacienda*, farm buildings, machinery and all the infrastructure', before proceeding to distribute implements and livestock to smallholders and cooperative workers, instructing some 200 of the latter to return to their communities of origin.[82] Similar assaults shortly ravaged neighbouring cooperatives. In Manrique's opinion, through these actions the PCP–SL aimed to:

> completely isolate the countryside. Not only has the presence of the state been eradicated, the same happened to all rural development projects in the zone. The principal idea is that only Sendero and the peasantry should remain in the rural districts – until the counter-insurgency forces intervene to provoke the migration and uprooting of large numbers of peasants, as has taken place in Ayacucho and its environs.[83]

The important point was also made that once it had assigned cooperative resources 'Sendero had nothing else to offer the peasantry in the economic sphere'.[84]

Opportunity to build on peasant goodwill nevertheless presented itself with regard to social matters. The detention and assassination of rustlers by PCP–SL units caused a sharp decline in delinquency and met with general approval, as did instructions to merchants to offer just prices and ensure fair weights in commercial transactions. Pressure on schoolteachers to perform their tasks more conscientiously, along with crackdowns on drunken and adulterous behaviour, proved equally popular. Likewise, efforts to mobilise communal labour in agricultural activities, such as the cleaning of irrigation channels and field clearance, won widespread backing. Although Manrique thought that the PCP–SL's imposition of a more austere 'public morality' signified a 'reduction in individual liberty', he held that these actions received 'unanimous acceptance' because *campesinos* believed they represented 'a worthwhile trade-off for the security that Sendero afforded them ... Hierarchical paternalism and authoritarian violence was seen as legitimate'.[85]

Thus, the PCP–SL was best able to generate support in the countryside because it brought services that state bureaucracies failed to deliver – personal security, a form of order, an efficient (but summary) system of 'justice' – rather than significant economic benefits. Unfortunately for the insurgents, this honeymoon period did not last long. A number of schisms between guerrilla organisers and the rural population arose when cadres acted to tighten Party control over the *puna* communities and impose their ideological agenda. Hostility built up around three main issues: (i) demands that agriculturalists cut market ties and move towards self-sufficiency; (ii) the outbreak of inter-community clashes over lands that had recently been 'liberated' from the cooperatives (although Sendero cadres made it clear that these would not be tolerated, the insurgents inevitably became embroiled and executed twelve *campesinos* who had participated in such land invasions); and (iii) growing tensions between PCP–SL-imposed 'authorities' and attempts by legitimate community leaders to reassert their rights and resist guerrilla demands.[86]

As a result of these difficulties, Manrique calculated that as of 1989, the polit-ical and military situation in Junín had become confused. On the one hand, the state had failed to respond adequately to the needs and aspirations of rural people. To compound matters, its unimaginative counter-insurgency policy involved little more than repression, which had contributed to a serious esca-lation in violence. For its part, the PCP–SL had expanded and acquired a social base – mainly by taking advantage of a post-agrarian reform power vacuum following the demise of the *hacendados* and adopting the authoritarian pattern of socio-political behaviour characteristic of old-style *gamonalismo*.[87] Despite making ground, one problem facing the PCP–SL whenever it moved into new areas such as Junín was that the *gamonal* system of political domination never attained the same pervasive force that it acquired in Ayacucho. Junín's commer-cially vibrant and 'open' peasant communities had long contested attempts by the regional elite to meddle in their affairs. Because the local populace enjoyed a higher level of economic development, possessed a 'lengthy tradition of demo-cratic organisation' and had a longer history of participation in labour and peasant unions, the PCP–SL faced greater difficulty gaining adherents in Junín than in more backward rural areas such as Ayacucho. Moreover, its excessive violence had a negative impact on most of Junín's citizens, with the outcome that 'in the short term Sendero's authoritarianism cannot prosper'.[88]

Ayacucho 1988–92: *campesinos* take up arms against Sendero

Manrique's article had the merit of being among the first to identify a phenom-enon that would shortly produce a sea change in the trajectory of the civil war: a rupture between *senderista* guerrillas and the Andean peasantry when, during the second half of the 1980s and the early 1990s, important contingents of country people adopted a position of open rejection and moved to expel rebel detachments from their districts. This development brought a halt to the expan-sion and intensification of the PCP–SL's campaign, which had characterised most of the 1980s. It is fitting that the best accounts of these events relate to the birthplace of the PCP–SL, the department of Ayacucho. In a fine article,

José Coronel noted that in the province of Huanta during the first phase of the conflict (1980–82), the PCP–SL managed to attract recruits (i.e., gain 'active support') among elements of the population settled in valley communities located adjacent to the provincial capital. Echoing Favre's 'deindianisation' argument, Coronel opined that these converts originated mainly among bilingual children in well-to-do peasant and small merchant households, who had come into contact with PCP–SL militants while attending local secondary schools or the university in the town of Ayacucho. Utilising these ties, cadres gained entry to the villages, where (usually operating in teams of three) they carried out agricultural work in return for food. Having established a degree of rapport, they spread Sendero's message and managed to garner 'passive support' from many smallholders, although some communities rejected the guerrilla organisers. In Huanta this backing was built up – just as Manrique noted in the department of Junín – largely via the PCP–SL's 'moralising' campaign against rustlers, sharp merchants and other targets of peasant reproach. Because few cooperatives existed in Huanta, opportunities to gain adherents through the reallocation of land were limited and, overall, the guerrillas had few economic benefits to offer agriculturalists in the valley.[89]

With regard to the more isolated, high-altitude pastoral communities located in the *puna* above about 3,000 metres, PCP–SL contacts remained minimal, since the organisation could not draw upon the services of student 'gatekeepers' to facilitate access to the peasantry. Even so, as a result of its moralising activities and by playing on resentment arising from the history of ethnic discrimination experienced by this sector of the population, by 1982 PCP–SL activists had acquired 'a degree of acceptance' in these villages.[90] Their implantation nevertheless remained weak, so it came as no surprise that points of friction between peasant and guerrilla quickly arose. According to Coronel, Sendero adopted a 'colonial attitude' (i.e., domineering, authoritarian) in its dealings with the *puna* communities. Conflict here stemmed not from exhortations to reduce commodity exchange, but primarily from the 'nonrecognition, replacement and even assassination' of community authorities who had been elected in open assembly and enjoyed widespread respect and legitimacy.[91] After the guerrilla column operating in the mountains removed or killed several of these leaders, in late 1982 a number of communities started to mobilise and coordinate activities in order to defend themselves and drive the insurgents out of their district. The outcome was a series of bloody clashes and large-scale migration as peasants fled to the towns (primarily Huanta and Lima). Hostility towards the PCP–SL in these upland villages persisted through the 1980s and into the early 1990s.[92]

If the rupture in peasant–guerrilla relations occurred as early as 1982 vis-à-vis the *puna* population, the situation in the valley, where the PCP–SL was better entrenched, proved more complex. Here, the indiscriminate brutality of naval marine detachments sent into the area to eradicate the subversives (1983–85) acted to increase sympathy and tolerance towards the guerrillas. Repression simultaneously induced a lack of cooperation with the state. By the late 1980s, however, attitudes started to change, to the degree that during the first months of 1990, smallholders began to organise into Comités de Defensa Civil (CDCs) – Civil Defence Committees. To this end, they collected funds for the purchase of arms and ammunition, established a watch system along military lines (ex-conscripts figured prominently in getting the CDCs up and running), and mobilised communal labour to built fortifications to protect their villages. Coronel identified a number of factors that explained this transformation among the inhabitants of rural areas where the PCP–SL had been best received:

(i) after seven years of conflict, a certain war-weariness had overtaken the population, who felt increasingly that they had received few benefits while having to endure high levels of risk to person and property;

(ii) the guerrillas committed a series of tactical errors that fanned peasant hostility (e.g., they commandeered vital supplies without payment; demanded accommodation; forcibly enlisted youths into PCP–SL military units; murdered several respected peasant leaders);

(iii) smallholders internalised the experience of CDCs already functioning in neighbouring provinces, where success in expelling insurgent columns brought a marked reduction in violence and greater personal security; and

(iv) when the marines withdrew from Huanta (1985), they were replaced by army personnel who pursued a policy of more selective repression (army commanders tried to negotiate agreements with village leaders and by the early 1990s encouraged actively the formation of CDCs as part of a more 'population-friendly' counter-insurgency strategy).[93]

According to Coronel, CDC peasant militias took the brunt of PCP–SL attacks and played a 'decisive role' in defeating rebel columns operating in Huanta.[94]

Furthermore, their effectiveness was a source of pride. Participation acted to raise confidence and self-esteem among the rural population, in addition to fostering social cohesion and a cooperative spirit at the village level. One consequence of this development was that community leaders were better able to put pressure on urban-based functionaries when requesting health, education and infrastructure improvements. The end product of more than a decade of civil war was, therefore, that peasants in Huanta had moved from a position of low levels of organisation and mobilisation capacity to one where they possessed a considerable ability to engage in collective action and defend their interests.[95]

The model eventually copied by *campesinos* in Huanta province, in their search for ways to repel PCP–SL incursions, was provided by farming communities nearby in the Apurímac river valley. This *ceja de selva* (jungle's eyebrow) ecological zone was populated by migrant colonisers from the highlands, whose household economy revolved around the cultivation of coca and, to a lesser extent, cocoa, coffee and subtropical fruits. Events in the River Apurímac valley have been described in some detail by Ponciano del Pino. In one of the best articles written on the conflict, del Pino noted that PCP–SL units first entered the area in 1982, attracted by its potential as a place of refuge and regrouping for combatants operating in the *sierra* of Ayacucho. Here, the guerrillas encountered a farming population that had succeeded against all the odds in constructing a peasant federation with 106 affiliated *'bases'*: the Federación Campesina del Valle del Río Apurímac (FECVRA) – River Apurimac Valley Peasants Federation. By 1982, FECVRA had grown to become one of the most important grass-roots organisations in the department of Ayacucho, whose chief *raison d'être* was to break the prevailing monopolistic exploitation by rapacious local merchants (low farm-gate prices, persistent under-weighing of harvests, harsh repayment terms for cash and other advances, etc.). Despite widespread local backing, in 1983 the Federation collapsed under intense pressure from both the PCP–SL and the military: FECVRA activists were threatened and assassinated by insurgent cadres intent on removing political competitors from the countryside as they strove to win peasant support; encouraged by malicious misinformation emanating from local merchants, the naval marines came to view the FECVRA as a 'terrorist front' and hunted down its members with their customary ruthlessness.[96] That same year also witnessed a precipitous fall in the price of cocoa, coffee and other commercial crops, provoking a spectacular expansion in coca cultivation and an attendant deepening of business dealings with international drug cartels via the export of *pasta básica de cocaine* (cocaine paste) to Colombia.

Amid a rising tide of political violence in 1983 and 1984, smallholders moved to defend themselves by spontaneously relocating their places of residence to create more defendable 'strategic hamlets', simultaneously establishing *rondas campesinas* (peasant militias) to repel PCP–SL columns. This phenomenon commenced in settlements located in the southern section of the River Apurímac (late 1983), and over the course of the decade spread northwards through the valley to embrace *ceja de selva* farming communities in the neighbouring department of Junín (formed 1991–93), so that by 1993 approximately 280 settlements and 20,000 armed country people were enrolled in the CDCs.[97] Initially their members had to confront PCP–SL guerrillas with rudimentary weapons, but over time they managed to acquire more sophisticated arms, some provided by the state, although most frequently sourced via their contacts with Colombian drug traffickers. Despite being disadvantaged in terms of firepower, by 1988 the CDCs were in the forefront of the struggle against Sendero. They eventually managed 'to defeat completely' the insurgents and in 1988 came to exercise political–military control over the River Apurímac valley.[98] As in the case of Huanta, the CDCs evolved from purely military entities to assume a wide range of administrative functions, including the settling of land and family disputes between smallholders, policing activities and development initiatives around health, education and agriculture.

According to del Pino, these militias first appeared as a grass-roots response to a pressing local problem. In many instances they could not be regarded as simple counter-insurgency organs imposed 'from above' by the Peruvian state – the view taken by the PCP–SL (to its cost) and much of the media.[99] He pinpointed several factors that motivated villagers to take up arms against the guerrillas. First, the economic difficulties experienced by smallholders post-1983 were compounded by PCP–SL assaults against infrastructure (such as the dynamiting of bridges and the blocking of roads), while the exhortation to 'encircle and starve' the towns proved incongruent to agriculturalists whose well-being depended increasingly on production for the world narcotics trade. Consequently, the rebel organisation's political message did not relate to the basic needs of the population – Sendero had little practical help to offer them economically, while the levy of 'revolutionary contributions' reduced household income. Subversive activity in the area was also viewed negatively by agriculturalists insofar as it attracted state attention, which potentially threatened the smooth operation of coca production and processing. Second, the PCP–SL practice of removing village leaders, of replacing them with their own cadres and killing individuals who refused to stand aside, provoked opposition. At the outset this was covert, but it soon found overt expression in the shape of the CDCs. Third, smallholder animosity towards Sendero arose from attempts to dragoon local youths into its military columns; while a final focus of grievance concerned the predisposition of rebel commanders to assassinate people who they (often mistakenly) believed to be informers. One of the reasons the PCP–SL committed these errors, del Pino maintained, was that the organisation entered the River Apurímac valley and commenced operations without undertaking any serious political groundwork. It therefore possessed a superficial understanding of local conditions and had shallow political roots.[100]

In del Pino's opinion, the ability of colonisers to mobilise effectively and challenge the insurgents, despite seemingly unfavourable odds, was in part due to their historical memory. When Chilean forces occupied Huanta province during the War of the Pacific (1883), their forefathers had formed armed columns to repel the invader; years later, they organised to expropriate and expel the most powerful landowner in the province (1923). These experiences could be drawn upon in the search for an appropriate response to current difficulties. Although they were recently settled colonisers, because of their Andean roots the valley population was deeply imbued with a tradition of communal decision-making and action, which enhanced their capacity to mobilise. Importantly, solidarity was also achieved as a result of religion. A high proportion of smallholders in the southern section of the valley where peasant militias first appeared belonged to evangelical sects, particularly Pentecostals led by Peruvian pastors purveying 'a fundamentalist message with apocalyptic overtones, which held that we were living on the eve of the second coming of Christ. Therefore, spiritual redemption was the only thing to attain in this world.'[101] PCP–SL exhortations to abandon religion and join in a different kind of crusade were ignored, their actions repudiated, and the guerrillas identified with the Antichrist. Given the depth of their convictions, Pentecostals frequently became leaders of the CDCs and ranked among their most fearless combatants.

Like the inhabitants of settlements located adjacent to the town of Huanta, villagers living elsewhere in rural Peru followed the example provided by the denizens of the River Apurímac valley. High-altitude communities surrounding the Mantaro Valley and other areas of the Central Sierra organised peasant defence patrols to oust PCP–SL platoons active in their districts (mid-1990). Two years later, a similar process commenced in Puno department against the backdrop of 'a deepening break between the guerrillas and the rural population'.[102] In addition to an upsurge of hostility towards the PCP–SL by elements of the rural population, another important factor that facilitated the creation of *rondas campesinas* in the early 1990s was a shift in counter-insurgency policy on the part of the Peruvian armed forces. It is to a consideration of this dimension of the conflict that we now turn.

State responses to insurrection: from 'dirty war' to 'non-genocidal authoritarianism'

Surprisingly, the counter-insurgency performance of the Peruvian state long remained a neglected topic for detailed analysis. Throughout the 1980s and into the early 1990s, comment on this important aspect of the civil war was typically confined to short articles published in Lima's newspapers and weekly magazines, mostly critical of the efforts being made to handle the rebellion. Carlos Tapia has written one of the few thorough examinations of this issue. Tapia noted that the outbreak of PCP–SL actions caught the armed forces insufficiently prepared. Initially, the military failed to appreciate the nature of the guerrilla movement, assuming that it could be suppressed as easily as those of the mid-1960s. Apart from committing the cardinal errors of misjudging and underestimating their opponent, the security forces did not possess an adequate level of training. Instruction at the officer training college prioritised the waging of conventional warfare (for the defence of Peru from outside attack), while the manuals used in counter-insurgency courses were outdated.[103]

Tapia also pinpointed other factors that hampered the state's ability to meet the challenge posed by the PCP–SL's insurrection in an effective fashion. For political reasons, between 1980 and 1982 the Belaunde government ordered the police to deal with the revolt, a task it failed to accomplish. Consequently, when the armed forces finally entered the fray in January 1983, Sendero had had two years' vital breathing space to acquire combat experience, gain recruits and build up its party networks at the very moment when it was most vulnerable. A second problem concerned intelligence data, a question of paramount importance if a state is to pursue successfully an unconventional war. Unfortunately for the Peruvian armed forces, upon their arrival in Ayacucho they possessed minimal knowledge about PCP–SL organisational structures and membership.

A third area of difficulty involved the security forces' relationship with the civilian population, another issue crucial in determining the outcome of this type of 'asymmetrical' conflict. For security reasons, most of the police and nearly all the troops sent into Ayacucho came from outside the department, did not speak Quechua and possessed little understanding of the cultural traditions and idiosyncrasies of the local population. To aggravate matters, many officers viewed the *serranos* with disdain, even though to make headway it was necessary to win their hearts and minds. One outcome of this particular concatenation of circumstances was the launching of a 'scorched-earth' policy similar to that employed in Central America: the military aimed to terrorise potential or actual support for the PCP–SL in an attempt to divorce the 'fish' from the 'river'. The predictable result was a series of well-publicised massacres in Andean villages, the abuse of human rights on a massive scale and widespread alienation among the civilian population, many of whom came to view the military as an army of occupation. With military brutality acting as a recruiting sergeant for the guerrillas, it was hardly surprising that the rebellion, instead of being controlled, spread over a wider area and intensified during Belaunde's term in office (1980–85).[104]

Inheriting a counter-insurgency campaign that was patently failing, in 1985 the newly elected APRA administration headed by Alan García attempted to end the worst excesses of the dirty war, called upon the military to respect human rights and was aware of the need for rural development. After the unearthing of several mass graves in August 1985, García requested the resignation of a number of commanding officers and demanded sanctions against those field operatives directly responsible. This created a climate of tension and distrust between the government, the police and the armed forces, which led to a scaling-down in the level of anti-Sendero activity. Faced with what they interpreted as a lack of political backing, some military and police personnel started to demand written orders before entering the field. Others failed to act when neighbouring bases came under attack and, on occasions, garrisons even brokered accommodations with local guerrilla units.

Tapia argued that the resulting 'paralysis in counter-insurgency actions' handed Sendero the initiative and facilitated a relentless increase in the number and geographical distribution of subversive actions in 1985, 1986 and 1987. So despite a greater awareness of the difficulties faced in challenging the PCP–SL and the policies that needed to be implemented, the APRA administration, like its predecessor, proved incapable of 'developing a coherent and effective counter-insurgency strategy'.[105]

Against a backdrop of continued failure to halt the expansion of PCP–SL subversion, which attracted mounting criticism of the military's performance in Congress and the media, in 1989 the Peruvian armed forces finally took the bull by the horns. Fully nine years after the insurrection began, it moved to devise an integrated counter-insurgency policy, one that not only concentrated on military matters, but also gave emphasis to the socio-political, economic and psychological dimensions of waging unconventional warfare. After drawing together experiences from various theatres of conflict in the Andes and the *ceja de selva*, their new plan advocated a move away from what could be called a policy of scarcely controlled genocide and the adoption of a 'non-genocidal authoritarian' strategy that nevertheless involved selective repression. This entailed: (i) attempts to win over and organise the civilian population through Civic Action Programmes while simultaneously encouraging the formation of

peasant militias; and (ii) reorganising the state's intelligence services in an effort
to overcome the existing disorder and avoid a wasteful duplication of resources.
The latter involved improving coordination between the multiple and often
competing agencies engaged in the 'intelligence war' against the PCP–SL via
the establishment of a unified command structure and the pursuance of a
commonly agreed strategy.[106]

The new proposals were accepted and implemented efficaciously by the
Fujimori government that assumed office in July 1990. Between 1991 and 1992,
new legislation was enacted to legalise the peasant militias formed to confront
the PCP–SL and permit them to post arms. Additional resources were ploughed
into a reorganised intelligence service. A cluster of new laws was enacted to
facilitate judicial procedures against suspected subversives and to increase the
flow of information on their organisations (e.g. special courts to try cases of
terrorism presided over by 'faceless judges', the Repentance Law of May 1992,
etc.). These initiatives soon yielded fruit. Sendero's armed columns in many
parts of the highlands were already on the defensive owing to the activities of
the *rondas campesinas*, and in September 1992 the security forces managed to
capture Abimael Guzmán and other Central Committee members. Abundant
documentation seized in the raid on Guzmán's hideout led to the dismantling
of a number of important party structures. Guzmán's detention also proved
vital in other respects, because:

> the idea that terrorism could be defeated and that an adequate strategy was
> being pursued became implanted in the minds of the population. This key
> government success in the psychological sphere permitted a reversal in the
> scepticism and lack of confidence widespread among the population ... also,
> the capture of Abimael Guzmán enabled the counter-insurgency forces to
> move onto the offensive on all fronts. For the first time, it was evident that
> the strategic initiative lay with the state.[107]

Given this sea change in fortunes, many cadres were captured over the
following three years, handed themselves in to the authorities, or simply abandoned the struggle, so that by the mid-1990s the guerrilla campaign was much
reduced in scale and intensity, although not eradicated completely. The
PCP–SL no longer had a realistic chance of toppling the government and seizing
power. For its part, the Fujimori administration could, with some justification,
proclaim that the task of 'pacifying' the countryside was well advanced.

Conclusion

From the preceding review, it can be appreciated that in Ayacucho, Junín, Puno
and other departments in Peru's central and southern highlands, the trajectory
of the civil war followed (with varying timescales), a broadly similar path.
Regarding the relationship between the rural population and PCP–SL guerrillas, rebel cadres managed initially to attract active support from a minority.
In addition, through attacks on individuals engaged in modes of behaviour that

met with popular disapproval (petty thieves, sharp merchants, etc.), Sendero garnered a broader level of acceptance and passive support. Once the rebel organisation moved to impose its authority and control over villagers in a partic-ular locality, however, serious tensions quickly arose around a wide range of issues (such as the requisition of crops, removal of community leaders and the propensity to kill). This produced a cooling of relations, particularly among those sectors of the population that had once offered only passive backing or mere acceptance. The third and decisive phase in the conflict (1989–1992) witnessed a haemorrhaging of passive support for the PCP–SL among the Andean population, accompanied by a rapid expansion in active opposition. Anti-Sendero peasant militias spread to many districts, survived determined insurgent attempts at their destruction and succeeded in expelling guerrilla detachments from their farms and villages.

The second factor that turned the years from 1989 to 1992 into a period of seeming victory but concealed defeat for the PCP–SL concerned the state's ability to design and implement an efficient counter-insurgency policy. An initial phase of indecisiveness and inaction (1980–1982) was followed by a bout of largely indiscriminate repression and bloodletting that alienated a consider-able swathe of the civilian population (1983–87). Confronted with an ill-devised and ineffective 'strategy', after 1989 the armed forces changed tack by reducing (although not eliminating fully) the level of state terrorism, while simultane-ously making attempts to win the hearts and minds of villagers and enlist their support in the struggle against subversion. This policy shift produced positive results and contributed substantially to heavy PCP–SL reverses during the first half of the 1990s.

Two contrasting but interconnected cycles in the trajectory of the civil war between 1980 and 1995 can therefore be perceived. On the one hand, the PCP–SL acquired a certain level of support among sectors of the rural popu-lation, but through its own inadequacies the organisation failed to build upon these initial advances and eventually saw its support melt way. On the other hand, the political and repressive organs of the state attracted suspicion and rejection over much of the 1980s, but the state eventually succeeded in placing itself in a position to take full advantage of the growing enmity between Sendero and the civilian population. As a result, by the early 1990s many country-dwellers in the highlands were cooperating with the state. Fatally for its prospects, then, Sendero distanced itself from the population at the very moment when the state was moving closer to it. The objective of the following chapters is to examine the extent to which the course of the civil war in the northern highlands mirrored the pattern of events found in other regions of the Peruvian Andes.

References

1   For details on the transition from military to civilian rule see Michael Reid, *Peru: Paths to Poverty*, London, Latin American Bureau, 1985; and Philip Mauceri, 'The

Transition to "Democracy" and the Failures of Institution Building', in Maxwell Cameron and Philip Mauceri (eds.), *The Peruvian Labyrinth: Polity, Society, Economy*, Pennsylvania, Pennsylvania University Press, 1997, pp. 13–36.

2   Additional information on events described here is available in: Ricardo Letts, *La izquierda peruana: organizaciones y tendencias*, Lima, Mozca Azul Editores, 1981, pp. 57–60; Rogger Mercado, *El Partido Comunista del Perú 'Sendero Luminoso'*, Lima, Editorial de Cultura Popular, 1982, pp. 18–19; and Lewis Taylor, *Maoism in the Andes: Sendero Luminoso and the Contemporary Guerrilla Movement in Peru*, Liverpool, Centre for Latin American Studies, Working Paper No. 2, 1983, pp. 6–13.

3   On the growing rivalry between Paredes and Guzmán, as well as developments taking place within Maoist circles in Ayacucho during the late 1960s and early 1970s, see Carlos I. Degregori, *Ayacucho 1969–1979. El surgimiento de Sendero Luminoso: del movimiento por la gratuidad de la enseñanza al inicio de la lucha armada*, Lima, Instituto de Estudios Peruanos, 1990, pp. 166–74. The PCP–SL derived its name from the student section of the organisation in Ayacucho: the Frente Estudiantil Revolucionario por el Sendero Luminoso de Mariátegui.

4   The best discussion of these issues can be found in Degregori, *Ayacucho 1969–1979*, pp. 184–92.

5   Born in 1894, José Carlos Mariátegui was the foremost Marxist theoretician in Latin America during the late 1920s. After a visit to Europe (1919–23), where he witnessed the debate within the Partito Socialista Italiano, attended the Livorno Congress of 1921 and came into contact with the L'Ordine Nuovo group around Antonio Gramsci, Mariátegui returned to Peru and became involved in the 'popular universities' run to provide educational programmes for Lima's workers. In 1926 he established *Amauta*, one of Latin America's leading cultural and political journals, as well as contributing to other publications aimed at promoting popular organisations in Peru. Mariátegui also played a leading role in the foundation of the Peruvian Socialist Party (1928) and the following year he helped create the Confederación General de Trabajadores del Perú (CGTP) – the General Confederation of Peruvian Workers, Peru's main labour federation. After a protracted illness, he died in 1930 aged 35. He became a guru of the Peruvian left, and during the 1970s and 1980s all groups claimed to be the true heirs to Mariátegui's political thought and project. Accessible introductions to Mariátegui's life and writings are Diego Meseguer, *José Carlos Mariátegui y su pensamiento revolucionario*, Lima, Instituto de Estudios Peruanos, 1974; Jesús Chavarría, *José Carlos Mariátegui and the Rise of Modern Peru, 1890–1930*, Albuquerque, University of New Mexico Press, 1979; and Harry E. Vanden, *National Marxism in Latin America: José Carlos Mariátegui's Thought and Politics*, Boulder, CO, Lynne Rienner Publishers, 1986.

6   Further details regarding the PCP–SL's shrinking presence within these grass-roots organisations and its largely unsuccessful attempts to counter its marginalised status by establishing parallel bodies dominated by the Party are provided in Carlos I. Degregori, *'Sendero Luminoso': Parte I: Los hondos y mortales desencuentros; Parte II: Lucha armada y utopia autoritaria*, Lima, Instituto de Estudios Peruanos, Documentos de Trabajo Nos. 4 and 6, 1986, pp. 33–35; and Degregori, *El surgimiento de Sendero Luminoso*, pp. 191–99. It is important to note, however, that this was not a unilinear process, for in 1976 the PCP–SL list managed to regain control of the Federación de Estudiantes at the UNSCH.

7   V. I. Lenin, 'Better Fewer, But Better', in *Collected Works*, Vol. 33, Moscow, Progress Publishers, 1966, pp. 487–502. Among the key texts on organisation figure V. I. Lenin, 'An Urgent Question', ibid., Vol. 4, Moscow, Foreign Languages Publishing House, 1960, pp. 221–26; 'What is to be Done?', ibid., Vol. 5, Moscow: Foreign

Languages Publishing House, 1961, pp. 347–527; and 'One Step Forward, Two Steps Back', ibid., Vol. 7, Moscow, Foreign Languages Publishing House, 1961, pp. 203–415.

8   Among the groups that gravitated towards the PCP–SL was Puku Llacta (a Quechua name meaning 'Tierra Roja', or 'Red Land'), a faction that had broken away from the PCP–Patria Roja in 1979 and whose membership was concentrated in the mining zones of the departments of Junín and Cerro de Pasco. Other minuscule groups that took the same route included the MIR–Cuarta Etapa, based around Chosica on the outskirts of Lima; the Nucleos Marxistas–Leninistas, a group that had split from the PCP–PR in 1967 and whose main area of activity was the town of Chimbote on the northern coast; and the VR–Político–Militar centred in Lima. Another important source of cadres who entered the ranks of the PCP–SL in 1979–80 and were well experienced in political organisation in the countryside was the VR–Proletario Comunista (VR–PC). Further details on this development in relation to the northern highlands are given in Chapter Three. According to Mercado, 'Shortly after initiating armed struggle, the insurrectionary organisation was reinforced by the constant recruitment of revolutionary elements who resigned from other parties and solicited membership of Sendero ... The political work of Sendero had also been productive and succeeded in absorbing considerable sectors of other parties, who on an individual basis, requested to be included in the Party, accepting its discipline, its ideological stance and bringing with them the knowledge acquired from working in their previous organisations'. Mercado, *El Partido Comunista del Perú*, p. 20. This assessment overestimates the number of individuals who switched from other left parties to the PCP–SL at this juncture. However, Mercado's monograph is useful, as it provides a broadly sympathetic account and thus acts as an antidote to the mostly hostile literate on the PCP–SL published at the time.

9   Gustavo Gorriti, *Sendero: historia de la guerra milenaria en el Perú*, Lima, Editorial Apoyo, 1991, 4th edition, pp. 49–58.

10   Ibid., p. 110. Degregori aptly used the metaphor of 'dwarf star' – small but burning very bright – to describe the organisation's evolution. See Carlos I. Degregori, 'A Dwarf Star', *NACLA Report on the Americas* 24: 4, 1990–91, pp. 10–19.

11   Gorriti, *Sendero*, p. 140.

12   On this issue, see the discussion surrounding the publications of Henri Favre mentioned below in notes 58–61.

13   José Carlos Mariátegui, *Seven Interpretive Essays on Peruvian Reality*, Austin, TX, University of Texas Press, 1974, p. 16.

14   Ibid., p. 12.

15   Ibid., p. 15.

16   Ibid., p. 16.

17   Ibid., p. 18.

18   Ibid., p. 34.

19   See 'Principios Programáticos del Partido Socialista', in José Carlos Mariátegui, *Ideología y política*, Lima, Empresa Editora Amauta, 1971, pp. 159–64.

20   Mariátegui, 'Principios Programáticos', p. 159; 'El problema de las razas en la América Latina', in *Ideología y política*, p. 34. Also see Marc Becker, 'Mariátegui y el problema de las razas en América Latina', *Revista Andina* 35, 2002, pp. 191–220.

21   Mariátegui, *Ideología y política*, pp. 40–46. The term *gamonal* originates from the word *gamonito*, a short, thick, parasitic sucker that grows near the roots of vines and other trees, absorbing sap meant to feed the fruit.

22   Meseguer, *José Carlos Mariátegui*, pp. 199–208. Mariátegui's position here was influ-

enced by his experiences in Italy during the rise of fascism, post-Revolution developments in Mexico and the polemic that took place in the late 1920s with Víctor Raúl Haya de la Torre, who founded the Alianza Popular Revolucionaria Americana (APRA) – American Popular Revolutionary Alliance – a radical nationalist party. APRA doctrine held that given the existence of an 'infant industrial proletariat' and a 'numerous but ignorant peasantry' in Peru, the anti-imperialist movement would be headed by the 'impoverished middle classes'.

23 Mariátegui, *Ideología y política*, p. 161; Vanden, *National Marxism*, pp. 66, 68. On Mariátegui's problematic relationship with the International, which came to a head at the Buenos Aires Conference of the Latin American sections (June 1929), see Alberto Flores Galindo, *La agonía de Mariátegui: la polémica con la Komintern*, Lima, DESCO, 1982.

24 See Fernando Claudin, *The Communist Movement: from Comintern to Cominform*, Harmondsworth, Penguin Books, 1975, pp. 152–66.

25 Matters came to a head in June 1929 at the First Congress of Latin American Communist Parties, held in Buenos Aires. The theses drafted by Mariátegui came under sustained criticism from the rigid apparatchiks who ran the Comintern's South American Secretariat. Flores Galindo, *La agonía*, pp. 33–36, 73–90.

26 Mao Tse-tung (Zedong), 'The Chinese Revolution and the Chinese Communist Party', *Selected Works*, Vol. 2, Beijing: Foreign Languages Press, 1967, pp. 309–14.

27 Mao Tse-tung (Zedong), 'Analysis of the Classes in Chinese Society', *Selected Works*, Vol. 1, p. 13.

28 Ibid., pp. 14–15.

29 Ibid., p. 16.

30 Ibid., pp. 16–18.

31 Ibid., p. 18.

32 Ibid.

33 Ibid., p. 19.

34 Ibid.

35 Mao Tse-tung (Zedong), 'The Chinese Revolution', pp. 318–29; 'Introducing The Communist', *Selected Works*, Vol. 2, pp. 289–90.

36 Mao Tse-tung (Zedong), 'Report on an Investigation of the Peasant Movement in Hunan', *Selected Works*, Vol. 1, p. 25.

37 Ibid.

38 Ibid., p. 24.

39 Claudin, *The Communist Movement*, pp. 271–83.

40 The key texts on political and military questions utilised in this and the following paragraph, are: 'Why is it that Red Political Power can Exist in China?', *Selected Works*, Vol. 1, pp. 63–72; 'Problems of Strategy in China's Revolutionary War', *Selected Works*, Vol. 1, pp. 179–254; 'Problems of Strategy in Guerrilla War Against Japan', *Selected Works*, Vol. 2, pp. 79–112; 'On Protracted War', *Selected Works*, Vol. 2, pp. 113–94; and 'Problems of War and Strategy', *Selected Works*, Vol. 2, pp. 219–35.

41 'The principle for the Red Army is concentration, and that for the Red Guards dispersion.' Mao Tse-tung (Zedong), 'The Struggle in the Chingkang Mountains', *Selected Works*, Vol. 1, p. 85.

42 'Problems of Strategy in China's Revolutionary War', *Selected Works*, Vol. 1, pp. 237, 239.

43 'Problems of Strategy in Guerrilla War Against Japan', *Selected Works*, Vol. 2, pp. 102–109; 'On Protracted War', pp. 119, 136–45.

44 'On Protracted War', p. 143; 'Problems of Strategy in Guerrilla War Against Japan',

pp. 109–11.

45 PCP–SL, '¡Retomemos a Mariátegui y reconstituyamos su partido!', October 1975, in Luis Arce (ed.), *Guerra popular en el Perú: el pensamiento Gonzalo*, Brussels, n.p., 1989, pp. 72–73.

46 Ibid., pp. 73–76. PCP–SL, '¡Contra las ilusiones constitucionales y por el estado de nueva democracia!', April 1978, in Arce (ed.), *Guerra popular en el Perú*, pp. 96–111.

47 '¡Retomemos a Mariátegui!', pp. 73–75. PCP–SL, 'Programa general de la revolución democrática', 1988, in Arce (ed.), *Guerra popular en el Perú*, pp. 412–13.

48 PCP–SL, 'La guerra popular es una guerra campesina o no es nada', February–March 1981, reproduced in Mercado, *El Partido Comunista del Perú*, pp. 28–47. According to this document, 'because in semi-feudal and semi-colonial countries towns comprise the bastions of counter-revolutionary forces while rural areas form the weak link in the system of domination, it is here that we find the principal motor force of the national–democratic revolution: the peasantry. The task of the revolution is to become strong in the countryside, which implies agitation among the peasantry, opening guerrilla warfare, establishing rural support bases, and utilising the countryside to encircle the towns and finally conqueror them'. Ibid., p. 45. The '*batir el campo*' quote is an extract from Guzmán's speech to the II National Conference of the PCP–SL (May 1982) and is transcribed in 'Las conferencias senderistas', *Quehacer* 30, August 1984, p. 20.

49 PCP–SL, '¡Desarrollar la guerra popular sirviendo a la revolución mundial', August 1986, in Arce (ed.), *Guerra popular en el Perú*, pp. 220–21, 238–39, 246–47.

50 This point was brought home to me forcefully in September 1982, during a conversation about Sendero's insurrection with an acquaintance who had been a member of Bandera Roja and would shortly join the PCP–SL. I was told that: 'All we need is the party, the united front and a mass political line. Everything else is froth.' A stress on intense activism rather than analysis has been a characteristic of most Maoist parties throughout the world, including those in Peru – which, typically, produced very few internal discussion documents or theoretical journals, despite the admonitions of the 'Great Helmsman' to do 'some hard thinking'.

51 For Lenin 'the chief mistake made by revolutionaries' is 'that they look backwards at the old revolutions'. *Collected Works*, Vol. 24, p. 141.

52 The first substantial document released (indirectly and in mimeograph format with a limited circulation) by the PCP–SL, entitled 'La Guerra popular es una Guerra campesina o no es nada' ('The popular war is a peasant war or it is nothing'), commenced circulation in 1981. It comprised a review of the main military actions undertaken by the insurgents, a call to arms against the state and a justification for insurrection. This was followed by 'Desarrollamos la guerra de guerrillas' ('Let us develop guerrilla war'), which appeared in March 1982.

53 Among the first general publications on the PCP–SL figured Rogger Mercado, *El Partido Comunista del Perú*, and in English, Lewis Taylor, *Maoism in the Andes*. Early examples of quality journalistic accounts that discussed events at a district level are Sonia Goldenberg, 'Los montoneros de Huanta: una jornada en las alturas navalizadas', *Debate* 28, September 1984, pp. 40–45; and Gustavo Gorriti and Abilio Arroyo, 'La guerra de Sivia', *Caretas* 838, 18 February 1985, pp. 36–38, 72. In October 1982, Raúl González published the first of several informative articles in the bi-monthly magazine *Quehacer*. After 1985 his reports concentrated increasingly on the complex conflicts unfolding in localities as diverse as Puno and the Upper Huallaga Valley. A number of these texts are reviewed later in this chapter.

54 Cynthia McClintock, 'Why Peasants Rebel: the Case of Peru's Sendero Luminoso', *World Politics* 37:1, 1984, p. 48.

55 Ibid., p. 74. In a classic text, Wolf posited that 'middle peasants' and smallholding populations located in 'peripheral' areas, who enjoyed relatively high degrees of autonomy from state control comprised 'the pivotal groupings for peasant uprisings'. These 'tactically mobile' social actors were crucial, because they had 'independence' from both landlords and state officials; they also possessed resources with which to mount and sustain a rebellion. When their subsistence household economies came under threat from demographic increase and the 'dance of commodities' that accompanied the spread of 'North Atlantic capitalism', 'middle' and 'peripheral' smallholders provided the 'spark' for revolution. A number of similar positions surfaced in the work of James Scott, who, in an influential monograph also placed 'the subsistence ethic at the center of the analysis of peasant politics'. For Scott, peasant 'indignation', mobilisation and revolution occurred when smallholders faced a threat to their subsistence minimum. Resentment might be provoked by: (i) environmental pressures (droughts, floods, etc.); (ii) excessive demands by the state (via taxation, conscription, labour drafts); and (iii) the expansion of 'North Atlantic capitalism', which brought greater 'individualism'. The spread of non-cooperative mores into village life undermined kinship ties and grassroots reciprocal insurance systems, or the communal 'moral economy' that traditionally enabled household economies to survive during times of stress. See Eric Wolf, *Peasant Wars of the Twentieth Century*, London, Faber & Faber, 1971, pp. 276–302; James Scott, *The Moral Economy of the Peasant: Rebellion and Subsistence in Southeast Asia*, New Haven, CT, Yale University Press, 1976, pp. 1–34.

56 McClintock, 'Why Peasants Rebel', pp. 49, 58, 82.

57 Ibid., pp. 76–81. For a trenchant critique of McClintock's argument, see Deborah Poole and Gerardo Rénique, 'The New Chroniclers of Peru: US Scholars and their "Shining Path" of Peasant Rebellion', *Bulletin of Latin American Research* 10: 2, 1991, pp. 133–91.

58 Henri Favre, 'Sendero Luminoso y horizontes oscuros', *Quehacer* 31, October 1984, pp. 29–30. In this regard, Popkin makes a poignant observation: 'revolutionaries who expect peasants to have no interest in market production as long as their subsistence floor is secure are likely... to have problems maintaining control when peasants in liberated areas seek to enter the markets with their newly recovered surplus'. Samuel Popkin, *The Rational Peasant: the Political Economy of Rural Society in Vietnam*, Berkeley, CA, University of California Press, 1979, pp. 28–29.

59 Favre, 'Sendero Luminoso', pp. 30–32.

60 Ibid., pp. 32–34.

61 Ibid., pp. 26, 34. The basic argument was restated in Raúl González, '"Desexorcizando" a Sendero: una entrevista con Henri Favre', *Quehacer* 42, August–September 1986, pp. 44–48. Favre's general thesis was reproduced, without proper acknowledgement, in Alain Hertoghe and Alain Labrousse, *Le Sentier Lumineux de Pérou: un nouvel intégrisme dans le tiers monde*, Paris, Editions la Découverte, 1989.

62 See Mario Vargas Llosa, Luis Millones et al., *Informe de la Comisión Investigadora de los sucesos de Uchuraccay*, Lima, Editora Perú, 1983. An intelligent discussion about the nineteenth century and contemporary experiences of these *puna* communities is provided by Cecilia Méndez-Gastelumendi, 'The Power of Naming, or the Construction of Ethnic and National Identities in Peru: Myth, History and Iquichanos', *Past and Present* 171, May 2001, pp. 127–60.

63 Degregori, *Sendero Luminoso*, p. 41.

64 Ibid., p. 42.

65 Ibid.

66 Ibid., p. 43.

67 Ibid., p. 44.

68 Ibid., pp. 46–47.

69 Ibid.

70 Ronald Berg, '"Sendero Luminoso" and the Peasantry of Andahuaylas', *Journal of Inter-American Studies and World Affairs* 28: 4, Winter 1986–1987, pp. 165–96. A revised version of this article appeared as 'Peasant Responses to Shining Path in Andahuaylas', in David Scott Palmer, *Shining Path of Peru*, London, Hurst and Company, 1992, pp. 83–104. Quotes are from the latter.

71 Ibid., p. 96.

72 Ibid., pp. 96–97, 102.

73 José María Salcedo, 'Puno: ¿esperando a Sendero?', *Quehacer* 36, August–September 1985, pp. 55–58.

74 Ibid.

75 Ibid., p. 55.

76 Ibid., p. 57.

77 Raúl González, 'Puno: el corredor senderista', *Quehacer* 39, February–March 1986, pp. 49–51.

78 Ibid., p. 56.

79 Ibid., p. 58. Other articles that examined events in Puno at this juncture included Fernando Vásquez, 'Las alturas de Sendero: informe de Puno', *Debate* 40, September 1986, pp. 29–38; and Lewis Taylor, 'Agrarian Unrest and Political Conflict in Puno, 1985–1987', *Bulletin of Latin American Research* 6: 2, 1987, pp. 135–62. The last focused on the complex conflicts between the PUM (an organisation of the legal left with considerable rural support in Puno), the PCP–SL and the ruling APRA party. A well-crafted piece that brings the story more up to date is José Luis Rénique, 'Apogee and Crisis of a "Third Path": *Mariateguismo*, "People's War" and Counterinsurgency in Puno, 1987–1994', in Steve J. Stern (ed.), *Shining and Other Paths: War and Society in Peru, 1980–1995*, Durham, NC, Duke University Press, 1998, pp. 307–38.

80 Nelson Manrique, 'La década de la violencia', *Márgenes* 3: 5–6, 1989, pp. 137–82. An abridged version of this article was also published under the title 'Sierra Central: la batalla decisiva', *Quehacer* 60, August–September 1989, pp. 63–71.

81 According to Manrique: 'Among agriculturalists in the lower-lying valley lands, the reaction to the blows received from Sendero has been one of indignation and the decision to resist, if necessary by resorting to arms. This is the case, for example, of the small- and medium-scale dairy producers organised in FONGAL [the local producers cooperative], who were affected badly by the destruction of the processing plant Leche Mantaro'; 'La década de la violencia', p. 151.

82 Ibid., pp. 152–54.

83 Ibid., p. 155.

84 Ibid., p. 156.

85 Ibid., pp. 157–58.

86 Ibid., pp. 161–62.

87 Ibid., pp. 164–66.

88 Ibid., pp. 169–70, 175, 180.

89 José Coronel, 'Violencia política y repuestas campesinas en Huanta', in Carlos I. Degregori (ed.), *Las rondas campesinas y la derrota de Sendero Luminoso*, Lima, Instituto de Estudios Peruanos/Universidad Nacional San Cristóbal de Huamanga, 1996, pp. 43–44, 77–78. Because the majority of PCP–SL recruits in Huanta originated from the households of merchants and well-to-do peasants, Coronel argued

that 'no direct correlation existed between the degree of [rural] poverty and the degree of support for political violence'. Ibid., p. 104.

90 Ibid., pp. 43–47, 70–71, 90–91.

91 On this point Coronel stated that: 'It has been frequently claimed that *senderista* attempts to close rural markets provoked confrontation with the *comuneros*. However, in a series of testimonies that we have collected, the prime cause of peasant rejection of SL was shown to be the non-recognition, removal and even assassination of community authorities. In some cases, our interviewees associated attacks on traditional leaders with the attack on "our father" '. Ibid., pp. 47–48, 71, 105.

92 According to Coronel: 'in January 1983 the peasants of Huaychao in an act of reprisal killed seven young members of the *senderista* column that circulated in the zone … already agreements existed to coordinate resistance against Sendero. At this moment the *"sinchis"* [counter-insurgency police] appeared, with all the paraphernalia of war – machine-guns, grenades, rifles, ammunition – which was in stark contrast to the arms carried by the *senderista* columns. This may have reinforced the determination of the villagers to confront SL, but it is necessary to stress that the initial decision had already been taken'. Ibid., pp. 47–48.

93 Ibid., pp. 46, 61–62, 73, 83, 93–94.

94 Ibid., pp. 97–98, 103, 106.

95 Ibid., pp. 102–104. These issues are also addressed in Orin Starn, 'La resistencia de Huanta', *Quehacer* 84, July–August 1993, pp. 34–41; and extensively in Mario Fumerton, *From Victims to Heroes: Peasant Counter-rebellion and Civil War in Ayacucho, Peru, 1980–2000*, Amsterdam, Rozenberg Publishers, 2002, chapters 4 and 5.

96 Ponciano del Pino, 'Tiempos de guerra y de dioses: ronderos, evangélicos y senderistas en el valle del río Apurímac', in Degregori (ed.), *Las rondas campesinas*, pp. 125–27, 132–34.

97 Ibid., pp. 138, 148, 152. On the organisational structure of the CDCs, see ibid., pp. 152–56. The *rondas* formed in the southern section of the valley were a spontaneous creation of the local population; those established during the early 1990s in the northern part of the valley had more of a military input.

98 Ibid., pp. 167–68, 170, 176.

99 Ibid., p. 135.

100 According to del Pino: 'Among other causes, the reaction against SL can be explained by the fact that even though its militants arrived late in the zone, they made demands almost immediately. Already in 1982 Sendero's Central Committee had decided to *"batir el campo"*, expel all representatives of the state and command a greater degree of collaboration from the population and youth. For this reason, the assassination of authorities began shortly after the arrival of SL in the zone. However, to implement this party policy without prior political groundwork carried greater risks of an adverse reaction from the locals, as in effect happened'. Ibid., pp. 133, 135–36, 138–39.

101 Ibid., p. 131.

102 Rénique, 'Apogee and Crisis', p. 331. Details on the Central Sierra can be found in Orin Starn, 'Sendero, soldados y ronderos en el Mantaro', *Quehacer* 74, November–December 1991, pp. 60–68; and Nelson Manrique, 'The War for the Central Sierra', in Stern (ed.), *Shining and Other Paths*, pp. 193–223. This article is also published in Nelson Manrique, *El tiempo de miedo: la violencia política en el Perú, 1980–1996*, Lima, Fondo Editorial del Congreso del Perú, 2002, pp. 187–226. Official figures originating from the Peruvian armed forces claimed that by 1993 some 525 CDCs mobilising some 34,537 people had been established in the depart-

ment of Junín. A further 198 and 68 were operating in the neighbouring departments of Huancavelica and Cerro de Pasco. See del Pino, 'Tiempos de guerra', p.
181.
103 Carlos Tapia, *Las fuerzas armadas y Sendero Luminoso: dos estrategias y un final*, Lima,
    Instituto de Estudios Peruanos, 1997, pp. 27–31, 37. On the (often tense) relation-
    ship between the military and civilian governments during the 1980s, which created
    a far-from-perfect environment for formulating counter-insurgency policy, see
    Philip Mauceri, *Militares: insurgencia y democratización en el Perú, 1980–1988*, Lima,
    Instituto de Estudios Peruanos, 1989. According to one commentator, when the
    insurrection broke out 'the armed forces did not possess expertise in conducting
    anti-guerrilla warfare … their theoretical knowledge on counter-insurgency was
    limited to copies of two US army manuals dating from the 1950s'. Enrique Obando,
    'Diez años de guerra antisubversiva: una pequeña historia', *Quehacer* 72,
    July–August 1991, p. 47. An analysis of the Peruvian military's counter-insurgency
    performance in relation to arguments about the conduct of unconventional warfare,
    forwarded by Robert Thompson, is available in Lewis Taylor, 'Counter-insurgency
    Strategy, the PCP-Sendero Luminoso and the Civil War in Peru, 1980–1996',
    Bulletin of Latin American Research 17: 1, 1998, pp. 35–58.
104 Tapia, *Las fuerzas armadas*, pp. 27–37. One document from the high command that
    was leaked to the press in 1991 indicated that the military had been operating on a
    'shoot-to-kill' basis. It advocated counter-insurgency actions 'of a highly offensive
    and aggressive nature, without losing sight of the fact that the best subversive is a
    dead subversive. Therefore, no prisoners will be taken'; ibid., p. 79. Also see
    Mauceri, *Militares*, pp. 35–50; and Taylor, 'Counter-insurgency Strategy', pp.
    41–44. A harrowing account of military and security service incompetence, torture
    and extra-judicial killing in Ayacucho and other theatres of conflict during the 1980s
    is provided in Ricardo Uceda, *Muerte en el Pentagonito: los cementerios secretos del
    Ejército Peruano*, Bogotá, Editorial Planeta, 2004.
105 Tapia, *Las fuerzas armadas*, pp. 39–42. Also see Mauceri, *Militares*, pp. 50–57;
    Obando, 'Diez años', p. 49; and Taylor, 'Counter-insurgency Strategy', pp. 45–47.
106 The new manual, entitled *Guerra no convencional. Contrasubversión*, was approved
    by the high command on 9 August 1990. It argued that 'the strategic problem of
    the counter-insurgency forces is to find the favourable minority and organise it to
    mobilise the neutral majority against the opposing minority'. As well as winning
    civilian support, it recognised that: 'In a war against subversion, intelligence counts
    for 80 per cent and military operations 20 per cent'. The document is discussed in
    Tapia, *Las fuerzas armadas*, pp. 43–55. This change in approach has been interpreted
    as a shift from '*la guerre révolutionnaire*' model pursued with bloody consequences
    by the French army in Algeria (and copied during the dirty war in Argentina in the
    1970s) to the so-called 'British doctrine' developed in Malaya during the
    'Emergency'. In 1989 the Peruvian armed forces translated into Spanish texts by
    established figures such as Robert Thompson and Richard Clutterbuck. See Tapia,
    Las fuerzas armadas, p. 44. For Clutterbuck's opinions on the insurrection in Peru,
    see Richard Clutterbuck, 'Peru: How to Defeat SL?', *Army Quarterly and Defence
    Journal*, October 1992. With the counter-insurgency campaign faltering, the search
    soon began for alternative policies. In this regard, see the interview with Thompson
    that appeared in Peru's best-selling weekly magazine, *Caretas* 935, 22 December
    1986, pp. 34–37. For a wider discussion contrasting British and US approaches to
    asymmetrical warfare, see John A. Nagl, *Counterinsurgency Lessons from Malaya and
    Vietnam: Learning to Eat Soup with a Knife*, London, Praeger Publishers, 2002.
107 Tapia, *Las fuerzas armadas*, p. 79.

CHAPTER TWO

Landscapes and History

The aim of this chapter is to provide the reader with an understanding of the geography of the Cajabamba–Huamachuco region. A basic knowledge of topography and climate is important. They influence the trajectory of the civil war in this part of the northern highlands on a number of levels, from providing a terrain that affords certain advantages for conducting a guerrilla campaign, to exercising an impact on relations between the local population and the insurgents. The chapter also outlines key features of the area's socio-economic and political history, giving particular focus to events dating from the late nineteenth century. It concludes with an assessment of the impact of land reform in Cajabamba and Huamachuco, along with an account of the social conflicts generated by the expropriation of haciendas in the years immediately preceding the PCP– SL launch of armed insurrection in 1980.

The setting

The area of Peru's northern highlands where the events examined in this book occurred is a zone of outstanding natural beauty that will be partly familiar to readers acquainted with one of Latin America's most popular novels, Ciro Alegría's *Broad and Alien is the World*. Within the Cajabamba–Huamachuco region, a number of contrasting ecological zones can be identified. The landscape is dominated by a succession of imposing mountains that rise to more than 4,000 metres above sea level. On bleak, windswept moors lying at 3,200–4,000 metres (called *jalcas* in this part of the sierra), sheep and sturdy cattle graze on sparse natural pastures. Potatoes, along with other indigenous varieties of tuber (*ocas, ollucos*) and grains (*quinoa*), are sown in modest quantities, for despite the presence of an adequate water supply flowing from the numerous shallow lakes that dot these uplands, the climate is not generally conducive to husbandry. As a result of rapid demographic growth and accelerating land hunger, however, settlement and agricultural activity have been increasing steadily at these high elevations in recent decades.

Nestling between the mountains, narrow valleys at altitudes of 2,200 to 3,200 metres have more fertile soils, warmer temperatures and an environment amenable to agriculture. Not surprisingly, the bulk of the rural population resides in this, the *quechua* ecological zone. Here, cultivation revolves around the production of cereals (chiefly maize, barley and, to a lesser degree, wheat), pulses, potatoes and vegetables. Livestock-rearing also plays a central role in the farming system. Scattered through the countryside, a myriad of adobe dwellings topped with terracotta tiled roofs and surrounded by a dense patchwork of small fields can be seen. The peasant freeholders who inhabit these modest constructions typically live on privately owned smallholdings, for unlike many other areas of Andean Peru, in Cajabamba–Huamachuco most of the rural population is settled in dispersed hamlets, not in sizeable villages. The valleys also house the main urban centres, such as San Marcos, Cajabamba and Santiago de Chuco, although Huamachuco (located at 3,160 metres above sea level) has a less benign climate (see Map 2). While not having large populations (Cajabamba, the most populous settlement, had 3,196 inhabitants in 1940 and 5,946 in 1972), these small country towns have always been vitally important for rural people. In addition to forming the hub of administrative and political power, they provide essential mercantile, educational, legal, medical and religious services.

At a slightly lower elevation (2,000–2,200 metres), the fast-flowing River Condebamba, which rises in the mountain range that divides Cajabamba from Huamachuco, has gouged out a flat valley bottom 3–4 kilometres wide. The fluvial soil is extremely productive and, when combined with an agreeable subtropical climate, permits the cultivation of sugar cane, cassava, chilli, bananas and citrus fruits destined for sale in regional markets. Intensive cattle-rearing also occurs. Two to three days' walk from the towns of Cajabamba and Huamachuco on an easterly path, the Andean range falls away in spectacular fashion to meet the Amazon lowlands, the area that formed the setting for Ciro Alegría's novel *El serpiente de oro*, an allusion to the River Marañón. In the intermediate ecological niche that joins these contrasting geographical areas – the *ceja de selva*, or 'jungle's eyebrow' – subtropical temperatures permit the production of coca and exotic fruits, along with small quantities of coffee and cacao. The nature of this zone's socio-economic relationship with the sierra is succinctly captured through a character in the opening chapter of *El serpiente de oro*, set in the small settlement of Calemar perched on the banks of the Marañón:

> from the mountains outsiders come, and we go to the fairs at Huamachuco and Cajabamba, taking coca to sell, or simply to make the trip ... [the Indians] ... come from the mountains ... to exchange potatoes, *ollucos* and any other highland product, for coca, chilli, bananas and the numerous fruits that grow here ... Here life is good. Even death breathes life.

Despite its fecundity, this zone traditionally supported few inhabitants due to the threat of tropical diseases, but during the second half of the twentieth century it became a permanent place of residence for constantly increasing numbers of land-starved smallholders migrating from the densely populated highlands.

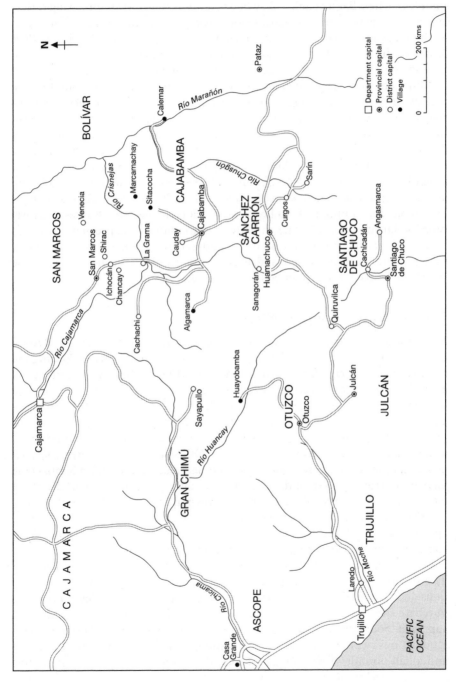

Map 2 *Cajabamba–Huamachuco: Provincial and District Capitals*

Travelling in the opposite direction, on the western fringe of the Andes the mountains meet the coastal desert. Here the two most important rivers running down to the Pacific, the Chicama and the Moche, rapidly lose altitude. On their middle reaches, flat irrigable valley floors support the cultivation of sugar, rice, cassava, citrus fruit and mangos, before giving way to the broader cane fields of the large sugar estates located in the Chicama and Santa Catalina Valleys (Map 2). In recent decades, given the attractive farm-gate prices, the illegal planting of coca bushes for processing into cocaine paste has expanded.

Although these clearly demarcated ecological zones are to be found in this part of the *sierra*, it is important to appreciate that an extremely rugged mountainous terrain and proximity to the equator cause a wide variety of microclimates to exist in close proximity. This special Andean geography allows farmers to plant crops as diverse as coca, bananas, potatoes and temperate cereals, all within a day's walking distance of one another. Smallholders consequently try to access land at different ecological levels in an attempt to insure against potential crop failure and broaden the choice of foodstuffs available for household consumption. Families without plots at varying altitudes regularly mobilise kinship links in order to barter commodities. The precipitous topography also makes communication by land tortuous, especially in the rainy season (October–April) when landslides frequently block the dirt roads and the numerous donkey tracks that criss-cross the mountains.

Estates, farms and smallholdings

Historically, the great estate (hacienda) has exercised a determining influence on the agrarian structure of the Cajabamba–Huamachuco region. During the colonial period, a significant proportion of land fell within the boundaries of extensive properties covering many thousands of hectares, whose principal economic activity was sheep-rearing for the production of wool. In an early, eighteenth-century, example of vertical integration, this commodity was processed into cloth in *obrajes* (wool manufactories) located on around thirty of the region's most important haciendas.[1] Other large rural enterprises, such as the Araqueda estate (in Cajabamba) and San José de Porcón (in Santiago de Chuco), operated mines for the extraction of silver and copper. Typically, these *latifundia* survived intact the economic depression and political chaos that characterised most of nineteenth-century Peru, so that until the 1960s, approximately two-thirds of land fell within hacienda boundaries, although in some districts the proportion was considerably higher.[2]

Prior to 1930 agricultural practices on local haciendas remained backward. The situation started to change in the following decade, when sugar corporations located in the lower Chicama and Santa Catalina valleys moved to purchase substantial properties in the highlands. Their motive was to secure a supply of foodstuffs to feed the thousands of labourers employed on their plantations (most workers received a daily ration of half a pound of meat and one and a half pounds of rice on top of their daily wages). The key estate in this regard was Chusgón, an immense latifundium covering more than 100,000 hectares, which originated in a land grant made in 1581 by the Viceroy to the Augustinian monastery in Lima. Over ensuing centuries, the hacienda avoided dismemberment and eventually passed into the hands of the Pinillos family (April 1861), who, on the initiative of the family head (Francisco Pinillos Martín), rented Chusgón in 1918 to José Ignacio Chopitea for the sum of 10,000 *soles* per annum.

Chopitea had well-founded motives for leasing properties in the *sierra*: he owned Laredo, the largest sugar-producing enterprise in the Santa Catalina valley (by 1915, the property already had 2,024 hectares under cane). With its considerable resident population, Laredo consumed substantial quantities of foodstuffs. Regarding labour requirements, many hands were also needed in the sugar plantation's (still largely non-mechanised) fields. Having acquired the lease, Chopitea directly administered several of Chusgón's *anexos* (sections) and sublet (for 4,000 *soles* per annum) the Chusgón, Ahijadero and Cochabamba *anexos* to the Northern Peru Mining and Smelting Company, which operated mines at Pataz, located on the Amazonian side of the Marañón. For its part, 'The Northern' was keen to rent parts of Chusgón in order to acquire grazing facilities to feed the many pack animals plying silver and materials to and from the coast and to gain access to supplies of labour, foodstuffs and timber. Company employees could also be accommodated on the estate when making the arduous, week-long journey between Trujillo and Pataz. However, as the mining enterprise and sugar corporation were merely leaseholders, no sustained investment programme took place.[3]

The catalyst for socio-economic change in Chusgón came in 1937, when Peru's largest and most efficient sugar corporation, the Empresa Agrícola Chicama Limitada (owned by the Gildemeister family), sought to expand its interests and purchased the Laredo plantation. As the contract with Chopitea was due to expire, and since the Northern Peru Mining and Smelting Company had no interest in extending its lease because the Pataz mines were nearing exhaustion, Chusgón's landlord entered into discussions with Laredo's new owners with a view to selling the property. Following labyrinthine negotiations (Pinillos Martín pretended to include in the sale more land than he intended, while the sugar corporation's representatives tried their utmost to drive down the asking price), Pinillos Martín eventually agreed to transfer the Cochabamba, Chusgón, Ahijadero, Pampatac, Tayanga and Santa Rosa *anexos* to the Gildemeister family. Simultaneously, he bequeathed the Yanasara and La Succha sections to his son, Francisco Pinillos Montoya. Shortly afterwards, the Bazán Lynch family, who owned Moyán (an estate adjoining the Ahijadero *anexo),* sold out to Juan Gildemeister, so that when these deals were completed (1941), the Empresa Agrícola Chicama emerged as the largest landowner in the Cajabamba–Huamachuco region, with properties extending over 75,000 hectares.

A new company, the Sociedad Ganadera Acapana Limitada (later renamed the Empresa Andina San Leonardo), was established to operate the recent acquisitions. Almost immediately an investment process commenced, with the aim of extracting the maximum possible return from the land by increasing the flow of commodities to Laredo and other sugar estates owned by the corporation (these included Casa Grande, the most extensive sugar enterprise in Peru, with 11,000 hectares under cane). Corriedale and merino sheep imported from Britain, Chile and Argentina were cross-bred with selected local stock and acclimatised to the highest pastures on the estate. Substantial expenditure on pedigree Shorthorn and Brown Swiss cattle, which were introduced to lower-level meadows, led to a rapid increase in milk yields for processing into cheese and butter. By the mid-1950s an average of 5,000 kilograms of cheese and several dozen boxes each containing 100 kilograms of butter were being despatched to Laredo every month. In order to expand meat production, the owners purchased Galloway, Scottish Highland, Santa Gertrudis, and Zebu stock, placing the various breeds throughout the hacienda in the appropriate ecological zone.

Hand in hand with these investments, land was drained, fenced into suitably sized meadows and (in favourable locations), sown with improved pastures – typically a ryegrass–clover mix or alfalfa. Irrigation ditches, stables, corrals, sheep dips and roads were constructed; a large-scale reforestation scheme that built up to plantings of 100,000 trees per annum, was also implemented. Modern herd-management techniques supervised by qualified personnel became widely practised. As a result of these investments, the carrying capacity of the land rose significantly, so that by 1962 the number of cows being milked on the enterprise averaged between 9,000 and 10,000 per day. Efforts were also made to increase food production on lands exploited directly by the hacienda and the plots farmed by sharecroppers.

In addition to the capitalisation of Chusgón and other of the region's most extensive properties, a process of agrarian transformation occurred between 1940 and 1960 on a number of smaller haciendas, particularly in relation to dairying. One pioneer in this endeavour was Pio Rosell, who first introduced Holstein and Brown Swiss cattle to the hacienda Jocos (around 6,000 hectares) in the 1930s and, over the next decade, invested in all the related improvements necessary to run a modern dairy enterprise. Other proprietors in the San Marcos–Condebamba–Cajabamba area copied Rosell's example. They originally concentrated on butter and cheese production because of difficulties with rapid access to markets and high transport costs, but after 1947 this sector received an important boost in that the road network was upgraded and a Nestlé milk-processing plant opened outside the town of Cajamarca.[4] Following these developments, by the 1960s this part of the *sierra* housed some of the most technically advanced and efficiently administered estates in the Peruvian Andes, operated by shepherds, stockmen and other employees, who were paid cash wages and had become well accustomed to working within a disciplined capitalist labour process.

Among the most prized and intensively farmed areas in the Cajabamba–Huamachuco region figured the fecund Condebamba Valley, where most of the land lay inside the boundaries of sizeable estates or medium-scale properties, whose owners resided in Cajabamba, Cajamarca or Trujillo. Sugar cane, the main crop in this valley by the 1930s, was processed into *chancaca*, a crudely refined sugar utilised primarily in the fermentation of *chicha* (maize beer). Cane fields cultivated directly by the landowner were worked by hiring wage labourers. Workers engaged in milling operations also received cash payments. On a minority of the more decentralised properties, sharecropping prevailed. Under the former labour system, it was customary for direct producers to receive a cash advance (*socorro*), which they paid off through a stipulated number of days' work at the going rate. For their part, sharecroppers had to hand over half of their output of *chancaca* to the owner as payment for access to land, the use of oxen for ploughing and transportation operations. To cover milling costs, an additional 15 per cent of the harvest was also charged when crushing took place utilising animal traction (oxen). If the mill was motor-powered, this proportion rose to 25 per cent, the remainder of the crop being sold to the landlord at slightly below the prevailing market price.[5]

One consequence of the deepening commodification of local agriculture in the decades after 1920 was an expansion in the ranks of medium-scale farmers and well-to-do peasant households, for during these years villages became more socially stratified. A number of upwardly mobile families succeeded in establishing commercial dairy enterprises, putting most of their land under improved pasture and purchasing pedigree livestock. Others moved away from traditional mixed farming practices and became more specialised in potato, citrus fruit, pulse or vegetable cultivation, selling their produce at weekly markets attended by merchants from as far away as Trujillo and Lima. Typically, these market-orientated farmers and peasant-entrepreneurs combined agricultural pursuits with trading activities in both town and country.

One of the most colourful of such characters was Rosario Contreras (b. March 1888), who commenced his working life in the late 1900s as a muleteer contracted to transport precious metals from the mines of Sayapullo and Quiruvilca to Trujillo.[6] Rumour had it that the fortunes of Contreras brightened considerably one dark night when a string of mules under his supervision 'disappeared' mysteriously into a precipitous gorge en route to the coast. Putting his illegally acquired capital to good use, Contreras started to invest in agriculture and trade. At regular intervals over the ensuing decades he purchased a new farm, installed a 'wife' and started a fresh family. By employing a high degree of astuteness to overcome the disadvantage of illiteracy, Contreras had accumulated eleven farms at the time of his death in 1971. He had also acquired eleven 'wives', who, in the company of ninety-three of his children, headed the impressive funeral cortège that wound its way through the streets of Cajabamba to warm acclaim from the local citizenry.

Clearly, Contreras passed an eventful life and accumulated a sizeable amount of wealth, even if it was constantly being – literally – eaten away by ever-expanding family commitments. Nevertheless, for most country-dwellers of humble origin, earning a living became progressively more difficult and complex

as the twentieth century progressed. A combination of the monopolisation of
the soil by large estates, rapid demographic increase (peasant households averaged five children), and inheritance customs (siblings usually shared land and
other household resources on the death of the family head), produced the fragmentation of smallholdings, leading to semi-proletarianisation and outright
proletarianisation on a massive scale.[7] After 1940, countless pauperised freeholders consequently abandoned the highlands and sought their fortunes in
Trujillo and other coastal cities, returning only infrequently to celebrate
carnival, make merry during the annual festival in honour of the local patron
saint, or attend a family bereavement.

Tens of thousands of other *minifundistas* sought to keep their precarious
farming activities afloat by migrating on a seasonal basis to work for several
months of the year on coastal sugar and rice estates. Some took up waged
employment or sharecropping facilities inside an adjacent highland hacienda.
Temporary work in Araqueda, Sayapullo, Quiruvilca and a number of lesser
mining camps operating in the Andes provided another source of income for
rural men, while women sought to raise household revenues through handicraft
production, occasional trading activities or entering domestic service in nearby
towns. Between 1920 and 1960, therefore, households belonging to all strata of
the peasantry found themselves more deeply integrated into labour and
commodity markets and evolved ever more intricate survival strategies in the
pursuit of capital accumulation or mere subsistence. Out of necessity, the population became considerably more mobile. This degree of occupational
multiplicity and high level of engagement with the market economy presented
a challenge to PCP–SL cadres, who operated within an anachronistic 'semi-
feudal' *Weltanschauung*. Such a simplified vision of Andean society produced a
divorce between ideology and lived experience that would eventually help
contribute to their demise.

Social and political traditions: factionalism

An unsophisticated perception of the historical tradition and contemporary
reality of everyday life in this part of the northern Andes was not just the prerogative of blinkered Maoist activists. In one of the few publications on the study
area, anthropologist Solomon Miller stated that 'the long docilized Peruvian
Indian has been politically inert since before the Spanish Conquest'; consequently, local elites were 'passively accepted as the overlords'.[8] Even ignoring
the fact that by the mid-twentieth century an overwhelming majority of the local
inhabitants were Spanish-speaking *mestizos*, this assessment conveys a mistaken
image, for the denizens of the Cajabamba–Huamachuco region possess a record
of considerable social and political turbulence. Local elites would not have
recognised the portrayal of their supposed subordinates as 'docile' or 'passive'.
This has been particularly true for the post-1870 period, which has seen elite
rule contested at regular intervals; non-elite social actors were by no means as
docile or as passive as Miller suggested. Indeed, they have long engaged in a

wide variety of overt and covert activities in an attempt to manipulate the prevailing hierarchical social order to their minimum disadvantage. During the colonial era, for example, outbursts of discontent occurred in Huamachuco (1751, 1752) and Usquil (1752, 1756), provoked by the abusive working conditions prevalent in *obrajes* and haciendas. These events culminated in a widely supported uprising by Indians and *mestizos* centred on Otuzco and Huamachuco (1758), against attempts by the authorities to update tax rolls and enforce the collection of tribute. Apparently, the revolt was quelled with great difficulty only after militia reinforcements were drafted in from Cajamarca and Lima. Such was the intensity of opposition that the authorities were forced to flee to Trujillo and plans to collect taxes were jettisoned.[9]

In more recent times, a defining moment in the social and political history of the Cajabamba–Huamachuco region proved to be the War of the Pacific (1879–83). By the 1870s, a factional mode of political organisation and competition had emerged out of the social dislocation caused by the Independence Wars fifty years earlier. A central feature of this system included the integration of all sectors of the population into vertically constructed clans, headed at a provincial level by prominent figures from the local landed elite or wealthier mine owners. Leadership positions in the districts were usually occupied by less powerful *hacendados*, medium-scale farmer-merchants or the occasional quack lawyer (*tinterillo*). The third tier in a faction's informally organised, hierarchical structure most commonly comprised *coqs de village* – richer peasants – or the more prosperous artisan-farmers, who nurtured their own and their superiors' political and economic ambitions within the hamlets.

Normally two (sometimes three) rival factions would be found in each province, with patron–client bonds forged and sustained through the practical medium of individual economic advancement rather than loyalty to a commonly held set of political beliefs. Patrons built up clientele networks, which they mobilised to seize and monopolise power in the province. If the member of one faction succeeded in being named as subprefect, the clan would manoeuvre to place its supporters into the position of district governor, lieutenant governor (in each parish housing more than 300 inhabitants), and mayor (presiding over a majority of local notables on the town councils). These officials were charged with collecting taxes, marshalling collective labour for public works, participating in the selection of conscripts for the army, deciding the composition of town-based militias and influencing the appointment of local magistrates. They therefore had ample opportunity to make financial gain, engage in illegal land-grabbing, or pursue inter-familial vendettas to a satisfactory conclusion. Faction rivalry was consequently intense, especially during elections. These formally involved small numbers of voters (women, illiterates and the poor were disenfranchised), with victory at the hustings depending, more often than not, on bribery (a small electorate increased the scope for malpractice). Alternatively, armed assaults would be launched against the voting tables by (usually inebriated) gangs led by *pistoleros* in the pay of faction leaders.[10]

Between elections, the normal practice was to hound the opposing clan at every opportunity. In one typical incident, on the afternoon of 17 September 1878 members of the anti-government faction resident in Cajabamba insulted and then assaulted the staff of the subprefecture when plans to collect the *contribución personal* (head tax) were being announced in the town square. They seized the tax rolls and ripped them up, before leading a demonstration against the authorities around the streets. Throughout that afternoon tensions smouldered on in the local bars, before escalating into a full-scale riot during a firework display to honour the town's patron saint.[11]

Although such events occurred quite regularly in the years prior to the War of the Pacific, disorder and lawlessness were far from endemic. Nor did inter-clan antagonism spin out of control. The Chilean invasion was, however, to drastically transform this situation and produce real pyrotechnics. When the Chilean army entered northern Peru in September 1880, rival *caudillos* found it impossible to establish a common front against the enemy and they pursued separate campaigns. By 1882, after the fall of Lima and a series of predictable reverses, the main point of schism within the Peruvian camp revolved around the question of whether to broker a peace accord with Chile or continue the struggle to expel the enemy. Miguel Iglesias, a prominent landlord from Cajamarca, headed the faction favouring negotiation, while José Mercedes Puga (owner of the La Pauca and Huagal haciendas in San Marcos) led those who advocated further resistance. Animosity between the opposing bands deepened to such a degree that in January 1883, Miguel Iglesias ordered Colonel Manuel Callirgos to hunt down Puga and destroy the forces under his command. At the head of 230 cavalry, Callirgos attacked the La Pauca and Huagal estates, executed summarily three of Puga's close associates (one of whom was his nephew), then proceeded to slaughter all the livestock and incendiarise hacienda buildings.[12] Furthermore, during the battle of Huamachuco (10 July 1883), Iglesias cooperated actively with the Chilean troops against Puga and his allies, contributing to their defeat. Relations between the rival factions were soured further when, in October 1883, Iglesias was declared president of Peru with Chilean backing and signed a humiliating peace treaty.

These events unleashed a full-blown civil war in the northern highlands. Between 1883 and 1885, columns of armed *montoneros* (irregular fighters) swept through Cajabamba and Huamachuco, bringing high levels of despoliation, death and destruction that continued after Puga's assassination by *iglesistas* in the town of Huamachuco (March 1885). The last large-scale confrontation took place on 7 October 1885, when Puga's followers attempted to storm the town of Cajamarca. During this clash, a sizeable force of rebels (allegedly 1,800 strong) was repelled by government troops after several hours of street fighting that left 109 of Puga's men dead. Following this failure, the most intense phase of the civil war came to an end, but the deep animosities spawned by the conflict continued to simmer to the end of the century and beyond.

Instability post-1885 was enhanced by the collapse of the Peruvian state and erosion of the legitimacy of the traditional elite. In this environment, vendetta-style feuds could run unchecked. A proclivity for ongoing factional violence became compounded by a wide distribution of weapons among the population and the not inconsiderable numbers of once-pacific individuals who had become embroiled in bloody conflicts, adept at handling guns and accustomed to settle disputes by resorting to force of arms. Finally, in addition to politically motivated violence, economic dislocation when allied to a breakdown in state control also occasioned an upsurge in brigandage and a generalised lawlessness that the authorities were powerless to contain.

Against this backdrop, in January 1886 the *iglesista* subprefect of Cajabamba, Alejandro Ravines, perished in a revenge killing carried out by members of Puga's *parentela* (clan).[13] Although in subsequent years affiliates of both factions managed to occupy the post of subprefect – the result of the changing sands of political fortune in Lima – their position was never secure (this was particularly the case with those tainted with the 'collaborator' brush). The nineteenth century ended fittingly with the subprefect of Cajabamba having to flee to San Marcos, as most of Cajabamba and Huamachuco lay at the mercy of an anti-government *montonera* column headed by Agustín Verastegui (as discussed below).

Social and political traditions: inter-landlord conflict

The new century opened with serious inter-landlord disputes festering away in many localities. One happened to be the district of Sitacocha (Cajabamba province), where Gaspar Mantilla maintained an armed band of between ten and twenty retainers on his Yanás estate. In July 1900, this group invaded the neighbouring property of Sitacocha, owned by Enrique Otoya, looting and torching hacienda buildings before making off with seventy-three head of cattle. Replying in kind, on 8 August 1900 Otoya mobilised his mercenaries, attacked Mantilla's hacienda and set fire to its installations. According to the subprefect, no land conflict existed between the two men, but 'the landowners of Sitacocha and Yanás are personal enemies. They are provoking the mutual destruction of their estates ... it is these landlords who have caused the total anarchy that reigns in the district of Sitacocha.'[14] Significantly, the subprefect lacked a police force to control the volatile situation.

As a result, this type of feud persisted well into the twentieth century. One of the most bitter concerned the owner of the hacienda Calluán (Julio Cacho Gálvez) and the proprietor of Choquizongo (Alfonso González Orbegoso). Both extensive estates, Calluán was located in the province of Cajabamba, while Choquizongo lay across the administrative divide in Huamachuco province. For his part, Cacho was one of the most influential landowners in Cajamarca; González ranked among the elite of the department of La Libertad. Animosity between Cacho and González over questions of land intensified in the mid-1910s and by 1924 had developed to such an extent that their rivalry had transcended regional bounds and was attracting national attention through articles in the Lima press. Their vendetta even became the topic of debate in

Congress. To strengthen his position, Cacho used family and personal connections to gain the support of Cajamarca's senators, the departmental prefect and the subprefect of Cajabamba province. González was equally successful in securing the backing of parliamentarians representing La Libertad, along with that of the subprefects of Huamachuco and Otuzco.

Under the protection of their respective political allies, Cacho and González felt confident enough to launch armed assaults on each others' estates with impunity from official sanction. Tempers became further frayed when Cacho won a long-drawn-out land dispute against his rival in Lima's Supreme Court on 9 October 1918. The situation degenerated into a state of open warfare upon González's return from Spain in late 1923 – he had been attempting to persuade potential Spanish colonisers to settle on his hacienda. During the following five years, tenants acting on Cacho's orders destroyed crops, robbed livestock and razed houses belonging to retainers of the González camp, and vice versa. Given the absence of any official sanction, an anarchic situation developed rapidly, which, in August 1924, moved the governor of the district of Cachachi to inform his superiors that, 'gun fights are continually taking place between the hacienda Choquizongo and Calluán'.[15] Throughout 1925 and 1926 the generalised mayhem progressed unchecked, the opposing bands even going to the trouble of digging trenches and constructing small stone fortresses, from which they fired on each other over the disputed lands. By the time the violence was finally brought under control in late 1927, much blood had been shed.

Social and political traditions: brigandage

Rather than exhibiting 'docility' and 'passively' accepting their lot, many of the poor in Cajabamba and Huamachuco were quite prepared to embrace banditry in order to earn a living. Participation in illegal activities during the late nineteenth century and the early decades of the twentieth century was facilitated by the weakness of the state in terms both of legitimacy and coercive capacity, as well as by divisions within the regional elite. A fragmented power structure offered greater opportunity for the astute outlaw to pursue an inverse strategy of 'divide and rule' by exploiting intra-landlord animosities: it became easier to gain effective protection from influential backers, play one faction off against the other and so operate with relative impunity.

Individuals who had participated in the War of the Pacific and the succession of post-war *montonera* rebellions found it difficult to return to their humdrum existence on the family smallholding and consequently adopted banditry as their preferred profession when not engaged in quixotic attempts to topple the central government. For example, August 1898 saw Agustín Verastegui lead some 100 irregulars in one of his frequent revolts. He succeeded in capturing Cajabamba for a short period, but when troops loyal to president Nicolás de Piérola entered the province, Verastegui's force dispersed into several bands, each between six and twenty strong. They lived by rustling and highway robbery, carried out over an area extending from the Condebamba

Valley to Huamachuco.[16] Official attempts to curb such widespread outlawry rarely proved successful. This was demonstrated by a joint operation mounted in July 1901 by the subprefects of Cajabamba and Huamachuco to apprehend 'the famous assassins Manuel and Asunción Cardenas', natives of Huamachuco, whose activities centred on the hamlet of Marcabalito, sited strategically between the two towns. Although the authorities recovered some stolen livestock, the brothers managed to evade capture.[17]

Matters became so bad that even the urban population felt threatened. This situation provoked the 'merchants and property owners' of Cajabamba to address a petition to the authorities in November 1901. The town's *'gente decente'* complained that nobody was safe to walk the streets after nightfall due to the lack of a local police force, 'which leaves our lives and interests unprotected in a town where bandits circulate around the outskirts. Robberies and all manner of scandalous events are being committed daily'.[18] Although the nervous townspeoples' requested that a detachment of troops be stationed in Cajabamba, the plea went unattended owing to a lack of funds. Some indication of the insecurity of daily life can be ascertained from a memorandum penned by the subprefect of Cajabamba in January 1902, who notified his superiors about:

> the alarming state that exists in this province, due to the activities of a gang of armed malefactors. Organised in bands, they commit scandalous robberies, engaging in combat with groups of citizens who go after them to recover their animals and other stolen goods ... they have forced the governor of Huamachuco to flee and have consequently become the lords and masters of that locality. They have formed a band of ten or twelve individuals who once belonged to the *montonera* led by Domingo Cruzado and Domingo Díaz Farfán. Although favoured by the amnesty law, they did not return to honest labours. Instead, accustomed to the marauding lifestyle, they have dedicated themselves to rustling. As a result, complaints from landlords and other cattle owners are constantly being made to this subprefecture.[19]

One of the latest incidents involved the robbery of forty-five head of cattle from the hacienda Sitacocha by the Cardenas gang. When the owner discovered where the livestock were being hidden, the subprefects of Cajabamba and Huamachuco combined their forces and in company with a group of armed men from the estate, went after the rustlers. In the ensuing gunfight, an employee from Sitacocha and one soldier were gravely wounded. Two of the bandits received fatal bullet wounds and the remainder escaped with the stolen cattle.[20]

Not long after this incident, the subprefect was once again complaining about what he regarded as the anarchic situation in Cajabamba province:

> The horrendous vice of drunkenness reigns among the inhabitants of this town, who have no will to work and not the slightest notion of the principle of respect for authority. Rustling is so common that it has been developed to

a fine art: the bands of armed criminals that circulate throughout the whole province have their accomplices in the zones where livestock are pastured. When the criminals receive word from these associates, they pounce, deliver the certain *coup de grâce*, and hide the cattle in the forests that cover the Cordillera. They later transport the livestock to the coast. sure in the knowledge that there is no force that can impede them. This crime has generalised to such an extent that it is even committed by women dressed up as men.[21]

According to the subprefect, the urban militia responsible for policing the town consisted of a group of 'undisciplined incorrigible drunkards' who provoked, rather than prevented, disorder.

Although most brigands took up the profession as a means of attaining better pay for less work, a minority engaged in rustling, highway robbery and similar activities for more complex motives, including labourer revenge. One such case involved Lorenzo and Gerado Goicochea, notorious footpads active in Cajabamba–Huamachuco around the turn of the century. These brothers had been labourers on the hacienda Calluán. After an altercation with the administrator, they fled the estate, taking off without repaying the cash advances they had received when starting work, and subsequently wreaked revenge on the landowner by lifting more than 100 Calluán cattle. Not content with this, they also plundered systematically livestock belonging to tenants settled on the hacienda, in addition to the animals and possessions of any traveller who had the misfortune to cross their path.[22]

Representatives of the state frequently became targeted for assassination by outlaws. In May 1924, one gang was regularly causing explosions and general mayhem in the streets of Cajabamba. They tried to blow up the subprefecture and hurled dynamite (acquired from local mining camps) at the house belonging to the deputy mayor, who had survived four previous attempts against his life. Cajabamba's subprefect reminded the departmental prefect that his predecessor had resigned owing to fear that he would be killed, while current endemic lawlessness signified that 'the lives of the authorities and honest citizens of this province cannot be safeguarded'.[23] As usual, pleas for police reinforcements went unheeded, so high levels of brigandage continued to plague the area until the 1930s, when a strengthening of the state and more forceful demands by landlords to control criminal activity led to a decrease in outlawry. Rustling and similar acts of thievery were never extinguished fully, however, compelling travellers to adopt inventive ways to try to safeguard their property. For example, when on the road with a mule train, the ever-resourceful Germán Contreras used to stuff money up the backsides of his pack animals. Although the need to resort to such measures became less common, outlawry remained a feature of rural life until the late 1970s, when PCP–SL guerrillas began to infiltrate the area.

Social and political traditions: conflict with the state

In addition to engaging in banditry and related forms of lawbreaking, the rural population came into conflict with the authorities over other issues. Conscription into the army was resented almost universally by country people and by no means 'passively accepted' by many men of military age. One common ploy to avoid being seized when the recruiters appeared was to flee the district and gain employment in coastal plantations. Others sought a position in a highland estate or a mining camp, where the owners would resist attempts by the authorities to carry off their employees. When the authorities did manage to snare some conscripts, it was not uncommon for groups of local women armed with staves and stones to ambush the gendarmes, overpower them and release their menfolk.[24]

The rural population could also become involved in confrontations with the state through being enmeshed in patron–client relations. One case where this occurred concerned the inhabitants of the hacienda Araqueda, one of the most extensive in the region (57,407 hectares). By the 1910s, the fortunes of the landowner, Juan Manuel Velezmoro, had taken a turn for the worse and he was heavily in debt to a Trujillo-based commercial house, having negotiated a substantial loan to purchase equipment for the Algamarca mines located on his estate. Owing to a combination of technical difficulties, low world metal prices and bad management, the investment failed to produce the anticipated return. Velezmoro consequently found himself unable to meet his financial commitments, whereupon the creditors opened legal proceedings (1911) and finally gained ownership of Araqueda, plus all its non-fixed assets, in April 1914. Velezmoro refused to recognise the court's ruling, however, and proceeded to organise the tenants settled on Araqueda to resist the takeover of his properties.

Estate foremen spread rumours to the effect that if they were successful in their suit, the new owners would raise rents drastically while simultaneously reducing the size of the plots allocated to each tenant. Patron–client ties were also manipulated to strengthen resistance, so that when in May 1911 the judge and the court inspector journeyed to Araqueda with the objective of making an inventory and a preliminary valuation of the property, Velezmoro assembled his followers and threw the officials off the hacienda. Reporting the incident to the subprefect of Cajabamba, the thwarted judge stated that Velezmoro:

> appeared in the hacienda Chuquibamba [an *anexo* of Araqueda] and brusquely interrupted our march, forcing us to withdraw due to the multitude of people he had assembled in the aforementioned estate. Velezmoro told us that he would never allow us to undertake the audit and impound his property. Even when it was pointed out to him that we could return with the assistance of the police force, Velezmoro told us that he did not care if we returned with all the police in the universe. He would resist everybody rather than permit them to set foot on his estates.[25]

The judge added that they would need the backing of at least 50 troops to enforce the court order, his party having been faced by Velezmoro and 200 of 'his people'. They had fled when the landowner had ordered his foremen to 'Go along with the men and chase them away'.[26]

Undeterred by threats emanating from the authorities, Velezmoro steadfastly maintained his position of resisting any move to impound Araqueda. Thus, in 1912, a detachment of troops sent by the prefect in Cajamarca to bring Velezmoro to heel and enforce a valuation of the estate and its mining complex was prevented from fulfilling its mission by several hundred Araqueda tenants armed with rocks, clubs, guns and dynamite expropriated from the hacienda mine.[27] Subsequent attempts to enter the hacienda in 1913 and 1914 met with a similar lack of success. In one of several incidents, six rural police officers (gendarmes) and the local judge endeavoured to penetrate the estate, only to be frustrated by 200 peasants under the command of Velezmoro. Upon arriving at the River Condebamba, which marked Araqueda's boundary, 'we could see many people lined up in trenches on the opposite bank, from where they hurled various sticks of dynamite at us', so making it 'impossible to continue'. The police officer proceeded to voice the opinion that:

> it is very strange that in estates belonging to well known landowners who form part of Decent Society, people who are accustomed to go around armed with weapons belonging to the state are allowed to band together. This creates a real danger, not just to the tranquillity of this neighbourhood, but also because it can result in disturbances of a far greater magnitude.[28]

After a year of further rebuffs at the hands of Velezmoro, the authorities concluded that enough was enough and decided to send a substantial force to dislodge him. On 27 October 1915, some 200 troops crossed the river. Scouts sent ahead on a reconnaissance mission 'encountered armed men hiding in a wood. The troops were ordered to advance towards them to determine their attitude. They were fired upon and had sticks of dynamite thrown at them.'[29] Under pressure from the advancing soldiers, the *campesinos* were forced to retreat further into the hacienda, in the process leaving one of their dead colleagues behind. More armed men were grouped on an adjacent mountain-side and when these had been overcome, the subprefect and his party proceeded to occupy the estate.

Although they had finally managed to take possession of the property, the authorities found themselves obliged to maintain a garrison of fifty soldiers stationed in Araqueda, for Velezmoro had managed to avoid being collared and continued to incite the tenants into resisting the new owners. At this stage, however, events took a turn that was not to the landowner's liking. Instead of blindly pursuing Velezmoro's interests, the Araqueda peasants were now following their own agenda – an anti-landlord movement had emerged. This development produced an abrupt change in attitude. The head of the mine informed the officer commanding the troops that 'Andrés Cueva, the principal leader of the indigenous insurrection in the estates, is to be found in

Corralpampa'.[30] According to the subprefect's report, when the military went to apprehend Cueva, he tried to escape and they were forced to shoot at him. The 'fugitive' was hit in the back by a bullet and died a few hours later. As if to justify the soldiers' actions, the subprefect informed the prefect that Araqueda's administrators had notified him that 'Cueva's presence in the hacienda was extremely dangerous. He had good reason to suspect that his presence was due to a desire to provoke new disorders that could have grave consequences.'[31]

Social and political traditions: *aprismo*

The manner in which unrest unfolded among *campesinos* settled on the hacienda Araqueda offered a portent of future socio-political developments in Cajabamba and Huamachuco. The late 1920s and early 1930s witnessed mounting dissatisfaction about the living conditions endured by the poor, with ethnic discrimination and a political system based on paternalism, exclusion and the monopolisation of power by a narrow elite. In this propitious environment, a new political force appeared on the scene, the Alianza Popular Revolucionaria Americana (APRA) – American Popular Revolutionary Alliance, which grew in explosive fashion between 1930 and 1932 to become the dominant political party in the northern highlands.

APRA's message of land redistribution, nationalisation, democratic reform, 'social justice' and anti-imperialism appealed strongly to a wide variety of classes and occupational groups resident in Cajabamba and Huamachuco. Many strategically placed middle-class professionals, such as lawyers and school-teachers, were attracted by the party's nationalist rhetoric and programme of 'anti-feudal' modernisation. Especially useful in terms of building up rural support was backing given to APRA by key intermediate social agents. These included medium-scale farmers, merchants, cattle dealers, labour contractors and even the occasional turbulent priest – individuals who were usually literate, closely connected with the mass of the rural population and who exercised considerable influence in the countryside.

APRA's rapid growth was also facilitated by extensive semi-proletarianisation among the farming community, which, when allied to a scarcity of attractive job opportunities in nearby Andean towns, engendered yearly migration on a massive scale. When smallholders entered temporary employment in coastal sugar plantations and highland mining camps, they came into contact with trade unions. Driven by the economic depression and the downward pressure on wages, these syndicates entered frequently into bitter labour disputes with the owners of capital. By 1932 they were APRA-dominated. The constant flow of migrant labour between the *sierra* and the littoral proved crucial in building up party support, as it provided a conduit for APRA's message to reach even the most isolated Andean hamlet.

Apart from the peasantry, artisans comprised another important section of the population that embraced *aprismo* at a time when, due to the economic depression, they were experiencing hardship in the shape of a fall in the demand for their goods and lower prices. The party also won backing among 'new' sectors of the working and middle classes (i.e. lorry drivers, telegraph operators and white-collar employees), and even gained a following among the recently formed Guardia Civil. Significantly, it was the first political group in the northern highlands to attempt to organise two other key components of the population that had hitherto been marginalised by the traditional political system: women and students.[32]

An indication of APRA's impact can be gleaned from the fact that in the 1931 election (which took place only a year after the organisation was founded in Peru), the party garnered two-thirds of the votes cast in the northern highlands. From then until the 1980s, it remained the dominant political force in the region, regularly attracting between 60 and 70 per cent of the ballot in municipal or national elections. Playing an important role in embedding the party in the local popular culture was the mystique the organisation's early members had attained through participation in anti-state rebellions and their subsequent repression.

Amid a national political environment embittered by rumours of widespread fraud aimed at preventing APRA from winning the 1931 general election, the pro-APRA result for the department of Cajamarca was declared null and void. In response, the party staged an uprising centred on the town of Trujillo and planned similar insurrections in the northern *sierra* to coincide with the main event on the coast. Accordingly, on 9 July 1932, a group of thirty well-armed men rode out of the hacienda Sitacocha to attack the civil guard post in Cajabamba. Forewarned that a large *aprista* force was approaching, the police abandoned the town to the rebels without a shot being fired. This produced 'a simple change in position. Now the *apristas* were in the town and the police were in the hills that overlooked it.'[33]

Receiving strong support from the local population, but neglecting to keep on the offensive and carry the battle to the police, the *apristas* remained in Cajabamba. They consequently lost the initiative and failed to extend the rebellion to the city of Cajamarca in the north or Huamachuco to the south, as originally planned, an error that effectively sealed the fate of those occupying Cajabamba. Four days later, army and police reinforcements were drafted into the province and began to draw a tight net around the town. In the ensuing confrontation, the *apristas* fought at the barricades and defended their positions street by street. Heavily outnumbered, they suffered many losses and eventually were compelled to surrender after running out of ammunition. Thirty-seven survivors were captured by the police and detained overnight in the local jail. The following morning they were marched off to the outskirts of town, where they were executed by firing squad.

Involvement in this and other attempts to overturn the status quo launched during the 1930s and 1940s earned APRA activists a considerable degree of respect and legitimacy; their legacy being that compared to other localities in the Peruvian Andes (such as Ayacucho, Apurímac and Huancavelica), the denizens of Cajabamba and Huamachuco possessed a longer and much deeper identifi-cation with a national political party.³⁴ Such a history of involvement with *aprismo* and 'modern' politics signified that quite sophisticated political operators were to be found at all levels of the population in town and country. As will be seen, the deeply embedded APRA tradition was to play an important role in determining attitudes towards PCP–SL recruiters and guerrilla fighters after 1980.

Social and political traditions: anti-landlord mobilisation

Another consequence of the activities of the first generation of APRA militants was an expansion of anti-landlord mobilisation and rural unionism. With regard to this feature of rural life, peasant and labourer resistance in the face of elite attempts to exploit their agricultural resources and labour power clearly predated the rise of APRA. Indeed, economic turbulence during the 1920s provoked a number of conflicts across the Cajabamba–Huamachuco region. Two examples will suffice to illustrate the type of incident that occurred.

By 1923, the villagers of Cauday were engaged in a rapidly escalating dispute with the neighbouring hacienda bearing the same name. Land-hungry smallholders rented plots and pasture rights from the landowner, who, after carrying out the customary twice-yearly rodeo, refused to return embargoed livestock to the tenants until they had paid the increased pasturage fees he had imposed arbitrarily. This demand was rejected by the *campesinos*, who promptly declared a rent and labour strike, during the course of which they started to take the occasional pot-shot at estate administrative staff. After a particularly concerted armed attack on the hacienda, the subprefect of Cajabamba decided to intervene. According to this official, when he journeyed one evening to Cauday, accompanied by the police, with the objective of mediating in the dispute, groups of peasants followed in their path. Silhouetted against the moon, they shouted threats such as 'It's the subprefect with his cops. Let's kill them. Long live the strike!' Having arrived safely at the *casa hacienda,* the subprefect and his party soon found themselves surrounded by the peasants, who proceeded to hurl rocks at the windows. They then set fire to the roof and discharged their firearms at the occupants. During the ensuing exchanges, villager Aurelio Gormás was killed and several people wounded on both sides. The subprefect managed to flee at 3 a.m. the following morning.³⁵

Similar developments took place on the hacienda Julcán in the province of Otuzco. Trouble had been brewing on this property since the early 1920s, but matters came to a head soon after the Northern Peru Mining and Smelting Company became the lessee on 25 February 1925. The Company immediately moved to reorganise the estate so as to make it more profitable, a policy that entailed a break with the hitherto paternalistic work environment, an expansion in the demesne lands directly utilised by the hacienda enterprise and a related attack on the tenants' household economy. Attempts were made to dislodge a number of peasant families from their plots and expel them from the estate. Levies on land and livestock were raised substantially and the Company even imposed an additional rent of 24 *soles* per annum on the rustic dwellings inhabited by the tenants. A ban was introduced on all small-scale commerce inside Julcán's boundaries, so denying the peasants easy access to market. These actions met with hostility from the estate's work force, which organised resistance to the Company's demands, both inside and outside the property. A rent strike commenced and support was also enlisted from radical pro-peasant *indigenista*-influenced lawyers practising in Huamachuco and Trujillo, who pursued their case through the courts. Via these intermediaries, contacts were mobilised to get the issue debated in the Senate, where sympathetic parliamentarians denounced the Company's provocative behaviour. Despite the negative publicity, the Company maintained its policy and succeeded in imposing its will – a police detachment drafted into the hacienda 'restored order' by gunning down several tenants and arresting the 'ringleaders'. This proved to be a pyrrhic victory, however, for peasant opposition to what was viewed as unjust exaction was never wholly overcome and, eventually, the mining enterprise rescinded its lease.[36]

Over the 1930s and 1940s, APRA labour organisers, lawyers and rural schoolteachers intervened in these kinds of disputes in order to promote party-affiliated *campesino* unions on an estate-by-estate and village-by-village basis. At times when APRA was proscribed and state repression forced party members underground, these organisations functioned clandestinely. Under such adverse conditions, peasant demands were usually pursued through the courts by the party's lawyers without reference being made to the existence of peasant syndicates. Simultaneously, the disaffected would resort to covert modes of anti-landlord activity (including poor labour effort, absenteeism, petty thievery, the unauthorised grazing of livestock on hacienda land and similar 'everyday forms of peasant resistance'). During intervals when the political climate proved more favourable, such as between 1946 and 1948, open mobilisation around issues of wages, rents, working conditions and land rights would surface. These collective initiatives invariably met with a hostile response from landowners. During the 1950s, however, tensions eased as APRA moved to the right and adopted increasingly anti-communist positions in an effort to gain respectability and the opportunity to govern. Within a less confrontational atmosphere, party-affiliated unions were to be found on many of the region's haciendas. Tenants and labourers who occupied leadership positions in these syndicates travelled to Cajabamba, Huamachuco or Santiago de Chuco (and as far afield as Trujillo) on a regular basis to discuss local difficulties and undertake routine party business. In this fashion, lasting bonds along patron–client lines were nurtured between provincial APRA leaders and pivotal social agents settled throughout the rural districts.

A review of developments on the hacienda Chusgón provides an indication of the dynamic here. The bête noire of many rank-and-file APRA members was the Empresa Agrícola Chicama sugar corporation, so that when this company purchased Chusgón in September 1941 it logically became a target for agitation and recruitment.[37] Labour-organising was facilitated by the serious economic and social disruption that accompanied the new owner's drive to capitalise this property. Almost immediately after taking control of Chusgón, the recently installed German administrator embarked upon a process of relocating tenants and reducing the size of their holdings. His motive was to fence off extensive blocks of the best land and transform them into meadows that could be irrigated, sown with cultivated pastures and populated with productive pedigree livestock. This move to strengthen the landlord enterprise at the expense of the peasant enterprise became especially conflictual as a consequence of the particular pattern of social relations that prevailed inside Chusgón. Among the hacienda residents a relatively privileged strata of *arrendatarios* ('quit-rent' tenants) enjoyed access to substantial stretches of land and generous grazing rights. According to one report written in August 1913, by that year this group already numbered 471 households spread over six sections of the estate, and these were in the fortuitous position of being able to rent plots to sub-tenants called *agregantes*. Each *arrendatario*, the report noted, had at least 'one or two *agregantes*, but most possess eight, ten and as many as twenty ... owing to the negligence of the owners, a situation exists whereby the *arrendatarios* have taken over hacienda resources and almost consider themselves to be the masters of the property'.[38]

This state of affairs remained unchanged until the Empresa Agrícola Chicama acquired the hacienda, but was quickly addressed by the new proprietors. In only his second report penned to the general manager of the Laredo sugar estate (the capitalisation of Chusgón was directed from Laredo), the administrator resident in the Cochabamba *anexo* recorded that 'four *arrendatarios* and three *agregantes* have been personally informed by me that they have to relocate by 1 December, as the land has been earmarked for pastures'.[39] Similar notices to quit were served on a regular basis over the following months.

Attacks on the tenant economy also occurred on other fronts. The underlying motive for these was that the hacienda administration wanted to shrink the 'peasant' aspect of household reproduction, while simultaneously increasing its 'labourer' dimension. If this could be achieved, the estate would reduce the autonomy of the tenants and be able to gain access to the larger amounts of labour time required to undertake the ambitious investment programme necessary to modernise the property. To this end, cash rents were raised to two *soles* per annum for each head of cattle (or every ten head of sheep) pastured on the hacienda, with the added stipulation that tenants had to provide six days' unpaid labour with rations per unit of livestock. Moves were set in motion to introduce a new labour regime whereby all *arrendatarios* and *agregantes* were obliged to work fifteen days per month for the estate in return for a daily wage of fifty *centavos* plus food rations. As the manager of Laredo put it in a letter to the farm manager resident in Cochabamba:

> Through this policy we will see who wants to work and who does not want to work. After several warnings the latter will have to vacate the hacienda, removing them a few at a time. We recommend that you proceed energetically, but also with tact, in order to avoid disorder.[40]

As part of the clampdown, the administration prohibited hacienda residents from engaging in labour recruitment for operations outside the estate, an activity that under the old regime had provided an extra source of income for a number of the more prosperous *arrendatarios*. When, in October 1942, the charge-hand (*mayordomo*) of the Cochabamba *anexo* (who was also an *arrendatario*) disregarded this instruction, he was dismissed and thrown off the hacienda, the objective being to 'make an example of him to everybody'.[41] Others experienced a similar fate during 1942 and 1943. A ban was introduced on all trade conducted by tenants inside the estate, so that commercial activity became the prerogative of the administration. It was also decided to phase out quit-rent tenancy agreements and extend the more profitable labour system of sharecropping throughout Chusgón's various *anexos*.

This raft of measures, imposed without consultation and implemented with haste, had a massive negative impact on the 'peasant' side of the tenant household economy. Modernisation especially threatened the well-being of the wealthier *arrendatarios*, who were usually literate. To complicate matters, several even occupied lower-ranking positions within the estate's administrative structure. Additionally, many *arrendatarios* (through family ties and their commercial operations) possessed good contacts in the town of Huamachuco. They were consequently able to use these connections, as well as exploit the influence they exercised over the *agregantes*, to defend their interests. It came as no surprise, then, that this group led the fight-back against the new labour regime being introduced inside Chusgón. Opposition took a wide variety of forms. Offers of employment as shepherds and stockmen were turned down. Tenants refused to pay labour and cash rents. Hacienda livestock disappeared at regular intervals. Angry peasants also vented their frustration by poisoning the company's animals, a course of action that was anathema to most rural people, but reflected the degree of hostility to the changes under way. In 1943 another source of grievance appeared when the administration attempted to curtail the activities of estate-based *arrieros* (muleteers), demonstrating their purposefulness by shooting several pack animals 'in order to not waste pasture needlessly'. The disgruntled *arrieros*, who had previously earned a decent living, since the estate was strategically sited on east-west trade routes, set fire to hacienda buildings in Cochabamba.[42]

Playing a central role in developing the anti-landlord movement was one Celso Urquizo. Urquizo had been administrator of Chusgón when the Northern Peruvian Mining and Smelting Company leased part of the estate, a post he combined with employment as a labour contractor (*enganchador*). Exploiting his position, Urquizo also carved out for himself a considerable amount of cultivated land and operated a moderately prosperous cattle business. All of this came to an abrupt end when the new owners took over Chusgón, as one of the first decisions they made was to dismiss Urquizo and banish him from the hacienda. In July 1943, in response to this humiliation and in an effort to recuperate his economic losses, the ex-administrator (assisted by a group of disaffected *arrendatarios*), circulated rumours that the government planned to purchase Chusgón, divide up the estate and hand the land over to its tenants. Therefore, it was suggested, nobody should pay rent or turn up for work – advice that was heeded by many direct producers and that, in the eyes of the hacienda administrator, amounted to 'rebellion'.[43]

Dissension between the hacienda administrator and its residents reached fever pitch on 23 April 1946, when several hundred peasants descended on the *casa hacienda* at Cochabamba with the objective of airing their grievances. Following a heated altercation, during which no concessions were offered, the German administrator (Kai Krogh) was seized and thrown from the first-floor balcony and then clubbed to death on the cobbled patio below. In this and subsequent clashes that arose upon the arrival of a police detachment from Huamachuco, ten people lost their lives. Managers remained convinced that the whole affair had been orchestrated by a coterie of scheming *arrendatarios*, who had cynically manipulated their supposedly 'ignorant' subordinates in an attempt to protect their own advantageous position. One such character was Fernando Chamorro, charge-hand at the Ahijadero *anexo* who, the new administrator claimed, had been 'the first to suggest that Mr Krogh should be thrown from the balcony and issued the order to carry out the act'.[44] In the aftermath of Krogh's murder, the alleged 'ringleaders' found themselves arrested and languishing in jail in Huamachuco. They and a number of other individuals suspected of 'disloyalty' were expelled from the estate.

Unfortunately for the owners, however, the removal of suspected 'trouble-makers' failed to re-establish order. In July 1946, 'a group of tenants congregated in the upland section of the hacienda and marched along the path leading to the hacienda buildings, firing rockets into the air and shouting that they would not pay their rents'. During the following year a *levantamiento de gente* – a rent and labour strike accompanied by demonstrations – took place in the Aricpampa and Moyán *anexos*. Further stoppages over wages, working conditions and the quality of daily food rations provided by the estate broke out in the Uchubamba, Santa Rosa, Cochabamba annexes.[45]

This wave of protest, whose effectiveness depended on coordination, planning and solidarity, was facilitated by the unionisation of the estate's work force. Urquizo and his associates established contact with APRA activists in Huamachuco during the early 1940s, which led to the foundation of peasant syndicates on all sections of Chusgón, each with its recognised leadership and the invariable official stamp (*sello*). Although the first syndicates were established clandestinely in 1943 and 1944, they did not show a public face until 1946. In that year a post-World War II pro-democratic political environment led to a lifting of the ban on APRA after fifteen years of repression and the election of a reform-minded president, José Luis Bustamante y Rivero. Despite initial management hostility and a refusal to engage in collective bargaining (in 1946, for example, Andrés Gordon, the organiser of the Sindicato de Colonos de Uchubamba, was thrown in jail for his efforts), negotiations of wages and conditions eventually became an accepted feature of employer–employee relations. The union was tolerated – although never enthusiastically – by Chusgón's administrators.

The Empresa Agrícola Chicama was far from the only landowner forced to come to terms with direct-producer organisation. Over the 1950s the network of hacienda-based unions continued to expand throughout Cajabamba and the *sierra* of La Libertad. In August 1957, for example, Jorge de Orbegoso, landowner of Araqueda and associated sugar-producing enterprises located in the Condebamba Valley, complained to Cajamarca's prefect that: 'for considerable time my Marabamba estate has been convulsed by labour unrest. In large part this is due to the actions of various agitators settled on the property, who incite the workers to not fulfil the contracts I have made with them'.[46] Orbegoso further alleged that the farm labourers were being visited regularly by Hilario Centurión, a 'self-proclaimed defender of the workers' resident in Cajamarca, whose political aim was 'to incite the working masses to revolt'.[47] In riposte, Circuncripción Vigo, one of the union leaders, noted that the Sindicato de Yanaconas de la Hacienda Tabacal y Anexos had been formed with the assistance of three migrants from the Condebamba Valley, who now resided in Trujillo. The organisation had presented its papers before the Ministry of Labour for official recognition. In addition, Vigo claimed that the union was:

> attempting to reach a compromise with the proprietor on labour and rent issues, as he has refused to receive a third of the harvest as rent, as agreed initially. Our union is fulfilling its role of defending its membership and is not pursuing a subversive campaign against the *hacendado*.[48]

Shortly afterwards, the Orbegoso family confronted labour unrest in other sectors of the hacienda Araqueda. Union officials lodged the usual complains about being hounded by management, while in his report, the governor of Cachachi district noted that unauthorised political meetings were taking place in the hacienda. Demonstrating standard prejudice, he further opined that these activities 'run the danger, given the lack of culture and drunken condition of the participants, of causing personal injury to the administrative personnel and damage to the private property of this enterprise'.[49] Like the Empresa Agrícola Chicama and the owners of Araqueda, other landlords in the region had to cede during the 1950s, albeit reluctantly, the right to organise and the existence of labour unions on their properties.

Syndicalisation brought important benefits. Through affiliation with the Federación Regional de Campesinos del Norte and the Federación Nacional de Campesinos del Perú (both established by the APRA party), grass-roots representatives came into regular contact with similar organisations functioning on neighbouring highland estates and along the northern coast. Participation in these bodies enabled rural people to keep abreast of local and regional political events. Rather than being 'docile' and 'passive', *campesinos* in the Cajabamba–Huamachuco area had a stronger sense of party affiliation than their counterparts in many other Andean departments. They also had a longer history of involvement with anti-landlord peasant unionism and were well aware of political developments at local and national level.

Hacienda dissolution and land reform

This political nous became evident in 1963, when Fernando Belaunde was voted president of Peru following electoral support for a programme that promised the modernisation of the country. Land reform was to occupy a central plank in the new government's agenda. Only two months after Belaunde took office, the Sindicato de Trabajadores de la Hacienda Cochabamba petitioned the Ministry of Labour and Indigenous Affairs in Lima with a request for the expropriation of all the properties of the Empresa Andina San Leonardo. These should be handed over to the enterprise's *'campesinos–yanaconas y pequeños arrendatarios'* ('peasant labourers and small-scale tenants'). The union representatives argued that 'the time has come to put an end to the numerous abuses that we have suffered at the hands of the Company, now that the peasant class – which has been forgotten and neglected for many years – is today protected and helped by our government'.[50]

Much to the chagrin of most of Chusgón's residents, this appeal remained unanswered, an experience identical to that of countless other estate workers in the northern highlands – and, indeed, throughout Peru – for despite all the rhetoric, the Belaunde government failed to deliver on land reform. In part, this was due to a lack of political will and administrative incompetence. Matters were not helped by certain practical difficulties facing Belaunde's administration: the executive held a minority position in Congress, with the result that the agrarian reform legislation was watered down by AP's parliamentary opponents. Exclusion clauses for (ill-defined) 'efficient' *latifundia* were written into a bill, which, in any case, contained a plethora of loopholes that might easily be exploited by an astute lawyer. As they could hire well-connected attorneys and operated productive estates, landowners such as the Empresa Agrícola Chicama expected to avoid total expropriation.

Talk about the need for land redistribution, however, sparked off important modifications in tenure patterns in Cajabamba–Huamachuco during the 1960s and 1970s, changes that would in the following decade influence the course of the civil war in the northern highlands. Several large estates started to fragment owing to the threat of expropriation and moves by landlords to concentrate investments on smaller areas of more fertile soil. Others reinvested their capital outside the agricultural sector altogether. Driven by such considerations, in May 1963 the Orbegoso family began to divide the hacienda Araqueda, selling individual plots to those settled on the property, as well as to any outsider who was able to pay the (inflated) asking price. A similar process took place on the Yanasara and La Succha estates in Huamachuco, where the eccentric landowner, Francisco Pinillos, handed over smallholdings of 10–30 hectares to the peasants. Meanwhile, the owners of Chusgón began to divide up and sell some of the less valuable sections of their hacienda in an effort to secure boundaries, settle disputes with surrounding villages and reduce discontent among the workforce.[51]

Although considerable amounts of land began to change hands in the 1960s, it was widely held that the Belaunde government was failing to address Peru's 'agrarian question' in a sufficiently robust fashion. It was also felt that his administration was incapable of modernising the productive structure and state apparatus. Consequently, opposition to Belaunde mounted, resulting in a military coup on 3 October 1968, headed by General Juan Velasco. This takeover ushered in twelve years of military rule that proved to be a watershed in twentieth-century Peruvian politics. Unlike other military interventions in Latin America at this juncture, the progressive faction of the Peruvian army that ousted Belaunde moved to push through key structural reforms aimed at modernising the country. It hoped to reduce substantially the power of the oligarchy, minimise external economic dependence, promote industrialisation and lay the foundations for the construction of a more democratic society. Revolution from above was to forestall revolution from below. Central to this project was the need for a far-reaching agrarian reform. New legislation was consequently promulgated in June 1969, with large-scale expropriations occurring through to 1976.

These rapidly unfolding political developments at the national level produced a marked acceleration in private land sales in the northern highlands after 1969, as owners scrambled to sell their properties before they were taken over by the state. The (illegal) division and decapitalisation of estates was facilitated by the slow progress of land reform in Cajabamba and Huamachuco. For example, as late as September 1974, only two haciendas in the provinces of Cajabamba and San Marcos had passed through all the various stages of adjudication (Malcas in the Condebamba Valley with 533.29 hectares and 59 beneficiaries; and La Pauca, which covered 47,354 hectares and housed 578 beneficiaries).[52] Malcas was converted into a Cooperativa Agraria de Producción (CAP) – Agrarian Production Cooperative. On expropriation, the ex-hacienda La Pauca became a Sociedad Agrícola de Interés Social (SAIS) – Social Interest Agricultural Society, a cooperative structure designed for the highlands that typically integrated modern livestock enterprises with neighbouring peasant communities. Through the SAIS mode of organisation, it was hoped that improved farming practices and economic surplus generated in the former could be transferred to poor *minifundistas* settled in the latter.

The slow start notwithstanding, expropriations gathered pace in 1975; most estates were adjudicated and converted into cooperatives (a few slipped through the net, thanks to connivance between landowners and functionaries in the agrarian reform section of the local Ministry of Agriculture). As a result, between 1960 and 1980 the degree of land concentration in this area of Peru's northern highlands was reduced significantly. The Agrarian Census of 1972 calculated that 2.8 per cent of holdings with an average size of 390.7 hectares controlled 77 per cent of land in the southern provinces of Cajamarca department. A combination of private sale and land reform weakened the hacienda sector, which shrunk to around 30 per cent of agricultural land. Simultaneously, the weight in the rural social structure of medium-scale farms of 20–50 hectares in size increased (Table 1).

Even so, despite the retreat of hacienda boundaries, a large majority of peasant households remained unaffected by the implementation of agrarian reform. Land redistribution benefited primarily labourers and tenants settled on expropriated properties. It also improved the position of more prosperous smallholders who possessed the wherewithal to purchase the plots that landowners put on the market. This brought a consolidation in the ranks of the rich peasantry, hand in hand with increasing proletarianisation among a majority of their less-fortunate neighbours. According to the 1994 Agrarian Census, while in Cajabamba province farming enterprises of less than 5 hectares comprised 72.2 per cent of holdings, these *minifundios* only controlled 18.7 per

Table 1 *Land Distribution: Provinces of Cajabamba and San Marcos, 1994*

Size *hectares*	No. Holdings	% Holdings	Area *hectares*	% Land Area	Average Size *hectares*
Cajabamba					
0.0– 0.5	1315	10.2	309.01	0.4	0.2
0.5– 4.9	7968	62.0	15483.85	18.3	1.9
5.0– 9.9	1861	14.5	12465.56	14.8	6.7
10.0–19.9	1001	7.8	13407.20	15.9	13.4
20.0–49.9	527	4.1	15131.91	17.9	28.7
50.0+	179	1.4	27607.88	32.7	154.2
TOTAL	**12851**	**100.0**	**84405.41**	**100.0**	
San Marcos					
0.0– 0.5	1285	12.9	286.72	0.6	0.2
0.5– 4.9	6555	66.0	12015.86	24.9	1.8
5.0– 9.9	1239	12.5	8294.66	17.2	6.7
10.0–19.9	580	5.8	7706.90	16.0	13.1
20.0–49.9	223	2.2	6395.30	13.2	28.7
50.0+	58	0.6	13588.39	28.1	234.1
TOTAL	**9940**	**100.0**	**48287.83**	**100.0**	

Source: Elaborated from *III Censo Nacional Agropecuario, 1994 – Cajamarca: Resultados Definitivos*, Lima, Ministerio de Agricultura, 1996, pp. 603–4, 613–14.

cent of agricultural land. Their average area stood at a paltry 1.7 hectares. In San Marcos, the respective figures were 78.9, 25.5 and 1.6 (Table 1). A similar pattern was to be found in Huamachuco, Santiago de Chuco and the other highland provinces of the department of La Libertad, although here the amount of land controlled by larger properties was greater owing to the presence of very extensive cooperatives (Table 2).

Table 2 *Land Distribution: Andean Provinces of La Libertad, 1994*

Size *hectares*	No. Holdings	% Holdings	Area *hectares*	% Land Area	Average Size *hectares*
0.0– 0.5	3492	4.8	792.40	0.1	0.23
0.5– 4.9	43824	60.0	96812.81	12.4	2.21
5.0– 9.9	14667	20.1	97515.55	12.5	6.65
10.0–19.9	7165	9.8	93619.35	12.0	13.07
20.0–49.9	2917	4.0	82069.34	10.5	28.13
50.0+	915	1.3	407505.99	52.5	445.36
TOTAL	**72980**	**100.0**	**778315.44**	**100.0**	

Source: Elaborated from *III Censo Nacional Agropecuario, 1994 – La Libertad: Resultados Definitivos*, Lima, Ministerio de Agricultura, 1995, pp. 306–12.

Unlike the situation encountered in the Central Andes, La Libertad cooperatives were not surrounded by dense clusters of well-organised peasant communities. They did, however, coexist alongside large numbers of land-hungry smallholders. In the province of Otuzco (which possessed the highest number of agricultural enterprises in La Libertad – 22,510), a mere 1.1 per cent of holdings accounted for 49 per cent of the land. At the other extreme, some 13,963 households (62 per cent) were unable to meet familial needs from on-farm resources. This latter figure rose to 72 per cent in the second most populous province, Sánchez Carrión (the province centred on Huamachuco). As a result, when the PCP–SL launched its 'protracted people's war' in the northern highlands, most rural families continued to live in dire poverty and suffered a debilitating 'subsistence crisis'. In terms of land-tenure patterns, therefore, General Velasco's agrarian reform had transformed rural society to an important degree, while paradoxically changing little. As far as the majority of rural households were concerned, earning a decent living from farming proved impossible and opportunities for upward social mobility remained limited.[53]

Social conflict and peasant organisation in the 1970s

Nor did the implementation of the military regime's land reform programme achieve the intended pacification of peasant unrest. Indeed, it exacerbated a number of long-standing disputes and spawned new conflicts. Two mutually reinforcing developments underpinned the rising tide of mobilisation during the 1970s. First, government propaganda proclaiming that 'Peasants, landlords will never again eat at the expense of your poverty' and promises of 'land to the tiller', coupled with a haemorrhaging of landlord power in the countryside, fuelled *campesino* expectations while simultaneously allowing greater scope for political engagement. The favourable environment created a new layer of (mainly) young political activists in the villages (many influenced by liberation theology clerics) and gave an added impetus to peasant organisation. A second key factor was an upsurge in urban radicalism influenced by the Cuban Revolution, conflict in Vietnam and the unusual spectre of a military government attacking the agrarian elite and expropriating the assets of foreign petroleum and mining companies. Against this backdrop, sectors of the urban poor, the provincial middle class, students and employees of the recently opened university in the town of Cajamarca became politicised. Many of these radicalised social agents rejected the two reformist parties traditionally influential in the northern sierra (APRA and the pro-Moscow Communist Party) and gravitated towards recently established new left political organisations keen to change fundamentally Peruvian society, particularly the condition of the supposedly 'marginalised' Andean peasantry.

These developments in town and country had their impact inside local peasant organisations. Of key importance here was the Federación Departamental de Campesinos de Cajamarca (FEDECC) – Departmental Peasants' Federation of Cajamarca. This body had been founded in 1961 by APRA, but as the party adopted more pro-landlord policies (for opportunistic political reasons APRA opposed Belaunde's 1963 land reform legislation), it experienced difficulty in maintaining its grip on the Federation. Internal tensions accentuated after the passing of the 1969 Land Reform Act and in that year the Federation split, the APRA minority was defeated and the majority came out strongly in favour of support for expropriation of the landlords.

Playing a leading role in this division was the pro-Moscow Partido Comunista del Perú-Unidad (PCP–U), which assumed control of FEDECC and led it in accordance with its national political line of 'critical support' for Velasco's military government. Against a backdrop of slow progress on land reform, which gave landowners ample time to decapitalise their properties, a sizeable group opposed to the organisation's PCP–U leadership emerged within the space of two years. Their platform rested on demands for an acceleration of hacienda takeovers, along with a halt to private land sales and estate decapitalisation. It was argued that a more rigorous anti-landlord strategy should be pursued in the countryside and that expropriations should take place without financial compensation and, if necessary, be accomplished through land invasions. Grass-roots delegates within FEDECC began canvassing for the removal of the Federation's PCP–U directive, wishing to replace it with members who were prepared to make the organisation fully independent of government influence and follow more robust anti-landlord polices.

Disagreement came to a head at a delegate assembly held in the town of Cajamarca on 27 January 1973, when the existing leadership was voted out by a ratio of approximately four to one. A motion was passed calling for a policy of building up FEDECC at the district level and increasing rank-and-file participation. Another motion was approved that proposed the affiliation of FEDECC to the national Confederación Campesina del Perú (CCP), in which Peru's largest revolutionary group, Vanguardia Revolucionaria (VR), was the major political force.[54] These developments indicated growing sympathy for the positions of this new left organisation among the most politicised sectors of the peasantry. Indeed, one of the key figures in ousting first APRA and then the PCP–U from influence in FEDECC at this juncture was Félix Calderón, a leader from the peasant community of Huacataz and member of VR. During the early stages of the PCP–SL's insurgency, he was to become one of Sendero's key cadres in the northern highlands (an issue addressed in Chapter Three).

Once in control of FEDECC, the newly appointed office-holders embarked on a campaign aimed at promoting a 'via campesina' solution to the agrarian question through tomas de tierras (land invasions). To this end, a network of Comités de Campesinos (Peasant Committees) was established at the village level as a medium for raising political awareness and grass-roots participation.[55] A number of successful land invasions were subsequently launched. Prominent among them figured the occupation of the hacienda Pomabamba in San Marcos (April 1974) by approximately eighty households, an event followed by many similar incidents.

Meanwhile, in the adjacent ex-hacienda La Pauca, which had undergone expropriation in October 1972, a complex array of conflicts emerged. Many socios (members of the newly established cooperative) attempted to expand illegally their individually farmed holdings by encroaching on lands earmarked for collective exploitation. Simultaneously, land-hungry members of peasant communities and freeholders settled along La Pauca's boundaries, who had gained nothing from the agrarian reform, strove to remedy their dire situation by undertaking a series of invasions. Their objective was to recuperate land they considered had been usurped by the ex-landlord (a number of squatter households felt particularly aggrieved because they had been evicted by the hacendado when he began to capitalise the estate in the 1940s).

The occupations were opposed vigorously by the leaders of the nascent cooperative, the outcome being a succession of violent clashes. One of the first confrontations involved 40 families from the community of Coriorco, who invaded 300 hectares. Cooperative leaders responded by mobilising some 185 socios: in August 1973, armed with machetes and staves, they evicted the squatters, burning their humble dwellings and driving cattle on to their crops.[56] Over ensuing years, land occupations extended to most sections of La Pauca and the resulting disputes became increasingly acrimonious. It became commonplace for cooperative leaders to block off irrigation channels within an invaded area, shoot the squatters' cattle, try to carry out a rodeo, or confiscate livestock and charge exorbitant levies for their return – all in addition to organising platoons of their followers to drive the occupiers out.

One of the most fought-over areas was Yerba Buena, where a succession of invasions and expulsions occurred. Here, a leading figure in the ranks of the squatters, Estanislao Vargas, was murdered on 15 November 1979 by a band headed by the administrator of La Pauca, Leoncio Bazán. This was followed by a second death on 2 November 1980. During an attempt to lift squatters' livestock, peasant activist Juan Abanto was shot in the stomach by one of the *pistoleros* in the pay of the cooperative, who were reputedly egged on by shouts of: 'If these Indians resist, go ahead and kill them. The cooperative will sort things out.'[57] Driven by an intense desire to expel invaders from outside and within, the group that came to dominate the SAIS enlisted the support of the police and, on occasions, the army, in addition to arranging the imprisonment of local FEDECC supporters. Despite their best efforts and the backing they obtained from key state institutions, the land occupations became more successful over time as the peasantry prevailed in what amounted to a long-drawn-out war of attrition.

Other factors contributed to an accelerating disintegration of the SAIS La Pauca during the late 1970s and early 1980s. Managerial incompetence led to a steep fall in production. Economic decline was exacerbated by corrupt administrators appointed by the Ministry of Agriculture to run the enterprise, who pocketed investment capital and income derived from the two most profitable activities of the cooperative (the sale of fighting bulls to *plazas* throughout Peru and milk to Nestlé). The malversation of funds extended to the leadership clique, whose members had come to control the enterprise by exploiting the ascendancy they enjoyed as a result of their positions of authority gained as confidants of the ex-*patrón*. Abuse of power was the norm as cooperative leaders tried to force those who had been sharecroppers to work for the SAIS, attempted to collect illegal rents and left wages unpaid for months on end.

With the leaders operating in such a Mafia-like fashion and establishing themselves as *gamonalillos* (small-time political bosses), disillusion with the SAIS spread rapidly. Private parcelisation of land accelerated after 1975 at the expense of collective cultivation, as the leaders managed to carve out for themselves holdings of 50–100 hectares of the best land, suborning Ministry of Agriculture officials in the process. On the other hand, most *socios* received plots of less than 5 hectares. This sorry tale of corruption and opportunism caused deep resentment among the populace and led to a proliferation of personal hatreds.

Similar problems arose in cooperatives in the *sierra* of La Libertad. The SAIS Tahuantinsuyo, created from highland properties belonging to the Empresa Agrícola Chicama, centred on the ex-hacienda Cochabamba and covering

70,561 hectares (nearly 59,000 hectares being natural pastures), was the largest enterprise in the department. It boasted 1,448 beneficiaries at the time of expropriation. Some 194 members were stable workers and the remainder were former tenants who acquired usufruct rights to their holdings. The SAIS Inti Raymi (based on the ex-haciendas Chota and Motil) covered 22,947 hectares on adjudication in September 1972 and housed 560 members, of whom 77 were permanent workers. The SAIS 3 de Octubre, although smaller (12,985 hectares), was similar: only nine of its 308 *socios* were permanent workers. Typically, on all SAIS in highland La Libertad, former tenants gained most direct benefit from the agrarian reform, obtaining rights to exploit far larger plots on an individual basis than the farm labourers. Expropriation, however, did not quench their thirst for land. Smallholders who were formally cooperative members and outsiders encroached on fields adjudicated for collective exploitation, provoking a series of bitter confrontations with the permanent work force, most of whom favoured collective farming. During a clash at Tallanga in November 1976, five *campesinos* were shot dead and many others were arrested for 'attacks against the armed forces'.[58]

A myriad of disputes were also unfolding in neighbouring districts. In Cajabamba, for example, the community of Chorobamba sustained a bitter struggle with the adjacent cooperative of Chingol for control over some 200 hectares of mainly poor-quality grazing land, which was nevertheless of vital importance to the *comuneros'* precarious farming economy. In April 1978, a land invasion was launched, sparking off a new round in this dispute. Cooperative members responded by enlisting support from the authorities. On 20 October 1978, two of Chorobamba's leaders were thrown in jail.[59] The community was also embroiled in a conflict with the Juez de Tierras (Land Judge) in Huamachuco and the Ministry of Agriculture in Cajamarca over land titles and official recognition. Such alienating experiences would shortly convert Chorobamba into a PCP–SL bastion. Another struggle was being waged in the hacienda Igosbamba–Ninabamba. Using his influence with bureaucrats in the Ministry of Agriculture, landowner Guillermo García had not only managed to stall the expropriation of his property, he had also illegally sold 200 head of cattle (March 1980). When in May 1980 the Deputy Land Judge of Huamachuco decreed that he remained the rightful owner of the enterprise, labourers and sharecroppers occupied the estate.[60]

Apart from the usual *mélange* of clashes over land and other farming resources, the rural population found themselves embroiled in altercations with the state on different fronts. In 1978, for example, the local police and authorities levied fines, on bogus pretexts, on the denizens of the community of Llucho, near Cauday. Those who refused to succumb to abuse and pay found themselves thrown into jail. To compound the injustice, they failed to receive protection from Cajabamba's judiciary.[61] In August 1980, the head of the Ministry of Agriculture office in Cajabamba was charging 1,000 *soles* to legalise land titles, when these should have been issued gratis. Yet again, local judges did nothing to protect smallholders from such blatant venality. As shall be seen, corruption in the judicial system formed another important source of rural discontent that the PCP–SL attempted to exploit.

Conclusion

From the preceding account it can be appreciated that by the 1970s the Cajabamba–Huamachuco region housed a wide variety of agricultural enterprises in terms of size, levels of technical modernisation, efficiency and intensity of production. Backward *minifundios* coexisted alongside some of the most developed estates in the Peruvian highlands. On these properties, wage labour relations had been commonplace since the 1930s and hacienda residents were well accustomed to labouring in a 'modern' work environment. Sharecropping formed the second most prevalent form of exploiting direct producers and was particularly in evidence for the cultivation of highly marketable crops such as sugar cane or potatoes. An overwhelming majority of farms, whether large, medium or small, had a long history of involvement in regional commodity and labour markets. Due to agrarian reform, between 1970 and 1976 most landlords lost their properties and much of their influence; the new 'owners of the countryside' were medium-scale farmers, kulaks and leaders of the cooperatives recently established by the military government. Consequently, despite the existence of widespread rural poverty, the socio-economic situation encountered in Cajabamba–Huamachuco when the PCP–SL started to infiltrate the zone proved to be very different and far more complex than the one-dimensional image of Andean 'semi-feudalism' drawn by Abimael Guzmán and his followers.

In the socio-political sphere, the inhabitants of Cajabamba–Huamachuco possessed a rich history of engagement in anti-elite and anti-state activity. Brigandage had been endemic and continued to plague farming communities, while there had never been any difficulty in mustering recruits for *montonera* uprisings against Lima governments. Migration had long acquainted *serranos* from all walks of life with new work experiences and ideas. Indeed, the region's most celebrated scion, poet César Vallejo, had been radicalised when he left his native Santiago de Chuco to work in the offices of the Quiruvilca mine (1910) and the accounts department at the Roma sugar plantation in the Chicama Valley (1912).[62] More recently – since 1930 – numerous individuals had experienced 'modern' politics through membership of labour unions or participation in party politics: primarily (but not exclusively), *aprismo*.

During the decade immediately prior to the launch of PCP–SL armed activity in the area, the political antennae of its inhabitants had been fine-tuned as a result of the considerable amount of controversy, debate and mobilisation that surrounded the implementation of land reform. Instead of putting an end to rural unrest, this policy heightened political awareness and radicalised a sector of the peasantry. It also spawned a plethora of new schisms among different sectors of the rural poor, in addition to conflict between peasants and the state – as illustrated by developments in the SAIS La Pauca and other cooperatives.

In short, when the PCP–SL commenced local recruitment in 1979, an environment existed that presented many possibilities for the insurgent organisation. It simultaneously contained many potential pitfalls. To register success, the Party would have to operate in an astute and sagacious fashion. How, then, did Sendero set about the task of building up its network of cadres in Cajabamba–Huamachuco and launch its 'protracted people's war'?

References

1   See Monica Zaugg, 'Textile Production and Structural Crisis: the Case of Late Colonial Peru', unpublished PhD thesis, University of Liverpool, 1993. To give an indication of the size of these enterprises, one source noted that the Chuquizongo estate (later known as Choquizongo) in Huamachuco covered, 'an area of approximately 1,940 square kilometres. The hacienda was blessed with many microclimates, so its owners could cultivate a wide variety of crops typical of the coast and the sierra (coca, bananas, avocados, sugar cane, coffee, cotton, potatoes, quinua, maize, etc.) … In addition to these products, Chuquizongo housed enormous numbers of cattle, horses, mules and sheep. Its pastures were so extensive that they could support comfortably 100,000 head of sheep and goats in the eighteenth and nineteenth centuries. Its *obraje* was one of the most productive in the province and maybe in the whole of northern Peru.' Quoted from Waldemar Espinoza Soriano, 'Geografía histórica de Huamachuco', *Historia y Cultura. Organo del Museo Nacional de Historia* 5, 1971, pp. 53–54. The same author claimed that in 1860 the hacienda Chusgón (in Huamachuco province), 'still contained 30,000 sheep despite its economic decline'. Ibid., p. 37.
2   For background information, see Lewis Taylor, 'Main Trends in Agrarian Capitalist Development: Cajamarca, Peru 1880–1976', unpublished PhD thesis, University of Liverpool, 1979.
3   Information in this and following paragraphs comes from Archivo del Fuero Agrario/Correspondencia de la Empresa Agrícola/Chicama/Cochabamba. These documents are not yet classified and are currently kept in sacks in the basement of the Archivo General de la Nación, Lima.
4   Taylor, 'Main Trends', chapter 4.
5   See the minutes of the 'Asociación de Productores de Chancaca del Valle de Condebamba', ADC/FDP/SpCb, 6 July 1943.
6   Rosario Contreras later changed his first name to Germán, reputedly because of his pale skin: gringo engineers employed at the Quiruvilca mine started to call him *hermano* ('brother'), which induced him to adopt the nearest Spanish equivalent. Information kindly supplied by his granddaughter, Cecilia Contreras.
7   Taylor, 'Main Trends', chapters 4 and 5.
8   Solomon Miller, 'Hacienda to Plantation in Northern Peru: the Processes of Proletarianization of a Tenant Farmer Society', in Julian H. Steward (ed.), *Contemporary Change in Traditional Societies, Vol. III: Mexican and Peruvian Communities*, Urbana, IL, University of Illinois Press, 1970, p. 144. This work examines the impact of socio-economic change on properties owned by the Empresa Andina San Leonardo (ex-hacienda Chusgón), to which he gives the pseudonym 'Ganadabamba Inc.'.
9   Espinoza, 'Geografía histórica de Huamachuco', pp. 8–23. Following this rebellion, the colonial authorities created Huamachuco as a separate administrative area in order to tighten their control. According to Espinoza, after 1758: 'maintaining the

peace in the province of Huamachuco required considerable caution and astuteness ... in addition to the significant Indian population there was a large number of *mestizos* who [in the eyes of the authorities] were "very uppish" ... The province was a cauldron of discontent, disorder and regular rebellion owing to the injustices perpetrated by *obraje* owners, landlords, officials and tax and tithe collectors'. Ibid., p. 23. Espinoza may exaggerate, but the general point stands.

10 For further information on this mode of politics in the northern highlands, see Lewis Taylor, *Bandits and Politics in Peru: Landlord and Peasant Violence in Hualgayoc, 1900–1930*, Cambridge, Centre of Latin American Studies, 1986; and Lewis Taylor, 'Sociedad y política en Contumazá, 1876–1900', in Lewis Taylor, *Estructuras agrarias y cambios sociales en Cajamarca, siglos xix–xx*, Cajamarca, Asociación Obispo Martínez Compañón, 1994, pp. 45–104.

11 The subprefect of Cajabamba to the prefect of Cajamarca, ADC/FDP/SpCb, 17 September 1878; 1 October 1878.

12 See 'Carolina Puga, viuda de Puga, contra coronel Manuel Callirgos Quiroga por los delitos de tres homicidios, flagelación, robo e incedio de las casas de las haciendas Pauca, Huagal y sus caseríos', ADC/CSJ/CC, *legajo* 40, 1886, fols. 2–4, 11–18, 115v–118, 319–20.

13 ADC/FDP/SpCb, 19 January 1886.

14 Ibid., 9 September 1900; 29 December 1900; 12 July 1901.

15 Ibid., 4 January 1926. Further details on the Calluán–Choquizongo dispute can be found in ibid., 1 August 1924; 22 March 1926; 20 May 1926; 6 February 1927. An extensive commentary on this conflict is also given in *El Perú*, 11 December 1927, a newspaper published in the town of Cajamarca. The state of open warfare between these landlords and their peasant followers provoked heated debates in Congress. See *Congreso Ordinario de 1925. Diario de los Debates del Senado*, Lima, Casa Editora E. Rávago, 1925, sessions held on 10 August 1925; 17 August 1925; 16 October 1925; 6 November 1925.

16 ADC/FDP/SpCb, 25 August 1898; 27 August 1898; 14 September 1898; 16 September 1898. For a participant's view of this rebellion, see V. Ortega, *Un episodio de la revolución de 1898*, Lima, Imprenta Luz, 1947.

17 ADC/FDP/SpCb, 10 July 1901.

18 Ibid., 8 November 1901.

19 Ibid., 15 January 1902.

20 Ibid.

21 Ibid., 31 March 1902.

22 ADC/FDP/P, 24 March 1900.

23 ADC/FDP/SpCb, 28 May 1924.

24 Recurring examples of this kind of event can be found in ibid., 7 May 1880; 28 January 1904; 7 September 1910. Not all the denizens of Cajabamba were hostile to the army's recruiting squads, however. Germán Contreras, for example, used a novel ploy to rid himself of offspring who eschewed physical agricultural work and possessed a general penchant towards idleness. He would invite them to his birthday celebrations, attendance at which could not be refused, but also arrange for the military to appear at a certain hour during the festivities so that the errant sons could be seized. Contreras reasoned that two years in the army would improve their work ethic.

25 Ibid., 8 May 1911.

26 Ibid.

27 Ibid., 2 December 1912.

28 Ibid., 14 September 1914.

29 Ibid., 30 October 1915.

30 Ibid., 11 July 1916; 12 August 1916; 25 August 1916.

31 Ibid., 29 August 1916; 4 September 1916.

32 Further information on the early development of APRA in the northern highlands, see Lewis Taylor, 'The Origins of APRA in Cajamarca, 1928–1935', *Bulletin of Latin American Research* 19: 4, 2000, pp. 437–59. For an informed analysis of similar political change in the neighbouring department of Amazonas, see David Nugent, *Modernity at the Edge of Empire: State, Individual and Nation in the Northern Peruvian Andes, 1885–1935*, Stanford, CA, Stanford University Press, 1997.

33 Guillermo Thorndike, *El año de la barbarie: Perú 1932*, Lima, Mosca Azul Editores, 1973, p. 160. The most thorough account of the 1932 revolt in Trujillo is Margarita Giesecke, 'The Trujillo Insurrection, the APRA Party and the Making of Modern Peruvian Politics', unpublished PhD thesis, University of London, 1993.

34 In January 1946, for example, the subprefect of Cajamarca informed his superiors that the district governor and all the lieutenant governors in Cauday were *apristas*. Every representative of Cajabamba's municipal government – ten councillors – belonged to APRA. ADC/FDP/SpC, 29 January 1946.

35 For their part, the villagers of Cauday claimed that the landlord was attempting to force them to perform unpaid labour. They complained to the prefect in Cajamarca that the subprefect [Demetrio Iparraguirre, a member of the local landowning elite] had taken the side of the *hacendado* and was 'committing all kinds of abuses against us. He has threatened us with death.' The subprefect replied that the bullet holes in the hacienda residence testified to the attacks perpetrated by the peasants. The prefect ordered the subprefect to provide guarantees to the villagers. ADC/FDP/SpCb, 24 November 1920; 4 December 1920; 17 December 1923; 5 January 1924.

36 For debates in the Senate on this conflict, see *Congreso Ordinario de 1925. Diario de los Debates del Senado*, sessions held on 28 September 1925; 3 December 1925; 12 January 1926.

37 On the link between the rise of APRA and social conditions in coastal sugar estates, see Peter Klarén, *Formación de las haciendas azucareras y orígenes del APRA*, Lima, Instituto de Estudios Peruanos, 1976.

38 See M. E. Espinosa to José Ignacio Chopitea, AFA/EACh/C, 8 August 1913. Espinosa had been contracted to make a confidential report on the economic and social situation found on the hacienda Chusgón because Chopitea was interested in leasing the property as a potential source of foodstuffs and workers to supply the Laredo sugar plantation. Espinosa estimated that Chusgón and its various *anexos* covered approximately '104 square leagues'. He considered the rents paid by Chusgón's tenants to be 'very low and I think that they could be at least doubled, but not immediately, because that would be dangerous'.

39 Letter of V. Wetti, administrator in the Cochabamba *anexo*, to Arend Kulenkampff, manager of the Laredo sugar plantation, ibid., 31 October 1941.

40 Kulenkampff to Wetti, ibid., 21 November 1941.

41 Ibid., 10 October 1942.

42 Ibid., 15 August 1943; 28 August 1943; 30 November 1943; 13 February 1944.

43 Ibid., 18 July 1943; 15 January 1944; 23 May 1944; 25 May 1944.

44 Ibid., 13 August 1946.

45 Ibid., 14 July 1946; 24 March 1947. Similar events occurred on other estates at this juncture. Throughout 1946, for example, sharecroppers and labourers who belonged to the Sindicato de Agricultores de las Haciendas Calluán y Monton refused to work and fulfil their tenancy agreements. ADC/FDP/SpC, 19 August 1946.

46   Jorge de Orbegoso to the prefect of Cajamarca, ADC/FDP/Pa, 21 August, 1957.
47   Ibid.
48   See the testimony of Circuncripción Vigo, ibid., 25 September 1957. The conflict arose from Orbegoso's desire to revise established labour and renting arrangements.
49   Pedro Rodríguez Cueva, General Secretary of the Sindicato Mixto de Yanaconas y Trabajadores de la hacienda Araqueda to the prefect of Cajamarca, ibid., 8 January 1959.
50   AFA/EACh/C, 26 October 1963.
51   On the sale of marginal lands belonging to Chusgón, see the letter by Enrique Gildemeister to the Administration of the Empresa Andina San Leonardo, ibid., 21 May 1963. On peasant protest against the high price demanded for this land, see ibid., 26 October 1963. On the process of hacienda land sales in general, see Taylor, 'Main Trends', pp. 337–41.
52   For additional details on the slow implementation of land reform and its political consequences, see Taylor, 'Main Trends', pp. 320–82; and Carmen Diana Deere, *Household and Class Relations: Peasants and Landlords in Northern Peru*, Berkeley, CA, University of California Press, 1990, pp. 234–61.
53   According to the Director of the Ministry of Agriculture's Huamachuco office, some 70 per cent of the rural population in highland La Libertad suffered from malnutrition in 1988. *La Industria*, 20 October 1988.
54   Policy initiatives were laid out in 'Acuerdos de la IV Convención Campesina de la FEDECC', mimeo, Cajamarca, February 1974.
55   On land invasions in the northern sierra, see Diego García-Sayán, *Tomas de tierras en el Perú*, Lima, DESCO, 1982, pp. 49–71.
56   Federación Departamental de Campesinos de Cajamarca (FEDECC), *Luchas Campesinas en Cajamarca*, Cajamarca, 1975, n.p. For further data on events in the SAIS La Pauca, see Taylor, 'Main Trends', pp. 387–93.
57   On the assassination of Vargas and the events leading up to it, see the FEDECC newsletter *Lucha Campesina*, issues 13, December 1978; 15, May 1979; and 16, December 1979. Also see the newspaper of the CCP, *Voz Campesina* 14, May–June 1979, and the Lima monthly *El Sol Andino*, February 1981.
58   Six of the detained were sentenced to eight years' detention by the court in Trujillo in December 1979. See *Lucha Campesina* 16, December 1979.
59   These events are reported in *Lucha Campesina* 12, November 1978.
60   'Informe de la Federación Provincial de Cajabamba', mimeo, presented to the Asamblea de Bases de la FEDECC, Cajamarca, July 1982.
61   *Voz Campesina* 11, October 1978.
62   Vallejo's novel *El tungsteno*, published in 1931, is supposedly set in Cusco, but draws heavily on personal observations of social conditions and labour relations made while he was employed at Quiruvilca. Even the name of the fictitious mine, 'Quivilca', illustrates this influence.

CHAPTER THREE

Early Moves to 'Reconstruct the Party', 1979–82

Five major strategic considerations led the PCP–SL to designate the northern highlands a priority area for recruitment and future guerrilla operations during the planning stage of its 'protracted people's war'. First, Party doctrine held that peasants formed the 'principal motor force of the revolution'; and since, by 1980, the department of Cajamarca and the Andean provinces of La Libertad housed the largest and most densely inhabited concentration of smallholders in Peru, it was to be expected that Sendero would target the zone. Second, if the Maoist goal of 'encircling the towns from the countryside' was to be achieved, the mountain hinterland of Peru's second most populous city, Trujillo, was a logical area of activity for launching armed actions. Third, the PCP–SL leadership anticipated correctly that a number of guerrilla fronts would need to be opened up in order to disperse the armed forces and so relieve pressure on political cells and military units operating at the nodal point of the organisation's operations: Ayacucho and its environs. Fourth, if the PCP–SL could tap the local population's dissatisfaction with the state, its social base and overall prospects in the 'protracted people's war' would be enhanced significantly. Fifth, the existence of extensive cooperatives and a few haciendas that had escaped expropriation during Velasco's land reform signified that this was not a uniformly impoverished region, as were most highland districts of Ayacucho and Apurímac. In the northern highlands there were significant amounts of land, livestock and other farming resources that could be redistributed to peasant households, consequently providing greater opportunity for the PCP–SL to build up support among the rural population.

Sendero exploit divisions within the left

For these reasons, clandestine recruitment commenced in earnest in 1979, when cadres from Ayacucho, Lima, Trujillo and Chiclayo were sent into Cajamarca and the *sierra* of La Libertad with instructions to attract new members and build up a political apparatus. Their task was complicated by the fact that, unlike in Ayacucho, the PCP–SL possessed no history of political activity in the zone and could access a minimal network of contacts. The insurgent organisation had played no role in the main peasant syndicate, FEDECC, and did not participate in the land invasions launched during the 1970s. A similar situation existed in Huamachuco and Santiago de Chuco. The Party's position was further weakened as a result of insignificant *senderista* influence among students attending the university in the town of Cajamarca (where student and staff associations were dominated by rival left groups). Neither had the PCP–SL any presence within the various trade union and artisan associations operating in the three key urban populations of Cajamarca, Cajabamba and Huamachuco.

The PCP–SL could employ to its advantage, however, a split originating inside Vanguardia Revolucionaria (VR), the most important leftist party active in the northern highlands (and the group with the strongest peasant base). Over the latter months of 1976 and early 1977, VR was in turmoil due to a bitter internal factional battle. Disagreement centred on two related issues: the characterisation of Peruvian society; and the policies required to advance the party's revolutionary project in the current political conjuncture. With regard to the former question, more Maoist-influenced cadres active in the less-developed regions of the Andes (such as Andahuaylas, Cajamarca, Huamachuco, Ayacucho and Cusco) adopted a strong *campesinista* ('peasantist') position on the basis that Peru remained essentially the 'semi-feudal' nation depicted by Mariátegui during the 1920s. This being the case, the argument went, peasants were the key class to target for proselytisation. By contrast, most of VR's Lima-based national leadership posited that Peruvian society was predominantly 'capitalist', with the working class the chief agent of social transformation. Militants in Cajamarca and Huamachuco who were opposed to the national line also argued that the military regime was being terminally undermined by a legitimation crisis. The high levels of popular unrest currently taking place (in 1977 a wave of regional and national strikes swept the country) signified that Peru was entering a 'pre-revolutionary' situation. Leading on from this particular reading of events, an important proportion of cadres in the northern highlands further criticised VR's leadership for not giving sufficient priority to preparing the party militarily for the seizure of power. Following several months of heated debate, a clear majority of VR activists in the northern highlands left the organisation to establish a new party, named Vanguardia Revolucionaria–Proletario Comunista (VR–PC).[1]

In accordance with their contention that revolutionary conditions were ripening in Peru, VR–PC adopted an ultra-left stance vis-à-vis the 1978 Constituency Assembly elections, calling for a boycott of what they labelled an 'electoral farce'. Nevertheless, once VR–PC's leaders saw how strongly the various left fronts polled (the Trotskyite Hugo Blanco received 12.3 per cent of the vote; overall the left garnered 30 per cent), the organisation performed an abrupt volte-face. During early 1979 VR–PC joined the Union of the Revolutionary Left (UNIR) – Unión Nacional de Izquierda Revolucionaria – coalition and participated in the 1980 general election.[2]

Such a blatant U-turn, taken without proper consultation with the rank and file, in addition to disagreements on other policy matters and personality clashes, created a high degree of confusion and disenchantment among VR–PC cadres at the very moment when PCP–SL activists started to target the northern highlands for recruitment. Guzmán's followers infiltrated VR–PC in 1979–80 and successfully courted part of its membership. In Cajamarca, an important component of the *Comisión Campesina* (Peasant Section) of VR–PC decided to break with the (primarily urban) leadership of the local party. By mid-1979 it had aligned with Sendero.[3] The most prominent figure to be 'captured' over these months was Félix Calderón, an activist from the peasant community of Hacataz (located some 16 kilometres from the town of Cajamarca), whose route into the PCP–SL came via VR and VR–PC. His political history mirrored that of a number of Sendero's most important peasant cadres operating in the northern Andes and, therefore, merits attention.

The activism of Calderón, a former catechist, dated from 1972, when he played a central role in the community's struggle to force the Ministry of Education to provide extra teachers for the village school. Successful mobilisation on this issue provided a stimulus for debate concerning other problems confronting the local population, a dynamic that led to *Comités Campesinos* being established in Huacat05 and six surrounding villages. These organisational advances were shortly followed by affiliation to FEDECC, the invasion of a neighbouring farm (Tres Tingos) on 24 April 1973 and occupation of the *fundo* Muyoc on 12 September 1973. In the following years the inhabitants resisted several efforts by landlords to recuperate their assets. They were also suspicious of attempts by officials from the agrarian reform section in the Ministry of Agriculture to intervene in the dispute with the objective of reallocating the squatters' plots and legalising land titles. Rightly or wrongly, the *campesinos* believed that the functionaries were in cahoots with local landowners and collaborating in a manoeuvre to evict them.

The ongoing conflict produced a tragedy in 1977. On 12 September, personnel from the Ministry of Agriculture were chased out of Huacatz by a group of residents brandishing staves and machetes, only to return on 28 December accompanied by a police detachment. In the ensuing confrontation, four peasants were shot dead, a number of leaders jailed and legal proceedings opened against them for a supposed '*ataque a las fuerzas armadas*' ('attack against the armed forces').[4] Such a bitter experience hardened Calderón's repudiation of the social status quo and helped propel him towards the PCP–SL, a trajectory eased by a similarity of ideological perspectives on key questions. This affinity can be traced through a reading of documents published in 1978 and 1979.

After the split with VR, Calderón became General Secretary of a FEDECC dominated by VR–PC. At the Federation's Congress, held in Huacatz over 18–20 August 1978, motions were approved stating that 'semi-feudalism' still prevailed in Peru's northern Andes; the argument being that the agrarian reform had 'consolidated large-scale landed property and raised feudal rents under state monopoly control'. As a consequence, 'the semi-feudal CAPs and SAIS' established by the Velasco government needed to be destroyed.[5] It was further posited that 'in Latin America the revolution develops from the countryside to the town, from the rural areas of backward semi-feudal countries, to encircle the cities', with the peasantry providing the 'motor force of the revolution' – which was supposedly on the horizon, given that Peru was living through 'a revolutionary situation'.[6] These Maoist-inspired positions, which mirrored those held by the PCP-SL, were soon being propagated through FEDECC's publications: in November 1978 the Federation's newsletter, edited by Calderón, opined that 'the land question is the principal problem. Therefore, the task is to carry through an agrarian revolution. The revolution will come from the country to the city in the form of popular war'.[7]

Having adopted this line, Calderón found it impossible to accept VR–PC's sudden willingness to participate in electoral politics, so becoming open to the blandishments of Sendero. By June 1979, cadres sent up to Cajamarca from the northern coast had recruited him into the Party. Although Calderón's new organisational allegiance was not widely known outside leftist circles, it could have been detected by the perceptive observer. Clues offering a glimpse of future developments, for example, were published in a freely available *Lucha Campesina* editorial written under Calderón's direction:

> Today it is impossible to sit back. Storm clouds embrace the Andes. The poor cannot continue living under the shoe and boot of a bunch of thieves. We need to develop the struggle. Nothing will stop us. This is a sign of the approaching storm.
>
> Ten years of false agrarian reform have passed. Now the land is in possession of the state. The state makes the peasants work like beasts of burden. Previously the boss was called a landlord, today the boss is the bureaucratic–landowner state ['*Estado terrateniente–burocrático*']. The hacienda of yesterday is now baptised with the name of CAP or SAIS ... We peasants are exploited and oppressed by local political bosses, who do not allow us to exercise our rights. They forbid us to do anything. If we get together to discuss our problems, they tell us it is prohibited. When we organise, mobilise and publish our newspapers and leaflets, we are persecuted, imprisoned, tried, sentenced, and on numerous occasions, assassinated mercilessly. They say we disturb the social peace and that we are against the nation. You cannot have social peace when you kill people through hunger. For this reason, the struggle will continue ... the Federation should work together with our grass-roots organisations to ... develop the revolutionary organisation of the peasantry.[8]

Shortly after issuing this call to arms, Calderón went underground. His recruitment represented a major coup for the PCP–SL. Through years of involvement in FEDECC, Calderón enjoyed a high level of prestige among the most politicised sectors of the rural population. Possessing a dynamic and charismatic personality, he was the best-known and most respected peasant leader in Cajamarca. Importantly, his participation in the 1970s drive to unionise the rural population meant that Calderón had built up a large network of contacts throughout the northern highlands, in addition to having acquired a national profile via activism in the CCP. Calderón's usefulness to Sendero, however, was to be relatively short-lived.

Sendero target *rondas campesinas*: Chota and Hualgayoc, 1981–82

Initially, Calderón and his comrades engaged in 'study group' activities aimed at assessing the post-agrarian reform situation in the *cajamarquino* countryside, disseminating the Party line and attempting to win over known leftists who might be sympathetic to Sendero's political project. This effort targeted activists settled in villages around the town of Cajamarca, as well as members of the local university acquainted with Calderón through their common history of militancy in VR or VR–PC. Outside resources were allocated to this task, in the shape of Sendero members drafted into the *sierra* from the shanty towns that surrounded Chiclayo and workers from rice plantations sited adjacent to Chepén on the northern coast. When, by mid-1980, a skeletal apparatus had been established, comprising two cells (one urban, the other rural), the local cadres began to devise an operational plan aimed at building the Party. Flowing logically from its strategic analysis, emphasis was placed on proselytisation in the countryside.

   Not surprisingly, one zone where the insurgents initially focused their attention was the northern provinces of Cajamarca department, where *rondas campesinas* (village-based vigilante patrols) had sprung up outside state control. First established in the province of Chota in December 1976, these organisations proved highly effective in combating rural crime. They became especially adept at curbing the activities of well-organised gangs of rustlers, who had previously operated with impunity owing to collusion with corrupt police officers and judges.[9] Following on their success in Chota, *ronda* committees spread quickly to the neighbouring provinces of Hualgayoc and Cutervo, where they also acquired widespread support. This level of legitimacy enabled the *rondas* to extend their activities from crime control to adjudicating on land and water disputes, questions of debt, physical altercations between freeholders, domestic rifts and community development initiatives on matters such as health, education, the provision of irrigation and similar agricultural improvements. Achieving near-universal participation at the hamlet level, *ronda* committees gave the peasantry enhanced power over local affairs. Crucially, they also provided an on-the-spot, quick, cheap and, above all, honest 'peasant justice', which was substantially superior to that administered by the state and enjoyed a far higher level of legitimacy. As they operated through communal decision-making processes via assemblies, encouraged open debate and practised the transparent election of office-holders, with leaders rotating every two to three years, these grass-roots organisations became a source of considerable peasant pride. People in the rural areas identified strongly with 'their' local committees.

   If the PCP–SL could gain a foothold among the hugely popular, well-organised and semi-militarised *rondas campesinas*, its apparatus and political influence could expand rapidly. The construction of a base in the populous provinces of Cutervo, Chota and Hualgayoc would also reinforce the Party's organisational efforts in the shanty towns that encircle Chiclayo, the commercial hub of Peru's northern coast and destination point for countless migrants from its mountainous hinterland. Thus motivated, in 1981 Félix Calderón, accompanied by several peasant associates from the province of Cajamarca and cadres who had been sent into the highlands from Chiclayo, made regular incursions into the Chota–Bambamarca area. The *senderistas* addressed *ronda* assemblies and attempted to persuade leading figures in the local organisations to join the Party. Overall, however, their calls for support for armed struggle failed to elicit an enthusiastic response. In the ensuing debates, the *ronderos* held that they had succeeded in building up autonomous organisations that possessed their own political agenda and functioned in a democratic fashion (unlike the PCP–SL). Participants in the nightwatch patrols held a wide range of political views, from IU to APRA and President Belaunde's Acción Popular (AP). Activists attached to these parties (APRA and Patria Roja in Chota; APRA and VR in Bambamarca), acted to block the PCP–SL from gaining a foothold; a powerful argument was that the *ronderos* were already experiencing serious difficulties with the authorities, which would increase significantly in the advent of guerrilla activity. In consequence, while many peasants voiced sympathy with the PCP–SL's goal of social transformation, an overwhelming majority remained unconvinced about their operational methods or chances of success.

One *campesino* who had been instrumental in establishing vigilante patrols around Bambamarca and was active in peasant politics at the local and departmental level, expressed these sentiments in the following manner:

> On a previous trip to Cajamarca, I'd been told about Sendero and what was being planned, so I'd been expecting a visit from Félix and had time to think about our conversation. Whenever we had met at FEDECC and other meetings we got on very well. He was a good man and I liked him despite our political disagreements. He was honest and could be relied upon to support peasant struggles. However, over recent years we'd gone our separate ways. I'd stayed with Vanguardia, while he left in 1977. Anyway, we had a long discussion sat on the edge of my maize field. Félix argued that the *rondas campesinas* were an important advance for peasants, but only went so far. They had a defensive usefulness. What we also needed was an offensive struggle to change Peru. Only that would improve the situation of the poor. I concurred that big changes were required in Peru. But to achieve this it was necessary to build up the movement – at present we were too weak to confront the state. On this we didn't agree. So, after a lengthy discussion we said a friendly goodbye and went on our different paths.[10]

A neighbouring *rondero* voiced other doubts:

> I knew Félix and respected him. But who were his *compañeros?* Could they

be trusted? They were not from our area. I had had no previous contact with his new organisation and didn't know what their plans were. Did they want to take over our *rondas* and use us? We were suspicious because we peasants have been tricked so many times in the past and promised so much. We were tired of being taken for fools. Those days have passed. Things had to change for the better in Peru – but were they the ones to do it? Was their path the correct one?[11]

Such misgivings resulted in Calderón and his comrades receiving a considerable degree of sympathy, but minimal active support, which must have been most frustrating. Undeterred by this far-from-satisfactory situation, however, the PCP–SL determined to press on with its plans and began to initiate low-level armed actions in the area in the hope of concentrating minds and impressing on the local population that they possessed serious intent and led by example.

Peasant–*senderista* relations subsequently became strained. Villagers mobilised to prevent the dynamiting of a bridge linking the towns of Bambamarca and Chota – it was, after all, useful for travelling to and from local markets. This incident was followed shortly by a severe reversal for the insurgent organisation. At dawn on 23 August 1982, Calderón and four of his comrades raided the hacienda Santa Clara, traditionally one of the better-farmed estates in Chota province and one that had managed to avoid expropriation under Velasco's land reform. After commanding the occupants: 'Don't move! We are guerrillas. Hand over all the arms and money you've got. We're not going to harm you', the attackers fled the scene in the landowner's pick-up truck, taking with them a significant haul of cash and other valuables. Two days later they had the misfortune to be spotted by Guardia Civil personnel stationed in the small town of Socotá, to the north of Chota, who pursued and cornered the insurgents when the dirt road they were racing down came to a dead end. In the ensuing firefight, two insurgents fell wounded and all five were captured.[12] Through beginning overt actions in a precipitous fashion, before establishing a social base and gaining a detailed knowledge of local conditions and topography, the PCP–SL's hopes of building a presence in Bambamarca and Chota were stillborn.

Why did so experienced a cadre as Calderón, who possessed an intimate knowledge of the rural population's psyche and would have comprehended their misgivings regarding the *senderista* project, commit such a basic error? An explanation is to be found in the internal politics of the PCP–SL, particularly the strategic decisions adopted at its Second National Congress held in May 1982. At this event it was agreed to embark on the '*batir el campo*' policy, outlined in Chapter One, whereby the countryside would be 'churned up' in order to force the rural elite and state functionaries to flee to the towns. In the words of General Secretary Guzmán, 'the key is to raze to the ground, and to raze to the ground is to leave nothing'.[13] Sendero's Central Committee determined that the destructive phase of this plan was to commence forthwith, with its constructive dimension – the 'conquering of support bases' – scheduled to start in January 1983.

At the Congress, the head and second in command of the PCP–SL's Northern Regional Committee argued that a 'one size fits all' approach was not appropriate, for in the area under their responsibility, 'conditions were not ready' to implement the 'churn up the countryside' policy. Despite this cautious assessment, the Party leadership overruled the regional commanders' objections. To add insult to injury, Guzmán censored severely his northern-based lieutenants for disputing the organisation's line, before forcing them to undertake a humiliating 'self-criticism'.[14] Failure to heed cautionary advice from cadres with local knowledge subsequently had fatal consequences for Félix Calderón and his comrades. As will be shown, this was not the only occasion when the PCP–SL's national leadership failed to strike the right balance between centralised command and decentralised decision-making.

Establishing a 'Red Zone': Cajabamba and Huamachuco, 1980–82

Following this setback in Cajamarca's northern provinces, the PCP–SL's gaze shifted more firmly southwards, to the extent that after 1982 its organisational efforts became almost wholly concentrated on the Cajabamba–Huamachuco region.[15] Indeed, well-rehearsed recruitment procedures had been under way in the area since 1979, when initial contact was made with a few local schoolteachers already known to *senderista* cadres from their student days at colleges in Cajamarca, Trujillo and Lima. One teacher who worked in a peasant community located between Cajamarca and San Marcos recalled being:

> Visited by an old friend from my college days who I had not seen for quite some time, so it was something of a surprise. We had fought side by side on the streets during the strikes against the military regime. He was waiting on a street corner by my house one weekend when I was in town to visit the family. I invited him in to eat and then we went out to a local bar for a drink. After chatting on family matters and exchanging news about mutual friends, we got on to the political situation in Peru. He told me about his militancy in Sendero and that armed struggle was planned to begin shortly. He urged me to join up. Peru was in a mess and the coming elections [in May 1980] would not change anything ... We met twice that weekend and about a month later he turned up one night unexpectedly in the village, accompanied by two men who were unknown to me. I was angry and told him it was dangerous to come to the community, for the *campesinos* might see them and start gossiping ... His efforts came to nothing. I did not really believe that Sendero was serious about beginning guerrilla war. Neither did I know much about Sendero. Also, I had recently got married and become a father – with these new responsibilities I couldn't just disappear up into the mountains. After persisting for a while, they left me alone.[16]

Although this informant (who sympathised with a rival left organisation but was inactive at the time), did not hold a favourable view of the PCP–SL, a small number of rural schoolteachers working in districts between San Marcos in the north and Santiago de Chuco in the south, became clandestine activists. This occupational group would be targeted for recruitment throughout the 1980s.

Teachers were considered to be particularly valuable cadres, for individuals who fulfilled their responsibilities assiduously held a strategic position that garnered social prestige and authority among the rural population, particularly vis-à-vis the young. A further important source of potential recruits was staff employed at the Colleges of Further Education and Technology (Institutos Superiores Pedagógicos) in the towns of San Marcos, Cajabamba and Huamachuco. Pupils attending these institutions not only came from urban families and the more prosperous rural households but also included young people from the ranks of the poor peasantry, who saw education and learning a trade as a means of supplementing their meagre farming incomes and attaining social advancement. Some of these students walked daily to college, while others returned to their homesteads at weekends. What they did provide was a conduit for spreading ideas and contacts throughout the countryside.

Serious efforts were made to enrol other 'gatekeepers' who commanded respect within the hamlets (although some would later become a target for attack): village-based Catholic lay preachers; staff attached to medical posts; and Ministry of Agriculture employees. NGO personnel engaged in rural development and welfare projects, whose activities started to proliferate during the early 1980s, formed a new group of well-educated professionals the Party wished to attract.[17] Potential militants were visited clandestinely two or three times, a few eventually joining the Party. As usual, the pattern was to rely on local knowledge and personal contacts (frequently members of extended families) when deciding who to approach.

Since the PCP–SL held that peasants provided the motor force of the revolution, *campesino* activists with a history of struggle against landowners during the pre-land reform era and those currently engaged in conflict with corrupt administrators and leadership cliques within the cooperatives found themselves especially targeted for recruitment. With regard to the peasantry and rural proletariat, guerrilla goals were facilitated by the process of political fragmentation and deactivation under way in the countryside during the late 1970s. Why had the Cajabamba–Huamachuco region shifted from an area of relatively high levels of rural unionisation during the 1940s and 1950s to one characterised by weak peasant organisation in 1979–80? Part of the answer lies with APRA, the party that had provided the initial impulse for syndicalisation after 1930. APRA's opposition to Belaunde's agrarian reform during the 1960s led to decay among its grass-roots organs at both the individual hacienda and provincial level. These entities became further marginalised when the Velasco administration (1968–75) established the Confederación Nacional Agraria (CNA) – National Agrarian Confederation – in 1972 to provide support for the military government among land reform beneficiaries and favoured producer groups. Through the 1970s, cooperative leaders from all the large CAPs and SAIS in

Cajabamba and Huamachuco became affiliated to the CNA, whose members contained many erstwhile APRA sympathizers.

After Velasco's ousting (August 1975) and the winding down of hacienda expropriations during the military regime's more conservative 'second phase', the CNA was disbanded by official decree in June 1978. Army generals feared that its original co-opting function had failed; an increasingly independent organisation was undergoing a process of radicalisation and adopting an ever-more critical stance vis-à-vis government agricultural policy. Against this back-drop, a number of national leaders (such as Avelino Mar) stopped being favoured by official patronage and became the target of state repression. Although illegal, the CNA continued to exist into the early 1980s, a situation that logically sowed confusion and disillusion among *campesino* activists in Cajabamba and Huamachuco's cooperative sector. Nor had Peru's other national peasants federation, the CCP, or the major left parties, managed to expand their presence significantly to fill the vacuum left by APRA's rightward drift and the CNA's demise. Indeed, these Marxist groups were striving to expand their presence in the region at the same time as the PCP–SL.

An appreciation of the relative weakness of peasant organisation at this juncture can be attained through an examination of the *rondas campesinas*. After proving their efficacy in Chota, the formation of *ronda* committees spread steadily northwards to the *sierra* of Piura, as well as southwards to the province of Cajamarca and beyond to the department of Ancash (see Map 1). By 1990, approximately 3,400 committees were in existence throughout the northern Andes.[18] The first to be established in San Marcos province was in the community of Licliconga in 1980. Part of this community, located in the district of José Sabogal, had fallen within the boundaries of the hacienda La Pauca. In the sector of Lanchepampa descending towards the river Marañón, sugar cane was processed into *chancaca* under sharecropping and quit-rent tenancy agreements. Prior experience in resisting landlord labour and rent exactions (including several violent confrontations with the police) stood local small-holders in good stead when confronting contemporary problems. After suffering a series of livestock thefts and turning the rustlers over to the authorities, only to see the felons released after paying a bribe, a group of exasperated *comuneros* took matters into their own hands and started night patrols.[19]

Licliconga, however, remained an isolated case, for nightwatch patrols did not appear in most other rural districts of San Marcos until the mid-1980s, by which time Sendero had established a presence in the zone. A similar situation was encountered in Cajabamba. Further south, in the *sierra* of La Libertad, the formation of *rondas* was weaker, but with a local characteristic. The few *rondas* in existence operated in a less democratic fashion than their mentors in Chota and typically fell under the sway of small-time *coqs de village*, who utilised the organisation to further their economic ambitions and settle personal scores. Many of these leaders were APRA supporters, who engaged in fierce political competition with the left. Internal schism undermined their effectiveness. In contrast to Chota and Hualgayoc, therefore, the PCP–SL did not encounter in

Cajabamba and surrounding provinces a dense network of autonomous, grass-roots *ronda* committees that had the capacity to hinder its activities during the vulnerable preparatory phase leading up to the launch of armed actions.

Other forms of rural socio-political organisation were equally frail. On top of the diminution of APRA activity in the countryside and the CNA's dissolution, the acrimonious 1977 split in VR produced a significant reduction in village-level proselytisation on the part of the legal left. Under these circumstances, among the cadres of VR, VR–PC, the MIR and other groups, energies were understandably being expended on theoretical and strategic questions – essentially inward-looking activities. As far as VR was concerned, it was not until 1979 that a sufficient reallocation of human resources occurred to permit a process of rebuilding to begin. This proved a slow affair. Only in May 1981 did militants attached to this revolutionary group deem it opportune to form the Federación Provincial de Campesinos de Cajabamba (FEPCCAJ) – Provincial Peasants Federation of Cajabamba which affiliated to the CCP.[20] Although the event represented a certain advance, the as yet limited influence of FEPCCAJ was indicated by its founding congress: this was attended by just thirty-five delegates from fifteen bases. Consequently, when the PCP–SL began clandestine recruitment in Cajabamba and its environs, it arrived at an opportune conjuncture. Following a series of post-1977 splits, grass-roots organisation had been weakened. *Senderista* cadres were not confronted – as in Puno and certain other highland areas – with a well-organised peasantry at the village level, reinforced by a solid network of province-wide unions and sister coordinating bodies. On the contrary, FEPCCAJ and similar entities were destined to collapse shortly after the start of serious armed activity.

Sendero initiates its guerrilla campaign, 1982

Having established without infiltration or repression a skeleton apparatus based on local recruits reinforced by cadres drafted into the highlands from Chiclayo, Trujillo and Lima, in 1982 the PCP–SL could commence the second phase of its party-building exercise in Cajabamba and Huamachuco. This involved less secretive propaganda activities directed at the rural and urban poor. Here, a common tactic was to take over a rural school, assemble all the pupils and teachers and deliver speeches outlining the Party's programme and objectives. One teacher described this experience as follows:

> They came out of the blue at about ten o'clock in the morning. A column of eighteen headed by a young woman. The *senderistas* forced us all to leave the classrooms and line up outside the school. We were in a state of shock and worried about what was going to happen. Some of the younger children started to cry and the guerrilla leader told everyone to be calm. Nothing was going to happen to us. After a little while one of the *terrucos* [terrorists] delivered a speech saying that the government was incompetent and the authorities corrupt. The Peruvian people were living a miserable existence

and the agrarian reform had not made things better. So, the only way to change things was to overthrow Belaunde. Sendero was going to make a revolution to give everybody good schools and education.

After about an hour they packed up and left. Some of the older children were excited by the event, but my colleagues and I were pretty scared. Luckily they did not take any of the kids ... We began to worry about what would happen. When I told my family, they wanted me to resign and get a job in town.[21]

Meetings would also be held with smallholders in secret at night, when the chances of disturbance were minimal. In more isolated villages and hamlets (typically sited on the eastern slopes of the Andes, where only a nominal state presence existed), day-long *escuelas populares* (popular schools) were held with the aim of propagating Party doctrine to consolidate the political convictions of recently enrolled cadres and attract new members.

Simultaneously, low-level armed actions, primarily of a symbolic nature, were launched to demonstrate to the local populace that Sendero possessed resolute political ambitions and also to accustom its overwhelmingly greenhorn operatives to combat conditions. On the evening of 6 May 1981, small explosives were detonated in three public squares in the town of Cajamarca, causing a certain degree of fright, a more intense level of gossip, but no physical or material damage. Twelve days later, a bomb exploded at the entrance to the Banco Agrario offices in Cajabamba – timed to send an unsubtle message to leaders of the legal left, who happened to be on a visit to the town. This was followed by several incident-free months before more serious attacks commenced in spring 1982. A portent of future events occurred on 4 April 1982, when a twenty-strong *senderista* column entered the settlement of Marcabalito, some 40 kilometres from Huamachuco and birthplace of novelist Ciro Alegría. After storming the local police station, the insurgents seized armaments and uniforms but did not kill the occupants. During the following hour they looted stores, distributing clothing, electrical goods, schoolbooks and stationery to the local population, before taking off towards Cajabamba in a stolen pick-up truck.

In June 1982, the television transmission mast perched on the hill overlooking Cajabamba was dynamited at the start of the football World Cup taking place in Spain. Several bridges were destroyed on minor routes in Cajabamba and Huamachuco between June and July 1982. In a similar act of sabotage, a Nestlé milk tanker travelling between Cajabamba and the processing factory outside Cajamarca was stopped at gunpoint and rolled off a cliff. No physical harm was inflicted on the driver or his assistant, although they were told the act formed part of a guerrilla campaign.

The same PCP–SL detachment followed up this incident with an assault on the SAIS La Pauca in July 1982. Approximately fifteen armed *senderistas* occupied the cooperative's main administrative complex and farm buildings that surround the old *casa hacienda*, destroying agricultural machinery, office equipment and estate records. Before abandoning the scene, the guerrilla commander gave a speech to the farm workers denouncing corrupt behaviour by the admin-istrators, exhorted them to seize control of the enterprise and called for support for armed struggle. As the cooperative manager happened to be absent on offi-cial business, he escaped harm. Further south in the *sierra* of La Libertad, meanwhile, another PCP–SL column soon moved the insurrection to a more serious level.

While killings had been carried out in Ayacucho department on a regular basis since the latter months of 1980, the delayed build-up of guerrilla forces in the northern highlands meant that bloodshed had hitherto been avoided. This changed in July 1982. During the previous month, a number of raids similar to the one launched against the SAIS La Pauca had occurred without loss of life. In June, for example, a *senderista* group entered the Serpaquino *anexo* of the SAIS 3 de Octubre. After destroying cheese- and butter-making equipment, an act soon to be repeated with the assault on the Allpachaca experimental farm belonging to the University of Huamanga in Ayacucho (August 1982), the insurgents slaughtered pedigree Brown Swiss and Holstein dairy cattle. Other cooperative assets, including land, implements and livestock, were handed over to cooperative members and neighbouring smallholders, who received orders not to work for the SAIS. To shouts of *¡Viva la lucha armada!* (Long live armed struggle!), the rebels managed to leave the scene unscathed and the local civilian population was unharmed.

Although no fatalities occurred on this occasion, a more fateful incident unfolded on 12 July 1982, when a detachment of approximately twenty *senderistas* overran Angasmarca, a small district capital in the province of Santiago de Chuco. Once the police post had been captured, the corporal commanding the local Guardia Civil unit was assassinated. Wounded, the unfortunate corporal's subordinates were stripped of their weapons and roughed up, but escaped execution – presumably because the assailants wished to drive a wedge between the ranks and their officers. After five hours, the insur-gents finally abandoned the township in two pick-up trucks, taking to the mountains with foodstuffs and other supplies requisitioned from local store-keepers.[22] A week later the same contingent raided the SAIS 3 de Octubre for a second time, emptying its granaries and killing livestock, the booty being distributed to local *campesinos*. Later the same day, the column travelled the 15 kilometres to Sarín, where they sacked the settlement's three main stores, again handing out goods to the inhabitants as the guerrilla leader gave a speech denouncing the Belaunde government and calling for armed struggle.

Despite the considerable amount of public attention these events attracted locally, over the next three months guerrilla units entered neighbouring villages and farms to carry out propaganda and recruiting drives with a surprising degree of impunity. As noted in Chapter One, the sluggish response to guerrilla activity by the coercive arms of the state at this juncture reflected political calculations being made in Lima. Fearful of ceding authority to a military that had only recently returned to the barracks, several of whose high-ranking generals were openly hostile to his administration, President Belaunde chose to sideline the

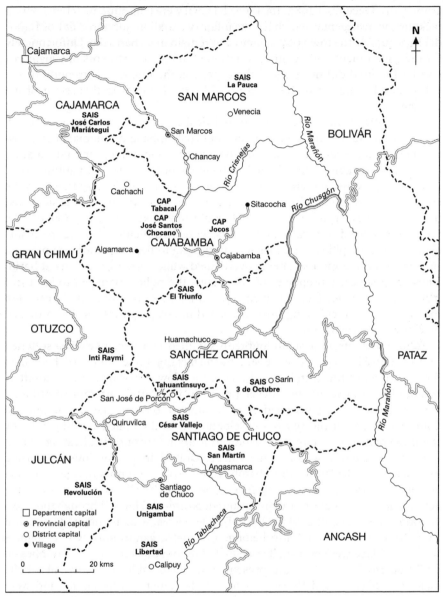

Map 3 *Cajabamba–Huamachuco: Agrarian Production Cooperatives*

army. Until December 1982, the Guardia Civil were consequently charged with tackling the insurgency, which led the infantry battalion quartered at Los Baños del Inca outside the town of Cajamarca to remain in its barracks. Unfortunately for the government, police officers stationed in the departments of Cajamarca and La Libertad did not possess the expertise, the numerical strength, or the will to handle effectively the build-up of PCP–SL forces in this sector of the highlands.

As a result of these political and logistical constraints, it was not until 28 November 1982 that the Guardia Civil in Cajabamba and Huamachuco registered any real success in combating the guerrilla. Upon receiving information regarding an assault on the Cochabamba *anexo* of the SAIS Tahuantinsuyo by a column of twenty *senderistas*, a police platoon was hastily despatched to the cooperative. Luckily for the local lieutenant governor, who was being subjected to a *juicio popular* (popular trial) and would most likely have been killed, the Guardia managed to locate their quarry without difficulty, forcing the insurgents to beat a rapid retreat. Despite attempting to flee and elude its pursuers, the rebel group found itself being overhauled while crossing the puna at Sarín. Employing superior firepower to advantage, the police managed to kill three insurgents in the ensuing engagement and capture an additional fifteen (ten men and five women). Only two succeeded in escaping to the safety provided by cover in nearby ravines.[23]

While this confrontation undoubtedly signified a reverse, defeat was softened for the PCP–SL's regional leadership by the fact that no senior cadres had fallen into the hand of the authorities. Indeed, the blow was shortly to be counterbalanced by an encouraging development in the Party's attempt to attract a rural following – the acquisition of a support base in the community of Chorobamba. Over the 1970s, participation in land conflicts accompanied by the usual ham-fisted state repression (arbitrary imprisonment, beatings, etc.), acted to radicalise a sector of the village. Out of these consciousness-raising experiences, leaders from Chorobamba came to play a prominent role in helping establish Cajabamba's peasants' federation (FEPCCAJ), as well as becoming active in left politics at the provincial and departmental level. Through the intervention of an ex-member of the PCP–Bandera Roja, who maintained links with PCP–SL cadres who had also belonged to that organisation, two key figures from the village were eventually persuaded to join the guerrillas: Sixto Nicasio and Roberto Barrios. As the present author was able to testify, like Félix Calderón, Nicasio and Barrios possessed charismatic personalities and were viewed with considerable esteem in the countryside. These qualities assisted the spread of the *senderista* message throughout Cajabamba and its environs.[24]

Conclusion

Through operating with forethought and working in a rational, well-organised fashion, by the end of 1982 the PCP–SL had managed to surmount the difficulties caused by its prior lack of participation in regional peasant, labour, or student movements. Despite experiencing initial failure in the provinces of Chota and Hualgayoc – partly owing to opposition from the *rondas campesinas* as well as the Party's own hasty voluntarism – it had, from inauspicious beginnings, succeeded in constructing a skeletal apparatus in Cajabamba and the *sierra* of La Libertad. Boosted by cadres drafted into the zone from the northern coast and Lima, two small guerrilla units of approximately twenty members had been formed, with links established to supportive elements in the rural population. Although the PCP–SL's adherents included school-age adolescents, students and teachers, at the local level, the Party was more than a group of alienated members from the urban petty bourgeoisie. It had incorporated into its ranks some of the most politically aware and experienced peasant activists in the region.

Counter-insurgency literature holds that a guerrilla movement is particularly vulnerable during its 'build-up phase' (i.e., when the insurrection is still being planned).[25] In common with developments in Ayacucho and other theatres of conflict in the Peruvian *sierra*, between 1980 and 1982 the state's security services had failed to monitor adequately, let alone infiltrate and check, the PCP–SL's activities in the northern highlands. Indicatively, Félix Calderón had not been captured through a carefully designed intelligence or 'search and destroy' operation, but as result of travelling along a public highway in a stolen vehicle. Such deficiencies enabled the PCP–SL to acquire a foothold in Cajabamba and the *sierra* of La Libertad relatively unhindered. Hand in hand with a failure of the state's intelligence services, the military dimension of its counter-insurgency effort also proved inept. The army was not deployed. The Guardia Civil rarely ventured far from their urban installations, only undertaking the occasional daytime foray into the countryside. This left the insurgents with unencumbered access to a rural population that lacked the organisational means to banish them from their villages. A platform from which to expand Sendero's 'protracted people's war' could therefore be established. How, and with what degree of success, did the PCP–SL attempt to 'churn up the countryside'?

References

1   Additional information on this split can be found in Letts, *La izquierda peruana*. The debate between the two organisations is summarised in 'Aportes a la discusión del problema agrario en Cajamarca', mimeo, Comisión Campesina de Cajamarca de Vanguardia Revolucionaria, Cajamarca, July 1982.
2   Letts, *La izquierda peruana*; Reid, *Peru*, pp. 65–80.
3   Nora Bonifaz, 'Las rondas campesinas, el estado y la política', mimeo, 1985, n.p.
4   An account of these events can be found in 'Acuerdos del Primer Congreso Departamental de la FEDECC', mimeo, Huacataz, August 1978, pp. 6, 8, 22–23.
5   Ibid., pp. 6, 14. At this juncture FEDECC supported the minority radical faction within the Confederación Campesina del Perú, headed by Julio César Mezzich (whose base was in the department of Andahuaylas) and Carlos Hancco (an activist in Cusco). Mezzich would become a leading PCP–SL cadre in the Ayacucho-

Andahuaylas zone, but at one stage was rumoured to be in command of the organisation's 'Second Army' in the northern highlands. For Hancco's perspective on Andean rural society post-agrarian reform, see Carlos Hancco, 'Lauramarca y el movimiento democrático revolucionario del campesinado por la tierra y contra la semifeudalidad', *Crítica Andina* 3, June 1979, pp. 157–73.

6   'Acuerdos del Primer Congreso Departamental de la FEDECC', mimeo, Huacataz, August 1978, pp. 6, 14.

7   *Lucha Campesina* 12, November 1978.

8   *Lucha Campesina* 16, December 1979.

9   Key publications on the *rondas campesinas* include John Gitlitz and Telmo Rojas, 'Peasant Vigilante Committees in Northern Peru', *Journal of Latin American Studies* 15: 1, 1983, pp. 163–97; Orin Starn, '*Con los llanques todo barro': reflexiones sobre rondas campesinas, protesta rural y nuevos movimientos sociales*, Lima, Instituto de Estudios Peruanos, 1991; and Ludwig Huber, '*Después de Dios y la Virgen está la ronda': las rondas campesinas de Piura*, Lima, Instituto de Estudios Peruanos, 1995. The most comprehensive analysis is Orin Starn, *Nightwatch: the Politics of Protest in the Andes*, Durham, NC, Duke University Press, 1999.

10   Interview # 17, 8 April 1997. This *rondero* reaction to the guerrilla is also noted in Orin Starn, '"I Dreamed of Foxes and Hawks ...": Reflections on Peasant Protest, New Social Movements, and the Rondas campesinas of Northern Peru', in Arturo Escobar and Sonia Alvarez (eds.), *The Making of Social Movements in Latin America: Identity, Strategy and Democracy*, Boulder, CO, Westview Press, 1992, pp.108–09.

11   Interview # 19, 10 April 1997.

12   This incident was recorded by the Policía de Investigaciones del Perú (the Peruvian CID at the time) in Chota (reference number 14–JP–SE). Félix Calderón was one of the last to perish in the massacre perpetrated at the El Frontón island prison on 19 June 1986. After surviving the fighting, Calderón was among the *senderistas* shot in cold blood by naval marines. They were despatched in batches of five shortly after laying down their arms. On this, see PCP–SL, '¡Gloria al día de la Heroicidad!', mimeo, Lima 1987, pp. 27, 55; and Agustín Haya de la Torre, *El retorno de la barbarie: la matanza en los penales de Lima en 1986*, Lima, Bahia Ediciones, 1988. Five years later, the hacienda Santa Clara was to witness a tragedy. On 23 March 1983, smallholders whose holdings surrounding the estate invaded the property, leaving the landowners, the Acuña family, in possession of around 60 hectares instead of the 856 hectares that had survived expropriation through land reform. On 13 June 1987, the estate's fifteen-strong work force occupied the remaining section with backing from their neighbours. In response, approximately eighty policemen arrived on the scene on 15 June and in the ensuing confrontation eight *campesinos* were shot dead and fifteen arrested. See Daniel Idrogo, 'Informe sobre la masacre de la Guardia Civil a los ronderos de la ex-hacienda Santa Clara', mimeo, Camara de Diputados, Lima, 26 June 1987. Information on Santa Clara was kindly supplied by Orin Starn.

13   'Las conferencias senderistas', *Quehacer* 30, August 1984, p. 20.

14   'Alberto', the leader of the Northern Regional Committee, was accused of 'lying to the Central Committee ... being insolent to the Central Committee ... of speaking like a landowner ... he paints a pessimistic picture of the situation in the north'. Gorriti, *Sendero*, pp. 272–77.

15   Although the PCP–SL established cells in the province of Jaén (adjacent to the border with Ecuador) and Chongoyape (in the hinterland between Chiclayo and Piura), these detachments never received the human and material resources dedicated to the Cajabamba–Huamachuco zone. In October 1981, personnel from the PIP discovered a guerrilla training camp approximately 13 kilometres outside Jaén.

The following month, a guerrilla unit dynamited the local transmission mast of the Panamericana TV station. *El Comercio* 7 October 1981; 27 November 1981.

16 Interview # 8, 30 March 1997.

17 Individuals from these backgrounds proved important during the first phase of building the Party apparatus in Huamachuco and Santiago de Chuco. For ethical reasons, further details cannot be provided.

18 Starn, 'I Dreamed of Foxes and Hawks ...', pp. 89–90.

19 Víctor Acosta, 'Historia de la comunidad de Licliconga', mimeo, San Marcos, August 1988.

20 *Voz Campesina* 23, July 1981.

21 Interview # 10, 3 April 1997.

22 *La Industria*, 13 July 1982.

23 *La Industria*, 1 December 1982.

24 Sixto Nicasio and Roberto Barrios were later arrested, and, like Calderón, died in the June 1986 prison massacre at El Frontón.

25 This point is made in Robert Thompson, *Defeating Communist Insurgency*, London, Chatto & Windus, 1966, p. 50.

CHAPTER FOUR

'Batiendo el Campo':
Guerrilla Expansion, 1983–92

Despite a steady ratcheting up of PCP–SL political and military activity throughout 1982, an overwhelming majority of the population who had settled in the southern provinces of Cajamarca and the *sierra* of La Libertad as yet held little inkling regarding the level of violence that was to shortly afflict their lives. Leftist activists, although cognizant of the insurgents' goals, felt that the *senderistas* did not possess enough cadres, military knowledge or popular support to enable them to survive for any length of time, yet alone expand their guerrilla campaign. For its part, the Belaunde government dismissed the PCP–SL as a gang of 'bandits', who would soon be routed by the security forces in much the same uncomplicated manner as their *guevarista*-inspired predecessors had been scattered during the mid-1960s. Like the present author, ordinary citizens went about their normal business, travelling the roads of Cajabamba and Huamachuco freely, demonstrating little concern for their personal safety. No one – except a few individuals attached to the police or army – made any adaptation to their lifestyle or daily routine. Even predictable targets, such as the post land reform remnants of the traditional landed elite, continued to live in their properties during the week and at weekends walked openly around the streets of highland towns engaging in their usual social pursuits.

Among the minority who gave any real thought to recent developments, the prevailing mood was that events in Ayacucho were particular to the south-central Andes. Whereas Ayacucho was Indian and Quechua-speaking, the predominantly *mestizo* and more Hispanicised north was different; it did not provide fertile terrain for Sendero's brand of Maoist fundamentalism. This complacency was epitomised by the subprefect of Huamachuco, who, in April 1982, drolly christened the PCP–SL column that was circulating in the province *'la banda de los veinte'* ('the gang of twenty'), even though it was known that they carried five machine-guns, in addition to rifles and revolvers, possessed a sizeable stock of dynamite and had recently been penetrating villages to deliver propaganda and enlist recruits.[1] Such insouciance was to evaporate after 1982, as the PCP–SL proved able to step up its guerrilla campaign to an unforeseen degree, bringing fear, suspicion, further economic hardship and a not inconsiderable amount of suffering and bloodshed to this area of the northern *sierra*. How, then, was the rebel organisation able to expand its operations during the mid- and late 1980s?

Batiendo el campo: attacks against civilian arms of the state

A key component of Abimael Guzmán's policy of 'churning up the country-side' involved the 'cleansing' (i.e., elimination) of the Peruvian state from rural districts. Following Mao's prescription, this entailed a three-pronged assault against: (i) its political structure; (ii) employees engaged in public-service delivery (education, health, transport, development assistance, etc.); and (iii) its coercive apparatuses (police, army, judiciary). Once Party strength had reached a point where the leadership calculated that more complex armed operations could begin, 'selective terrorism', aimed at government functionaries, soon followed. Prime targets included subprefects (the highest political authority at provincial level), district governors and lieutenant governors appointed to oversee affairs in the villages. Municipal elected representatives comprised another group that was viewed as legitimate game for assassination.

Accordingly, in May 1983 the hitherto underestimated '*banda de los veinte*' entered the small district capital of Sanagorán, one hour distant from Huamachuco, where they submitted the mayor and lieutenant governor to a *juicio popular* prior to carrying out an execution before a horrified group of forcibly assembled townspeople. On 31 August 1983, a similar scene unfolded in Curgos, the mayor and lieutenant governor being killed in like fashion. A written warning was left alongside the bodies: 'That's how the traitorous authorities and collaborators of the reactionary Belaunde die!' The blood-stained paper also contained a chilling promise as to future behaviour: 'And how they will die!' These functionaries were unfortunate enough to be seized without warning. Others were given notice to resign through anonymous letters pushed under doors and messages painted or pinned on walls. Those who failed to heed the ultimatum ran the risk of a violent death.

After commencing in 1983, assassination attempts on office-holders and local political figures, particularly those representing the governing party, increased year on year (see Table 3). Officials from the district of Sanagorán, located within easy striking distance of the principal bolt-hole of the PCP–SL's Ejército Guerrillero Popular (EGP) in Huamachuco province, were especially vulnerable to attack. A *senderista* column re-entered the settlement on 15 May 1985 and assassinated the APRA mayor and Acción Popular-nominated lieutenant governor. The mayor's successor, a veteran *aprista* no less than seventy-five years of age, was shot in the chest at 11.45 p.m. on 5 May 1986 by a hit squad that forced entry into his home.[2] On 27 May 1987 a guerrilla detachment once again occupied the town, burned down the municipality and forced the recently appointed mayor (on this occasion, a supporter of Izquierda Unida) to resign.[3] Faced with these traumatic events, approximately one-third of the population

Table 3 *Political Figures Assassinated, 1986–91*

Date	Location	Office
7 May 1986	Sanagorán	Mayor (APRA)
April 1987	Shirac (San Marcos)	Mayor (APRA)
24 April 1987	Santiago de Chuco	General Secretary (APRA)
2 July 1987	Santa Cruz (S. de Chuco)	Mayor (APRA)
21 July 1987	Cajabamba	General Secretary (APRA)
1 November 1987	Angasmarca	Lieutenant Governor (APRA)
1 November 1987	Chusgón	Provincial leader (APRA)
5 January 1988	Huamachuco	Subprefect (APRA)
3 August 1988	Santiago de Chuco	Subprefect (APRA)
7 March 1989	Huamachuco	General Secretary (APRA)
9 April 1989	Cachachi (San Marcos)	Mayor (APRA)
1 October 1989	Huamachuco	Mayor (APRA)
5 November 1989	Santiago de Chuco	Mayoral candidate (APRA)
23 March 1990	Santiago de Chuco	Organisation Secretary (APRA)
9 April 1990	Venecia (San Marcos)	Mayor (FREDEMO)
4 August 1990	Ichocán (San Marcos)	Ex-APRA councillor
5 June 1991	El Espinal (Sayapullo)	Lieutenant Governor (APRA)
8 December 1991	Venecia (San Marcos)	Deputy Mayor (FREDEMO)

Source: Elaborated from police and newspaper reports.

fled the area to the relative safety of Huamachuco town, or sought refuge with relatives living in Trujillo and other coastal urban areas.

Between 1983 and 1985, minor government representatives living in outlying localities proved the chief victims of PCP–SL assaults, but from 1986 higher-ranking figures based in larger settlements entered the firing line. The morning of 28 May 1986 witnessed an unsuccessful attempt on the life of the mayor of Santiago de Chuco. This was followed by a similarly frustrated attack on the mayor of Cajabamba (September 1986), who survived despite being hit by four bullets. However, on 24 April 1987, an assassination squad directed by a woman succeeded in killing Luis Geldres, general secretary of APRA for the province of Santiago de Chuco. Geldres was gunned down while in a meeting at his place of work, the local hospital – an action soon repeated with the elimination of his counterpart in Cajabamba (July 1987). On 5 January 1988, the PCP–SL murdered Víctor Sotomayor, a retired schoolteacher and long-standing APRA activist, who had been recently appointed subprefect of the province of Sánchez Carrión after the resignation of his predecessor following death threats. He was shot by two individuals at 6.40 a.m., only two streets distant from the police station in Huamachuco town.[4] During the same month, another prominent APRA functionary, who had been charged with directing the García government's public works programme in Santiago de Chuco, was killed. The province's subprefect was subsequently gunned down by five *senderistas* (four women and a man) in early August 1988, after just two weeks in post. Adding an element of pathos to the crime, the victim, who was lucid beyond his seventy-eight years of age, happened to have been a lifelong *aprista* who had been imprisoned for his radical political beliefs during the 1930s and 1940s.[5] A similar fate befell APRA's general secretary for the province of Huamachuco in March 1989, while on 16 August 1989 the town's *aprista* mayor died from a bullet in the head under mysterious circumstances.[6]

Over the period 1987–91, assaults on individuals holding public positions in localities outside the so-called 'red triangle' formed by Cajabamba–Santiago de Chuco–Sayapullo became more frequent as the PCP–SL expanded its theatre of operations south towards the department of Ancash and north to the province of San Marcos (see Map 2). In San Marcos province, the mayor of Shirac and his wife were shot in April 1987, after a group of approximately fifty *senderistas* took over the settlement and subjected the couple to a *juicio popular*. Also in San Marcos, the mayor of Cachachi and his wife were killed by four *pistoleros* on 9 April 1989, a fate that befell the FREDEMO (Frente Democrático)-supporting mayor of Venecia (district of José Sabogal) on 5 April 1990. He was dispatched while walking between home and the municipality, after having ignored a number of demands to resign.

As far as the PCP–SL was concerned, these homicides had the desired effect. They sowed panic and provoked widespread resignations from public positions, to an extent that by 1990, about 80 per cent of the rural districts of San Marcos, Cajabamba, Huamachuco and Santiago de Chuco lacked lieutenant governors, justices of the peace, land judges and other low-ranking authorities. In July 1989, for example, the mayor of Santiago de Chuco announced that he and the mayors of Quiruvilca, Santa Cruz de Chilca and Angasmarca, along with the subprefect, the *fiscal* (public prosecutor), judges and other public servants from the locality had received death threats. On 26 June a large explosion had destroyed part of the municipal building at Cachicadán, whose mayor had been given an ultimatum of twenty days to resign and abandon town.[7] The following April, the head of APRA's party organisation in Huamachuco was forced to flee to Trujillo following intimidating telephone calls.[8] That the threats were not illusory was demonstrated with tragic effect in the November 1989 municipal elections, when the *aprista* candidate for Santiago de Chuco, a seventy-one-year-old retired farmer, was gunned down six days prior to polling day. He had recently resigned as subprefect to fight the election.[9]

At this juncture, the Peruvian state exercised no more than a tenuous political presence over large swathes of the countryside. Such a worrying situation was recognised in a secret intelligence assessment on one province in the Cajabamba–Huamachuco region: 'In the years 1991 and 1992, the districts of WWWW, XXXX, YYYY and part of ZZZZ did not have any authorities (lieutenant governors), due to the subversive activities of Sendero Luminoso'.[10] A similar vacuum of political authority prevailed in surrounding provinces. Regarding the major urban settlements, although the principal public posts (prefect, provincial judge, etc.) remained filled, both office-holders and towns-people felt increasingly threatened and under siege. A generalised sense of insecurity became accentuated as the insurgency gathered momentum, the sound of gunfire regularly pierced the night-time quiet and full-scale assaults became more frequent. One such incident occurred on 11 November 1988, when several guerrilla columns penetrated Cajabamba, where they dynamited and raked with bullets the prefecture, town hall and court building. While these targets were being hit, another detachment ensured that the local police remained pinned in their barracks.

As the governing party during Alan García's presidency (1985–90), APRA logically found itself the main target for PCP–SL attacks when the insurrection escalated in the late 1980s. In this regard, one cannot help but note the commitment and courage of party members belonging to the *aprista* old guard, who, despite being in their seventies, were prepared to accept public office under extremely perilous circumstances. Although those occupying high-profile positions such as subprefect or mayor were settled in urban areas where there were police units and provided regularly with a bodyguard, as indicated by the afore-mentioned assault on Cajabamba, these only afforded a modicum of security. APRA's candidate in the mayoral elections of November 1989, for example, was shot while crossing the main *plaza* in Santiago de Chuco. Others suffered a similar fate on the streets of the region's provincial capitals in broad daylight. Lower-ranking authorities living in rural districts were obviously in a far more hazardous situation. One informant from a hamlet in San Marcos, which was visited regularly by PCP–SL columns, accurately summed up their predicament as being akin to:

> ... clothes hung out to dry, flopping helplessly in the wind. They had no protection from the authorities in the town or the police. At any moment the *senderistas* could grab them. Some lieutenant governors bought a gun. Others slept in their maize fields, but it was all in vain. If the *senderistas* wanted to get you, you were buggered (*jodido*). The situation was impossible – the only thing to do was to resign, keep your head down and hope you would be left in peace.[11]

With the PCP–SL claiming to have '*mil ojos y mil oídos*' ('a thousand eyes and ears') throughout the countryside, in addition to usually demonstrating a detailed knowledge of local affairs when its columns entered a hamlet, pressure on the state's representatives at the grass roots proved immense. Understandably, by the early 1990s most had opted to protect their physical safety over considerations of social prestige or the (usually meagre) financial reward an official appointment might afford.

A marginally less difficult situation confronted public sector employees working in rural areas. Schoolteachers found themselves in an especially delicate position. On the one hand, the security forces regarded them with suspicion, believing that many *profesores* held pro-Sendero sympathies and that rural schools provided a focus for propaganda and recruitment. Such attitudes are indicated in the following document, penned by the counter-insurgency police:

> In the secondary schools located in this province's towns, villages and hamlets, prior to 1993 the majority of pupils were subject to proselytisation and indoctrination by cadres of 'SL'. This even extended to primary school children who could read and write.[12]

Rural schoolteachers experienced regular harassment from the police and, since they were important 'gatekeepers', they were also subjected to pressure from the PCP–SL to join its ranks and help recruit their pupils into the organisation (discussed in Chapter Three). Staff in schools in outlying districts, many of whom were poorly trained and paid, were also in the habit of working only a three- or four-day week (absenting themselves on Monday and/or Friday), a lack of diligence that ran the risk of sanction by *senderista* detachments keen to win support among a disgruntled populace. These circumstances caused fear among schoolteachers and in the years after 1986 they quit their positions in a flood of resignations in Cajabamba, Huamachuco and throughout the neighbouring *ceja de selva* provinces of Bolívar and Pataz. In September 1986, for example, the suspicious death of two *campesinos* adjacent to Sayapullo provoked every teacher to flee the town, leaving the education system paralysed.[13] Staff employed in the network of small rural medical centres likewise felt threatened by both sides: guerrillas would come searching for bandages, medicines and occasionally treatment, while the military swore drastic retribution against anybody who provided even minimal medical assistance to the rebels. Faced with the intractability of their situation, those *posta médica* personnel who could do so relocated to the towns.

A similar withdrawal from the countryside by the state could be seen vis-à-vis the Ministry of Agriculture and functionaries employed by other agencies charged with bringing aid to farmers. Faced with death threats, extension work and related forms of technical assistance had ground to a halt by the late 1980s. To reinforce the message, whenever PCP–SL detachments raided a provincial capital, attempts were usually made to dynamite the offices, stores and workshops of the local Agencia Agraria (Agriculture Office), as occurred on May

Day 1986 in Cajabamba. Explosives were also placed outside the house rented by the provincial development agency, inside the electricity generating plant and in other public buildings. On 14 July 1989, the offices of the Banco Agrario (Agrarian Bank) in Huamachuco suffered another such assault. Material damage aside, the highest-profile victim of these actions was the head of the Ministry of Agriculture in Cajamarca, Jorge Chiclayo, who was assassinated on 30 September 1987.[14]

Against this backdrop, in August 1990 staff working for the Agrarian Bank in Cajabamba and San Marcos wrote a desperate report to their superiors that captures forcibly the dilemmas experienced by countless civil servants over these years. Their petition was partly stimulated by a bomb attack on the Bank's offices in Cajabamba (7 June 1990), but a more recent development had heightened concern. A PCP–SL communiqué nailed up in one of the town's squares not only denounced the Bank's work force as 'enemies of the people' but it also threatened them with assassination for being 'accomplices of the government's dastardly agrarian policies'. In view of this development, the Bank's regional managers in Cajamarca were informed about:

> The reality in which the Bank's personnel are undertaking their work, exposing our physical integrity continuously, as well as that of our families. This situation also carries implications for the issuing, tracking and recovery of loans, which impact negatively on our books of loans made and recouped ... We are faced with a dilemma as to whether to approve loans where problems with subversion exist. Experience tells us that if we decide to not make loans to agriculturalists, they then complain to the subversives, who meet with them at night in the schools. We are informed about this by many of our clients, who have been forced to attend numerous such meetings. Logically, we can fall victim to reprisal attacks. Alternatively, if we do opt to distribute credits, we run the risk that the farmers will not meet their contractual agreements, especially if interest rates increase. We know this as it has already occurred with regard to the supervision of zero interest credit. The subversives are indoctrinating the farmers to refuse to pay their loans, arguing that 'it is the people's money and therefore belongs to all the people'. On this matter, some clients have told us that the subversives tell them that the Bank first tricks them with the loan, only to later raise the interest rate, in this fashion maintaining 'the exploitative bourgeois order which pauperises the peasantry'.[15]

The Bank's employees ended their petition with a list of demands, including police protection, transfer out of Cajabamba and San Marcos after two years' service, higher salaries and the provision of basic foodstuffs at subsidised prices.

The withering away of the state over much of the countryside during the late 1980s was accentuated by the severe economic problems currently engulfing Peru. Aware that the best long-term strategy to counter the guerrilla threat was through social and economic advancement, Alan García's administration pursued a heterodox economic policy between 1985 and 1987, which aimed at reactivating a productive apparatus that had been languishing in deep recession since the onset of the 1982 debt crisis. Among a raft of measures adopted to achieve these goals figured increased government investment, in which the Cajabamba–Huamachuco region participated – it did, after all, lie at the heart of APRA's *sólido norte*, the party's birthplace. Political loyalty needed to be rewarded and patron–client relations maintained. Money was consequently pumped into extending basic infrastructure, such as electricity provision to outlying settlements in Otuzco province and improvements to the road link to the coast. Attempts were made to enhance the provision of public services, including new equipment for schools in Sánchez Carrión province and a refurbishment of the hospital in Santiago de Chuco by a team of Cuban doctors and technicians (September 1988). The productive apparatus was also targeted, with monies allocated for extending irrigation facilities, the provision of selected seeds, state support for purchases of pedigree livestock and attempts to open new lines of husbandry, such as alpaca breeding. Agriculturalists had access to credit at zero interest rates.

These well-intentioned efforts to improve living standards were undermined not only by *senderista* dynamite. Economic collapse in 1988 brought rampant inflation, rising unemployment and plummeting incomes.[16] Civil service salaries were the worst affected, as the government strove to close the gap between its expenditure and steeply declining tax receipts, so that by 1989–90 the average schoolteacher, agronomist or health worker employed in Huamachuco and its environs was earning a paltry US\$30 per month. Such a dire scenario understandably produced a severe slump in morale among state employees, which in turn stimulated their exodus from the countryside. Who would be foolhardy enough to risk their life for a princely US\$30 per month?

Batiendo el campo: attacks against coercive arms of the state

Hand in hand with attempts to establish a political vacuum, the PCP–SL made concerted efforts to create a void of coercive authority by expelling the police from the rural districts. Following the model tested to satisfaction since 1980 in Ayacucho (and Mao's admonition to strike 'with one "fist" in one direction at one time', under 'conditions favourable to ourselves'), the insurgents launched a series of surprise assaults on isolated police posts. The standard practice was to engage superior numbers and concentrate firepower in an attempt to guarantee a favourable outcome. Normally, a local police station would contain a detachment of five, at most seven, *guardias*; Sendero would assemble twenty or more combatants to launch an attack, having carefully planned the operation beforehand. Favoured times for conducting these assaults was at night or sunrise, periods calculated to catch the police unawares. The insurgents would strive to get as close to their target as possible without being detected, then strike decisively, employing a combination of dynamite and machine-gun fire before the defenders had time to react and organise effective resistance. Wherever possible, the policy was to take out the officers first, so as to spread panic among the ranks and encourage a quick surrender.[17]

From small-scale beginnings in 1982, the number of such attacks increased relentlessly and occurred over a wider area. Initially concentrated in the environs of Santiago de Chuco and Huamachuco, after 1984 they attained regularity in the provinces of Cajabamba and San Marcos and in the *ceja de selva* zone adjacent to the River Marañón. Strikes against the police could range from audacious assassination attempts against individuals (such as that mounted by the two insurgents who killed a corporal accompanying an Easter religious procession at Julcán in April 1989) to full-scale assaults against permanent installations. At times, the PCP–SL succeeded in storming a police station; on other occasions they were repelled (as was the twenty-strong guerrilla attack against the base at Usquil on 12 May 1990); but overall, the initiative lay with the insurgents. Some police stations were shut down. One of the first was Angasmarca (1986), after it was hit by a PCP–SL column. Its closure was followed by a larger number in 1987–89 (e.g. Huaranchal, Araqueda, Cachachi and Marcamachay). Occasionally, police facilities would reopen, only to be destroyed a second time. This scenario occurred on 8 March 1992, when a substantial guerrilla force attacked the post at Angasmarca. After a sustained confrontation, the *senderistas* managed to kill five out of seven defenders before taking off with their weapons and communications equipment. Confronted by an enemy that could strike anywhere and at any time, the Guardia Civil beat a strategic retreat to concentrate its forces in the region's provincial and district capitals. Although the guerrillas failed to expel the police completely, by 1988 they had managed to place the government's forces on the defensive. Spending most of the time barricaded in town, the *guardias* ventured out only sporadically to patrol the surrounding countryside by day. Many villages were consequently left without an effective police presence. After nightfall, the PCP–SL could usually move around and organise meetings with impunity.

What explains the inability of the Guardia Civil to confront effectively the PCP–SL between 1983 and the early 1990s, despite its possession of a number of apparent advantages (access to larger quantities of superior weaponry; a more sophisticated communications system and transport)? Remembering Mao's dictum that 'it is people, not things, that are decisive', over this period the esprit de corps of the PCP–SL's cadres proved to be higher than that of the police. Various economic and political factors contributed to this situation. Constant stress at work and home produced falling morale among the Guardia Civil, which was exacerbated by a pay packet of rapidly declining value when inflation rocketed between 1988 and 1990. Like other public employees, an ordinary policeman or woman was earning a risible US$30 per month by the turn of the decade; a high-ranking commander US$75 or less. In addition, the theoretical superiority of the police to the PCP–SL in firepower was often disproved by reality. Fear of allowing weapons to fall into guerrilla hands meant that handheld machine-guns and high-powered rifles were stored in the better-defended garrisons and were not always available to front-line officers stationed in rural locations. Bullets were rationed and firing more than the set quota could lead to deductions from pay packets. The economic valetudinarianism of the

Peruvian state also resulted in threadbare uniforms, broken boots and non-existent or inadequate rations for Guardia Civil out on patrol, none of which helped alleviate a pervasive pessimism among the ranks, a situation noted by a *cajabambino*, whose brother works in the police force:

> When the police left Cajabamba to patrol the countryside, they made a sorry sight. It was almost possible to pity them. Some wore patched up trousers, others needed their boots repairing. You could see from their faces that their heart was not in the job. They would have preferred to stay in town. Many cops had been sent up from the coast and could not handle the physical aspect of hiking in the *sierra* ... After a few hours wandering around the countryside they would return looking more bedraggled than ever, all covered in dust and exhausted. Even carrying their guns looked an effort. In the rainy season they were in a worse condition, as there was not enough rubber boots or plastic ponchos to go around.[18]

The dire financial and equipment deficiencies affecting the Guardia Civil as an institution did not just produce low morale. It also resulted in a cautious and a non-aggressive approach to their counter-insurgency responsibilities.

Although no evidence has been uncovered of active collaboration between guerrillas and police in the Cajabamba–Huamachuco region (as occurred in parts of Ayacucho), several incidents illustrate their defensive mindset. When, in June 1988, the detachment of police stationed at Chancay (near Ichocán) heard rumours that a column of thirty *senderistas* was approaching the settlement, the *guardias* opted to make a hasty retreat. Rationalising their actions, they informed the inhabitants that: '*Preferible es desertor vivo que policía muerto*' ('A living deserter is preferable to a dead cop').[19] The following April, police in San Marcos were informed by local residents that PCP–SL cadres had – once again – entered a hamlet near Azufre, about an hour by foot from the provincial capital.[20] Fearful of engaging the insurgents, they refused to act on the information and stayed in town, leaving the population to cope with the incursion as best they could. Such tergiversation did little to endear the police to ordinary citizens:

> When Sendero started to get active here, the cops got really scared. They acted very macho in their dealings with the *campesinos* and other defenceless people, but when faced with Sendero they were a bunch of cowards. Even when they knew where the guerrillas were hiding, the cops did not dare to go after them. The usual excuse was that they had not been given orders and had to defend the town, but we all understood that the real reason was a lack of balls. Most just wanted a quite life and to not take any risks.[21]

Apart from inadequate pay and quartering, police reticence in confronting the PCP–SL was deepened by a lack of expertise in counter-insurgency tactics, their training having focused on crime detection and social-control duties. Matters were not helped by a shortage of human resources. Planners understandably concentrated expertise and manpower in Ayacucho, surrounding departments in the south-central Andes, and Lima (by the late 1980s, increasing numbers of armed attacks were occurring in the capital). For commanders in the northern Andes, such a prioritisation signified understaffing: during the second half of 1985, for example, government control and public order in Otuzco and its environs was supposed to be maintained by sixty-five mostly inexperienced *guardias*. Given the mountainous terrain, poor roads and the difficulty of moving quickly from one area to another, no effective police presence existed, other than in the provincial capital. Operational considerations also resulted in the rural areas being largely unprotected: fearful of dividing their troops and leaving a weakened urban base exposed to attack when out on patrol, officers chose to barricade themselves behind defensive positions in the highland towns.

Efficacious police action in the war against the PCP–SL was further hampered by a paucity of accurate intelligence data about the rebels' membership and activities, a factor of crucial importance in waging a successful counter-insurgency campaign. Difficulties in this regard were compounded by the soured relations that often existed between country-dwellers in particular and the (at times misleadingly named) 'forces of law and order'. What were the roots of the rural population's animosity towards its supposed protectors? Distrust was fuelled by perceived ethnic divisions between the '*cachacos*' ('cops') and local residents, sentiments that from the *campesino* perspective became reinforced by immoral behaviour on the part of individuals who were supposed to provide security and justice. Questions of corruption, the arbitrary lifting of scarce possessions, and physical abuse – both petty and serious – carried out by undisciplined personnel, produced a reluctance to cooperate with the police. The seemingly straightforward act of entering a police station could result in unforeseen and unfortunate outcomes, especially if one conformed to a popular *senderista* stereotype, i.e. a young male *campesino* or a student (female or male).

Concerning the ethnic issue, for many *guardias* of urban coastal origin who had been inculcated from childhood with the standard prejudices, the denizens of Cajabamba and Huamachuco were '*serranos de mierda*' ('shitty highlanders'). When referring specifically to the peasantry, either in their presence or behind their backs, the derogatory label '*indios de mierda*' ('shitty Indians') would be commonly employed, even though an overwhelming majority of country people were Spanish-speaking *mestizos*. These complications notwithstanding, the *Weltanschauung* of many ordinary policemen stationed in the Cajabamba–Huamachuco region included a strong sense of class and ethnic superiority vis-à-vis their rural cousins. One smallholder, who had on different occasions in the past been on the receiving end of a policeman's boot, summed up the mutual antipathy:

> The cops don't treat us justly or with respect. They look down on country people and think they can do what they like. They shout '*cholo*' this and '*cholo*' that and insult you all the time with 'son of a bitch' and worse. Moneyed people from the town don't have to put up with this. They get less abuse,

less punches, less kicks ... At weekends when the cops get drunk, it's worse
– and that's when we go to town to do our weekly market. There's not much
a *campesino* can do about it. If you complain the authorities usually don't take
any action and the *guardias* come after you again, threatening and maybe
giving you another beating. You just have to keep your head down and try
and avoid them as much as possible.[22]

Within a tense social environment conducive to negative stereotyping, the
local populace ended up being viewed with a degree of suspicion that verged
on outright hostility. That such attitudes were not confined to the more poorly
educated, lower-ranking personnel may be surmised from a report written by
an undercover agent charged with producing intelligence assessments for San
Marcos and Cajabamba. Indicating a social-science background and a more-
than-passing acquaintance with Karl Marx's *Eighteenth Brumaire of Louis
Bonaparte* of 'potatoes in a sack' fame, he opined that the peasantry:

Forms the largest and most dangerous class, a sector of which is affiliated to
FEDECC, a part of the CCP and led by extreme leftist elements ...
Approximately 60 per cent of the peasants are illiterate, easy to influence,
indoctrinate and manipulate ... Concerning the provinces of Cajabamba and
San Marcos, it has been found that in the rural areas (populated principally
by peasants and related occupational groups), about 90 per cent of the inhabitants are indoctrinated (*concientizada*) by cadres of the PCP–SL ...

For approximately the last twenty years, the peasantry has been developing
an attitude of complete rejection vis-à-vis the prevailing social order. They
are struggling constantly to alter their situation. Such a change in belief by
sectors of our society highlights the emergence and strength of new power
structures within their ranks. Thus, traditional peasant agitation was always
characterised by its spontaneous, fleeting and partial nature, as well as being
confined to a small, restricted locality. However, the contemporary peasant
movement has extended over the greater part of our zone and is not isolated.
It possesses an ongoing dynamism and gives every indication of being in a
process of heightened development, as illustrated by widening unionisation,
the growth of so-called *rondas campesinas* and activism in political parties.[23]

While there was a tendency for police officers to see a bloodthirsty subversive inside every poncho, for their part, country people were provided with
ample reason to fear the Guardia Civil and hold them in low esteem.

Otuzco province was characterised by particularly tense civil–police relations
due to corruption and a lack of discipline. A complicating factor here involved
drugs. Since the late 1970s, increasing numbers of smallholders, cultivating
plots in narrow, low-lying valleys at altitudes between 1,800 and 2,000 metres,
had been responding to depressed agricultural prices and rocketing input costs
by planting coca bushes. On a minimum of 150 enterprises scattered throughout
El Huayo, Sacamaca, Huayobamba and neighbouring parishes, production had
been steadily expanding during 1980–85, to the point where the zone became

popularly known as '*el Uchiza liberteño*' ('La Libertad's Uchiza'), after the Amazonian boom town famous nationally for its involvement in the narcotics business.[24] Apart from refining locally grown leaves into cocaine paste, traffickers used Otuzco as a staging post between their Amazonian headquarters and exporting points along Peru's northern coast.

Despite Otuzco's growing importance in the drug trade, police units stationed in the province appeared unconcerned and rarely mounted operations against producers or dealers, even though a wealth of information concerning locations and identities circulated freely among the province's citizens. Whereas cultivators and their associates obviously viewed this situation with satisfaction, many inhabitants of the small towns and surrounding countryside who fell outside the coca circuit regarded these developments with alarm. Disquiet stemmed primarily from the connection between drugs and violence: the usual bloody settling of accounts between rival gangs aside, a *senderista* column was already circulating in the province; it was likely to become more powerful if fed by 'revolutionary contributions' levied on cocaine entrepreneurs. Similar scenarios in the Upper Huallaga Valley in the department of Huánuco and the department of San Martín had been given ample publicity through the national media. The denizens of Otuzco were naturally keen to avoid travelling along the same path.

Against this backdrop, police inaction on the narcotics issue brought widespread criticism, since it was generally believed that they had succumbed to bribery. Such sentiments culminated in a mass protest in Otuzco on 9 September 1989. One specific complaint raised by the population centred on the inability of the police to seize even one kilo of cocaine over the preceding twelve months, although sizeable shipments had passed regularly through the town.[25] No positive action materialised, however, with the result that complaints were made at frequent intervals over the following three years.

Members of the Guardia Civil stationed in Otuzco certainly faced a great temptation to augment their reduced stipends with backhanders from drug traffickers, but this was by no means the only source of public dissatisfaction with their behaviour. A proclivity for drunkenness, combined with the purposeless mistreatment of the local populace, created additional friction. Faced with such indiscipline, the commander of the local station felt compelled, in March 1986, to ban his men from drinking in uniform in order to 'stop the scandals that some bad police provoke, abusing the poor people, especially those who come to town from the countryside'.[26] The measure had but temporary effect. In March 1990, complaints were again being raised about their conduct:

> You can observe constantly police in uniform in an inebriated state. To make matters worse, they commit abuses against the population, especially the peasantry ... Last Tuesday sergeant Pretell, accompanied by another three members of the Policía General [ex-Guardia Civil] assaulted an employee of the Education Department with kicks and fists. When they got him to jail, he was beaten around the head and forced to strip naked.[27]

Nor was regard for the police enhanced by the activities of one of their former colleagues, who, in search of higher wages, had assumed employment as bodyguard to the local mayor. Taking advantage of his position, the ex-officer robbed the municipal offices and fled to the coast in a police vehicle. Although detained with his booty and brought back to Otuzco under escort, he was released by the local judge, a decision that provoked 'dismay and general protest among the populace'.[28]

Incidents of a far more consequential nature acted to undermine civil–police relations, especially extreme violations of human rights. One infamous abuse of authority occurred on 11 May 1985, when two captains in the Guardia Civil stationed in Huamachuco punched and kicked to death a school student whom they believed had robbed a policeman's wife. Having witnessed the murder, the victim's brother was then kidnapped by the officers. His remains (severely mutilated by dynamite detonated by the officers in an attempt to complicate any judicial process) appeared outside the town seven days later. Understandably, such 'brutal assassinations caused widespread protest, condemnation and revulsion amongst the townspeople'.[29]

Multiple factors, therefore, created a situation whereby the Guardia Civil proved unable to halt the expansion of PCP–SL activity in Cajabamba and Huamachuco. Although on occasions the police managed to inflict quite telling reverses on the insurgents (to be discussed below), these remained infrequent compared to the build-up of PCP–SL forces. Between 1985 and 1992, in consequence, the authorities failed to prevent sections of the so-called 'red triangle' becoming de facto 'liberated zones', where the state's political and coercive presence was ephemeral in the extreme. Additionally, significant areas of territory were, in effect, 'semi-liberated', insofar as they might be contested by the state during the day, but fell under guerrilla control after nightfall. This increasingly disadvantageous correlation of forces necessitated the deployment after 1988 of larger numbers of army personnel, a measure that prior to 1992 appeared to make little alteration to a picture of rebel advance and state retreat.

Batiendo el campo: attacks against the *gamonales*

The third component of the PCP–SL's 'cleansing the countryside' strategy, entailed the neutralisation or elimination of a rural elite that had already been weakened severely upon implementation of General Velasco's agrarian reform. As noted in Chapter Two, amid a political environment increasingly favourable to hacienda expropriation, key pillars of the region's traditional landowner class (the Iparraguirre, Orbegoso, Pinillos and related families) started to divide and sell off their highland properties during the 1960s. Most took their relatives and capital to Trujillo, Lima, or coastal valleys, where they established modern enterprises in dairy farming, asparagus cultivation for export and intensive horticulture to supply demand in coastal cities. By 1980, an important transformation had therefore occurred in the composition of the local agrarian bourgeoisie. Established *parentelas*, who proudly traced their roots back to the colonial era, had been replaced by a layer of medium-scale farmers of less 'aristocratic' lineage, whose agricultural activities revolved around the market and profit maximisation.

Momentarily bucking the historical tide, a small number of landowners identified with the 'old' order had mobilised contacts and influence within the Ministry of Agriculture to cling on to all or most of their estates. Given the important symbolic significance these individuals represented in the eyes of the local peasantry, they quickly became prime targets for PCP–SL death threats. One prominent case involved the Otoya brothers, whose family had owned the hacienda Sitacocha since the mid-nineteenth century, if not before. Sited between Cajabamba and the *ceja de selva* subtropical zone bordering the River Marañón, this estate was not only isolated and thereby vulnerable to *senderista* incursions but it also lay directly along a favoured guerrilla supply and disengagement route between the highlands and the Amazon. Furthermore, a precipitous terrain encompassing lofty peaks and steep gorges, coupled with a negligible state presence, made the area attractive to the PCP–SL as a centre for its operations in Cajabamba and San Marcos. Its strategic position meant that rebel columns could strike out to Huamachuco and Santiago de Chuco in the south, as well as northwards towards Cajamarca. Such inducements signified that between 1982 and 1984 a guerrilla presence grew ever more noticeable in the zone. After receiving a number of menacing warnings, the Otoya brothers finally fled Sitacocha, first relocating to their house in Cajabamba and, after the provincial capital became, in turn, too dangerous, lodging with family in Cajamarca. Since they had a reputation for drunken, aggressive behaviour and for acting very much in the fashion of the stereotypical Andean *gamonal*, their departure was not lamented by *campesinos* settled in parishes around Sitacocha and Marcamachay, or the residents of Cajabamba town.

A somewhat different scenario arose in the adjacent hacienda, Jocos. Here, a youthful member of the expropriated landowning (Rosell) family, who happened to be a qualified agronomist imbued with progressive ideas, was employed as administrator of the recently established Agrarian Production Cooperative (CAP). Despite the good working relationship and mutual respect existing between the administrator and cooperative members, the situation eventually became too dangerous and in 1983 he was forced to leave for the coast, where he managed a dairy enterprise in the Virú Valley, located south of Trujillo.

This development illustrated a general trend: by 1986–87, the escalation of PCP–SL activity and its attendant heightened risk meant that all members of the traditional agrarian elite had abandoned the countryside to seek refuge in Andean towns or outside the highlands. A long-established source of power and social control had consequently disappeared, contributing to a substantial weakening of traditional structures of political authority in the countryside.

The fertile Condebamba Valley and its environs comprised an area where the medium-scale agrarian bourgeoisie was particularly well entrenched. These landowners proved more reluctant to quit their properties, given that they were less likely to possess sufficient alternative sources of income outside agriculture. Some attempted to keep businesses afloat by constantly switching residence between their farm and nearby towns, which offered greater protection (in this case Cajabamba, San Marcos and Cajamarca). By 1986, however, *senderista* activity around the Condebamba Valley had reached a stage where, after receiving assassination threats and fearful about future developments (including possible guerrilla influence among their workforce), a number of owners ceased administering their *fundos*, which, in practice, passed into the hands of tenants and agricultural labourers. Such a fate befell several of the agricultural enterprises established decades earlier by the colourful Germán Contreras. Others bought a modicum of protection and manoeuvred desperately to hang on to their interests through the payment of 'revolutionary contributions' to the PCP–SL and by undertaking to provide workers with improved conditions.

One fraction of the rural bourgeoisie, however, did not have the negotiation option open to them. Farmers with close links to sources of political power were particularly at risk from rebel detachments. Some, determined to maintain control of their assets, chose to ignore the obvious dangers, with fateful consequences. For example, on 23 August 1987, in the district of Cachachi, a PCP–SL column attacked the *fundo* El Montón. This property belonged to Alberto Negrón, a prominent member of Acción Popular (AP), who served as senator during the second Belaunde government (1980–85). Although Negrón happened to be absent when the raid took place, the farm's administrator, his son and the neighbourhood lieutenant governor were executed, while a schoolteacher, whose wayward behaviour elicited complaints from the populace, suffered the indignity of undergoing a public dressing-down and having his head shaved. After undertaking these acts, the rebels proceeded to divide up El Montón's land and farm equipment among the assembled *campesinos*.[30]

Perhaps the most infamous case of a strike against politically connected, medium-scale agriculturalists involved Alipio Arroyo, the owner of Campo Alegre, a *fundo* sited near La Grama on the northern edge of the Condebamba Valley. In September 1992 the farmer fell victim to a *senderista* hit squad. Arroyo's demise was not only provoked by his class position. He belonged to one of the 'historic' *aprista* families in the department of Cajamarca and Francisco Arroyo, the farmer's son, was currently mayor of Cajamarca (1990–92) on the APRA ticket. The father's homicide was partly the result of his well-known party affiliation, but equally it represented a symbolic strike at the political influence wielded by his son.

Pointing to a wider problem, guerrilla activity in and around the Condebamba Valley was facilitated as a consequence of particularly strained relations between local inhabitants and the Guardia Civil. Demonstrating a perverse sense of humour, the populace labelled the police post strategically sited at La Grama, the main crossing over the River Condebamba, '*El Engordero*' ('The Fattening House'), in reference to the constant exactions they suffered at the hands of their supposed protectors. Smallholders moving produce by mule between the Valley and markets in Ichocán and San Marcos would be regularly stopped and relieved of part of their harvest. Vehicle owners plying the San Marcos–Cajabamba route were likewise compelled to pay bribes in cash or kind before being allowed to continue their journey. Such behaviour understandably lent credence to insurgent claims apropos the corrupt and unjust nature of the Peruvian state.

A comparably dangerous situation to that encountered around the Condebamba Valley prevailed in the *ceja de selva* zone that ran alongside the course of the River Marañón, although here rebel forces tended to pursue a policy of accommodation as opposed to outright assassination. Once a presence in the Cajabamba–Santiago de Chuco–Sayapullo triangle had been established, PCP–SL activity in this subtropical area intensified significantly after 1987. Among the attractions figured a minimal state presence and a peasantry with an ambivalent (and, at times, hostile) attitude towards the state. Additionally, large areas of dense vegetation and the local topography offered relative security from attack – from a strategic vantage point, any approaching force could be detected at one or two hours' distance. Linked to Sitacocha and Marcamachay, the locality afforded a corridor for the relatively unimpeded movement of cadres and supplies east–west from the jungle to the highlands and south–north along the Andes mountain range. A final source of attraction was financial – the resources generated by coca and (on a smaller scale) poppy cultivation.

Since 1976, an expanding area of land bordering the Marañón had been planted with coca bushes, as in the province of Otuzco. At slightly higher elevations, poppies thrived. The drugs, processed locally into cocaine paste and heroin, were then either taken by mule along the northern exit route to Celendín, San Marcos or Cajabamba, for transport by truck via Cajamarca to the coast; or, further south, the illicit cargo travelled through Huamachuco to Trujillo. In the face of government neglect and the zone's inaccessibility, the narcotics business had been developing largely unimpeded for around a decade when *senderista* columns began to percolate into the area. They encountered a smoothly functioning commodity chain, staffed at the base by smallholders and knitted together by middle-ranking facilitators, who supplied chemical inputs and technical assistance, arranged payments and organised shipments to the *cosca* head (usually a family member) living on the coast. As in other drug-producing areas where the Party operated, the PCP–SL sought better returns for direct producers and levied 'taxes' on drug consignments heading to market. According to one police interviewee, rates varied in proportion to the size of cargo. A string of mules departing for a rendezvous with a coast-bound lorry at a discreet location along the Cajabamba–Cajamarca road would reputably be charged up to US$1,000; larger quantities attracted payments up to US$5,000.[31] Although the PCP–SL did not get directly involved in production and distribution, its purely parasitic business relationship with drug-traffickers became an important source of the more sophisticated weaponry the insurgent organisation acquired from the late 1980s.[32]

PCP–SL attempts to establish *bases de apoyo*: the cooperatives

From the preceding account, it can be appreciated that over the mid- and late 1980s the PCP–SL attained a considerable degree of success with regard to the destructive dimensions of General Secretary Guzmán's 'churning up the countryside' policy. The state political and bureaucratic apparatuses had ceased to operate effectively in most areas, its coercive agencies forced on to the defensive and the agrarian bourgeoisie rendered impotent in the face of a cumulative guerrilla advance. Alberto Fujimori's celebrated intelligence adviser, Vladimiro Montesinos, aptly summed up this train of events: Peruvian governments in the 1980s 'were playing "draughts", while Sendero Luminoso was playing "chess"'.[33] In accordance with Guzmán's entreaty, rural areas in the Cajabamba–Huamachuco region had indeed been 'thrown into confusion', but how successful was the insurgent organisation in pursuing the constructive component of its strategy, namely, the building of a social base among the peasantry and other sectors of the population?

Given the plethora of land disputes, bitter personal rivalries, mismanagement and constant accusations of corruption affecting the region's CAP and SAIS farming cooperatives, soon after establishing a political presence, the PCP–SL made a concerted effort to intervene in these conflicts with a view to gaining adherents. According to Party doctrine, Velasco's agrarian reform programme had maintained the traditional land tenure structure intact, with the result that these enterprises represented one dimension of the 'semi-feudalism' that allegedly persisted in Andean Peru. For the PCP–SL, a continuing 'feudal concentration of land' signified that 'the land question is the motor of class conflict in the countryside' and represented a structural problem that could 'only be solved by the peasantry, under the control of the Communist Party, taking and defending the land with arms in their hands via the popular war'.[34] Furthermore, *campesino* leaders and managers administering the cooperatives had risen into the ranks of the agrarian elite. They had, it was argued, largely supplanted the traditional landlord class to become the 'main exploiters' of peasants and rural proletarians; they comprised newly empowered *gamonales*, who dominated the rural poor. Under the slogan 'land to the tiller', the PCP–SL's task entailed the destruction of the cooperatives by means of mass invasions from without and within their boundaries. The immediate aim was to distribute land, livestock and implements to the *campesinos* on an individual basis, wreck farm plant and machinery, and remove, by threat or assassination, cooperative leaders and administrative personnel. This supposedly 'anti-feudal' struggle against the cooperatives would, it was anticipated, enable the party to win support among the so-called 'principal motor force of the revolution'. In the words of a PCP–SL leaflet circulating widely in Cajabamba and Huamachuco during 1984 and 1985, the objective was to: 'Sabotage production, take over land, attack the rich, encourage personal feuds and stimulate land hunger'.[35] As indicated in Chapter Three, steps to implement this policy occurred as early as mid-1982 with armed interventions against the SAIS 3 de

Octubre (province of Huamachuco) and the SAIS La Pauca (San Marcos).

By this juncture, every large-scale SAIS in the *sierra* of La Libertad was beset by intractable structural problems that offered PCP–SL cadres a fertile terrain in which to operate. A typical situation existed in the SAIS Tahuantinsuyo (province of Huamachuco), where, despite the enterprise's growing economic difficulties, an influential minority of the ex-hacienda workforce wished to maintain the cooperative as a going concern. In opposition, most *socios* (backed by land-hungry households in surrounding *minifundio* zones) desired fragmentation and individual family farming. Collective–private divisions were further complicated by rivalry between *anexos*.

These tensions spilled over on 5 March 1982, when a force of thirty *socios* from the cooperative's productive core based on the ex-hacienda Cochabamba entered the Moyán *anexo* with the intention of evicting a number of households. Facing dogged resistance, the Cochabamba faction was repelled, only to return to Moyán on 21 May 1982 in greater numbers (approximately sixty mounted men), accompanied by a detachment of police. They managed to destroy several homes, trample crops and confiscate livestock. One *campesino* was detained by the Guardia Civil and various evictions were enforced.[36] Responding to these events, twenty insurgents raided the SAIS on 12 July 1982, commandeered foodstuffs and forced cooperative members to listen to a political discourse in favour of armed struggle. Despite the capture of some local guerrilla forces by a police detachment that arrived during an occupation of the Cochabamba *anexo* in November 1982 (see Chapter Three), the SAIS gained no respite from PCP–SL predation. Successive incursions during 1983 and 1984 reduced the enterprise's land base and caused the destruction of its capital equipment and its stock of pedigree cattle and sheep. Through the distribution of land and livestock, the PCP–SL was able to establish a support base among alienated cooperative members and a group of *minifundistas* who fulfilled their long-standing ambition to gain access to SAIS resources.

A comparable train of events unfolded simultaneously in the SAIS El Triunfo (structured around the ex-hacienda Chuquizongo), located in the neighbouring province of Otuzco. Created out of thirteen farms, four adjacent *minifundio* zones and extending over 21,760 hectares, this cooperative's complicated organisational structure made conflict almost inevitable, especially as, during the original expropriation in 1973, permanent workers had been allocated much less land than the estate's tenants. Faced with a dissident faction in San Vicente and neighbouring sections who wanted to split from the SAIS and establish a separate peasant community, cooperative leaders assisted by the police entered the area in July 1982 and attempted to embargo livestock belonging to the rival group. In the ensuing confrontation, a nineteen-year-old peasant woman was shot dead by a cooperative loyalist.[37]

Yet again, during the following months PCP–SL cadres strove to intervene in the conflict, seizing SAIS resources and allocating them to the local community to utilise on a private basis. Efforts to build on peasant goodwill in the first half of 1983 led to the formation of a *base de apoyo*. Likewise, in the SAIS 3 de

Octubre (Huamachuco province), a first *senderista* incursion in August 1982 brought the destruction of the enterprise's dairy and the redistribution of a considerable quantity of pedigree livestock. Individuals were warned not to go and work for the SAIS, a threat that most *socios* heeded out of fear, while others fled the area. Under these and other pressures (administrative incompetence and corruption) the cooperative began to disintegrate, a process that accelerated after August 1983, when a *senderista* detachment assassinated the president of the SAIS along with a fellow *socio*. The guerrillas concurrently established a support base, the cell reputedly including former members of the cooperative's administrative committees who, after being ousted in an internal power struggle, had entered into conflict with the enterprise's current leadership.[38]

Unsurprisingly, fragmentation and the advance of private farming did not bring an end to conflict. By mobilising personal contacts or making illegal payments, some *socios* acquired far larger holdings than others, while an unequal division of enterprise non-fixed assets (especially valuable pedigree bullfighting stock), engendered multiple jealousies. Obviously frustrated, by 1986 a clear majority of members were lobbying the Ministry of Agriculture for the cooperative's dissolution and the granting of individual land titles.[39] Although this train of events proved disastrous for the local economy (between 1982 and 1986. the SAIS Tahuantinsuyo, 3 de Octubre and El Triunfo lost up to 10,000 head of pedigree cattle to a combination of guerrilla actions and commonplace rustling), the PCP–SL did succeed in gaining backing among a sector of smallholders.[40] Being more committed to the cooperatives, rural labourers proved harder to convince about the benefits of armed struggle.

As with strikes against the state's political and law-enforcement apparatuses, assaults on cooperatives were concentrated initially in the 'red triangle' formed by Cajabamba, Santiago de Chuco and Sayapullo, but commencing in 1984–85, enterprises sited further afield came under serious threat. Control over the Condebamba Valley, which had the richest soils in the region, became an important insurgent objective. For residents of the CAP José Santos Chocano, this had profound consequences. Established legally on 20 June 1975, the cooperative was was created by combining six *anexos* of the ex-hacienda Araqueda (Chuquibamba, Corralpampa, Algamarca, Condorcucho, El Chingol and Ribera de Condebamba), covering 923.45 hectares of mostly prime agricultural land. In the following June, a further 36.87 hectares were allocated to the CAP, which at this stage possessed 1,063 head of pedigree cattle, as well as three sugar cane presses, tractors, ploughs and other implements. The enterprise flourished for a few years, but by 1983 it had begun to decay – despite the considerable assets at its disposal. Falling livestock numbers and the resultant diminished earnings from milk sales caused delays in the payment of wages that could last for several months. Such an unsatisfactory situation produced an advance of individual over collective farming activity, amid the usual mutual recriminations about corruption and free-riding to the detriment of the collective good. At the centre of these disputes figured Isabel Salvatierra, president of the cooperative from 26 April 1980 until his ousting on 25 April 1983.

Against this backdrop, a PCP–SL column entered the CAP on 14 January 1984 and killed the manager, Oscar Acón. Cane-pressing machinery, the electricity generator, tractors and other equipment were dynamited. Two months later, cooperative members headed by the president of the cooperative's Administrative Council (Teófilo Baltazar) appointed a new administrator (Crecencio Paredes). During another guerrilla incursion (September 1984), Baltazar was in turn assassinated on the grounds that he was 'a police informer and corrupt'. Miraculously, Paredes managed to escape detection and flee across the fields unscathed. Sendero's accusations contained a large element of truth, for since 1979 the enterprise's leaders had been selling cattle and arranging bank loans, supposedly to finance maize cultivation, yet most *socios* received no benefit and were owed several months' unpaid wages. Such opportunistic behaviour understandably provoked considerable resentment among ordinary members of the labour force and bred sympathy for the PCP–SL's actions. Support was also forthcoming from Isabel Salvatierra. Peeved at his loss of position in April 1983, Salvatierra threw in his lot with Sendero shortly afterwards and participated in attacking the CAP. Another component of the local *base de apoyo* comprised neighbouring *minifundistas* who, encouraged by PCP–SL cadres, launched invasions in the Chingol sector of the cooperative.

Under these pressures the enterprise disintegrated rapidly in 1985–86, when collective land was parcelled out on an individual basis. This course of action was formally agreed (although the minute book has been lost) by cooperative members and other interested parties at a General Assembly held on 24 September 1987, before the watchful gaze of armed PCP–SL cadres stationed around the room. As a result of the division, most households acquired plots of around 1.5 hectares, while a minority managed to carve out for themselves more substantial holdings, in one case an appreciable 32.20 hectares of prime agricultural land.[41] In the short term, Sendero's policy of 'land to the tiller' at the barrel of a gun would bring the Party support, but would in the longer term spawn a plethora of conflicts, as will be discussed in Chapter Five.

With a *senderista* column circulating around the Condebamba Valley almost constantly, the neighbouring CAP Tabacal suffered a similar fate. After the cooperative's leadership had received a series of threats, on 1 June 1986 a group of twenty-five insurgents raided the property. Four members of the enterprise were killed. These included the president, Marcial Quiroz, the administrator, the cashier and the shopkeeper. In an intentional act of public humiliation, the victims were forced to parade around the estate's main square singing songs in favour of the armed struggle, before being shot at point-blank range.[42] The insurgents then proceeded to destroy farm equipment. A second major assault occurred in late July 1987 to coincide with National Day. Approximately twelve guerrillas stormed the property and were busily distributing foodstuffs from its stores to the local populace when a police detachment from the Chaquicocha post (some 30 minutes away) arrived on the scene. In the ensuing confrontation two *senderistas* lost their lives. One was a pupil from Cajabamba's technical college. The second, schoolteacher Alberto Paredes, represented a more signif-

icant loss, as he occupied an influential position in the PCP–SL's local apparatus. Others who died included the cooperative's president (fatefully, the
brother of his forerunner killed in June 1986) and one policeman.[43] Although
the appearance of the police forced the insurgents to retreat towards the safety
of mountains near Araqueda, their attack sparked the final dissolution of the
enterprise, whose land base, livestock and surviving farm equipment was
divided among its thirty-six members and their children. 'Outsiders' squatting
on cooperative land, numbering around fifty households, also acquired holdings through the armed backing they received from the local detachment of the
EGP. Like the land-hungry families in the SAIS Tahuantinsuyo, SAIS El
Triunfo and CAP José Santos Chocano, these PCP–SL actions were viewed
favourably by members of this deprived section of Condebamba's farming
community.

In the first week of July 1988, a third cooperative in the province of
Cajabamba became the scene of assassination when a guerrilla column accompanied by smallholders from adjacent *minifundista* zones entered the CAP Jocos.
In Jocos, as in other cooperatives in the region, the PCP–SL hoped to acquire
a social base by exploiting contradictions arising out of the 1970s agrarian
reform. As noted in Chapter Two, this 6,080-hectare estate had been in the
forefront of the agricultural modernisation process in the northern highlands
that commenced in the 1930s. At final adjudication in June 1975, the property
held 171 hectares of fertile irrigated valley land sown with improved pastures,
which supported two sizeable pedigree dairy herds. Milk production, the main
business activity, was supplemented by sheep-rearing, an interest that had
attracted investment since 1960. Above the two principal irrigation channels
that gush down each side of the valley, the estate's waged workforce and tenants
produced food crops on the surrounding hillsides and grazed their livestock on
upland natural pastures. Smallholders settled around the boundaries of Jocos,
especially near Sitacocha, had long cast covetous eyes on the estate's resources
– a sentiment that grew in tandem with demographic increase post-1950 and
the resultant fragmentation of peasant property.

Hacienda records (since destroyed, but data is in the author's possession)
show that in mid-1973 Jocos still housed around 1,500 head of cattle, notwithstanding the uncertainties caused by land reform. The estate sold the
PERULAC factory 1,850 litres of milk per day and dedicated part of its production to butter-making and other uses (feeding calves, etc.). Despite subsequent
decapitalisation, at its expropriation cooperative members inherited 909 dairy
cattle and supplied PERULAC with 1,300–1,400 litres of milk daily. The fort-
nightly cheque from Nestlé allowed the enterprise to pay wages on time and
make some capital investments, which permitted the CAP to enjoy an initial
period of stability and growth. After 1983, maladministration and disruptions
in commerce caused by expanding PCP–SL activity led to a crisis within the
cooperative that members made a desperate effort to address in 1986 through
investment in additional livestock. In a classic dilemma common to production
cooperatives, this prioritisation of the *socios*' 'capitalist' role over their 'worker'

role led to cash-flow difficulties, delays in paying wages and bitter conflict between members, which ultimately forced the president of the CAP to resign. Thereafter, the situation deteriorated markedly: in March 1987, Eloy Robles assumed leadership of the enterprise but did nothing constructive to halt a decline in its livestock numbers and was eventually forced to stop the delivery of milk to PERULAC. Without a regular income flow, the payment of wages had to be suspended.

When a *senderista* detachment entered Jocos on 10 May 1987, therefore, widespread discontent existed among cooperative members and non-members alike. In an assembly that Robles attended, no opposition was voiced to insurgent demands for the dismantling of the CAP and the division of its land base along individual lines. It was also decided to sell off the remaining livestock and other non-fixed assets to meet unpaid wages. To mark the CAP's demise, the *senderistas* ordered the slaughter of three cows and the distribution of their meat among the *asemblistas*. Additional symbolic acts involved the torching of cooperative account books, the granary, a tractor, butter-making equipment and the milk-testing and artificial insemination laboratory.

Unsurprisingly, these developments failed to usher in a peasant (or Maoist) Valhalla. Simulating adherence to the assembly's policy agreement, Robles sold 12 oxen, 250 cattle and the cooperative's pick-up truck, but he omitted to distribute the money raised to those owed wages, which led to his prosecution and a jail sentence. Upon the detention of Eloy Robles, former chargehand Luis Paredes assumed a leadership role in July 1987 and started to implement PCP–SL directives. Over the ensuing months, private holdings (without legal land titles) were allocated to members and their offspring. More controversially, family members of ex-employees who now resided in Cajabamba also received land, while peripheral areas passed into the hands of *minifundista* squatters. Alienation deepened among the local peasantry when Robles was released from prison: avarice triumphed over foresight, as he allied with Paredes in an attempt to dispose of remaining cooperative assets for personal advantage. Informed of these developments by angry residents, on 6 July 1988 PCP–SL cadres penetrated Jocos and subjected Robles and Paredes to a *juicio popular* before executing them. The assembled population was admonished to behave in a moral manner, under threat of suffering a similar fate.[44]

These sanctions, although severe, were accepted by a sector of the district's inhabitants, who opined that the victims had been 'shameless opportunists', only interested in feathering their own nests at the expense of more needy peasant households.[45] Such sentiments enabled Sitachoca and its environs to become a PCP–SL bastion between 1988 and 1992. Over these years, guerrilla forces launched repeated attacks against Guardia Civil posts in Sitacocha, Lluchubamba and neighbouring hamlets, forcing closures and a police withdrawal to Cajabamba. The resultant vacuum of authority allowed the insurgents to enter settlements unhindered, organise *escuelas populares* and attract recruits. Effective state presence evaporated under a combination of threat and fear as Sendero imposed itself as the de facto authority in the zone. Several attention-grabbing acts sufficed to drive home this reality. In one, the foreman of a gang that maintained the Lluchubamba–Santa Rosa road was assassinated and heavy earth-moving equipment incendiarised. On 5 June 1990, a schoolteacher assigned to the hamlet of Pencachín was killed and a note declaring 'This is how informers die' was left beside the corpse to convey an unambiguous message to local citizens.

PCP–SL attempts to establish *bases de apoyo: minifundista* land hunger, Maoist morality and the demise of *rondas campesinas*

As events in Jocos indicate, PCP–SL cadres operating in the countryside utilised land scarcity and dissatisfaction vis-à-vis corrupt behaviour offensive to the peasantry's moral code when building sympathy among households living within and immediately around the cooperatives. These issues were also employed to gain adherents outside the cooperative sector. Approximately 75 per cent of holdings were less than 2 hectares in size, so that an estimated 70 per cent of farming households suffered from malnutrition. Access to additional land was therefore a prime aspiration among a population whose plight had been rendered more desperate following drought-induced crop failure during the agricultural years 1985–86 and 1989–90.

Activists strove to respond to this yearning for land by promoting the invasion of medium-scale farms, so that the *fundos* El Montón and Campo Alegre were far from the only such enterprises to be overrun by guerrilla detachments. Rumi Rumi, a property owned by Alberto Urrunaga in the district of Cajabamba, was overrun by guerrillas in 1989. Mounting a carefully planned operation, PCP–SL militants first assembled the workforce to hear a speech advocating agrarian revolution through armed struggle. Once they had concluded, and in the company of smallholders settled around Rumi Rumi's boundaries, they invaded the farm, forcing administrative personnel to take flight. Having taken control, the insurgents proceeded to allocate individual plots and distribute other resources among the participants. The granary was emptied of 600 kilograms of seed potato, 250 *arrobas* (23 kilograms) of wheat and 200 *arrobas* (18 kilograms) of barley. Agricultural implements and all the farm's livestock were also handed over to *campesinos* who supported the occupation.[46]

Such incursions were not restricted to enterprises owned by clearly identifiable members of the rural bourgeoisie. Households positioned more ambiguously on the divide between well-to-do peasant and medium-scale farmer could be singled out for attack. During the latter months of 1988, this fate befell two families who had acquired holdings of 75 hectares and 112 hectares of (mostly rain-fed, second- and third-grade) land when the hacienda Calluán fragmented during the 1960s. In an environment steeped in inter-household jealousies and after receiving a number of supplications from disaffected neighbours, the PCP–SL contingent circulating the zone authorised invasions of these properties and the redistribution of their assests.[47] Indeed, rich peasants frequently fell victim to the guerrilla. Scant sympathy for their predicament was likely to be shown among the wider community in cases where: (i) former administrative personnel under the defunct landlord regime established relatively prosperous enterprises through *hacendado* largesse; or (ii) a sizeable holding had been carved out via the illegal appropriation of cooperative land.

Both scenarios could be encountered in the SAIS La Pauca, encapsulated frequently in the life history of the same individual, which explains the following unpitying assessments regarding certain physical assaults and armed expropriations undertaken by PCP–SL detachments active in different *anexos* of the ex-hacienda:

> Through talking with the peasants, the *terrucos* became well informed about what had been going on around here. They soon discovered who had been close to Rafael Puga [the former landowner]. They knew what had occurred after the cooperative had been established. About who had been robbing its assets. About the mistreatment of those who did not support the leaders. About how they cheated the workers out of wages and got rich at their expense ... Over the years a lot of bitterness and resentment against the leaders had consequently built up, and not just among the cooperative's members. So when Sendero began to attack them, people thought: 'Well done! They had it coming! It's about time someone brought these crooks to account. They have been abusing us for years, now it's their turn to suffer'. Obviously, this was only stated to family and close friends – those you trusted. Otherwise you could be denounced as a terrorist supporter to the cops. But that is what many really felt.[48]

This informant's son voiced more straightforward approval of PCP–SL actions in this regard:

> After nearly twenty years of doing what they liked, those who got rich out of the SAIS from everybody else's sweat, got what they deserved. Many poor peasants had had to put up with their capriciousness and unjust demands for years, but did not have the power to oppose them. Sendero changed all that. We stood by and watched what happened, but applauded silently. The abusers were being taught a lesson at last. There was little sympathy towards them.[49]

As well as hitting the interests of kulaks, the guerrillas were also prepared to pit village against village and hamlet against hamlet. In localities where rival *caseríos* competed for land, water and other coveted resources, the standard approach did not involve a considered appraisal of local history and the veracity of rival claims made by the parties in dispute. Instead, cadres followed the far more expedient policy of throwing their weight behind the village – or faction within a village – that demonstrated greatest receptivity to the Party's message. Once this had been determined, land invasions aimed at benefiting pro-Sendero elements would be mounted. Threats and, if necessary, armed force, were to be employed to 'settle' disputes and so ensure the victory of the favoured group. Disgruntled individuals were left with no option but to feign agreement or abandon the area. This scenario characterised the PCP–SL's takeover of the *caseríos* of Corralpampa (1988) and Cruz de Algamarca (1991) in the province of Cajabamba, and was repeated wherever the organisation operated in the northern highlands. A similar train of events took place in the village of Quillispampa (district of Cachachi): cadres based nearby in the peasant community of Chorobamba – Sendero's principal stronghold in the district – pressured Quillispampa's authorities to back the Party and obey its instructions. After refusing to cooperate, the president of Quillispampa was executed on 1 May 1991 and a pro-Sendero leadership installed. A support base for the insurgents was subsequently built up in the village.[50]

Although of paramount importance for resource-scarce rural households, the land question was by no means their sole pressing concern. Thievery, especially livestock rustling, was another key preoccupation. While a scattering of *rondas campesinas* had been established in San Marcos by the mid-1980s, nightwatch patrols remained few and far between over much of Cajabamba, Huamachuco and other Andean provinces of La Libertad. High levels of rural crime consequently threatened the production of numerous smallholdings, a scourge that reached endemic proportions at times of drought and (as Starn described for the northern part of Cajamarca department) could provoke desperate responses. One particularly bloody case of peasant-enacted 'justice' in the face of official inaction occurred on 7 March 1982, when three young rustlers of between twenty and twenty-five years of age from Usquil journeyed to the parish of Porcón in the district of Quiruvilca to lift cattle. After being discovered and chased in the hamlet of Barrio Nuevo, one robber fell into the hands of the local populace, who dished out a severe beating before decapitating him with an axe.[51]

Fortunately, such extreme cases of frenzied retribution occurred infrequently. They did, however, illustrate the degree of frustration experienced by country people, who felt themselves not only abandoned by the state but actively prejudiced by its seeming indifference to *campesino* suffering. Even worse, with livestock playing a pivotal role in precarious smallholding economies, their farming communities and way of life appeared threatened as a result of collusion between the authorities and their predatory tormentors. Among the areas where such sentiments were most keenly felt were the westerly districts of highland La Libertad, especially in the environs of Lucma and Otuzco, home to smoothly functioning networks of *abigeos* (rustlers), who supplied stolen animals to slaughterhouses in Trujillo. Journeying back up to the *sierra*, these *abigeos* would rob mules and donkeys from smallholders in coastal valleys, which they sold in the highlands. When detained and handed over to the police by farmers, the foot soldiers of these bands would regularly be released by unscrupulous provincial judges.[52]

Possessing an attuned ear for peasant grievances, PCP–SL cadres strove to capitalise on the resulting high level of alienation. Whenever a guerrilla unit entered a new area, villagers invariably heard an unequivocal message that all stealing, whether professionally organised cattle-rustling or impromptu petty pilfering, was to cease forthwith under the threat of immediate and drastic sanction. Other forms of antisocial behaviour, including excessive drunkenness, domestic violence, malicious gossiping and 'witchcraft' (*brujería*) likewise became targets for suppression.[53] As elsewhere in highland Peru, these dictates were viewed positively by the majority. Nevertheless, it would be an exaggeration to claim that they attracted 'unanimous acceptance' in the northern highlands – as reputedly occurred in parts of Junín department in the Central Sierra – given a long-standing bandit tradition that in certain families ran through generations, and a reliance by a minority of households on illegal activities for their survival.[54]

One resident on the border between the provinces of San Marcos and Cajabamba captured eloquently the perspective of numerous local inhabitants regarding Sendero's clampdown on thievery:

> We did not have a well-organised *ronda* around here, so a lot of robbing went on. The *abigeos* would take our animals at night, sell them to the truckers or the livestock dealers in San Marcos and before you knew it, they were away to the coast. The cops in La Grama turned a blind eye, took their cut and did nothing to help us. Although some of us talked about getting a *ronda* committee formed, too many people were scared of landing in trouble with the authorities and chickened out ... We were too divided. This gave the rustlers lots of opportunity. However, when the *senderistas* turned up they threatened that anybody who robbed would be killed. As you never knew where they might be and people realised that the punishment would be implemented, there was a lot of fear. But it worked. Thievery stopped and we had one headache less. So the action achieved wide support in our *caserío* and throughout hamlets around here ...We could not do it on our own, but the *senderos* did it for us.[55]

Severe consequences threatened individuals who chose to defy the Party's directive, as evinced in July 1990 when a guerrilla column entered the hamlet of Membrillar (Otuzco province) and assassinated four rustlers after conducting a *juicio popular* designed to convey an unambiguous message to the local population.[56]

While not uncomplicated in that the PCP–SL did not follow the *rondas campesinas* custom of attempting to reform village-based lawbreakers, its uncompromising policy of meting out harsh 'justice' against resolute recidivists achieved a degree of resigned acceptance:

> What could you do? Things were complicated. The authorities in town offered no support. The Justices of the Peace were either too scared or not bothered. Often the rustlers possessed revolvers or hunting rifles and threatened their neighbours. Village leaders could not control them and enforce the will of the majority. Regarding *abigeos* who came from outside the locality, it was almost impossible to employ moral pressure to get them to change and

mend their bad habits. In these circumstances, where the situation was difficult to deal with, a few drastic measures were necessary to force bad individuals to comply with what most *campesinos* were desperate to achieve. One or two had to be sacrificed so that the majority could live in peace.[57]

While peasant-on-peasant violence might be tolerated and even welcomed under certain circumstances, wider support existed for tough action against dishonest members of the state bureaucracy. This sentiment was especially strong in cases where the populace believed vehemently that an official was behaving in an unethical fashion, but felt powerless to remedy the situation through legal channels.

Perhaps the most conspicuous example of a guerrilla attack eliciting high levels of approval involved Simón Damasen, the leading judge in San Marcos. After two years in post, Damasen had acquired a terrible reputation throughout the province. It was an open secret that civil cases about land conflicts, commercial disputes and debts, as well as criminal charges surrounding burglary or physical assault, would be decided in favour of the party who offered the highest bribe. One particular sentence that incensed the populace and enhanced Damasen's reputation for heartless venality concerned a conflict over property whose outcome resulted in a poor widow with several children to support losing her *minifundio*, even though the identity of the party who was the rightful owner was common knowledge. Against this backdrop, at dawn on 25 October 1990 a PCP–SL contingent entered San Marcos undetected and dynamited the front of Damasen's house, damaging the building and causing minor injuries to the occupants. The attack attracted almost universal approval throughout the province. A typical response opined that:

> He deserved it. The man was completely amoral. He was terrible and totally without shame. 'Justice' existed for whoever paid the most money. He only thought about money and had no pity for the poor. It was the poor who suffered most because they did not have the cash to win cases, even when they were in the right and should have had the law on their side ... Damasen consequently became known as a very bad character and became despised by many people. Lots of stories about his misdeeds circulated around San Marcos. Even protests about his conduct did not change anything. So when Sendero blew up his front door little sympathy was shown. The *senderistas* knew about his conduct and the population's hostile attitude, which is why they tried to kill him.[58]

In addition to outright accusations of corruption, other aspects of the judge's behaviour bred wholesale disapprobation in town and country. After a meeting held on 6 December 1986, the organising committee of *rondas campesinas* in San Marcos strove to establish new nightwatch patrols throughout the province. With difficulty and despite many operating deficiencies, the number of active patrols grew steadily between 1987 and 1988, bringing an increase in self-administered justice at village level, hand in hand with a decrease in the volume of cases being processed by the legal fraternity based in San Marcos town. This development obviously jeopardised the earning capacity of Damasen, who moved to redress the situation. Peasant leaders occupying official positions in the *rondas campesinas* were issued with detention orders for usurpation of functions, subjected to harassment and thrown in jail. One activist who suffered two incarcerations at the hands of Damasen related his experience in the following terms:

> That bloody judge knew I was deeply involved with the *rondas campesinas* and knew I had a big file because of my years working in the peasant movement. He therefore issued an order for my arrest. The first time I was picked up one Sunday when I went to town on market day. They got me inside and the cops gave me a good pasting, with their truncheons, kicking and all the usual stuff. They were asking about the *rondas* and insulting me, saying 'How can an ignorant peasant like you administer the law? What do you know?' After four days they got nothing out of me and threw me out into the street … The second time was much worse – now the threat was that they would accuse me of terrorism and send me to Cajamarca, where I would not get out for twenty years. Luckily for me, the chief of the local police station realised I had nothing to do with Sendero and so released me. He told me to clear off and keep out of trouble … We knew who was behind all of this. The real reason we were being persecuted so badly was that the judge and some local notaries wanted to get rid of the *rondas campesinas*. We were hitting their pockets and they didn't like it.[59]

In addition to raising the issue of judicial harassment, this testimony by an experienced organiser at provincial and departmental level pointed to another serious issue that participants in nightwatch patrols had to confront – accusations of collaborating with terrorism.

Since 1986, the PCP–SL's rival guerrilla movement, the Movimiento Revolucionario Túpac Amaru (MRTA), had been launching infrequent armed actions in Cajamarca and neighbouring districts. Despite conducting far fewer attacks, the *tupamaros* organisational structure proved less watertight than that mounted by the *senderistas*, with the result that its operational capability received a severe blow in 1989, when the counter-insurgency police captured the MRTA's local commander, lawyer Wilfredo Saavedra, along with most of the cell based in Cajamarca and its satellite town of Los Baños del Inca.[60] As Saavedra had acted as legal representative for the Provincial Federation of Rondas Campesinas of San Marcos, the watchful eye of the police fell naturally on local peasant leaders, four of whom were arrested under suspicion of MRTA membership. In another case, eleven *ronderos* from the hamlet of Pauca Santa Rosa were detained, charged with terrorism and sentenced to twenty years. Although these *ronderos* were later declared innocent and released because of lack of evidence, following a Supreme Court ruling in Lima (October 1993), these developments increased the vulnerability of anyone who occupied an official position in the *rondas campesinas*, while simultaneously providing Judge

Damasen with additional grounds on which to harass the anti-theft patrols.

Opportunity in this regard was enhanced unwittingly in 1991 by the Fujimori government, when Decree Law 635 passed on to the statute book. This piece of legislation aimed to protect the business community in Lima and other major cities from kidnap by guerrilla units and gangs of common criminals (incidences of which had increased significantly in the chaotic social and economic environment that arose between 1988 and 1990). In the hands of dishonest authorities at the provincial level, however, it could be utilised against night-watch patrollers. The months following enactment of Law 635 consequently witnessed lawyers acting for rustlers instructing their clients to charge prominent members of the patrol committees with '*secuestro*' and, as a result of this convenient legal pretext, most were issued with arrest warrants. Soon, many leaders found themselves languishing in jail, trapped in a hazardous political impasse, with most police far from sympathetic to their plight.[61]

Apart from repression originating from hostile individuals occupying strategic positions inside the local state apparatus, the functioning of *ronda* patrols between 1988 and 1992 was further complicated by the opportunistic behaviour of some of their own members – or those who purported to be members. After his release, one of the four leaders from San Marcos charged with belonging to the MRTA stole money from a foreign-funded NGO promoting rural development. Such peculation, news of which spread quickly around the province, not only elicited public condemnation levelled at his person but also discredited the wider movement. Lamentably, this was not an isolated case, for elsewhere, illegal and improper behaviour undermined the legitimacy of the patrol committees.

In this regard, the parishes of El Espinal and Colpa (district of Sayapullo) attained deserved notoriety. Here, a group named (purposely, to confound) the Rondas Campesinas Mariateguistas emerged in December 1986 and quickly grew to around eighty members. Structured on patron–client lines rather than the usual *ronda* practice of mass participation and consensual decision-making at hamlet level, this band pursued personal vendettas with an eye to enrichment under the guise of operating a *ronda campesina*. More Mafia than Mariátegui, the band seized livestock, crops and other property belonging to opponents, using the threat of violence, altered smallholding boundaries forcibly and meted out physical punishments in arbitrary fashion to members of rival families. Attacks on the lieutenant governor of El Espinal drove him from office in 1988, while in the same year a local schoolteacher received a beating so harsh that it left him seriously injured. These transgressions remained unpunished due to connivance between village-level caciques and police officers stationed in Sayapullo.[62]

A third factor compounded substantially the difficulties facing *ronderos* during the late 1980s: PCP–SL policy. On penetrating into a new area where *rondas campesinas* existed, *senderista* commanders pressurised the participants to disband their patrols. Henceforth, the guerrillas would suppress rustling and their appointees would administer those other aspects of village life for which the committees had been assuming responsibility. Sendero, its cadres informed the populace, intended to create a New Popular Democratic Republic parallel to that of the Peruvian state; organs of social power outside Party control could not be allowed to continue functioning. Individuals who ignored this directive faced the threat of assassination, as happened to the president of the committee at Otuto (Cajabamba province) and his son. Similar events occurred at the hamlets of Chigden, Chuco, Higosbamba and Pauca. Nervous *ronda* leaders consequently took to spending nights hiding in their maize fields or concealed in makeshift bush shelters on a nearby mountainside.[63] Other activists, through good fortune, managed to avoid being shot. Luck appeared to have deserted a main instigator of the *rondas campesinas* in Licliconga, among the best organ-ised in San Marcos and Cajabamba, who happened to be addressing a meeting to coordinate patrol activities in surrounding hamlets when:

> ... a column of around twelve *senderistas* arrived. Their leader, a robust-looking man in his late twenties, marched to the front of the assembly and shouted out 'What's going on here?' and put a pistol to the head of XXX. He then demanded to know who was speaking and who was in charge. XXX was thinking: 'How do I get out of this mess? I'm really buggered now.' Everybody was really scared and there was a lot of tension. Anyway, the *senderistas* were told that we had organised a meeting of *ronderos* to plan our activities. When their chief found out who was leading the discussion, he said: 'We have heard about you. We have been told that you are a good and honest militant who treats the peasants well. We will not harm you' and lowered his gun. That was a relief! Sendero's commander then ordered that the *rondas* be disbanded. From now on, the Party was going to deal with crime and sort out other problems.[64]

Most *rondas campesinas*, harried from without by hostile elements in the local bureaucracy and the PCP–SL, while simultaneously undermined from within by warranted fear and dishonest behaviour, ceased to function between 1988 and 1990 throughout Cajabamba, San Marcos and the *sierra* of La Libertad. Unlike the situation in Chota and Hualgayoc during the early 1980s, these less 'organic' entities proved unable to confront successfully the substantial pres-sures emanating from guerrilla and state. Illustrative here was the situation encountered in highland La Libertad. Local activists aided by national leaders sent from the Lima-based Confederación Campesina del Perú attempted to promote *rondas campesinas* in the zone and in November 1989 even managed to mobilise the grass roots to hold the *Primer Congreso de Campesinos y Rondas Campesinas* for the province of Santiago de Chuco. The initiative failed to prosper – fear of reprisals kept participation low and no movement became consolidated.[65]

Nevertheless, organisational collapse was not the whole story. Notwithstanding the extremely unfavourable environment, in a few districts where opportunity allowed and a crime wave demanded urgent action to protect peasant livelihoods, villagers strove to establish nightwatch patrols. This scenario arose at Jollucos (district of Cascas) in January 1988 and five months later around the hamlets of Unigambal, Cahuide and Casapampa (province of Santiago de Chuco), where four *ronda* committees were established. On occasions, grass-roots patrollers felt confident – or incensed – enough to move on to the offensive. One such incident arose on 1 February 1990 involving the community of Quinal (Unigambal). After a policeman shot dead a 22-year-old *campesino* he had accused falsely of stealing cattle, approximately 400 *ronderos* stormed the local police station and drove the *guardias* out of the district.

Over the period 1988–92, therefore, a complicated situation could be found regarding grass-roots peasant organisation. In most cases the picture was one of disintegration. A small number of *rondas campesinas* managed to continue operating openly, while others maintained a precarious existence, functioning covertly below the radar of the police, judicial authorities and PCP–SL guerrillas. Overall, however, the *rondas campesinas*, like the CNA-affiliated unions formed in the 1970s and centred on ex-haciendas and provincial peasant federations, did not possess the organisational solidity to counter a relentless expansion of insurgent forces in the Cajabamba–Huamachuco region.

PCP–SL organisational structure: Cajabamba–Huamachuco, 1991–92

Although it was denied in most of the mainstream media, by 1992 the PCP–SL had established an ascendant presence in both town and country. One outward sign of the Party's expanding operational capability came in the form of the increasingly regular blackouts of Trujillo and Andean urban settlements after 1988, as electricity pylons and generating plants became immobilised by dynamite, much of it seized from local mining camps. Secret reports penned by counter-insurgency agents indicate that several cells, each holding from five to eight cadres, had been formed in the towns of Cajabamba, Huamachuco and Santiago de Chuco. Single cells were also operating in San Marcos and Otuzco, despite the urban milieu occupying a 'complementary' status to the rural in the Party's strategic model. Regarding the provinces of Cajabamba and San Marcos, *bases de apoyo* were also identified by the security services in a string of villages and hamlets. Among these figured Santa Rosa–Sitacocha, Choropampa, Chugurbamba, El Carrizal, settlements along the banks of the River Calluán, Totorilla, Las Melgas, Cerro Chugo, Shirac, Quillispampa, Algamarca, Tingo and Pauca. A similar scenario existed in the province of Sánchez Carrión, where agents located *bases* centred on the hamlets of Collona, Vilca, Sanagorán, Suro Grande and Shalcapata, in addition to cells in the main agrarian production cooperatives, to a total of approximately thirty. According to knowledgeable informants, at least ten others remained undetected.

An account written in 1991 by a well informed journalist working in Cajabamba captured the extent of PCP–SL activity in the province at the peak of its influence:

> Fifty per cent of the rural districts … are controlled by 12 of the aforementioned support bases. A further 20 per cent are under threat of becoming so,

while the remaining 30 per cent have been infiltrated by the dynamic activity of both the urban and rural cells. The town houses eight support bases that are centred in the educational establishments – secondary schools and the technical college.⁶⁶

Official and unofficial sources consequently indicate that by the early 1990s the organisation was pushing through the party-building dimension of its *batir el campo* strategy with no small measure of success. It had enrolled members from a wide range of ages and occupational backgrounds: peasants, artisans, petty traders, casual labourers, schoolteachers, public employees, ex-members of the armed forces and police, young people and university students.

Working from the lower echelons of the organisation upwards, participants in the base groups (most of whom were not full Party members), provided accommodation, storage facilities, food and similar back-up facilities to cadres, in addition to assisting with recruitment. Those who impressed were selected to staff a number of specialist units. A logistical support cell was charged with collating information for transmitting up the chain of command, arranging the storage of arms, explosives and medical supplies as well as providing secure hiding places. Cadres allocated propaganda responsibilities engaged in wall-painting, producing leaflets, organising *escuelas populares* and recruitment. A third section provided material assistance and legal advice to combatants and their families (*Socorro Popular*), while cadres with the appropriate skills were assigned to a specialist assassination squad (see Figure 1). Members of these groups fed into the *Fuerza Local* (Local Force) – the district-level guerrilla company, which organised *paros armados* (armed strikes) aimed at closing down trading in neighbouring towns. They also mounted ambushes against the army and police and engaged in acts of sabotage (dynamiting bridges and electricity pylons, blocking roads, etc.), as well as participating in the takeover of villages and farms. Cadres used one pseudonym when engaging in these types of propaganda and other activities related to the general population, but used another inside the Party in their effort to confuse the police and minimise detection. A rigid cell structure was another aspect of this strategy.

Elements of the *Fuerza Local* liaised closely with the *Comité Zonal* (Zonal Committee), which comprised middle-ranking cadres who planned political and armed activities throughout a province and worked hand in hand with the *Fuerza Principal* (Principal Force), the main detachment of the PCP–SL's Popular Guerrilla Army operating in the region. Militarily, the *Fuerza Principal* was the best-prepared and equipped element of the Party. Following Mao's prescription, their brief was to operate with a high degree of mobility, striking unexpectedly in one locality and withdrawing quickly to a predetermined location before the security services could react. Over the late 1980s and early 1990s, the most utilised retreat of this platoon centred on Cachicadán, San José de Porcón and surrounding parishes in the province of Santiago de Chuco. When under serious pressure from the army and police, however, it would split into two or three columns in an effort to evade contact under disadvantageous condi-

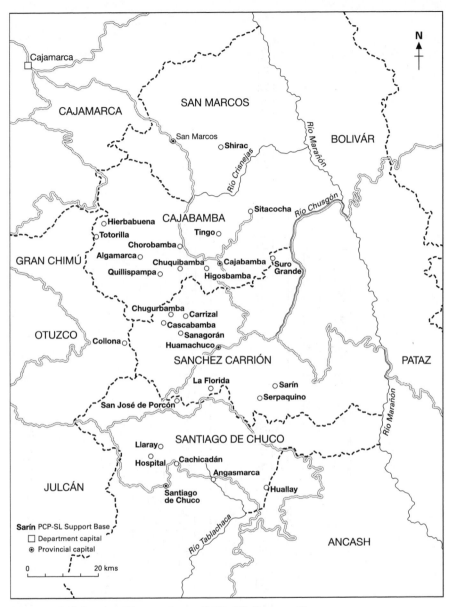

Map 4 *Cajabamba–Huamachuco: PCP–SL Support Bases, c.1992*

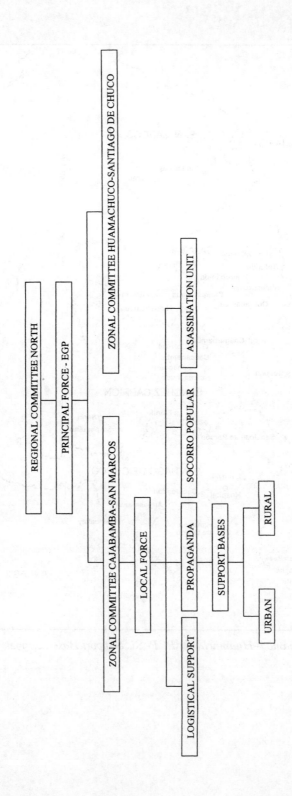

Figure 1 *PCP–SL Organisational Structure: Cajabamba–Huamachuco, 1990*

tions. According to army intelligence personnel engaged in writing the infamous *Plan Verde* (Green Plan), designed to establish an authoritarian military–civilian regime, the PCP–SL's core guerrilla troop in the zone in early 1990 numbered thirty tested combatants. Their assessment of the capability of this and similar guerrilla detachments concluded that: 'They are well trained and disciplined. They possess a high level of morale and are very ideologically committed. Their training takes place on the battlefield.' The *Fuerza Local*, by contrast, 'is not capable of sustaining prolonged engagements with the armed forces', while the support bases 'are made up of local inhabitants dedicated principally to logistical activities, simple intelligence-gathering and delivering messages'. The report also opined that 'pursuing its aim of operating along the whole length of the Andes chain', in the *sierra* of La Libertad, Sendero 'is increasing its actions'.[67]

Responsibility for implementing Party strategy lay with the Northern Regional Committee.[68] While the base of the organisational pyramid in Cajabamba–Huamachuco was overwhelmingly local in origin, after the detention of home-grown peasant leaders during 1983–84, high-ranking positions were usually allocated to trusted cadres drafted in from Ayacucho, Lima or the northern coast. From mid-1984 until his capture in central Lima on 11 June 1988 when attending a national coordinating meeting, Osmán Morote, Central Committee member and long-standing comrade of Abimael Guzmán, headed this organ. It was incumbent on Morote and his fellow *mandos* (commissars) to educate the membership about the PCP–SL's political platform, strategy and tactics ('Gonzalo thought'). In turn, from the *serranos* they learnt about the local social scene, the prevailing power networks and kinship relations, in addition to the location and content of conflicts. The outsiders provided basic military training in the art of ambush, how to conduct attacks and ordered retreats, the planning of assaults on urban targets and the use of firearms. Improving physical fitness and developing a detailed knowledge of local topography comprised other essential tasks. Recruits consequently had to endure long marches through the mountains, surviving on basic rations, getting accustomed to living outdoors exposed to the elements and surviving the cold Andean nights.

PCP–SL numerical strength in Cajabamba–Huamachuco is impossible to gauge with any degree of accuracy, since personnel levels fluctuated constantly due to capture, combat loss, desertion and the exigencies of particular operational demands that might require the drafting of extra cadres into the highlands from the littoral or jungle. Documents seized along with Osmán Morote nevertheless provide a partial snapshot of the Party's shape at the moment of his arrest. They suggested that EGP strength in Huamachuco stood at fifteen combatants, augmented by eighty-one centred on Cajabamba–San Marcos. In terms of class extraction, the La Libertad detachment was recorded as being comprised of eleven 'peasants' and four 'petty bourgeois' combatants (i.e., artisans, informal sector earners, teachers, students and similar occupations). For Cajamarca, sixty-four were categorised as 'peasants', two as 'workers' and fifteen as 'petty bourgeois'. Three *mandos políticos* and an equal number of *mandos militares* were operating in the *sierra* of La Libertad, divided equally in terms of background between 'peasants' and 'petty bourgeois'. Three *mandos* directed the insurgency in the southern provinces of Cajamarca department, all of 'petty bourgeois' roots. Regarding gender, two and five women were enrolled in the EGP in La Libertad and Cajamarca respectively, while two women occupied leadership roles in each zone.[69]

Recorded levels of detentions, casualties and desertions between 1993 and 1996, as well as classified police reports, suggest that the true number of individuals connected to the Party apparatus at all levels was considerably larger than the Morote documentation indicated and ran into the hundreds – even when taking into consideration that not all those arrested and killed were guilty as charged, or indeed, real combatants. Uncertainty about its size notwithstanding, what cannot be disputed is the capacity of the insurgent organisation to expand the spread and scale of its guerrilla campaign. Police assessments recognised that: 'since 1984 in the provinces of XXX and YYY, PCP–SL terrorist activity has been increasing progressively, both in quantitative and qualitative terms', with 1992 representing a high point, when the whole region was declared a *Zona Convulsionada* ('Lawless Zone') and month-long *Estado de Emergencia* (States of Emergency) decrees affected regularly the region's provinces.[70] In police jargon, the Cajabamba–Huamachuco zone was considered *'altamente roja'* (deeply red). Between 1984 and the end of 1992, some 675 guerrilla actions were recognised officially in the provinces of Cajabamba and San Marcos, having causing 166 deaths among the civilian population, the police and the military. In La Libertad, a total of 569 recorded subversive incidents occurred from 1980 to 1987, after which the figure shot to over 1,200 by 1992. By no means all guerrilla actions, especially those conducted in outlying rural districts, reached the ears of the authorities. Another indication of developing Party strength was that by 1992 the single EGP column of thirty combatants identified in the Green Plan compiled in 1990 had divided into two detachments, each of a similar size.

Significantly, Party growth was able to occur over these years despite regular losses, for although they were on the defensive overall, the police and the army managed to mount a number of successful operations. Aside from the capture of valuable cadres such as Félix Calderón and Osmán Morote, and the frequent removal of one or two members through detention or death, a number of pivotal counter-insurgency actions deserve mention. One setback in the vulnerable build-up phase of the PCP–SL's armed campaign took place during its initial assault on the SAIS Tahuantinsuyo (28 November 1982). On this occasion, the police managed to shoot three and capture a further fifteen (presumably greenhorn) insurgents, thus decimating the Party's first EGP detachment operating in the northern highlands (see Chapter Three). A second significant blow happened on 24 June 1984 when a police platoon intercepted a column of fifty *senderistas* at Choquizongo shortly after they had destroyed the nearby police post at Huaranchal. In the ensuing confrontation, fifteen insurgents were killed, including *'la Gringa'* (also known as *'camarada* Norma'), the PCP–SL's *mando militar* in the Cajabamba–San Marcos area.[71] Another telling reversal took place on 8 December 1989, when a guerrilla contingent holed up in the hamlet of Yerba Buena, approximately one hour's hike from Calluán, found the house it was occupying surrounded by a police patrol. Induced by the heavy rain to stay put, the insurgents committed the elementary mistake of remaining in the same hideout for three days. In the ensuing firefight, at least five *senderistas* died, included among them Zonal Commander '*camarada* Patty'. Her demise represented a major loss to the local apparatus, for like *la Gringa*, this guerrilla leader had developed into something of a cult figure throughout Cajabamba and San Marcos, with a reputation for being *simpática* (likeable) but extremely ruthless. 'Patty' was admired and feared in equal measure: as one informant commented, she could be 'sweet and friendly, while at the same time hard-hearted and not afraid to kill. She was a very *macha* young woman.'[72]

A third important reversal occurred in August 1991. A series of assaults during preceding weeks culminated in an hour-long ambush of a military convoy in the vicinity of Cachicadán that left nine soldiers dead and fifteen wounded (12 August). In reprisal for this and other attacks that had caused sizeable losses among the army and police, a three-day operation named '*Tenazas*' ('Pincers') was launched across the conflict zone. One police platoon closed in on a PCP–SL refuge and training camp in a remote corner of the former hacienda La Pauca (district of José Sabogal). After exchanges lasting several hours and with PCP–SL forces running low on ammunition, the insurgents tried to actuate a controlled disengagement, but were intercepted by police reinforcements, the outcome being the capture of one *mando* and twenty-six combatants.[73] In a parallel operation centred on Cachicadán, soldiers (aided by a helicopter gunship) succeeded in locating and engaging the column responsible for the 12 August ambush, killing five out of an insurgent band more than twenty strong. A follow-up exercise launched against a rebel base in La Pauca (1 October 1991) left six *senderistas* dead and an undisclosed number wounded.

In addition to carrying out a number of efficacious attacks on the PCP–SL's military arm, the police managed to deactivate part of its political structure. The capture of a young peasant man from Araqueda in May 1989 provided information that permitted the arrest of several local cadres; their caches of arms and explosives were also impounded. According to official sources, that same year eleven *senderista* cells were disbanded in La Libertad and the neighbouring provinces of Bolívar and Pataz, while in April 1990 eleven cadres belonging to the Party's apparatus in the town of Huamachuco were caught. Intelligence data extracted from individuals detained during the August 1991 'Pincers' manoeuvre also led to the lifting of PCP–SL sympathisers settled in La Pauca, Shirac and adjacent districts. These losses in manpower and materials were, however, more than compensated by a steady flow of new recruits, with the result that between 1990 and 1992 the Party appeared to be pushing through its party-building programme effectively.

Conclusion

When the Peruvian army was belatedly directed to combat PCP–SL insurgents in December 1982, the then Minister of Defence, the hard-line retired general, Luis Cisneros, apparently informed his staff that: 'This will resemble a turkey shoot'.[74] A tendency to belittle developing guerrilla political and military capabilities characterised many sectors of the Peruvian establishment throughout the 1980s, to the extent that even respected independent and normally critical elements of the media postulated that 'Sendero does not have popular support'.[75] The true situation over much of the national territory was far more complex. For multiple reasons – ranging from gross failings on the part of key state agencies to the implementation of policies attractive to sectors of the highland population and a willingness to employ armed force to instil fear and secure compliance – the PCP–SL had managed, by 1992, to construct an apparatus in Cajabamba–Huamachuco that far exceeded its prospects when Party 'reconstruction' commenced with a handful of militants in 1979.

Roots had been laid down among various sectors of the population, with over thirty *bases de apoyo* having been established in town and country. The 'agrarian revolutionary war' seemed to appeal to groups of resource-scarce *campesinos*, while among elements of the urban population, the lack of adequate employment opportunities and socio-economic chaos afflicting Peru in the late 1980s appeared to enhance the attractiveness of Sendero's radical rejection of the status quo. Under pressure from guerrilla advances, mainstream political parties, peasant organisations, the Church and similar organs of civil society had all but ceased to function in the countryside. The PCP–SL had also forced itself to the centre of the local political stage, the apparent efficiency and sacrifice of its cadres standing in favourable contrast to the incompetence and self-seeking corruption that tainted an overwhelming majority of Peru's political class, most public institutions and the bureaucrats employed in them.

A supposed 'turkey shoot' consequently evolved into a much more labyrinthine affair than Cisneros and others anticipated. By early 1992, the insurgent organisation was operating both politically and militarily over an ever-widening swathe of territory and ostensibly implementing its *batir el campo* strategy according to plan. Employing Mao's tactical formula of 'swift advances and withdrawals' to good effect, it had driven state agencies and their representatives out of most rural areas and established, if not wholly 'liberated', at least 'semi-liberated' zones where government fiat held less sway than that of local guerrilla commanders. Yet three years later, the insurgent organisation was in serious retreat. By December 1995 the state had succeeded in gaining the initiative in both the political and military spheres through inflicting telling damage on the PCP–SL's apparatus and diminishing its offensive potential. It is to a consideration of this sea change in fortunes that we now turn.

References

1   The subprefect's comments were reported in *La Industria*, 7 April 1982. Exhibiting an equally relaxed attitude, police commanders in Huamachuco opined confidently that 'the guerrillas will be captured any day now', declaring the province 'to be under our control'. *La Industria*, 8 April 1982; 11 April 1982.

2   Ibid., 8 May 1986.

3   *Caretas* 1071, 21 August 1989.

4   *La Industria*, 6 January 1986; 8 January 1986.

5   Ibid., 4 August 1988.

6   *La Industria*, 26 August 1989; *Caretas* 1071, 21 August 1989. Although it was first reported that the mayor, Ricardo Woolcot, had been assassinated by the PCP–SL, it later transpired that he had committed suicide after a spat with his girlfriend. No doubt the psychological stress arising from his public position played a part in this unfortunate episode.

7   *La Industria*, 1 July 1989.

8   Ibid., 27 April 1990. Earlier (9 January 1990), the *aprista* leader had survived an assassination attempt despite being hit by two bullets.

9   Ibid., 7 November 1989.

10   Policía Nacional del Perú (hereafter PNP), 'Apreciación de la situación subversiva en …', mimeo 1996. To protect the informant's identity, the full title of this document cannot be provided.

11   Interview # 5, 26 March 1997.

12   PNP, 'Apreciación de la situación subversiva en …', mimeo 1996.

13   *La Industria*, 22 April 1986; 19 September 1986. One inspection, conducted by the governor and priest of Cachicadán in April 1986, found that in a local school only four of the nine teachers on the payroll had turned up for work. In another school, 40 per cent of the registered pupils were attending classes, while in a neighbouring institution this fell to a mere 5 per cent. *La Industria*, 12 April 1986.

14   *El Comercio*, 2 October 1987.

15   'Banco Agrario y violencia terrorista en Cajabamba', mimeo, Cajabamba, August 1990.

16   Background information is provided in John Crabtree, *Peru Under García: an Opportunity Lost*, Basingstoke, Macmillan, 1992; and Carol Graham, *Peru's APRA: Parties, Politics, and the Elusive Quest for Democracy*, Boulder, CO, Lynne Rienner, 1992.

17   Interview with counter-insurgency operative, Cajamarca, 12 April 1997. One intelligence document described the insurgents' operational procedures when undertaking 'Guerrilla actions in the rural theatre' as: '*Surveillance:* camouflaged in the selected area, wearing dark clothes, dominating the panorama. *Containment:* when attacked, they come out shooting. During daytime, they hold at a distance of 200 metres; at night or under cloudy conditions, from five to fifteen metres. *Scouts:* when government forces are detected, they keep a distance of 300 metres; at night or under cloudy conditions, they close in from five to fifteen metres'. PNP, 'Apreciación de la situación de inteligencia en …', mimeo 1993.

18   Interview # 6, 27 March 1997.

19   Interview # 7, 27 March 1997. That this phrase is quoted elsewhere indicates that news of the event had spread throughout the countryside and, as far as the rural population was concerned, became widely used to epitomise the police's half-hearted response to PCP–SL attacks. See Dirk Kruijt, *Entre Sendero y los militares: seguridad y relaciones cívico–militares, 1950–1990*, Barcelona, Editorial Robles, 1991,

p. 96.

20   Interview # 8, 27 March 1997.

21   Interview # 24, 14 April 1997.

22   Interview # 4, 26 March 1997.

23   PNP, 'Apreciación de la situación de inteligencia en ...', mimeo 1993. Information given in Chapter Three shows that this assessment contained inaccuracies. More important than the inexactitudes is the police mindset indicated in the text.

24   Much of the expansion in coca production was driven by Perciles Sánchez (alias 'El Padrino'), the infamous head of a powerful drug-dealing clan based in Trujillo, whose involvement in the trade increased post-1975. As part of a 'settling of accounts' between rival bands, he was assassinated in 1991. Interestingly, decades earlier this zone had been an important centre of bandit and montonera activity, suggesting a long-standing ambivalent attitude towards the state among a sector of the province's population.

25   La Industria, 17 September 1989. In 1986, a police sweep reputedly captured 8 kilo-grams of pasta básica de cocaine (cocaine paste) and led to the destruction of 5,000 kilos of coca leaves, while in April 1988 some 20 kilos of pasta básica were impounded – small amounts, considering the scale of local production. La Industria, 13 January 1986; 2 April 1986; 22 April 1988; 23 April 1990.

26   Ibid., 30 March 1986.

27   Ibid., 22 March 1990.

28   Ibid., 17 September 1989; 12 October 1989.

29   Ibid., 13 May 1985; 14 May 1985. In response, a human rights committee was estab-lished in Huamachuco and a monument was raised in their memory. The police officers concerned both received prison sentences of twenty-five years.

30   This event was reported in 'Banco Agrario y violencia terrorista en Cajabamba', mimeo, Cajabamba, August 1990.

31   Interview with counter-insurgency operative, 12 April 1997.

32   Ibid. In this regard, the PCP–SL copied the experience of the Communist Party of China (CPC), although the connection remained unknown until recently. When, in 1941, the poverty-stricken Yan'an base area experienced a crippling financial crisis caused by the KMT and Japanese army blockade, permission was granted to produce and export a 'special product', namely opium, to zones controlled by their enemies. While consumption within Yan'an was outlawed effectively, the historical association of the opium trade with imperialist domination made involvement a highly sensitive issue. Around 15 January 1945, Mao undertook a 'self-criticism' and 'confessed that the CPC had committed two grave mistakes in its history that could be excused only by circumstances. The first was taking Tibetan barley without consent during the Long March. If the party had stuck to its rule of military disci-pline, the whole Red Army would have perished. The second forgivable mistake was planting "a certain thing".' After this, the 'necessary evil' was no longer deemed necessary and was banned. See Chen Yung-fa, 'The Blooming Poppy Under the Red Sun: the Yan'an Way and the Opium Trade', in Tony Saich and Hans van de Ven (eds.), New Perspectives on the Chinese Communist Revolution, New York, M.E. Sharpe, 1994, pp. 263–98.

33   Quoted in Expreso, Special Supplement, 7 June 1994, p. 18.

34   '¡Desarrollar la guerra popular sirviendo a la revolución mundial!', in Arce (ed.), Guerra popular en el Perú, pp. 273–76.

35   Quoted in Oiga, 28 October 1985. In the 'interview of the century' published in the PCP–SL mouthpiece El Diario, Abimael Guzmán boasted that: 'The Party's policy has been to intervene around this problem [of land]. Implementing land invasions

has been a crucial issue we have addressed, which has been especially important in the department of La Libertad. There, over 200,00 hectares have been repartitioned and more than 160,000 people mobilised. Of all the actions we have undertaken, this is the largest in terms of the masses we have mobilised.' *El Diario*, 24 July 1988, p. 37. The number of individuals claimed to be involved in land takeovers represents a gross exaggeration.

36 *La Industria*, 25 May 1982.
37 Ibid., 4 July 1982.
38 *Caretas* 766, 19 September 1983, pp. 36–38.
39 *La Industria*, 24 January 1986. Also see *La Industria*, 24 February 1988; 6 January 1989.
40 Ibid., 6 June 1986.
41 See 'Informe técnico sobre la Cooperativa Agraria de Trabajadores José Santos Chocano', Instituto Nacional de Cooperativas, mimeo 22, March 1994.
42 *La Industria*, 5 June 1986; *La República*, 7 June 1986. This incident was reported most accurately in *La Industria*.
43 *El Comercio*, 31 July, 1987. Although Paredes was reported killed in action, local *senderistas* claim he was captured, tortured and then executed in the Chaquicocha counter-insurgency base. See Chapter Five, note 95.
44 'Banco Agrario y violencia terrorista en Cajabamba', mimeo, Cajabamba, August 1990.
45 'I heard that the men were a pair of thieves. It became common knowledge around here. Instead of trying to work for the betterment of the Jocos people, those rascals only wanted to grab the farm's assets for themselves. They were very greedy and thought it would be easy to dupe the *campesinos*, especially given all the confusion caused by the *terrucos* in the area. But they got it wrong. People soon worked out what was happening and that they were being cheated. When Sendero found out, their days were numbered. They died as a result of their own stupidity ... People believed that they had caused their own death.' Interview # 23, 14 April 1997.
46 The occupation of Rumi Rumi is recorded in 'Banco Agrario y violencia terrorista en Cajabamba'. 1 *arroba* = 11 kilograms.
47 J. Cortegana, *Sendero en Cajabamba: Cachachi*, Trujillo, Artes Gráficas Richard Burgos, 2001, pp. 73–74. Focused on Cachachi, this essay provides valuable data on events in this and the surrounding districts.
48 Interview # 7, 26 March 1997.
49 Interview # 9, 30 March 1997.
50 Events in Quillispampa are detailed in Cortegana, *Sendero en Cajabamba*, pp. 68–71. From 1998 to 1992, local PCP–SL commanders appeared to be striving to push through a strategy akin to Mao's policy of 'advancing in a series of waves'. Localities where this was perceivable included Lluchubamba–Sitacocha–Marcamachay; Cachachi–Algamarca–Sayapullo; Cachicadán–Angasmarca–Mollebamba; and Sarín–Curgos–Marcabal.
51 On similar incidents in Bambamarca and Chota, see Starn, *Nightwatch*, pp. 82–83. Events in Porcón were reported in *La Industria*, 16 March 1982.
52 One such case concerned Alfredo Arroyo, a rustler operating in the vicinity of Muchamarca in Otuzco province. Having been captured by the police and placed in jail, Arroyo's liberty was ordered by the district judge, much to the alarm of local agriculturalists. *La Industria*, 4 February 1988. The practice of taking stolen cattle to the littoral and returning to the highlands with livestock lifted from coastal valleys had been occurring since at least the nineteenth century. Farmers from all districts in Otuzco had been pressing the authorities to crack down on rustling since the early

1980s, with no success. See *La Industria*, 11 July 1982.

53   One surreal but tragic case of collective hysteria over 'witchcraft' occurred on 27 January 1985 in the village of Aricapampa (province of Sánchez Carrión). After being accused of practising illegal medicine and administering poisoned potions, Bacilia Layza was thrown in jail and mistreated for eight days before being taken to the village square and tied to a tree. She was then doused with petrol and set alight in the presence of the district governor, lieutenant governor, local Juez de Primera Instancia and more than 300 bystanders. Twenty of the perpetrators were later tried for this murder, when the provincial prosecutor demanded 500 years' imprisonment for the accused. *La Industria*, 12 June 1986.

54   Manrique opined that the PCP–SL clampdown on antisocial behaviour gained 'unanimous acceptance' in the Central Andean department of Junín. See Manrique, 'La década de la violencia', p. 157.

55   Interview # 12, 4 April 1997.

56   This incident was reported in *La República*, 22 July 1990. From this area, stolen livestock were transported down the Chicama Valley for sale in the Casa Grande sugar plantation or the town of Pacasmayo.

57   Interview # 7, 27 March 1997.

58   Interview # 5, 26 March 1997.

59   Ibid.

60   Between 1986 and 1990, the MRTA also conducted sporadic guerrilla actions in Cajamarca's northern provinces of Cutervo, Chota and Hualgayoc. After 1990, its activities intensified in the provinces of Celendín (Cajamarca), Bolívar and Pataz (La Libertad). This development is discussed in Chapter Five.

61   An inkling of attitudes towards the *rondas campesinas* among the security services can be gleaned from the following intelligence document: 'Taking advantage of their marginalisation and subsistence problems, elements of APRA and the extreme left have organised the peasantry into "*Rondas Campesinas*". These are well structured and undertake actions of Marxist–Leninist indoctrination, with a tendency to support subversion.' PNP, 'Apreciación de la situación de inteligencia en ...', mimeo 1993 [italics as in the original]. While police intimidation increased as the civil war intensified between 1990 and 1992, relations between the *rondas campesinas* and the Guardia Civil, had been strained since the mid-1980s, if not before. One case concerned the patrol organisations established in the *caseríos* of La Manzanilla–La Grama–Campo Alegre in April 1985. By the following year, *campesinos* who occupied official positions (such as Melquiades Arias) found themselves threatened by the police counter-insurgency battalion stationed nearby at Chaquicocha. Grass-roots activists suspected that the justice of the peace in La Manzanilla, police officers, lawyers in San Marcos and local rustlers were conducting a campaign against them, using terrorism as a cover, to protect their illegal earnings. Hostility from such an influential array of forces provoked the collapse of the La Manzanilla and neighbouring patrols, a development that worked to the PCP–SL's advantage. See, 'Encuentro provincial de rondas campesinas de San Marcos', mimeo, 1987.

62   These activities became something of a scandal, not just in highland La Libertad, but also in Trujillo. For reports on the Rondas Campesinas Mariateguistas, see *La Industria*, 4 June 1988; 20 June 1988; 9 July 1989. Later, the military converted this band into a Civil Defence Committee, although enhanced official recognition failed to produce a lessening of abuse.

63   One activist related his experience as follows: 'After 1988 things got really tough. I was getting a load of hassle from the *aprista* subprefect and the cops. Matters became

much more complicated when rumours spread that Sendero wanted to repress our organisation and *camarada* Patty was going to deal with us. So I began to take extra precautions. Whenever I went to town, I made sure I was with a group of neighbours. I kept a low profile, did my business quickly, kept away from the main square and left by the back path ... At home I kept an eye out for strangers moving about and started to sleep nights away from the house. I hid in the field, where I had buried a pistol just in case something occurred.' Interview # 5, 26 March 1997.

64   Interview # 12, 4 April 1997.

65   The ability to sustain grass-roots organisations in the countryside was further undermined by intimidation targeted against members of the legal left. An assassination unit run by army intelligence issued death threats to known IU militants in Santiago de Chuco, which, in order to obscure its activities used the name of the APRA-run paramilitary hit squad, the Comando Rodrigo Franco. See Uceda, *Muerte en el Pentagonito*, p. 212.

66   'Sendero Luminoso en el norte del país', quoted in Kruijt, *Entre Sendero y los militares*, p. 96.

67   Quotes taken from 'Plan Verde: apreciación de inteligencia', Lima, mimeo March 1990. Elaborated by an elite intelligence unit within the Peruvian army, the *Plan Verde* (Green Plan) aimed to overcome the corruption and incompetence of the Belaunde and García administrations, eliminate the threat posed by PCP–SL and MRTA guerrillas and reverse what its authors considered to be the 'social decomposition' of Peru. In its original version, the document envisaged a military coup to be launched in May 1990 to torpedo the anticipated election of a second APRA government allied to IU. In its place, a military–civilian regime committed to internal 'order', social discipline and 'national regeneration' would be installed. This authoritarian regime, the *Plan Verde* authors argued, would remain in power during 'fifteen to twenty years, for a whole generation, in order to create a new Peruvian man'. The plan contained strong fascist overtones. A 'GESTAPO' style security apparatus needed to be created in order to undertake the 'HISTORICAL NECESSITY' of applying the death penalty to eliminate the 'nation's enemies'. Furthermore, it was considered that Peru possessed a 'surplus population' that needed to be brought under control through a massive sterilisation campaign targeted at the poor and indigenous groups. During the 1990s, aspects of the Plan were adopted by the Fujimori government. [Words in capital letters as they appear in the original document.]

68   Other Regional Committees existed for Lima; the Central Andes (departments of Pasco and Junín); the 'Principal Zone' (consisting of Ayacucho, Huancavelica and Apurímac); the 'Eastern Zone' (comprised of Huánuco, San Martín and Ucayalí departments); and the Southern Andes (Cusco, Puno and Arequipa).

69   Data published in *Caretas* 1012, 27 June 1988. Questions must exist about the reliability of these figures. It seems incongruous that six commissars would be stationed in the *sierra* of La Libertad alongside a smaller guerrilla detachment to that based in Cajabamba–San Marcos, which possessed half as many of these key cadres. That these statistics were purposefully falsified in order to mislead in case of capture cannot be discounted. At the time of Morote's arrest, it was rumoured that his whereabouts had been passed to the police as a result of a policy disagreement with Guzmán – as yet an unsubstantiated allegation. Morote was sentenced to twenty years' imprisonment in November 1990, the punishment being raised to life imprisonment following a second trial conducted in April 1996.

70   PNP, 'Apreciación de la situación de inteligencia en ...', mimeo 1993.

71   Some dispute exists regarding the number and manner of these deaths. According

to *senderistas* formerly active in Cajabamba–Huamachuco detained in the Huacariz maximum-security prison, some seventeen guerrillas were assassinated after surrendering to a combined force of police and a band of armed cooperative members led by Angel Vargas. See the letter signed by twenty-seven 'Political Prisoners and Prisoners of War' in Huacariz to President Valentín Paniagua, 11 July 2001.

72 Interview # 13, 4 April 1997. In common with the situation found in other regions, the PCP–SL apparatus in Cajabamba–Huamachuco contained a high proportion of women occupying leadership positions. Following in the footsteps of *'la Gringa'* and 'Patty', in 1996 the *mando militar* attached to the Fuerza Principal in Cajabamba–San Marcos was 'Cristina', while according to counter-insurgency sources her counterpart in Huamachuco–Santiago de Chuco went under the pseudonym of 'Lucia' or 'Andrea'. On this issue and the wider question of the Party's appeal to women, see Robin Kirk, *Grabado en piedra: las mujeres de Sendero Luminoso*, Lima, Instituto de Estudios Peruanos, 1993.

73 Interview # 5, 26 March 1997 and # 7, 27 March 1997. This clash was also reported in *La República*, 13 August 1991; 14 August 1991.

74 Quoted in Uceda, *Muerte en el Pentagonito*, p. 34. Cisneros was the intellectual author of the Green Plan blueprint to establish a 'militarised democracy' after the 1990 general election.

75 *Caretas* 1084, 20 November 1989, p. 34.

CHAPTER FIVE

Seeming Victory, Concealed Defeat: Guerrilla Retreat, 1992–97

Intensification of the civil war throughout the Andean chain, reinforced by a growing military presence in the Huallaga Valley and other *ceja de selva* areas, along with a marked increase in guerrilla attacks in Lima and valleys lying immediately to the north and south of the capital, gave the impression that the PCP–SL was advancing on all fronts between 1988 and 1992. For the first time, informed political observers started to moot the possibility that the insurgency might triumph. Among cadres, the party slogan *'Presidente Gonzalo: garantía de triunfo'* ('President Gonzalo: guarantor of victory') gained resonance, as indicated in May 1988 by Isidoro Nunja, *mando político* in the Chancay and Huaral Valleys. After being arrested following an assault against the Andahuasi sugar- and fruit-producing cooperative located adjacent to Huaura on the coast north of Lima, Nunja declared that opinion among *senderistas* held that the Peruvian state's collapse would occur inside the next two to three years – the first notable departure from the official party line that the 'protracted people's war' could extend over several decades.[1]

Further evidence that the PCP–SL held an audacious, if rash, view of its prospects and was telescoping its original timetable for implementing insurrection appeared in May 1991. Through its mouthpiece, *El Diario*, the Central Committee announced that the organisation had moved from a situation of 'strategic defence' (the first main phase within the PCP–SL's military schema) and was embarking upon the period of 'strategic equilibrium' vis-à-vis the Peruvian state and its armed forces. This decision (coming out of an action plan adopted in 1989 and a Central Committee document approved in February 1991) was based on an assessment that the insurgents were in the process of attaining a position of political and military parity with the state. The 'old order' was crumbling fast, while the PCP–SL was growing numerically. Insurgent forces held the initiative in both the political and military spheres; guerrilla activity in the countryside had reached a stage where it could not be eradicated. 'Liberated zones' dominated by the Party were consequently expanding, as was its control over people and resources. As a result, the PCP–SL's organs of government in rural districts were being strengthened, along with EGP membership, which was moving to a position where the rebel army could assemble greater contingents and engage the state's forces in larger-scale and more open, conventional-style confrontations. The political and military balance was such that a 'war of movement' could commence, which (following Mao's prescription) would eventually usher in the 'strategic offensive' phase of the conflict, leading to the collapse of the state and the seizure of power.[2]

Hyperbolical leadership pronouncements and reality stood at variance, however. Outside the coca-producing Huallaga Valley, the Party's EGP remained at a clear disadvantage to the army in terms of both fighters and fire-power, making talk of involvement in set battles premature if not suicidal. Furthermore, despite presenting an aura of being unstoppable, of devising care-fully laid strategic plans that were methodically implemented, the PCP–SL confronted several rapidly mounting problems after 1988. In a number of high-land locations (particularly in and around the department of Ayacucho), a large proportion of the rural population had fled their homes, with the result that the 'river' was running dry, so leaving the 'fish' more exposed. To complicate matters, the Party was experiencing an erosion of its social base among those villagers who chose not to migrate – a development stimulated in no small degree by its unsophisticated view of Andean rural society. As noted in Chapter One, after initially supporting sanctions against corrupt officials, rustlers, dishonest merchants and kulaks who had prospered as a result of Velasco's agrarian reform, many peasants in Ayacucho and its environs began to resent and then rebel against the insurgents.[3] Attempts by the PCP–SL to impose a 'natural economy' on villagers, as part of a strategy of encircling and starving the towns, threatened the reproduction of numerous household economies and kindled opposition, as did demands to supply EGP detachments with food and conscripts. Anti-guerrilla sentiment was further fuelled by the arbitrary removal of established community leaders and their replacement with younger PCP–SL cadres, who were held in lower esteem and invariably acted in an authoritarian fashion. Hostility also arose because of the extreme violence that the PCP–SL employed when implementing its *batir el campo* policy. So while from the vantage of Lima the insurgency appeared to be expanding rapidly, the situation confronting rebel commanders operating in the mountains had become far more complex.

One of the first commentators to grasp the implications of this unfolding situ-ation was Raúl González, who in mid-1990 and early 1992 flagged several strategic problems facing guerrilla forces, encapsulating them aptly in the phrase 'Sendero grows but does not develop'.[4] How do these trends occurring else-where in the Andes compare with events in Cajabamba and Huamachuco after 1992?

Tension between peasant 'river' and Maoist 'fish': political factors

Crucially for transforming guerrilla fortunes in the northern *sierra*, the PCP–SL started to encounter limits to the 'support' its activities received from a majority of the rural population, and, by the early 1990s, engendered growing opposition as it strove to move the conflict to 'a higher level of struggle'. A similar situation arose to that found by Berg in the department of Apurímac. Individuals from various walks of life voiced broad agreement with the PCP–SL's overall goal of restructuring a society that condemned most of the region's inhabitants to desperate poverty and silently applauded the sanction of thievery, official corruption and other types of behaviour similarly deemed delinquent. A significant jump nevertheless existed between such passive 'sympathy' and higher levels of commitment (e.g., from providing transient insurgents with food and shelter, hiding propaganda and weapons, to eventually joining a Party cell or engaging in armed actions).[5]

Interview data indicates that reservations in the political sphere – broadly defined – centred on three issues. First, numerous inhabitants in the Cajabamba–Huamachuco region failed to cross the divide between 'passive' and 'active' involvement, in part because they remained unconvinced about the long-term viability of the *senderista* revolutionary project. Even at the zenith of insurrectionary activity, many people simply never believed in a guerrilla victory. This sentiment was expressed succinctly by one *minifundista* in the province of San Marcos:

> How were they ever going to beat the army? They told us that the army would be defeated. OK, the *terrucos* were tough and possessed the advantage of surprise, so they could give the police the run-around and take them on. But I've been in the army and know the score. We knew that the army would eventually have to come in and that they would have *serrano* (highland) conscripts and better arms. Then Sendero would have a real fight on its hands and be at a disadvantage.[6]

Incredulity about guerrilla claims clearly surfaces in the following statement:

> The *senderistas* said that they were winning the struggle and, if we gave support, would protect us against the forces of repression. But who could believe that? Their column circulating in San Marcos and Condebamba consisted of around fifteen to twenty people. Not all of them possessed modern weapons and some of them looked like weedy townies … Their main concern was to avoid direct combat with the military and police, so how were they going to protect us? Only a very naïve person could believe that![7]

Disquiet regarding the long-term prospects of the PCP–SL and the impact of guerrilla activity in the zone was heightened by an awareness of events occurring in other regions of Peru, particularly Ayacucho. Via the radio, newspapers, conversations held on Sunday when attending market and networks formed by the *rondas campesinas*, word spread throughout the region that further south the armed forces were operating a 'scorched-earth' policy and had perpetrated a number of massacres. Word about the fate of well-known personalities such as Félix Calderón and Roberto Barrios during the June 1986 prison disturbances also travelled throughout the countryside. For its part, the PCP–SL was acting in an equally ruthless fashion, the outcome being that peasants were caught in the crossfire and human rights violations took place on a grand scale. If such a bloody scenario was to be avoided in the northern highlands, the implication was that the civil war should not be allowed to escalate. One way to achieve this was to keep the PCP–SL at arm's length as far as possible. This issue was debated keenly among villagers understandably preoccupied about their physical safety and the message was also driven home by the liberation theology wing of the Catholic Church, which expressed the issues at stake in the following manner:

> In Ayacucho, *terrucos* and *milicos* (military) were killing peasants like flies. Whole villages were disappearing or having to flee to Lima. Did we want that here? No. So we decided to try and keep out of it, to only give food and shelter to the guerrillas when we couldn't refuse. The aim was to try and live as normal a life as possible, without antagonising either side.[8]

A voice from a neighbouring district conveyed a similar message:

> We didn't want to get involved. It was far too dangerous. Who cares if a peasant gets killed? Only his family and neighbours. Nobody else is concerned. Nobody bothers about the *campesinos* or defends them. So we had to look after ourselves and the best way to look after ourselves was to be wary of outsiders we did not know or trust. To have no contact with them, keep our heads down and just work our own fields – which is what we tried to do.[9]

Such misgivings led many rural people, particularly those over thirty, to tolerate the PCP–SL (often through fear), while minimising as far as possible their degree of collaboration with the insurgents.

A second factor that helps explain why 'a single spark' failed to 'ignite the prairie fire' in the way the PCP–SL leadership anticipated, was that country people in Cajabamba–Huamachuco were by no means as 'easy to persuade, indoctrinate and manipulate' as counter-insurgency operatives and less-reflective Party cadres both assumed. Entrenched political loyalties complicated Sendero's proselytising drive. Although many *campesinos* might be illiterate or possess a basic level of education, they did not represent a 'blank sheet' on which a particular set of political ideas could be imprinted readily. As noted in Chapter Two, from the 1930s this region had been an APRA bastion, which traditionally garnered between 60 and 70 per cent of the vote at election time. Since the early 1970s, a new generation had emerged in the villages, which supported the various left organisations. A substantial swathe of the population, although often highly critical of APRA and the left, retained their ingrained political sympathies throughout the 1980s and (despite the rise of independent 'movement' politicians, epitomised by the accession of Alberto Fujimori to the presidency in 1990) into the early 1990s.[10] Only a few established peasant leaders (viz. Calderón, Barrios and Nicasio) abandoned their party affiliation and threw in their lot with the insurgents. One astute activist, with a history of militancy in FEDECC, articulated a widely held opinion among the most politically conscious peasants that the PCP–SL was especially keen to recruit when he stated that:

> The Sendero people visited me on a couple of occasions, but I told them I supported Izquierda Unida and didn't agree with their policies or methods. The rural people did not want their kind of revolution. What we needed was to build up our own organisations, to get things done by ourselves and put pressure on the authorities to invest and improve our living conditions ... Anyway, you don't make a revolution by killing brother peasants or blowing up things. The *senderistas* started hitting the wrong target. They even killed comrades like Pedro Huillca and members of the CCP ... Peru is a poor country and needs better roads, bridges and electricity brought to the countryside.[11]

This question of ingrained political sentiments became particularly acute for the PCP–SL between 1985–90, when APRA formed the national government and monopolised the local power structure. Despite APRA's disastrous record in office, many citizens did not condone the assassination of *aprista* subprefects, mayors or district governors, whom they regarded as *compañeros* and who were perhaps personal acquaintances who had assisted them with some problem in the past and may not have been tainted by charges of corruption. Killing prominent APRA die-hards who had remained loyal since the 1930s and 1940s, such as subprefect Víctor Sotomayor in January 1988, proved especially counterproductive. Although after lifelong employment such figures had usually attained a reasonably comfortable retirement, they could by no means be regarded as wealthy, while their steadfast dedication to the APRA cause in the face of repression earned widespread respect and grudging admiration, even from political opponents holding firm anti-APRA views.

Further down the administrative chain, lower-level political appointees (lieutenant governors, justices of the peace, etc.) usually originated from humble backgrounds and were not readily indistinguishable from the mass of the rural poor. Furthermore, villagers tended to make a clear distinction between such an office-holder and an 'outsider', who was fleecing the state and/or the local population. The latter were viewed as a legitimate target, the former not. In this regard, a typical comment was that:

> I have always been an *aprista*. For thirty years I've been an *aprista*, along with all my brothers and sisters. It made me really angry when the *senderistas* started killing members of my party. We are not rich. We come from the common people and most of us are poor. Don ... was an ordinary person, a good person who tried to help people. He was just serving his people and his party. Yet they shot him like a dog in the street. That was unjust. He didn't deserve that.[12]

Patron–client ties encouraged these opinions. Such a situation was particularly in evidence in the Condebamba Valley, a locality where several of the medium-scale farmers who comprised the local elite were *apristas* of a conservative bent. Having been radical in their youth, they still held anti-oligarchic and nationalist attitudes, but tended to possess traditional views on social and religious matters. Belonging to the same party as most of the labourers and sharecroppers who worked their fields reinforced the social bonds forged by regular face-to-face contact on the farm. Additionally, owners occasionally provided monetary and other modes of assistance to employees during times of financial stress and attended the same religious and festive events. Direct producers also depended on their employers for their livelihood. Consequently, these medium-scale farmers were well placed to spread an anti-PCP–SL message among the local population. This they did in an effective fashion, to the extent that guerrilla attempts to assassinate members of this component of the agrarian bourgeoisie encountered disapproval, placing a strain on their dealings with APRA-supporting smallholders in and around the Condebamba Valley.[13]

A third source of tension in peasant–guerrilla relations connected with politics arose from the position adopted by the PCP–SL towards existing grass-roots organisations, especially the *rondas campesinas* and peasant federations. As noted in Chapter Four, upon commencing operations in a particular zone, the rebels strove to suppress all autonomous elements of civil society it encountered and replace them with Party-dominated organs. The resultant hostile attitude towards the *rondas* (according to the PCP–SL, they comprised 'reformist bourgeois' entities) spread alienation in parishes where the denizens had fought hard to get them functioning and, their many deficiencies notwithstanding, viewed the patrol committees as 'their' organisations, of which they were justly proud. Although robberies all but disappeared in areas under strong PCP–SL influence, due to the draconian sanctions meted out, in districts where a '*conciencia rondera*' had taken root, the eradication of many types of crime did not compensate for the suppression of an authentic grass-roots movement. An inkling of the discontent with this policy emerges in comments from two informants:

> I participated actively in the *rondas*. Robberies stopped and some of the worst rustlers became the best *ronderos*. We re-educated them. We sorted out our own problems and things were moving in the right direction. Then Sendero came along and tried to order us around. That brought difficulties with the police and the authorities. Many people got scared, stopped participating and the *ronda* ceased functioning ... Today we have a crime wave in the countryside that is driving the *campesinos* mad. This wouldn't have happened if it hadn't been for Sendero and the authorities. Neither of them helped the peasants. When Sendero came, things went downhill.[14]

> Here in ... the *ronda campesina* was working quite well. We had got ourselves organised and kicked out the rustlers. People felt more secure and you could sleep peacefully at night. But when the *terrucos* passed through, they told us they would take over from the patrol and control things. The president and the rest of the committee were threatened and resigned out of fear. Our *ronda*

ceased functioning. Most of us were unhappy about this, but what could we do? They had the guns and the power. We didn't possess the strength to do what we wanted. We couldn't resist them ... People resented their interference, but were powerless to do anything about it.[15]

Indeed, these attitudes were so deeply held that in some parishes of San Marcos and Cajabamba (notably, sections of the former hacienda La Pauca) smallholders attempted to defy PCP–SL exhortations and continued operating their committees clandestinely, despite the dire consequences that discovery might occasion. Measures adopted included meeting at night, posting lookouts to detect any approaching strangers and purposefully having no easily identifiable formal leadership that might present a target for repression, although such precautions did not prevent the assassination of *ronderos* in Otuto and other *caseríos*. As will be shown, this determination to try and maintain autonomous organisations also created friction between *rondero* activists and the military.

Similar sentiments took root among individuals who had participated in the CCP or CNA and had honed their political skills during the struggle for agrarian reform. Although by the early 1990s both these peasant federations were practically moribund owing to internal divisions, loss of membership, financial penury and hounding by government coercive agencies, the idea of autonomous, mass-based organisations devoted to furthering the peasant cause against local *gamonales* and state injustice still held resonance for this layer of activists. The PCP–SL's project and domineering modus operandi were consequently viewed critically by many of the most politically experienced members of rural society, as evinced by a participant in the 1970s land invasions:

Sendero was against all independent organisation and political action by the peasantry. They had all the answers and just wanted to order us about and use us as cannon fodder. Their mode of behaviour was just like the domineering landowners and political bosses we had fought so hard to get rid of ... We did not want to change one master for another. The way for us to develop was to build strong federations from the *caseríos* upwards, trying to involve as wide a section of the peasantry as possible. We needed to rebuild the FEDECC. But the *senderistas* wanted to prevent this and control everything.[16]

Such attitudes, held by influential 'gatekeepers' known and respected throughout the countryside, formed an important barrier against insurgent aims to push forward from a situation where they had constructed a sizeable party organisation, to one of attaining active support from a decisive proportion of the rural and urban population.

Research undertaken in Ayacucho, Junín and neighbouring departments in Peru's central and southern highlands indicates that the forced removal of legitimately chosen peasant community leaders played a central role in turning villagers against PCP–SL political and military units. Resentment developed towards the practice of replacing trusted people with Party appointees (some-

times 'outsiders'), who then acted in an arbitrary fashion and disrupted established customs, eventually provoking armed resistance to the insurgents.[17]

Although some anti-Sendero sentiment stemming from this policy was
expressed by several informants, interference in community organisation did
not emerge as a pivotal factor in souring peasant–guerrilla relations.[18] Regional
differences in agrarian structure come into play here. Just as Quechua has all
but disappeared from the northern highlands, the presence of legally recognised
corporate peasant communities is much weaker. While a number of settlements
called 'communities' are encountered in Cajabamba–Huamachuco, in reality,
the overwhelming majority exist in name only. Close inspection reveals that
they lack many of the characteristics found among peasants in other regions,
such as collectively owned and farmed areas, the operation of a communally
regulated fallow, frequent engagement in collective agricultural labour (*minga*),
the autonomous election of village leaders and decision-making through regularly convened assemblies.[19] Whereas in the centre and the south these
institutions may assume aspects of a state within a state, in the northern Andes
a more atomised smallholding peasantry forges links with national institutions
and organisations without the buffer of strong, long-standing communal structures. At the hamlet level, state-appointed or ratified positions (lieutenant
governor, justice of the peace, head of the neighbourhood irrigation committee,
etc.), invest individuals with standing and influence, as does involvement in
national or regional non-official bodies (APRA, peasant federations and, where
they exist, *rondas campesinas*).

Such a situation begets positive and negative outcomes. Grass-roots leaders
have ready access to power networks that can be utilised when problems arise,
so enhancing the populace's defensive and offensive mobilisation capacity.
Simultaneously, however, the position of official and non-official office-holders
becomes more overtly politicised, so that political rivalries frequently coalesce
with personal animosity to undermine the authority and ability for action of
local leaders – an acute problem, given the long history of factional conflict in
the region. Divided villages signify authorities whose position is less secure,
whose legitimacy is more likely to be contested, so providing the PCP–SL with
ample opportunity to play one faction against another. Factionalism also undermined the rural population's potential to develop a grass-roots 'peasant
counter-rebellion' (Fumerton) in the northern highlands, as evinced in
Quillispampa, Otuto and other 'communities' spread throughout the
Cajabamba–Huamachuco region (to be discussed below).

Tension between peasant 'river' and Maoist 'fish': economic factors

Another area of emerging stress between country people in the northern Andes
and the PCP–SL concerned the disruptive impact of insurgent activity upon
household economies. According to Favre, Manrique and other researchers
writing on Ayacucho and adjacent departments, hostility towards the PCP–SL
developed when guerrilla demands started to threaten the production of family

farms. Of particular note were attempts to impose a 'natural economy' on cottagers through the curtailment of market contacts, along with instructions to produce and provide food to sustain EGP detachments ensconced in the mountains. Parental protective feelings aside, *senderista* attempts to draft sons and daughters into the EGP also exercised a negative effect on the operation of a non-mechanised, labour-intensive farming system by removing much-needed hands.[20]

On the question of compelling agriculturalists to revert to self-sufficiency when implementing a strategy of encircling and capturing towns, PCP–SL commanders in the northern highlands adopted a flexible attitude towards its implementation. Around Sarín, Sanagorán and other parishes firmly inside the Cajabamba–Santiago de Chuco–Sayapullo 'red triangle', cadres exhorted smallholders to revert to a subsistence economy; in San Marcos, by contrast, no sustained attempt to separate farmers from the market occurred. How might this variation in policy be explained?

Since 1970 San Marcos province, which had long been a supplier of produce to highland and coastal markets, had witnessed a substantial increase in commercial activity. In addition to the popular Sunday market held in the provincial capital, a new weekly fair grew up at La Grama, placed strategically beside the main river crossing in the Condebamba Valley. At the opposite end of the province and at a higher ecological level, in 1987 a market attended by cattle dealers who earned a living transporting animals to the littoral opened in the *caserío* of Huanico. These developments reflected both the commercial tradition of the local peasantry and post-land reform agricultural intensification: after haciendas fragmented, newly established or newly autonomous medium- and small-scale agricultural enterprises started to plough land that had previously been extensively farmed and engage in more intensive livestock-rearing activities. Local PCP–SL commanders also applied a different policy vis-à-vis off-farm trade, according to lines of agricultural production. Given its importance as a source of Party income, no attempt was made to halt the expansion of coca cultivation in Otuzco and low-lying lands bordering the River Marañón. On the other hand, in the districts of La Libertad mentioned above, efforts were made to limit the supply of potatoes and cereals to markets in highland towns, with traffic on coast roads to Trujillo being disrupted on a regular basis through the dynamiting of bridges and felling of trees at strategic points along the route.[21]

Senderista insensitivity to local conditions surfaces regularly in accounts of peasant–insurgent relations in Ayacucho and surrounding departments. For the Cajabamba–Huamachuco region, however, criticism of prohibitions on commodity exchange appears unwarranted, as evinced by two testimonies, the first by a *minifundista*, the second from a *fiscal* (public prosecutor), who headed the judiciary at provincial level:

> We might be poor and have little cash, but we need to sell what we produce in order to buy goods manufactured in the towns. That's how we survive and

manage to have a few comforts in our lives. How else are we going to get clothes, soap, school books for the children and other necessary things? ... When Sendero was active in these districts, they talked about how the merchants and cattle dealers in town tried to cheat us. They said that we should do something about it – bartering more among ourselves, organising to sell our crops collectively, like a cooperative. But they did not try to stop us trading our potatoes, maize and livestock – it would have been an impossible demand.[22]

Here the terrorists did not attempt to shut down commerce in a sustained fashion. A few *paros armados* occurred in the town that had varying degrees of success: shopkeepers did not close their businesses voluntarily, they complied out of fear of reprisal against their persons and their livelihood. But the rural population has always come to market to meet people, as well as to trade. It is as much a social as an economic affair. I think Sendero realised this fact and therefore did not interfere. They never possessed the strength to prohibit thousands of people walking to town and attending the market.[23]

If, through expediency, PCP–SL cadres did not make a sustained attempt to impose a strict ban on trading over much of Cajabamba–Huamachuco, what about the forced recruitment of youth into the EGP and other units engaged in acts of commission? Yet again, no consistent pattern over time and place emerges. Occasional incidents of abduction occurred – in May 1986, to give one example, a *senderista* column shanghaied eight peasants and their livestock after occupying the *caserío* of Cosgabamba in Huamachuco – but they remained infrequent. Even so, as gossip circulated around the countryside, fear of being plucked from the homestead spread, instilling a sense of trepidation, which, in turn, bred animosity towards the insurgents. Worry about abduction also complicated the undertaking of routine (but essential) farming activities, as noted in the following statement:

> We have three children, two boys and a girl. As the boys reached military age in 1988–89, we became afraid that they could be conscripted into the army and carted off to Ayacucho ... A greater preoccupation was that they would be taken by the *terrucos*, which would have led to an almost certain death or a lifetime in prison. Every morning my wife prayed that nothing was going to happen to the children that day. She was very nervous and when times were particularly difficult, sent them to stay with our relatives in Cajamarca ... All of this was most upsetting. When they were all away, we felt better, but it also caused many problems around the farm – how could we pasture our animals safely? It was difficult for my wife and I to cope on our own.[24]

Oral testimony indicates that fear of kidnap far exceeded the likelihood of being taken. Indeed, from the perspective of guerrilla commanders, forced recruitment held important drawbacks – the victims were likely to prove irresolute combatants, might spread dissension among the ranks and attempt escape at the first opportunity, taking to the opposition valuable information about

Party membership and operational practices. A regular supply of fresh recruits also lessened the need to pursue a consistently applied policy of party-building via the barrel of a gun.

If a certain discrepancy between perception and reality clouded the issue of abduction, exhortations to supply guerrilla contingents with foodstuffs and other resources proved a more well-founded source of disharmony in guerrilla–peasant relations. Mao stated that 'The richest source of power to wage war lies in the masses of the people' – hence it was a matter of crucial import not only to eschew 'the abuses of press-ganging' but also to provision insurgent forces adequately without simultaneously placing onerous demands on peasant producers.[25] The question was addressed in 'The Three Rules and Eight Remarks', which laid down the principles governing guerrilla conduct towards the civilian population:

Rules:
1. All actions are subject to command.
2. Do not steal from the people.
3. Be neither selfish nor unjust.

Remarks:
1. Replace the door when you leave the home.
2. Roll up the bedding on which you have slept.
3. Be courteous.
4. Be honest in your transactions.
5. Return what you borrow.
6. Replace what you break.
7. Do not bathe in the presence of women.
8. Do not search without authorisation those you arrest.

The goal for the rebel army should be to 'become one with the people, so that they see it as their own army'.[26] This should be achieved by behaviour different from the locust-like rapaciousness of conventional conscript forces,

Unfortunately for their prospects, PCP–SL detachments operating in the Cajabamba–Huamachuco region never evolved a satisfactory solution to the provisioning conundrum. One method employed to secure rations involved the interception of lorries delivering Andean foodstuffs and livestock to the coast. Vehicles bringing rice and sugar up into the highlands formed another particularly attractive target. Resources were also acquired through the hold-up of inter-provincial buses and demanding 'revolutionary contributions' at gunpoint from startled passengers. These interventions nevertheless failed to provide the constant flow of foodstuff necessary to cover everyday requirements. In consequence, EGP fighters and other cadres based in the countryside not only experienced hunger from time to time but often needed to live off local smallholders, so that Rule 2 and Remark 5 of Mao's code were contravened on a regular basis. Pack animals for moving material were requisitioned without payment and, to compound matters, on occasions not returned to their owners;

overnight accommodation and food would be demanded, with no recompense forthcoming from cash-strapped insurgents. Such impositions on smallholders, at least 70 per cent of whom could not meet the household subsistence minimum from on-farm production, eventually provoked deep resentment. In this regard, a typical response opined that:

> The *senderistas* always wanted something from the people – a place to stay overnight, meals, food, firewood and the rest. One night, six of them arrived at the house of my friend and asked to be put up and fed. How could he refuse? At dawn they left taking one of his donkeys to carry their equipment, as well as a sack of maize ... My *compadre* was really aggrieved at this. He has four children to maintain and only three hectares, so food was scarce. He never saw the donkey again, so had to ask favours and borrow from friends and neighbours when goods needed moving.[27]

More forcefully, it was held that:

> The *terrucos* were like a plague and had no shame about exploiting us peasants. They would just take what they wanted, never compensate us and give nothing in return. Did they believe it was easy to make the land produce? Did they think that we could afford to feed them? No – they knew we lived a hard life, but this did not stop them taking our food and possessions. How could you believe in such people?[28]

Exasperated farmers could be driven to extreme lengths in defence of their livelihoods. One early expression of this phenomenon occurred in June 1983, when villagers from Llaygan (near Huamachuco) lynched two *senderistas* who they discovered lifting their livestock. As insurgent forces grew stronger, however, recourse to this kind of overt anti-guerrilla action carried greater risk and therefore remained very infrequent.

Naturally enough, not all householders held such a negative attitude: individuals who backed the PCP–SL provided shelter and sustenance without demur, as in Chorobamba, for example. Among farming families outside solid guerrilla base areas, however, extra demands placed upon an already inadequate food supply engendered discontent, especially when the loss of valued livestock essential for household reproduction occurred. Sendero's presence in a *caserío* consequently assumed a double-edged character. By clamping down on theft, the insurgents contributed towards household survival, while the requisitioning of foodstuffs and other commodities brought extra hardship to families already living on the edge, a paradox not lost on one perceptive smallholder:

> The *terrucos* brought some benefits, as well as a lot of sorrow, to the *campesinos*. They put an end to rustling, the robbing of our personal possessions and they dealt with corrupt authorities who made our life unbearable. But later their actions brought added difficulties by taking part of the harvests. Most families just manage to get by and do not have anything to spare. Sendero's presence thus changed from positive to negative and complaints against them grew.[29]

As the conflict escalated during the late 1980s and early 1990s, disruptions to the complex farming system operated by households occurred on other fronts, one being the cultivation of plots at complementary but differing ecological levels. As noted in Chapter Two, wherever possible, agriculturalists attempted to access land at varying altitudes in order to obtain additional output, minimise the consequences of crop failure and liven up their diet. These plots were often sited at several hours' distance from one another and when the civil war escalated, a chance encounter with a guerrilla column or police/army patrol could have fatal consequences. As it became increasingly dangerous to move around, plots sited away from the family house suffered neglect, with an adverse effect on peasant well-being. Such a dilemma confronted one small-holder who farms slightly less than two hectares in the *quechua* ecological niche, at 2,700 metres above sea level. The output from these plots is insufficient to support the family, so it is augmented by 7 hectares of natural pastures located at around 3,500 metres in the *jalca*, some six hours' walk uphill from the household's main residence. In sheltered spots interspersed among the hardy *ichu* grass, small patches of potatoes are cultivated, including seed potatoes, the sale of which comprises a vital source of income to cover off-farm purchases. This cottager described the problems posed by the threat of escalating violence in the following terms:

> One became scared of moving around. If you bumped into the police they might arrest you, beat the shit out of you, or even make you disappear. With the *terrucos* you never knew how they might react. So I didn't want my kids out on the road. Therefore, my wife stayed up top with two of the children for weeks on end. Things became very difficult because we depended on the potato harvest to get cash to buy rice, pasta and other necessities, but I couldn't go up to plough. We were broke and had a rough time. Fortunately, the situation has calmed down, so now we can grow potatoes for our own use and seed potatoes to sell.[30]

Although the rural population was equally fearful about being intercepted by government forces, most blamed the PCP–SL for begetting additional and ill-affordable hardships.

Further fissures between peasant 'river' and guerrilla 'fish' arose from the manner in which the PCP–SL chose to implement its 'agrarian revolutionary war'. As related in Chapter Four, moves to 'sabotage production, take over land, attack the rich, encourage personal feuds and stimulate land hunger' led to a full-blooded assault on the region's cooperatives, provoking their disintegration. Here, Sendero pursued the expedient policy of supporting the property-owning aspirations held by a majority of the farming community in parishes where CAPs and SAIS existed. Around every cooperative, numerous resource-scarce smallholders cast covetous eyes upon meadows sited on the other side of the wire, in the domain of former estates. An equally strong desire to grab extra territory could be found among the many independent farming families listed formally as cooperative *socios*, but who in practice had minimal contact with the enterprise via the sale of labour power or trade.

An appreciation of the social weight of tenants whose usufruct rights dated from the landlord regime is indicated by the situation encountered within cooperatives located in highland La Libertad. At adjudication in the early 1970s, some 386 permanent workers ranked among the beneficiaries, alongside 8,760 former quit-rent tenants.[31] Upon expropriation, the quit-rent tenants received considerably more individually exploitable assets than the permanent workers, but they were not content and sought to expand their holdings. For their part, stockmen, shepherds and other permanent labourers inured to a wage-labour process dating back to the 1930s and 1940s had a greater attachment – their multiple failings notwithstanding – to the cooperatives and collective work practices. While many considered that some restructuring was necessary and even desirable, permanent workers were typically opposed to the total demolition of 'their' enterprise. Like most individuals who work with their hands, they were instinctively appalled at the violent and seemingly pointless destruction of useful things. After a lifetime's work as a stockman, labourers understood fully the considerable dedication and investment that had underpinned the development of modern livestock enterprises; the decimation of herds and flocks was, in consequence, viewed with horror.[32] By pursuing this very strategy, the PCP–SL alienated an influential minority group in rural society, one endowed with what might be labelled a 'proletarian consciousness', politically aware as a result of a history of activism in the CNA or CCP, and adept at accessing local and regional power structures.

In most of the region's CAPs and SAIS, this component of the workforce did not have the numerical strength to resist *senderista* demands, their disagreement thus remained unspoken or voiced discreetly around a narrow circle of trusted family and friends. However, members belonging to one enterprise managed to organise successfully to protect its installations and non-fixed assets. Ironically, given the PCP–SL's chief ideological mentor of Peruvian origin, this happened to be the SAIS José Carlos Mariátegui, centred on the formerly Gildemeister-owned haciendas Huacraruco and Sunchubamba.

In the mid-1980s, as the civil war deepened and Cachachi, Calluán and neighbouring parishes along its eastern and southern boundaries became foci of persistent guerrilla activity, cooperative leaders moved to establish *rondas* to prevent unauthorised outsiders entering the property. Despite these precautions, on one occasion in 1987 lack of diligence by an employee allowed a *camioneta* (pick-up truck) to pass through the large steel gate that blocked the entrance to Huacraruco. The *camioneta* was halted when it reached the estate's main complex of farm and administrative buildings. Three unrecognised men descended from the vehicle and tried to pressurise cooperative members to allow them passage to Sunchubamba, from where they intended to travel via a little-used back road through to Cachachi. Although bulges beneath their jackets indicated that the impostors carried weapons, the *campesinos* held their ground. After a tense stand-off, the strangers were compelled to retrace their steps and abandon the hacienda. Only after his arrest in June 1988, when his picture covered the front page of every national newspaper, did Huacraruco's residents realise that they had faced down Osmán Morote and his two body-guards.[33]

A second area where *campesino* and *senderista* logic diverged over the manner in which Sendero chose to pursue its 'agrarian revolutionary war' concerned the practice of installing outsiders on occupied land. These families became popularly known as '*mitimaes*', after the Inca custom of transferring loyal ethnic communities to police recently conquered territory. Following a successful invasion of cooperative property, privately owned medium-scale farms, or takeovers that pitted one village against its neighbour, PCP–SL policy was to settle cadres or trusted sympathisers of peasant extraction in the newly seized area, often handing them larger parcels of land or the better-quality soils. The idea guiding this policy was that these 'colonisers' would form the nucleus of a new support base, extend Party influence and, by allocating them favourable plots, improve the food supply necessary to maintain EGP units in the field. Last, but not least, *mitimaes* could fulfil social-control functions and act as the organisation's eyes and ears, supplying information concerning the local populations' collective and individual behaviour, as well as movements by government forces.

While this policy was rational from the perspective of Party strategists focused primarily on building the organisation, assigning outsiders coveted assets over which they possessed no previous claim predictably stoked deep animosity among established residents, especially where smallholders felt they held valid historical ownership rights:

> If the land had been expropriated in the past by the landowners, it should return to us. That is right and just ... Where our brother peasants have strug-gled for years to recover what rightfully belongs to them, they should have received this property when the agrarian reform was undertaken. In many cases this did not happen. But when Sendero began to organise invasions of the cooperatives, it distributed land according to its own priorities, not those of the local people. Strangers were given plots, often the best fields, which did not go down well. It spread bad feeling ... With reason, people became resentful, even if there was not much they could do about it. Sendero tried to settle one injustice, but created another.[34]

When pursuing this policy, the PCP–SL frequently exhibited a lack of sensi-tivity that spawned disaffection, the price paid for being locked in a pre-agrarian reform mindset and stubbornly attached to a rigid ideology that was poorly adapted to messy realities. It was not comprehended sufficiently that post-Velasco, the apparently straightforward matter of taking land from one seemingly resource-endowed group and transferring it to the resource-penu-rious had become a complicated affair. Cadres frequently did not possess the necessary depth of knowledge about local circumstances, or were content to take at face value the narrative emanating from partial individuals who appeared most sympathetic to their cause. Either scenario stymied their ability to reach nuanced decisions derived from a judicious balance between the veracity of rival claims and an accurate consideration of varying household requirements.

Peasant–guerrilla discrepancies also appeared once households occupied land with *senderista* backing. Remembering Mao's dictum that 'the peasant thinks in harvests', upon acquiring new plots, the immediate concern of small-holders was to plough the soil, produce more food and address the family's subsistence deficit. While recipients were grateful to the guerrilla for facilitating access to additional resources, their interest in revolution tended to wane. More pressing everyday concerns understandably began to assume priority over esoteric concepts such as 'protracted people's war' and overthrowing the 'landlord–bureaucratic state'. One urban-based informant with a finely tuned ear for rural grievances explained the unravelling of guerrilla–*campesino* inter-ests on this score in the following terms:

> Talking to many people from the countryside, I was told that Sendero's attraction diminished once people had attained their main objective. After getting more land they would support the guerrilla for a time, but once they became caught up in the normal agricultural tasks – ploughing, planting and the like – the time they had for participation in Sendero's activities and their interest reduced. You could say that the peasants had got what they wanted and once that occurred, interest in politics declined.[35]

As if this was not enough, households located within support bases and recently invaded territory were also pressed to supply commodities to feed EPG contingents and other party activists. While necessary to sustain the apparatus, this demand did not attract universal approval. With approximately 70 per cent of the rural population experiencing hunger at some stage over the agricultural cycle, the control of food was a matter of vital importance: few smallholders, even kulaks, could afford the luxury of giving comestibles to non-family people on a regular basis. At a deeper level, such requisitioning contravened two inter-connected social mores that were widely accepted within peasant society: (i) the belief that to earn a right to food, adults must first contribute some phys-ical labour towards its production; and (ii) enjoying access to food without having to suffer the inconvenience of manual work carried a strong association with the hacienda regime. Although recently buried, the era of landlord domi-nation nevertheless remained imprinted strongly in the psyche of the local *campesinado*. Neatly expressing this link, a former estate worker opined that:

> Sendero acted like a *patrón*. They demanded food and other items, although they had not worked to cultivate or make them. Such behaviour was no longer possible ... The days of the hacienda have passed. As *el chino* Velasco said, 'Peasants: the landlords will no longer eat at the cost of your hunger'. Sendero wanted to exact goods without payment, to make people work for them and hand over part of what was produced. For what? Were they on our side or did they want to exploit and use us? People became suspicious of their motives.[36]

Given the century-old history of factional schism characteristic of regional society, guerrilla interventions aimed at intensifying rivalries between villages did not only produce winners and losers. Invasions and counter-invasions incited rancour among the latter coupled with initial euphoria among the former, followed by a re-evaluation of household objectives once fields had been partitioned. Commenting on this scenario, an activist noted that:

Getting one group of poor peasants to fight a neighbouring group of poor peasants opened up a can of worms. Many actions were not even targeted at people who had become rich during the land reform. The *senderistas* were told 'This land belongs to us', 'That *caserío* supports the government', or 'They took these fields from us', and boom – an invasion would be organised without much ado. At times it was difficult to understand who was using whom. Were the peasants taking advantage of Sendero, or Sendero taking advantage of the peasants? Things became very complicated ... Anyway, it was a short-sighted and ill-considered policy because a lot of bad blood was created and, in any case, once the people had seized the land, after a while they tried to disengage from Sendero and get on with their lives. So problems emerged on two fronts: with those who had been expropriated unjustly and those who had gained land through support from Sendero.[37]

When confronted with opposition on this and other issues related to economics, the PCP–SL's response was typically authoritarian – for their 'own good' the 'peasant masses' needed to obey Party instructions. The consequence of such behaviour was not hard to foresee. In the short-term, it produced compliance, but simultaneously called upon the population to engage in deeper reflection concerning the nature of guerrilla goals and their own household goals, a thought process that led to further questioning of the advisability and viability of the *senderista* revolutionary project.

Tension between peasant 'river' and Maoist 'fish': social factors

Concerning social matters, the PCP–SL's strategic and tactical modus operandi generated friction with the population on two main fronts: the provision of state services and the use of violence. Since at least the 1960s, rural dwellers throughout the Cajabamba–Huamachuco region had petitioned politically appointed authorities (essentially the prefect, sub-prefect and district governor) and civil servants based in local branches of the various ministries, demanding basic services already available to the urban population. Typical needs in the education field surrounded the creation of a village school, an increase in the teaching staff or additional equipment (books, desks, etc.), all of which were invariably in short supply. Regarding health needs, common requests included the opening of a medical post stocked with basic medicines, the provision of primary training for local residents in midwifery, the treatment of minor injuries and similar everyday needs. In the productive sphere, mobilisations would occur around road improvements, for investment in small-scale irrigation schemes, as well as extension programmes aimed at transmitting technical advances in livestock rearing and cropping systems.

Sendero's *batir el campo* strategy clearly instigated a significant contraction in service provision across the board, undermining the gains made in numerous hamlets through decades of struggle. Teachers and health workers fled the countryside. Agronomists, justifiably fearful, remained glued to their desks. By the late 1980s, activity by the Ministry of Transport, the Agrarian Bank and similar agencies had ground to a halt in rural localities, with negative consequences for the population. Naturally enough, the political class and the state bureaucracy received their share of disapprobation for abandoning the countryside, but it was recognised that guerrilla actions were principally responsible for the collapse of services and the resultant hardships:

> When Sendero became active, everyone fled to the town. The schoolteachers and the nurse all disappeared. We were left isolated. The kids had no school to attend and lost years of education. If someone got ill, what could they do? There was no alternative but to get to town – but what if you were too poorly to walk or could not get on a horse? ... The situation turned terrible. And to think we had struggled for a long time to get these services! So Sendero did us no favours. Clearly there had been problems in the past, like getting the teachers to be at school from Monday to Friday, with the supply of educational materials and the like, but Sendero made things much worse.[38]

Although frequently critical of the state and the lax behaviour often demonstrated by its front-line service providers, the overwhelming demand was for extra and improved provision, not withdrawal. When insurgents targeted teachers and similarly placed professionals, therefore, the rural population understood clearly who induced their flight out of the village. In this regard, perhaps the most high-profile incident to have reverberated around the region during the early phase of the conflict occurred on 16 March 1986 at Tulpo, a *caserío* sited adjacent to Angasmarca in Santiago de Chuco province. After occupying the settlement and massing villagers in the square to hear calls for armed struggle, insurgents subjected four women teachers, suspected of collaborating with the police, to a *juicio popular* and killed them before the stunned crowd.[39] Unsurprisingly, the cold-blooded nature of these assassinations not only provoked shock and sympathy towards the victims but also sparked a wave of resignations among professionals employed in surrounding 'red zones'.

This event brings into focus the question of violence and the population's response to the PCP–SL's willingness to act in a ruthless fashion. Research conducted in Ayacucho and neighbouring departments indicates that rural people usually preferred a 'punish but don't kill' approach towards thieves and others who violated the mainstream moral code. In most cases they eschewed the taking of life. Once the guerrilla contravened popular perceptions of right and wrong, backing ebbed and opposition spread.[40] Analysis of developments in the northern highlands reveals that a similar scenario unfolded during the late 1980s and early 1990s. Over the insurrection's early phase (1982–84), the probability was for the takeover of a village or small town to occur without recourse to bloodletting among the civilian population. After 1985, this situation began to change, with a marked rise in *senderista*-inflicted deaths noticeable in 1986. Within a fortnight in mid-March 1986, for example, a fifteen-strong rebel column shot six peasants who protested injudiciously against the rebels' presence in the hamlet of Pampa Regada, a four-hour hike from Usquil. This was followed shortly afterwards by the seizure of four brothers in Angasmarca; two managed to flee, the less-fortunate siblings were assassinated. In an act evoking Sicilian vendetta feuds, September 1987 witnessed eight members of one family put to death in Algamarca, a parish located across the valley from Cajabamba and within sight of the town.

The usual charge levelled by PCP–SL cadres against their civilian victims involved accusations of collaboration with the authorities. Such a fate befell a father and his two sons who resided in the hamlet of Recta Ponce, near the mining settlement of Quiruvilca. In March 1988, a guerrilla column entered the *caserío* where, following the standard speech and daubing of graffiti on walls, the rebels left after expropriating ten cattle belonging to local smallholders 'to feed our other comrades'. A villager informed *senderistas* bivouacked nearby that the Valderrama Castillo family had contacted the Guardia Civil – despite the fact that the villagers were warned against reporting the incident to the police under pain of execution. Shortly afterwards, the household's male members were pulled from their house and hanged from nearby trees.[41]

Thereafter, peasant deaths at insurgent hands became a regular occurrence. Disregard of the Party's directives was implacably subjected to sanctions, as seen in October 1989, when a woman suspected of collaborating with the authorities was shot in Sanagorán – being six months pregnant failed to save her. On occasions, violence perpetrated against the civilian population could assume a bizarre aspect devoid of apparent logic. Another incident that took place in Sanagorán illustrates this point. *Senderistas* overran the district capital in November 1992 and assembled the populace in the market square; there then followed a tableau reminiscent of a bygone age. Pandering to rural superstition and no doubt motivated by a desire to garner support, a *senderista* commander acting under the pseudonym of 'Paco' gunned down a middle-aged woman whom the locals had denounced as a *bruja* (witch).[42]

Others proved more fortunate, although they had good cause to curse their luck. One case that graphically illustrates Isbell's apt description of the Andean peasantry as being pinned between 'the wall and the blade', concerned a smallholder from the vicinity of Quillispampa, who, in March 1995 found himself accused by the security forces of participating in rebel-orchestrated land invasions launched against Cruz de Algamarca, Pampa de Arenilla and neighbouring hamlets between December 1990 and January 1991.[43] Before being detained by the military, this individual happened to have been charged with adultery and delation by *senderista* forces operating in the Araqueda–Condebamba sector of Cajabamba. Following a *juicio popular,* he managed to avoid assassination, but was compelled to endure a relatively light punishment consisting of several punches around the body, along with a public head-shaving – rudely administered and designed to humiliate, as well as convey a message to the assembled villagers. Prior to having his hands unbound, he received an admonishment to reform under pain of execution from Sendero's local *mando político*.[44]

How did the populace react to such rough treatment? The denizens of Cajabamba–Huamachuco were inured to hardship and not given to foppery, yet by the early 1990s PCP–SL violence had escalated to a level that was not only considered excessive but was also seen as iniquitous, in that many considered innocent by their family, friends and neighbours suffered severe castigation without good cause. Hostility on this score was even expressed by people who had not been affected directly, or lost a relative, at the hands of Sendero. Such a shift in attitude from neutrality or passive tolerance to repudiation is captured in the following statement:

> The *senderistas* claimed they were on our side, on the side of the poor and fighting for us. But how can you be on the side of the poor and kill so many innocent *campesinos*? It doesn't make sense. Some of them had a heart of stone and refused to listen to the ordinary people. They acted without pity and committed too many excesses ... Too many innocent people started to lose their lives. Therefore, feelings towards the *terrucos* started to change away from acceptance. Rural people began to have doubts. They became uncertain about how the *senderistas* might act, causing fear to spread over the countryside. Eventually many just wanted them to go away, so that they could be left in peace.[45]

As one thoughtful observer of the local scene commented, 'Sendero started out giving dreams, but ended up delivering a nightmare'.[46] Similar sentiments were expressed by a resident in Cajamarca town, who maintained close links with friends in rural San Marcos and Cajabamba:

> Sendero had within its ranks individuals who were bad and cruel. They operated in an arbitrary manner and abused the peasants to excess. Some were obsessed with their own power and appeared to be acting out of control and, it has to be said, against their own objectives. Many of their actions didn't make sense ... Once the killings committed by Sendero became more frequent, rural people became increasingly critical and turned against them ... Executing and chastising too severely cost the guerrilla a lot of support.[47]

A further potent element of tension surrounding peasant–guerrilla relations flagged by this and other informants concerned the mistreatment of peasant women: 'the *terrucos* committed the error of messing around with the *campesinas*'.[48] Indeed, after being arrested by an army patrol, one peasant woman from Huangajanga, a hamlet located in Sayapullo province, stated that she had been abducted and raped by 'terrorist elements' before being set free.[49] Given the social taboos, the veracity or frequency of such incidents is impossible to determine accurately. What remains beyond doubt, however, is that rumours of sexual abuse circulated persistently around the countryside, inflicting – whether justified or not – significant damage on the PCP–SL's reputation and credibility. On this and other dimensions of violence, the Party failed to operate wisely. Through omitting to heed rigorously the third of Mao's rules – 'Be neither selfish nor unjust' –the PCP–SL started to encounter problems, during the early 1990s, that were not immediately apparent to most national and international observers. The increasingly frequent charges of unscrupulous behaviour made against individual *senderistas* at this juncture also raises important questions about the quality of the Party's cadres and the efficacy of the organisation's internal control mechanisms, issues that will be addressed shortly.

Counter-insurgency: policy changes 1990–92

By 1990, therefore, stress points were developing on a wide array of political, economic and social issues between a broad swathe of the population and the PCP–SL. Particular issues or incidents might come to the fore at any time and carry more weight in one locality compared with another, but overall, the general trend in relations between 'river' and 'fish' tended towards oxygen deprivation rather than nourishment. Although cadres might mouth well-known slogans such as 'A single spark can start a prairie fire' and fantasise about 'strategic equilibrium', they ignored a Chinese maxim attributed to the seventh-century Emperor, Tang Taizong, which warns against the hidden dangers confronting outside organisations that rely on the peasantry for their survival: 'The water can make the boat float, but it can sink it too'. Over the quinquennium 1985–90, the Party had registered appreciable growth in membership and military capability, while its influence extended throughout ever-increasing areas of rural Cajabamba–Huamachuco. Crucially, however, the PCP–SL had attained what Ranajit Guha (following Antonio Gramsci) labelled 'domination without hegemony'. At root, Sendero's authority did not rest on consent, but on coercion.[50] A conjuncture had consequently emerged, within which a determined minority supported the guerrilla, an intimidated majority acquiesced to its activities through fear, while another minority group was becoming increasingly alienated by the PCP–SL's behaviour. Unfortunately for the guerrilla, the ranks of the third group happened to be expanding more quickly than those of the first and second.

Into this complex political situation, whereby the PCP–SL had established a social base while simultaneously attracting growing – but as yet latent – hostility from a broadening section of civil society, a new factor entered the equation, one that would exercise a crucial impact on the trajectory of the civil war in the northern highlands. The catalyst for change appeared in the shape of an improved counter-insurgency effort mounted by the state. Throughout the 1980s, the official response to the insurgency in Cajabamba–Huamachuco reflected the national picture in that it proved ineffective on all fronts. As discussed in Chapter Four, the Peruvian army and intelligence services proved surprisingly slow to learn how to 'eat soup with a knife' – to employ T. E. Lawrence's phrase. Initially, the police had been allocated responsibility for confronting the guerrilla, the army only making intermittent incursions into the zone when matters appeared to be getting out of hand, with the result that despite occasional reversals, the PCP–SL enjoyed a relatively free reign over significant stretches of the countryside.

As the insurgency mounted, piecemeal measures to boost the security forces were adopted by Alan García's administration. In June 1986, two corps of the Guardia Republicana (Republican Guard) were drafted into the highlands, one based in Huamachuco, the other in Santiago de Chuco. Unlike the average police officer, the members of these more militarised units had received elementary instruction in asymmetrical warfare and contained personnel with specialist skills, such as bomb disposal. Some upgrading also took place vis-à-vis equipment: June 1988 saw seven armoured vehicles of Israeli manufacture, each fitted with three machine-guns, sent up into the *sierra* from Trujillo, although anyone with even a fleeting acquaintance with Andean topography would realise that these were of marginal usefulness. Nor was the government above engaging in symbolic acts aimed at convincing a sceptical public that it was tackling the insurgency seriously. Late April 1986, for example, witnessed deputy Minister of the Interior and *aprista* party heavyweight Agustín Mantilla participate in a 'search and destroy' sweep in the *sierra* of La Libertad involving some 200 officers.

Additional manpower, increased firepower and political posturing nevertheless failed to make any significant impact on the insurgency. An overwhelming majority of counter-insurgency operatives remained stationed in urban installations sited in provincial and district capitals, for even as late as 1991 only one rural garrison had been established in the provinces of Cajabamba and San Marcos – the Chaquicocha police base in the Condebamba Valley. To compound matters, a poor military performance was mirrored in the administrative sphere of the state's anti-terrorist effort. Systemic chaos and corruption characterised the judicial apparatus, as illustrated by the case of Luis Geldres, the *aprista* general secretary for Santiago de Chuco, who was killed by a *senderista* hit squad in April 1987.

One María Luisa Ruíz (alias 'Ana') was captured by chance along with Osmán Morote in Lima on 12 June 1988. This particular *guerrillera* had previously been arrested in Quiruvilca in May 1987 and accused of participating in the assassination of Geldres. Surprisingly, Ruíz was freed after just one month in prison, it being rumoured that threats had been made against the judicial authorities in Trujillo charged with pursuing her case. The lawyers were persuaded to shelve the prosecution owing to 'lack of proof'. Undeterred by this experience, on her release Ruiz resumed her activities as a member of Sendero's *Fuerza Principal* operating in the Curgos–Sarín–El Pallar–Chusgón zone adjacent to Huamachuco, where, according to eyewitnesses, she participated in the killing of seven peasants in the *caserío*s of Huarana and Tulpo.[51] Such faint-hearted behaviour by the judicial authorities not only caused resentment among the security forces and encouraged the committing of human rights abuses but it also attracted substantial criticism from the civilian population and the mainstream media. On the military, political and legal fronts, therefore, the state was failing to respond adequately to the insurgency in the Cajabamba–Huamachuco region. Faced with a deteriorating situation, by the late 1980s the army's presence in the conflict zone necessarily assumed a more continuous character, but since no strategic rethink of counter-insurgency policy took place, no fundamental shift occurred in the established pattern of guerrilla advance and state retreat.

As noted in Chapter One, against a backdrop of escalating crisis following Alberto Fujimori's *autogolpe* (palace coup) in April 1992, a raft of more robust counter-insurgency measures designed to reverse the prevailing unfavourable balance of forces was introduced. In an effort to overcome intimidation and secure severe sentences, a system of military courts presided over by 'faceless judges' was adopted. Defendants found guilty of the new charge of *terrorismo agravado* (aggravated terrorism) now confronted perpetual incarceration, with minimal prospect of release. Henceforth, minors accused of terrorism would no longer be exempt from prosecution.[52] Given that, in guerrilla warfare, non-military factors play a key role in determining outcomes, with intelligence data and infiltration representing, according to counter-insurgency expert Robert Thompson, an issue 'of paramount importance', May 1992 saw the passage of a Repentance Law granting amnesty or reduced jail terms for individuals who chose 'voluntarily' to abandon armed struggle and collaborate with the authorities by betraying their erstwhile comrades.[53]

Meanwhile, behind the scenes, a number of complementary policy and administrative changes had been under way during the twilight of García's APRA government. The armed forces moved away from the ham-fisted practice of outright repression to a 'non-genocidal authoritarian' strategy. Crucially, the security services underwent a process of reorganisation and upgrading, achieving a notable success with the capture of Abimael Guzmán and other key Central Committee members in September 1992.[54]

How did these developments unfolding at the national level impact on the civil war in the Cajabamba–Huamachuco region? An early sign of new thinking on counter-insurgency matters occurred during the first half of 1991, when the generals finally tempered their natural reticence about arming the rural population and embarked upon a policy of establishing Comités de Defensa Civil (CDCs – Civil Defence Committees), more commonly referred to locally as Comités de Autodefensa (Self-defence Committees). One obvious tenet of non-conventional warfare is that the control of people (particularly in the countryside) is crucial. To this end, the 32nd Infantry Division was despatched from its base at Trujillo into the *sierra* of La Libertad to organise CDCs and train the inhabitants, with the 7th Infantry Battalion stationed outside Cajamarca being drafted into Cajabamba and San Marcos on a parallel mission.

Priority was initially given to localities deemed to be of strategic importance and those having a history of intense PCP–SL activity. All males between the ages of fourteen and sixty were enlisted (the minimum age was supposed to be eighteen, but this restriction was frequently ignored). A CDC might have from 30 to 200 members, who were supplied with low-grade weaponry; these were typically single-shot hunting rifles, although a smattering of six-shot pieces entered village armouries. Militiamen also received wellington boots and cheap plastic ponchos. Each CDC was directed by army advisers in coordination with local (military-appointed) committees, comprising a President, a Vice-President and individuals mandated to oversee particular aspects of an organisation's activity (discipline, record-keeping, economy, etc.). Responsibility for quartermastering, especially for monitoring the distribution of arms, was invested in this body, although it was subject to constant checks by army personnel. In order to encourage participation, youths eligible for conscription could undertake their military service in their home-village CDC.

By October 1994 some 955 CDCs, collectively having approximately 61,000 members, had reputedly been established in the mountains stretching from the department of Tumbes on the frontier with Ecuador down to Ancash. Logically, the greatest density (and most active) of these paramilitary organs occurred in Cajabamba–Huamachuco. By the end of 1993, a total of 443 Committees had been formed in the department of Cajamarca, which mobilised some 27,927 members; in La Libertad, around 14,018 individuals were enrolled in 219 units; by November 1995, this had grown to 260 with 20,000 participants.[55] An overwhelming majority of units operated in the countryside, but they could also be found in district capitals possessing a minimal police presence.

A variety of factors aided the rapid proliferation of the CDCs: (i) in many localities the population was familiar with the mechanics of organising patrols as a result of their experience with the *rondas campesinas*, or had at least heard about how these functioned; (ii) many individuals were willing to go along with their formation, owing to tensions that had been accumulating between the PCP–SL and the peasantry since the late 1980s; (iii) the army could call upon substantial numbers of ex-conscripts attuned to military discipline; and (iv) last, but not least, rural people joined the Committees out of fear, since those who refused to cooperate risked being labelled a '*senderista*'. However, although this particular concatenation of local circumstances allowed their numbers to expand impressively, the CDCs were constructed on shallow foundations, causing problems that will be addressed presently.

No matter what individual motives for joining might be, the CDCs nevertheless posed a significant challenge to PCP–SL cadres. Despite their access to limited weaponry, the Committees benefited from numerical strength and military backing, they possessed local knowledge and could function night and day, so depriving guerrilla forces of the operational freedom they had enjoyed throughout the 1980s. For the first time since the insurgency commenced in the early 1980s, the state attained through these organisations a position from which it could contest the PCP–SL for control of the population. Decisively, via the CDCs it could also provide a level of protection that allowed anti-guerrilla elements in the villages greater leeway to make their opposition public:

Map 5 *Cajabamba–Huamachuco: Main Counter-Insurgency Installations, c.1995*

The spread of the Comités de Autodefensa represented a hard blow to Sendero ... While they had a certain military capability and could mobilise to push the subversives out of villages and confine them to the *jalca* or other isolated spots, their most important impact was social and political. When the army formed Committees it forced the population to make a choice between the subversives or the military, and once they had made that choice there was no going back – so in a sense they had to confront Sendero in a more decided manner. Initially, many *campesinos* were wary about participating, but once the Committees were functioning, they had to integrate themselves into them.[56]

Alongside the enrolment of the local peasantry in the fight against Sendero, steps were taken to augment the permanent military presence in the conflict zone. By 1994, army bases had been established in the hacienda Sunchubamba (SAIS José Carlos Mariátegui), in district capitals where guerrilla activity was particularly strong (Sitacocha, Cachachi), and at Chuquibamba in the Condebamba Valley; a similar programme of constructing new garrisons and strengthening existing installations occurred in Huamachuco and Santiago de Chuco. Apart from representing additional personnel and firepower, the majority of infantrymen allocated to these installations came from rural Andean stock and so were better able to endure the rigours of sweep and search manoeuvres in the mountains than the police, many of whom were of coastal and/or urban origin. A parallel upgrading also took place in the quality of key personnel, in that many more officers had by now received specialist counter-insurgency instruction in Panama and elsewhere, as well as having gained combat experience in Ayacucho. By 1994, the same could be said of a number of police commanders stationed in the conflict zone, the outcome being that on the military front, the state was in a much stronger position to contest terrain with the PCP–SL and inflict greater physical damage on the insurgent organisation.[57]

Two final pieces in the counter-insurgency jigsaw involved neutralising a central element in the PCP–SL 'agrarian revolutionary war': the ability to garner support through land distribution; and attempts to address an important source of alienation that helped attract the disaffected to the guerrilla – official corruption. In order to help tackle the first issue, a policy of accelerating land titling was implemented, beginning in 1990, which affected both the cooperative sector and independent smallholders. One initial instance of movement on this question occurred in June 1990, when the SAIS Virgen de Rosario in Otuzco province was formally wound up, with 2,474 hectares distributed on an individual basis to 305 households. A further 4,616 hectares were allocated to neighbouring smallholders. As part of a 'hearts and minds' exercise, property titles were not the only thing handed out: sacks of basic foodstuffs were distributed to rural families suffering from the prolonged drought that afflicted the northern *sierra* at the time. Over the years 1991 to 1994, thousands of ownership documents were legally registered with the Ministry of Agriculture. Cognizant of the populace's penchant for formal ceremony and pieces of paper covered with impressive-looking stamps, land titles were presented to appreciative farmers at officially sponsored events attended by the appropriate bureaucrats and local military commanders. The underlying symbolic message they transmitted was that the state was addressing their wishes.

Following the *autogolpe* of April 1992, the Fujimori regime attempted to clamp down on corruption inside the civil service. It also strove to 'retool' the state and create a more efficient administrative apparatus. Throughout the 1980s, the venality of many judges, police, officials in state-run enterprises and government departments formed a major source of popular discontent, one that propelled numerous people into varying levels of sympathy and collaboration with the guerrilla. In response, the Fujimori regime removed a number of unscrupulous judges from the conflict area, transferred in better-trained functionaries, streamlined the ministries and tried to get key officials to work in a more coordinated and open fashion.[58] In San Marcos and other provincial capitals, for example, public meetings attended by the mayor, subprefect, public prosecutor and head of the local police detachment would take place each Sunday morning in the town hall, providing a forum for citizens to raise their concerns and voice complaints directly to important figures within the provincial power structure. While it would be ingenuous to assume that official corruption and nepotism had been eradicated (indeed, within the higher echelons of the regime it was mushrooming under the aegis of Vladimiro Montesinos), over the period 1992–95 the prevailing public perception held that graft was much reduced from the administrative chaos that characterised Alan García's final two years in office.

On different fronts, then, after 1990 the state appeared less of an 'enemy' in the eyes of many *campesinos* and new channels for cooperation arose, albeit within an increasingly 'militarised' political environment. To help cement patron–client ties with the rural population, during 1992–94, initial steps were also taken to reverse the retreat of the state. Using the military protective umbrella and often employing conscript corvée labour, moves began to implement small-scale development initiatives. Typically, these first involved road improvements; later on the army launched more overtly social projects, such as literacy schemes for peasant women, the aim behind both kinds of initiative being to lessen hostility towards the state and win 'hearts and minds', in order to assist the government's pacification programme.[59]

Counter-insurgency: turning the tide, 1992–94

While the array of new counter-insurgency measures helped create an overall environment more favourable to the state in its dealings with civil society, the real turning point in the civil war in Cajabamba–Huamachuco stemmed from two closely connected events. First, the passage of the Repentance Law in May 1992; and second, the capture of Abimael Guzmán in September 1992. Guzmán's detention represented a massive blow to the PCP–SL rank and file. During the 1980s, the mystique built up inside the organisation around the figure of '*Presidente Gonzalo*' and 'Gonzalo Thought' helped forge a high degree of internal party cohesion, discipline and *esprit de combat*. Nevertheless, the personality cult ultimately proved to be Sendero's Achilles' heel, in that the General Secretary's arrest dented severely cadre morale and undermined the belief of many grass-roots Party members in a victorious outcome – the slogan '*Presidente Gonzalo: garantía de triunfo*' now had a hollow ring. Aided and abetted by a press and propaganda campaign aimed at fomenting doubts within guerrilla ranks, the Repentance Law offered wavering combatants a relatively attractive, although far from risk-free, escape route out of the war and proffered the prospect of a more secure future.[60]

Although most high-ranking PCP–SL cadres in the northern highlands joined the organisation out of deeply held political convictions and fought resolutely until the end, they attracted followers with less altruistic motives. A number of the landless and urban unemployed (particularly young men) with uncertain prospects joined the Party amid the crisis of the 1980s out of a sense of adventure, as an avenue for earning a living and, importantly, as a path to acquiring power and peer recognition. After all, having grown up in the Cajabamba–Huamachuco region, they had become imbued with Andean traditions of *gamonalismo*, a belief system centred on the legitimacy of employing subterfuge and violence to further one's own interests and attain 'respect'. When guerrilla operations occurred, these individuals typically implemented the *batir el campo* strategy in a robust fashion and, in consequence, rose to occupy middle-ranking positions inside the PCP–SL. Now confronted with a more aggressive performance by military detachments reinforced by the recently formed CDCs, a number of them were arrested and quickly broke under the 'unscientific' interrogation methods the security services customarily administered to their captives. Taking advantage of the Repentance Law, they started to collaborate actively with the intelligence services. Others, behaving in opportunistic fashion (another characteristic of classic *gamonalismo* inherited from the days of factional politics), rapidly reassessed their prospects and surrendered voluntarily, especially after the capture of Guzmán brought a noticeable fall in morale.

Consequently, 1993 witnessed some sixty-eight *senderistas* adopting this path (only six of them women), a trend that snowballed during the following year. Between January and October 1994 a total of 292 (39 women) 'voluntarily' took advantage of the Repentance Law to negotiate a reduced sentence and, in some cases, avoid imprisonment altogether. As mentioned, the clear quid pro quo involved 'repentants' informing on the identity of their ex-comrades, PCP–SL hideouts, arms caches and channels of communication. Heightened military effectiveness and improvement in the quality of intelligence units stationed in Cajabamba–Huamachuco, alongside the impact of the Repentance Law, therefore increased appreciably the flow of information about the local PCP–SL apparatus available to the authorities, enabling the state to inflict far greater damage upon its political and military structure.

Hardly surprising, then, that whereas prior to 1992 yearly detention rates had been minimal, between 1993 and September 1996 some 557 *senderistas* were arrested in Cajamarca, an overwhelming majority in the provinces of Cajabamba and San Marcos. Some 360 of these turned themselves in and sought amnesty under the Repentance Law; over 600 captures were registered in the *sierra* of La Libertad.[61] Arrests were usually made either by police and army personnel combing the countryside with lists of names provided by informants, or took place in the company of a hooded 'repentant', who was escorted around villages with orders to finger Party members and collaborators. The typical scene involved all the inhabitants being forcibly assembled, whereupon the *arrepentido* would pass along the line, pointing out suspects.

One figure who traversed this route and whose actions caused significant damage to the insurgents was a young *campesino* named Santos Robles, who had been recruited into the PCP–SL when a teenager by no less a figure than Osmán Morote. After receiving military training in Ayacucho, Robles was then drafted back into Cajabamba as a *mando militar* in 1988. Following his arrest in 1990, he turned informer and eventually negotiated a reduced sentence under the Repentance Law, whereupon (exhibiting a touch of malicious irony), he adopted the pseudonym 'Morote'. Between 1992 and 1994, Robles was regularly seen being chaperoned around the streets and country lanes of Cajabamba, indicating supposed *senderistas* to his minders. As a result of these actions some 300 people were reputedly detained, including numerous innocents. Accusations also abound that Robles fed off the new-found power that his relation with the security services afforded, exploiting his position to blackmail the vulnerable. Even when he was well into his reduced sentence under the Repentance Law, intelligence agents would occasionally take Robles from the high-security jail at Huacariz, sited on the outskirts of Cajamarca, to traverse San Marcos and Cajabamba in search of additional *senderistas*. Although all informers were allocated a code (e.g. A1HO–17112, A1HO–72321, etc.), the scale and nature of 'Morote's' activities meant that his identity became impossible to disguise. Needless to say, his nemesis could not be long delayed: Robles was stabbed to death in his cell on 17 July 1997.[62] Once the informant's usefulness diminished, the authorities allowed some of his victims their moment of revenge.

Another individual who possessed the ability to attract fear and loathing in equal measure around the Condebamba Valley and its environs was Jesús Crespin. From a smallholding family in Quillispampa, Crespin had been active in the local Party apparatus from at least 1990. On 31 August 1991 he formed part of a twenty-strong *senderista* column that occupied the hamlet of Lloque, where the insurgents seized a middle-aged woman accused of collaborating with the authorities. Following a public denunciation, she was shot in the head, but continued breathing and was knocked to the ground and given the *coup de grâce* by Crespin. In a portent of future developments, the victim happened to have been involved in an ongoing land dispute with Crespin's father.[63] Thereafter, the young man's activities and reputation for violence grew, eventually to reach the ears of the security services, who redoubled their efforts to capture him.

With the police closing in, Crespin decided to surrender and in mid-1994 sought amnesty under the Repentance Law. The following account from a neighbour, who was arrested along with his three brothers-in-law and received a ten-year jail sentence for terrorism (all the while protesting his innocence), illustrates graphically the impact of this turncoat's activities:

> At 11 p.m. on 22 November 1994, police personnel entered the community of Quillispampa under the guidance of a repentant who responds to the name of Jesús Crespin Ruíz ... The aforementioned repentant denounced us as members of the Sendero Luminoso terrorist group. They pulled us from our humble abode and dragged us to the local football pitch, where they began to hit us hard before the gaze of our families. Seeing this, my wife started to cry.
>
> While beating us cruelly, the police asked about guns and told us to hand over our arms. So that my wife would not witness this insane act of torture, they removed her to a place where she could not see the cruel treatment I was suffering. While the police were torturing me they ordered that I repent. If I would repent, they said they would help me ... I replied that: 'I am not a terrorist. I have nothing to repent about!' So they continued with their maltreatment, insulting me repeatedly, calling me names like 'Motherfucker' and 'Son of a bitch' ... Afterwards they tied my hands and told me 'You are going to rot in prison', before taking me and my brothers-in-law to the *caserío* of Araqueda, where the police threw us all in a room. The next day we were beaten again, when they claimed I was a *mando político*, stating that Jesús Crespin Ruíz had told them this. This repentant accuses me of various terrorist attacks, which I cannot understand because at the time the incidents occurred (1992–1993), I was working for the Retamas transport company ... Following this, they took us to Cajabamba, where we arrived at 6 p.m. and they put us in jail. Later, at 12 p.m., the police brought us out and once again tortured us pitilessly, during which time they again accused me of being a *mando político*, even though I continued to deny it.[64]

According to this detainee, the informant's actions were driven by two factors. First, when Crespin was on the run, he had indicated to a police search party the house belonging to the mother-in-law of the former *senderista*. Second, denunciations had been lodged with the authorities by the *quillispampinos* after an insurgent force that included Crespin appropriated their crops. These events, the prisoner maintained, had bred 'hatred, hatred' and a thirst for revenge within Crespin, which he was able to assuage by exploiting his 'repentant' status. A petition signed by sixty-two residents from the vicinity of Araqueda claimed that Crespin possessed another reason for acting in this fashion: one of the detainees was a smallholder with whom he had entered into a sharecropping agreement; the informer's aim was to take advantage of the owner's incarceration to expropriate his land.[65] No matter what the motivation happened to be, over the second half of 1994 and throughout 1995, Crespin's word led to the incarceration of scores of people in Cajabamba province, by no means all of whom were PCP–SL activists or sympathisers.

As if the effect of individuals such as Jesús Crespin was not enough, the devastating impact of the Repentance Law on the rebel organisation was compounded by the fact that, in acts of *gattopardismo* ('leopardism') of Sicilian proportions, a number of strategically placed individuals not only became informers but also switched sides completely.[66] Swimming with the changing tide after the capture of Guzmán, they metamorphosed miraculously from autocratic *senderista* commissar to autocratic leader of a local Comité de Autodefensa. One infamous individual from the parish of Chuquibamba in the Condebamba Valley, who took this particular route in search of personal safety and enrichment, surfaced in the character of Isabel Salvatierra (Isabel can be a male name in the *cajamarquino* countryside). After being ousted as president of the CAP José Santos Chocano in April 1983, Salvatierra entered the local PCP–SL apparatus (see Chapter Four), participating in numerous armed and propagandistic actions before taking advantage of the Repentance Law in 1994. Accompanied by his brothers, Brígido and Juan – themselves both former *senderistas* transformed into *arrepentidos* – Isabel became active in Chuquibamba's CDC. In cahoots with certain avaricious policemen stationed in Cajabamba, he demonstrated his total abandonment of Maoist agrarian communism by attempting to blackmail local smallholders with the intention of seizing their property.

Indeed, Salvatierra possessed something of a track record when it came to violating guerrilla principles of rural egalitarianism. Following the assassination of Oscar Acón in January 1984, Crecencio Paredes became head of the José Santos Chocano cooperative and presided over the parcelling up of the enterprise, assisted by a *compadre* of Salvatierra's, one Alberto Urquiaga. As a result of the division, most cooperative members were allocated 1.5 hectares, whereas Urquiaga (backed up militarily by Salvatierra's PCP-SL connections) obtained 32.20 hectares of prime, irrigated, valley cropland. Not content with this windfall, Urquiaga assisted Paredes to dispose illegally of all the non-fixed assets remaining in the CAP and pocket the proceeds. To compound the injustice, Urquiaga was neither a farmer nor a cooperative member, but a townie from Cajabamba in possession of an oleaginous reputation, who, despite an *orden de captura* (detention order) issued against him for fraud in 1990, was able to go about his normal business owing to the connivance of corrupt elements inside the provincial police hierarchy.[67]

Once the Salvatierra brothers abandoned their guerrilla past, they ingratiated themselves with members of the police and, aided by Urquiaga, set out on the path of primitive accumulation. Smallholders were threatened with arrest under the anti-terrorist legislation, and also torture, followed by a lengthy incarceration, unless they gave what for the normal rural household amounted to significant amounts of cash, or made over the titles to their property. Such behaviour induced one of the intended victims to complain to the subprefect of Cajabamba:

... for more than three months to the present day, Isabel Salvatierra Valderrama has been coming to my house showing me a list of names, supposedly of terrorists who he intends to accuse. He has threatened me, demanding the sum of 500,000 *nuevos soles* in order to keep my name off the list ... In September 1994 my father ... was detained by the DIRCOTE of Cajamarca, where he is currently serving his sentence as a repentant. Taking advantage of my father's absence, and exhibiting the cunning of a freed repentant terrorist, Salvatierra forcibly persuaded my mother to pay him 600,000 *nuevos soles*. This money was handed over in Cajamarca, where he said the cash was to bribe a major in the National Police surnamed Aliaga, in addition to an officer who is charged with investigating cases of terrorism ... [Salvatierra] said that he possesses influence and works in close cooperation with the aforementioned officers.[68]

In a similar vein, no fewer than twenty-five former members of the José Santos Chocano cooperative addressed a petition to the head of the Human Rights Commission in the national Congress, arraigning him on the following charges:

Corrupting the military, political and judicial authorities, Alberto Urquiaga Rodríguez and Isabel Salvatierra Valderrama have been attempting to dispossess us of our land. For this reason, they have lodged a series of denunciations against us. These range from participation in the vilest terrorist acts to the charge of illegal squatting ... The first of the aforementioned individuals has accused us of being usurpers and terrorists, to which end he has utilised his influence with a PNP major whose surname is OJEDA PEÑA. This officer has engaged in blackmail. He threatens to accuse us of terrorism if we do not hand over our possessions ... Additionally, the aforementioned officer and his colleagues have abused their position by expropriating our cattle ... Among other police officers who are threatening us arbitrarily is one whose surname is SALAZAR HERNANDEZ and another called ARREA. They can be seen in the company of Judge Moreno Zavaleta, drinking liqor in different *cantinas*, as on 1 May, when we saw them imbibing in the bar above the Palacios Transport Company. As Salvatierra Valderrama was buying the alcohol, this is classified as corruption and is against the law ... Salvatierra Valderrama is a repentant terrorist and Urquiaga Rodríguez is a fraudster. The former sold all the land that he received in the cooperative and is now trying to get it back. The latter is a crook. He is not a peasant and does not live in the locality, but is from Cajabamba. Even so, they are now trying to open proceedings to take our land away. They have no scruples.[69]

Given Salvatierra's connections with strategic players within the local power structure, no action was taken to detain him, notwithstanding his reputation as a person *de alto vuelo* (a trickster) with a penchant for engaging in Mafia-style behaviour. Individual characteristics aside, the activities of turncoats such as Robles, Crespin and Salvatierra proved disastrous for the PCP–SL in the northern highlands. Although several hundred took advantage of the Repentance Law, it was the information supplied by approximately a dozen ex-combatants that truly devastated the regional Party organisation during 1993 and 1994.[70]

Counter-insurgency: flaws within the PCP–SL apparatus

How was it that the actions of a relatively small number of middle-ranking cadres could wreak so much havoc on the guerrilla organisation? Remembering Mao's observation that when engaging in 'prolonged and tangled' warfare, 'it is people, not things, that are decisive', political education represented an issue of fundamental importance. Established social mores, when allied to normal human passions and failings, produced behaviour that 'persists by force of long tradition', which might undermine the successful pursuit of revolutionary goals. Among these traits, Mao argued, figured 'localism', in which the extended family network ('clan') and village-based party branch became indistinguishable, leading to a harmful admixture of their respective interests. In addition to the dangers of conflating personal and party affairs, 'the defection of careerists' comprised another important problem facing an insurgent organisation, along with the prioritising of military over political matters.[71] Regarding violence, when commenting on criticism levelled at peasant associations in Hunan for 'going too far', he maintained that:

> The peasants are clear-sighted. Who is bad and who is not, who is the worst and who is not quite so vicious, who deserves severe punishment and who deserves to be let off lightly – the peasants keep clear accounts, and very seldom has the punishment exceeded the crime …To put it bluntly, it is necessary to create terror for a while in every rural area, or otherwise it would be impossible to suppress the activities of the counter-revolutionaries in the countryside or overthrow the authority of the gentry. Proper limits have to be exceeded in order to right a wrong, or else the wrong cannot be righted … now that the peasants have risen and shot a few and created just a little terror in suppressing the counter-revolutionaries, is there any reason for saying they should not do so?[72]

Nine years later, 'ultra-left' excesses committed during the later period of the ten-year agrarian revolutionary war that commenced in 1927 were viewed as 'wrong' and therefore targeted for criticism and rectification:

> Distinction should be made between the landlords, the merchants and the rich peasants, and the main point is to explain things to them politically and win their neutrality, while at the same time organizing the masses of the people to keep an eye on them. Only against the very few elements who are most dangerous should stern measures like arrest be taken.[73]

When dealing with 'traitors', an anti-espionage policy 'must firmly suppress', but equally:

... there must not be too much killing, and no innocent person should be incriminated. Vacillating elements and reluctant followers among the reactionaries should be dealt with leniently. Corporal punishment must be abolished in trying criminals; the stress must be on the weight of evidence and confessions should not be taken on trust. Our policy towards prisoners ... should be to set them free, except for those who have incurred the bitter hatred of the masses and must receive capital punishment and whose death sentences have been approved by the higher authorities ... and, if they fight against us and are captured again, should again be set free. We should not insult them, take away their personal effects or try to exact recantations from them, but without exception should treat them sincerely and kindly. This should be our policy, however reactionary they may be. It is a very effective way of isolating the hard core of reaction.[74]

Just as counter-insurgency expert Robert Thompson advocated that government troops should operate within the law and not indulge in human-rights violations, since such actions only served as a 'recruiting sergeant' for insurgent forces, Mao regarded excessive violence as self-defeating, because it spread alienation and encouraged opposition. As the Chinese maxim cautioned, needless brutality 'drives the fish into deep waters and the sparrows into the thickets'.

Bearing these points in mind, how might the quality of the PCP–SL apparatus in the northern highlands be evaluated? On the question of 'localism', given its clandestine nature, entry into the Party often followed a discernible pattern: recruitment was effected by close relatives or friends. Brothers or sisters would enrol their siblings and cousins, children their mothers or fathers and vice versa, so that extended *senderista* families developed in town and country. Under these circumstances (especially within a social environment steeped in a long history of factional and familial feuding), it was to be expected that Party political business and personal animosities could easily fuse. As the trajectory of Crespin and Salvatierra illustrate, quarrels predating a cadre's involvement in the insurgency ended up being pursued as part of a wider guerrilla campaign and then continued when individuals entered their post-insurgent phase – with the (at times unwitting) assistance of the security services. Crespin and Salvatierra were far from the only *senderistas* to travel this path. A cottager from the hamlet of Colcabamba (Cajabamba province) was assassinated for no apparent reason by a PCP–SL detachment in August 1992; two years later the victim's sister found herself arrested on terrorism charges through the testimony of Pedro Jacinto Soto, a repentant. Soto had previously been active in the district's Fuerza Local (on his arrest, police found arms hidden in his cottage) and, a member of a rival family, he informed the police that she had 'collaborated with food and accommodation'.[75]

Two related outcomes flowed from a tendency to indulge in 'localism': (i) some military actions were not conducted according to strict political criteria, 'politics' therefore, was not always 'in command'; and (ii) a number of civilian deaths resulted from non-political motives. As the life histories of Crespin,

Salvatierra, Soto and oral testimony demonstrate, the PCP–SL exhibited a tendency to take part in violence beyond that considered valid by most inhabitants, in violation of Mao's admonishment that 'confessions should not be taken on trust'. Punishments, in consequence, occurred on the basis of innuendo, with some units being too hasty in administering 'stern measures'. Such opportunistic action spawned hostility from those affected directly. Moreover, in a social setting where people have long memories and most of everybody's private business is common knowledge, combining the personal and the political in this fashion damaged the PCP–SL's credibility at village level. Keeping 'clear accounts' and being 'clear-sighted', rural people possessed the in-depth information to analyse the motives behind the actions mounted against particular individuals and to assess their legitimacy. Engagement in vendetta-style violence also facilitated the spread of 'black propaganda' aimed at undermining the Party's reputation by intelligence operatives engaged in psychological warfare. Equally, the high number of people who took advantage of the Repentance Law during 1992–94 indicates that the Party failed to address the – foreseeable – problems that might be created by 'the defection of careerists'.[76]

According to Mao, if an organisation was to avoid falling into these pitfalls 'the only solution is to intensify political training', for 'facts have shown that the better the company Party representative, the sounder the company'. Local commanders also needed 'to do some hard thinking', 'combine wisdom with courage' and 'be willing to learn', for 'the important thing is to be good at learning'.[77] Events in Cajabamba–Huamachuco indicate that during the late 1980s and early 1990s the regional PCP–SL apparatus was found wanting on all these counts. Indeed, one of the first commentators to pinpoint this potential weakness was journalist Gustavo Gorriti, who noted, perceptively, that the guerrilla lacked 'well-trained middle-ranking cadres'.[78] After the capture of Felix Calderón, Roberto Barrios and other politically experienced peasants of local extraction, leadership positions in Cajabamba and the *sierra* of La Libertad were occupied mainly by outsiders who, even when they originated from peasant stock, did not possess the same level of fine-grained knowledge about local affairs. As the Party expanded rapidly after 1985, relatively greenhorn individuals rose to occupy posts that conferred upon them responsibilities beyond their capability and wisdom. Too many of the Party's intermediate-level militants proved unable 'to do some hard thinking' and were too slow to learn. The outcome was a spate of injudicious actions that were counter-productive to the organisation's long-term goals. When problems arose, individually and collectively, the regional apparatus failed to exhibit an ability to analyse and rectify its modus operandi. Here, the local PCP–SL structure highlighted a failing common to all of Peru's Maoist and new left groups: within a rigidly hierarchical party political culture, the emphasis was very much on frenetic activism, with correspondingly little attention paid to promoting cadre education, theoretical debate and contemplative reflection regarding everyday praxis.

Indicatively, a similar situation appears to have arisen in Ayacucho and the neighbouring departments of Apurímac and Huancavelica. In a highly critical internal Party document penned by a leading cadre operating in Sendero's *Región Principal*, it was noted that the organisation's rapid growth had allowed:

> ... many opportunists to infiltrate our ranks, given the easy entry of the masses. Applying a mistaken policy, many comrades went too far in their treatment of class enemies, striking out in all directions and on the basis of faulty information. In this fashion, they killed many people who later could have made good comrades. Combatants who still conserved a petty bourgeois mentality and others who were badly oriented acted as if they were a gang of miserable thieves, becoming the scourge of each *pueblo* they entered. Tired of such abuse, the inhabitants denounced us to the enemy. Many comrades in our support bases brought these complaints to EGP commanders, protesting against this unacceptable guerrilla behaviour. But some *mandos,* instead of intervening to prevent such actions, have threatened these comrades, accusing them of being traitors ... The first thing this type of rotten and stupid combatant does on coming to a village is threaten the peasants with death so that they will not inform the enemy. Terrorised, the unfortunate inhabitants believe mistakenly that all *guerrilleros* act in this manner. Additionally, these combatants fell into indiscipline, especially with regard to the second cardinal rule [Mao's 'Do not steal from the people'], seizing without the masses' permission whatever they desired, undertaking banquets without restraint, in opposition to the interests of the populace. Furthermore, anybody who protested was accused of being a traitor, and if they persisted with their protest, it cost them their life. One would have to be stupid to condone such repugnant behaviour.[79]

Not only did 'green' recruits come to occupy the pivotal position of *mando*, despite having 'received little orientation', 'former thieves' and other undesirable elements managed to 'infiltrate the Party'. After 'simulating' a character reform, some of these 'hypocritical' individuals managed to 'trick' the organisation and were:

> ... even allocated leadership roles. They joined our ranks only to provoke unnecessary conflicts and taking advantage of their authority, exacted vengeance on their old enemies, so undermining the Party's prestige. When the situation became difficult, these were the first to desert and go over to the enemy. This kind of person has caused us great damage.[80]

To compound matters, the apparatus demonstrated 'too little interest in educating new recruits, overconfidence regarding its own position, combined with an exaggerated underestimation of the enemy'.[81] Apparently, then, many of the errors committed by the CPC during the late 1920s were being repeated by the PCP–SL in Ayacucho six decades later, and while no comparable document has been unearthed that evaluates with cold dispassion the Party's conduct in Cajabamba–Huamachuco, it would appear that similar deficiencies characterised the organisation's operation in the northern Andes. Over the quinquennium 1985–90, therefore, the guerrilla expanded quantitatively, but failed to improve qualitatively, so making the task of the security services correspondingly less difficult once the state mounted a more rational counter-insurgency effort in the early 1990s. To the external observer, the PCP–SL presented an image of efficiency, meticulous planning and coherent decision-making, but behind this façade the organisation's internal working arrangements and control mechanisms proved seriously flawed.

Counter-insurgency: flaws in the Comités de Autodefensa

According to the literature written on Huanta, the River Apurímac Valley and other parishes in the department of Ayacucho, following an initial failed attempt by the Peruvian army to establish 'strategic hamlets' in 1983-84, the rural population began to form CDCs largely under their own initiative during the late 1980s. Having proved their usefulness by the early 1990s, they then began to receive military support. The Committees eventually played a key role in defeating PCP–SL insurgents, achieving widespread support, high levels of participation and operational autonomy; they could not be regarded as mere *fantoccini* – mechanically worked puppets – created and manipulated at will by the military. Rather, demonstrating commendable 'agency', the CDCs were organs of 'peasant counter-rebellion' that contributed towards the rebirth of civil society after the devastating pillage and violence visited on villages during the civil war.[82]

If (with appropriate caveats), this is the story of CDC formation and trajectory in the central-southern Andes, the picture for the northern highlands differs in important respects. No largely spontaneous grass-roots 'peasant counter-rebellion' emerged in Cajabamba–Huamachuco, despite deepening points of rupture between the PCP–SL and growing numbers of the local population during the late 1980s and early 1990s. Several factors can be advanced to account for the population's inability to act autonomously in this regard. A first point concerns the vagaries of political history and organisational development. Compared to Ayacucho, villagers in the northern highlands had experienced greater involvement with parties (essentially APRA) in the decades after 1930 and, during Velasco's agrarian reform, participation in the CNA and CCP peasant federations. After Velasco's ousting in 1975, *rondas campesinas* had been established, with varying degrees of success. One consequence of these experiences was the emergence of a clearly identifiable layer of leaders, but, as the civil war escalated, this seeming advantage in terms of political 'social capital' metamorphosed into weakness. Known activists attracted the attention of both the PCP–SL and state coercive agencies. Threatened with collaboration or death by guerrilla forces on the one hand, while suffering persecution and imprisonment at the hands of the authorities on the other, the most politicised elements of rural society naturally feared for their personal safety. Such a difficult situation undermined their ability to act. The very individuals possessing the skills necessary to evolve a 'peasant response' to the unfolding crisis were, in consequence, rendered impotent by a vicious circle of violence over which they exercised little control and enjoyed limited possibilities for manoeuvre.

A second, but related, factor that reduced the potential for 'peasant counter-rebellion' in the northern highlands has to do with attitudes towards the state. On top of finding themselves in vulnerable and dangerous circumstances, many of the most politically conscious and able individuals who would normally have been expected to push grass-roots organisation to counter the PCP–SL were understandably wary of the state's military and political apparatus. Having experienced directly the operation of peasant federations and the *rondas campesinas*, or heard of them through the rural grapevine, they desired the establishment of autonomous organisations that operated in a democratic fashion. Simultaneously, however, they realised that the creation of such bodies was firmly off the political agenda, or would, at best, be a difficult project to sustain. The schisms that had arisen with officialdom over the nightwatch patrols left bitter memories. Under current circumstances, the state would not allow independent movements to operate in the countryside. Sitting back and keeping a low profile therefore appeared the most expedient available option. An unfortunate situation that enveloped a smallholder from the *caserío* of Higosbamba (Cajabamba province) in late 1993 illustrates the competing pressures and circumspect outlook in this regard. This smallholder was denounced as a terrorist by leaders of the local CDC because he refused to enrol and patrol. In reply, the accused protested that: 'I'm a *rondero* and am not in agreement with the Comités de Autodefensa'. This was no isolated case, for other denizens of Igosbamba, Ichabamba and surrounding hamlets in Cajabamba province also declined to participate in the neighbourhood CDC, resulting in their arrest and maltreatment.[83] An influential minority of smallholders, alienated and determined to maintain their autonomy, proved reluctant to collaborate with the state's dirty work.

Alongside an ambivalent attitude vis-à-vis the state, a third feature of rural society in the northern highlands that helps explain the absence of 'peasant counter-rebellion' relates to the nature of village life. As mentioned earlier, compared to the central and southern Andes, rural society in the north has traditionally been more atomised; the corporate peasant community figured less prominently in the rural social structure. To compound matters, the manner in which agrarian reform had been implemented accentuated long-standing divisions and spawned a plethora of new conflicts. Bitter inter- and intra-hamlet rivalries involving extended families and opposing land groups (often encouraged by the PCP–SL), created a level of social fragmentation that made the emergence of an independent, broad-based, anti-guerrilla social movement problematic. Nor could the inhabitants draw on other important 'organisational facilitators' who might have enabled mobilisation. Whereas in the River Apurímac Valley and surrounding districts Pentecostal churches sustained an active social network and a collective *Weltanshauung* that helped village militias to develop, in Cajabamba–Huamachuco the spread of Protestantism and, in tandem, the presence of sects possessing a strong sense of identity, remained far weaker.[84] Furthermore, the Catholic Church in the northern highlands opposed the PCP–SL, but, because of human rights concerns, remained guarded about close collaboration with state coercive agencies. Mustering the rural population around religion thus presented greater obstacles compared to the situation encountered in parts of Ayacucho.

A *mélange* of factors therefore determined that the creation of anti-guerrilla militias in the Cajabamba–Huamachuco region largely became an army- and police-driven initiative imposed from above. Needless to say, these entities suffered from a lack of legitimacy, unlike their counterparts further south, and after 1995 they quickly entered a process of decline. Indeed, by 1997 most had become inactive, while those still functioning were beset by a wide array of problems. An underlying difficulty facing the CDCs from the outset was that country people never regarded them as 'their' organisations. Against this backdrop, militia credibility was torpedoed by two common operational failings that the authorities consistently failed to address: (i) abuses perpetuated by military and police personnel charged with creating and overseeing their everyday activity; and (ii) corruption among those villagers who came to occupy leadership positions within the Committees.

Regarding the first issue, although the military top brass adopted a 'non-genocidal authoritarian' posture towards the highland population, not all officers wholeheartedly took on board a 'hearts and minds' approach in their dealings with civilians. Among some personnel, traditional patterns of behaviour persisted, including physical abuse and extortion.[85] The illegal activities of police officer Ojeda have already been noted in relation to attempted blackmail against former members of the cooperative José Santos Chocano. This was far from an isolated denunciation, for some eighteen months prior to this incident, an anonymous letter had been sent to the police chief in Cajabamba protesting against Ojeda's rapacious behaviour when on patrol in the surrounding countryside:

> According to the testimony of four inhabitants from Huayllabamba ... the police under the command of major Ojeda are carrying out a series of sweeps and committing abuses. Included among these figure raids on the properties of the poorest sector of the population in order to extract money from them. The police say: *'la justicia es sólo para el que paga'* ('justice is only for those who pay'). In other words, if these unfortunates manage to cough up the amounts demanded, they can go free. If not, they are transferred to [the high security prison at] Cajamarca ... The villagers also say that the poorest families live in a state of fear following the formation of the Self-defence Committees. The members of these organisations receive total backing from the police and civil authorities. They take advantage of their position to exact revenge. For this reason, the populace has to keep quiet and tolerate the multiple abuses that occur.[86]

Despite such complaints being lodged with the authorities, no sanction was forthcoming from Ojeda's superiors; to add insult to injury, he did not even get transferred out of Cajabamba. The Fujimori regime's attempts to curb low-level corruption clearly encountered limitations.

Money, moreover, was not the sole motive behind extortion. Disputes about women could also produce abuse. In Araqueda and surrounding districts, police sergeant Américo Barrueto acquired a justifiable reputation not only for robustness in taking the fight to the PCP–SL and organising the local CDCs. He was also in the habit of casting his eye over the local peasant women. This had dire consequences for a smallholder from the hamlet of Colcabamba who received a twenty-year sentence for terrorism. According to the accused, Barrueto had planted incriminating documents (a poster and a notebook) along with four sticks of dynamite in his house; the reason became clear at the moment of arrest, when the sergeant addressed the smallholder's partner in the following terms:

> 'You stupid peasant bitch! Your own capriciousness led you to get involved with this bastard instead of going out with me – a policeman' … I do not know what this officer's intentions towards my partner were. Undoubtedly he had an interest in her and once he knew that she was living with me, has maintained a deep hatred towards my person … This police officer wants to implicate us both in terrorism … he is exacting revenge.[87]

While it was not hard to foresee the negative impact on citizens of financial and other misdemeanours committed with impunity by the police, the arbitrary use of violence by supposed upholders of law and order provoked deeper popular rejection. Incidents here ran the gamut from perpetrating petty abuses designed to demonstrate power, such as kicking a civilian in the street, to undertaking serious crimes such as rape and homicide.

To give one example, on 24 November 1996 a conscript stationed at the Chuquibamba military installation in the Condebamba Valley deserted and, while on the run, raped a nine-year-old girl who was tending a flock of sheep nearby. With reason, the assault caused 'profound shock among the population'.[88] The officer corps also indulged in unacceptable behaviour. When two *campesinos* returned to Chuquibamba on 26 October 1996 after completing their patrol with the local CDC and handed in their firearms to the base quartermaster, a quarrel erupted with an army lieutenant named Jorge Salas. Salas, who was reputedly inebriated, attacked the peasants with apoplectic ferocity, severely injuring one of his victims and beating the other, Gregorio Vera, to death. Vera's body was then dumped beside the River Condebamba. Despite protests from the deceased's family and neighbours, the army took no action against the lieutenant, nor was he posted out of the district. Faced with this affront, the district governor was moved, two months later, to draft an official indictment against Salas to the departmental prefect. The document, whose contents were leaked to a local newspaper, complained about:

> The continuing series of abuses committed by the soldier, like being constantly drunk, forcing the inhabitants of Chuquibamba to purchase him alcoholic drinks and even arresting those who do not accede to his demands … In the same petition, lieutenant Jorge Salas is accused of using his official position to threaten people with his army-issued weapon. This occurred a

few weeks ago at the village of Tacshana in Cajabamba, when in an inebriated state, Salas drew his pistol and fired several shots in the air, causing
panic among the public. For his part, Pablo Secundino Vera Liñán, father
of the rondero *leader* Luis Gregorio Vera Aguilar, demands a full investigation into the death of his son.[89]

Despite the publicity surrounding these events, the officer continued to be
protected by his superiors.

Since military and police personnel appointed to direct the day-to-day
running of the CDCs set such a poor example, better behaviour could hardly
be expected from those civilians they selected to hold positions of authority
within the militias. Following the example of Isabel Salvatierra, it became
common practice for committee appointees to exploit their newly acquired
power to engage in extortion and settle long-standing vendettas, resulting in
bloodletting tangential to that caused on strict counter-insurgency grounds,
hand in hand with additional economic hardship for the targeted households.
One case concerned a seventy-five-year-old widow, who was arrested in 1993
in the parish of Araqueda, after being accused of terrorism by members of the
local CDC. Although the slow pensioner seemed an improbable guerrilla, police
officers acted against her without comprehending the subplot – she was involved
in a property dispute with an influential family within the Committee.[90] A
similar fate befell a smallholder from Tabacal in the Condebamba Valley, who
was denounced as a terrorist and arrested on 23 October 1993 by the hamlet
CDC. The detainee was in the unfortunate position of having ongoing personal
and land 'problems' with members of the Tabacal militia.[91]

Such a bleak state of affairs proved the norm in Condebamba and
surrounding districts. Similar events in the neighbouring settlement of Chingol
induced six smallholders to complain about:

> Julio Marquina Briceño, president of the Chingol CDC. Informing us that
> eight boxes of munitions have gone missing from his house, Marquina wants
> us to lie and state that the river carried away the boxes. In addition, he has
> forced us all to collaborate with two *nuevos soles* to purchase identity cards,
> which have not been issued to us yet. He has also demanded ten *nuevos soles*
> under the pretext of arranging the issuing of property titles.
>
> We would like to inform you that the aforementioned individual under-
> takes these acts because his real intention is to compel us to abandon our
> holdings, which we have acquired through legal purchase. With this in mind,
> he is not above intimidating us with being denounced as a 'terrorist', and
> threatens that he is 'going to plant papers in our pockets' with the aim of
> implicating us and securing our imprisonment. Marquina states that he has
> the support of the authorities on this matter, and has already bribed them
> with a bull.[92]

In order to curry favour, anticipate potential future difficulties and apply a little
moral pressure, the *campesinos* ended their petition by noting that regarding the

allegation of subornation: 'We do not believe this, because the authorities ought to be the first to contribute to Peru's pacification, prevent arbitrary abuse and uphold human rights'.[93] Apart from the usual competition over land and other agricultural resources, CDC militiamen and their military minders could find themselves bound up in personal imbroglios. One such case unfolded in the *caserío* of Ayangay (Cajabamba), where they arrested a youth for terrorism on the hearsay of an aggrieved mother, whose unmarried daughter had given birth to his child. While the detainee claimed that he 'supported the baby to the best of my economic capability', the mother did not view him as suitable son-in-law material and, in consequence, had 'threatened to denounce me on various occasions'.[94]

If dishonest behaviour on the part of office-holders undermined the credibility of the CDCs, as it did with the PCP–SL, a propensity to take part in gratuitous violence engendered hostility among the rural population. The harrowing experience of a smallholder from Rosa Huayta, near Liclipampa in the district of Cachachi illustrates an all-too-common pattern of behaviour:

At around 9 a.m. on 18 December 1993, I was detained by the army and *ronderos* from the hamlet of Tabacal. They approached my house in a threatening manner and encountered me eating soup with my wife and children. When my dogs started barking, I went outside and saw peasants and soldiers had surrounded the house, whereupon I moved to tie up my dogs and had half-turned when they started firing. The soldiers shot into the air and the *ronderos* at my body, hitting me twice in the elbow. I fell to the ground, at which they ran forward and tied my hands behind my back.

Then the soldiers and *ronderos* dragged me to the entrance of my house, threw me on the ground face down and started to beat me. I continued being beaten while they ransacked the house, scattering my food and possessions all over the floor. They asked 'Where are the guns?' and I replied that I knew nothing about arms. My wife was also questioned: 'Where are the guns that belong to your husband?' She replied that 'My husband doesn't have any guns'. They then beat her and still she said that we had nothing. Our attackers then looked at one another and exclaimed: 'This motherfucker hasn't got anything'.

After finding nothing in my house, they dragged me away with my hands tied, all the while hitting me with their rifles. We then met another group of soldiers, to whom they handed me over. Their commander ordered that I be untied and told me to take off my jumper so he could inspect my arm. They could see the wounds from the two bullets and the blood that kept flowing. I asked them why they had treated me so, to which the soldiers informed their commander that the *ronderos* had shot me. Thereupon, the officer ordered the *ronderos* to take me down to Tabacal on horseback.

I was bleeding profusely, but the *ronderos* showed no concern. When we arrived at Tabacal, they handed me over to the army, who again questioned me about arms. I replied that I knew nothing of guns and seeing that my elbow continued bleeding, ordered the *ronderos* to take me to Chaquicocha

... they turned me over to a police lieutenant at Chaquicocha at around 3 p.m. and still my arm was bleeding. Then the police continued interrogating me, asking lots of questions about guns. Four of them started to hit me on my injured arm and tied a rope across my mouth ... after so much torture, my clothing was soaked in blood. When I fainted, they transferred me to Cajabamba at around 6 p.m. – I was at death's door through lack of blood.'

Seeing that I was completely buggered (*jodido*), the police in Cajabamba took me to the public hospital. When I woke up the next day, a drip was attached to me, but the bleeding had not stopped. I was in hospital for three days and on the fourth day I was taken to the DIRCOTE in Cajamarca. While there, I received no medicines. That's how poverty-stricken peasants have to suffer ... I was not given food for 16 days.[95]

As if this treatment was not enough, as a result of the beating administered to his partner by the Tabacal CDC, she suffered a miscarriage. Such excessive behaviour provoked increased wariness of the CDCs, leading many people to restrict their involvement to the minimum expediently possible within prevailing constraints. Not surprisingly, in localities where militias came into contact with the drug trade, violence between civilians tended to be severe in the extreme, even beyond that considered tolerable by the military. One prime example involved the Comités de Autodefensa in Calemar and Nimpana on the banks of the River Marañón in Bolívar province (La Libertad), who had been given special training at the Trujillo army base in September 1994. By December 1995, counter-insurgency officers moved to confiscate the weapons they had distributed and disbanded the militias after a stream of complaints had been lodged with the authorities. In addition to accusations concerning collaboration with cocaine dealers, militia leaders had employed their positions to 'commit a series of abuses against the inhabitants', including the kidnap and extra-judicial assassination of two brothers rumoured to be members of the PCP–SL.[96]

Given the numerous injustices committed with impunity in their name, disillusion with the CDCs was quick to develop. It spread particularly fast because rural people possessed a benchmark against which to evaluate militia internal working practices and methods of treating ordinary citizens: the *rondas campesinas*. Despite official persecution and the less-than-model behaviour of several well-known leaders, the anti-theft patrols still enjoyed a positive image among the highland population. When analysed across a range of issues, from modes of participation to levels of accountability, the counter-insurgency militias compared unfavourably (see Figure 2), a situation noted frequently in the local press. In this regard, a typical report opined that the 'Self-defence Committees are losing strength. The people no longer believe in them due to the plethora of abuses committed by their leaders, many of whom use the Committee solely as a means of self-advancement under the guise of providing protection'.[97]

By 1995, in consequence, most CDCs were experiencing operational prob-

Rondas Campesinas	Comités de Autodefensa
Formed through peasant initiative 1976+ to eradicate rustling and other forms of rural crime; self-financing, although receive support from NGOs and political parties (Patria Roja, APRA)	Formed 1991+ by military to assist in the fight against the PCP–SL; occasionally receive foodstuffs from army; demand comestibles from peasants
Organised democratically: grass-roots participation at village level; two-yearly rotation of leaders; decision-making through regular assemblies	Non-democratic: key office-holders selected by the army or police; hierarchical; no internal democracy
Leaders accountable; low levels of corruption; leaders from all peasant strata	Leaders only accountable to the authorities; corruption widespread; vehicle for individual enrichment, acquisition of power and settling of personal vendettas by leaders; leaders tend to be kulaks or upwardly mobile landless
Legitimate: peasants view *rondas* as 'their' organisation; source of pride; expand functions to administration of justice; settle all manner of disputes; engage in communal work projects and rural development initiatives	Lack legitimacy: participation forced; viewed as organs of the state; legitimacy undermined by abuses of leaders and army/police
Struggle to keep functioning under difficult circumstances, as caught in the crossfire; 'terrorist' accusations against leaders by corrupt state officials; targeted for assassination by PCP–SL	Leaders targeted for assassination by PCP–SL; Comités decline post-1995 as do not have mass support
1996+ crime wave in rural districts; new, younger layer of leaders emerging, who hope to develop the *rondas*	1997+ attempts to revive the Comités in response to PCP–SL reorganisation, but reluctance on part of most of rural population

Figure 2 *Northern Andean Rondas Campesinas and Comités de Autodefensa Compared*

lems and many ceased functioning shortly afterwards, owing to widespread grass-roots alienation, a development with important implications for the rural population.

Against a backdrop of rapidly advancing peasant impoverishment, making ever-greater numbers of households dependent on EU and US food handouts, the demise of the CDCs (when taken in conjunction with *ronda campesina* inactivity due to ongoing state hostility) produced a rural crime wave of dramatic proportions. A flavour of the political complexities encountered at village level emerges in the following statement:

> Today we have gone backwards. Despite all the government propaganda about pacification, in many respects things around here are worse than ever ... Before, we had rustlers and other thieves, so we organised a *ronda*. Then, when people got scared owing to threats from Sendero and the police, the patrol fell apart. Later, we were forced into a Comité de Autodefensa, but it worked half-heartedly and once the *milicos* stopped forcing us to patrol, it practically died ... So now we are left with nothing – many peasants are frightened to build something up again, to get involved. But given the tremendous poverty, we are suffering greatly at the hands of big- and small-time thieves. There's no security. It is creating real hardship. There's a lot of frustration and anger – but as yet no response.[98]

As well as permitting theft to advance unchecked, the collapse in rural organisation provided the political space for the PCP–SL to start rebuilding its apparatus in Cajabamba–Huamachuco.

Batiendo el campo with modifications: Party reconstruction, 1994–97

Although between 1993 and 1994 the PCP–SL apparatus suffered considerable damage under the double blows of Guzmán's arrest and the Repentance Law, the provincial-level organisation managed to survive. According to intelligence service reports, by April 1993 leadership of Sendero's Northern Regional Committee had passed to a cadre operating under the pseudonym 'José'. Responsibility for the Zonal Committee covering San Marcos, Cajabamba and the province of Bolívar in La Libertad was exercised by a *mando político* called Imelda Chávez (alias 'Sandra'), assisted by a *mando militar* named 'Hugo'. The Local Force commander in San Marcos–Cajabamba was one Timoteo Medina ('Pablo'), assisted by another *mando militar*, 'Cristina'.[99]

Indeed, while members were being lost at a rapid rate and the number of attacks mounted by the PCP–SL fell dramatically, these guerrilla commanders still managed to rally their forces to deliver telling blows against their opponents. On 13 January 1993 at 8 p.m. a column estimated by the police to be ninety strong (surely an exaggeration), entered the *caserío* of Pomabamba in San Marcos, killing local merchant-farmer Alfredo Arana before taking off with eleven head of cattle and a horse belonging to his father. That same night, another detachment raided the Instituto Superior Pedagógico in Cajabamba, lifting office equipment and setting fire to the college upon their departure. The following month, three *senderistas* armed with machine-guns overpowered the operator of San Marcos's electricity generator and dynamited the installation. In early March 1993, the police discovered a significant cache of explosives laid alongside the road leading from Cajabamba to Algamarca. They were hidden in 20 holes, each containing 50 sticks of dynamite, connected by 150 metres of cable and a battery-operated detonator sited in a nearby field.[100] Significant loss of life occurred on 12 October 1993, when a fifteen-strong insurgent detachment led by 'Cristina' entered Chingol. They pulled CDC president Artemio Avalos from his house, along with a fellow member of the local Committee, took both to the small *plaza* and shot them for 'collaborating with the government'. Two hours later a similar scene unfolded in the neighbouring settlement of Chuquibamba, where three inhabitants were despatched.

The first half of 1993 also witnessed Party activity spreading to areas outside traditional strongholds such as Sitacocha, Araqueda, Sanagorán and Sayapullo, as attempts were made to establish a presence in the province of Celendín. Word reached the police that a group of between eight and ten guerrillas were conducting *escuelas populares* in the district of Oxamarca. It was speculated that they:

> ... hope to garner support for a possible attack on the police station at Sucre, and then after this action, assault the provincial headquarters of the PNP in Celendín, along with the town's authorities. The personnel are constantly changing. It is presumed that they rotate and enter from a neighbouring zone, such as the district of José Sabogal in San Marcos.[101]

In all likelihood, these insurgents formed part of a detachment fifteen to twenty strong, which was mainly bivouacked in the *caserío* of Tingo la Palla and, whenever opportune, crossed the Marañón to seek refuge in the hamlet of Chuquitén in the province of Bolívar.

Guzmán's surprise announcement from his prison cell in October 1993 that the armed struggle had reached a conclusion, and that it would henceforth be necessary to embark upon 'a war without bloodshed, a war without bullets', no doubt encouraged hesitant militants operating in Cajabamba–Huamachuco to take advantage of the Repentance Law. A determined minority nevertheless opted to continue fighting, following the so-called '*Línea Liquidacionista de Izquierda*' ('Left Liquidationist Line'), or 'Sendero Rojo', headed by Oscar Ramírez Durand.[102] Adapting to a difficult counter-insurgency environment throughout 1994, therefore, the Party found itself compelled to implement a number of shifts on the political and military fronts.

Modifying the military proved less complex. The immediate objective being survival, EGP combatants beat a tactical withdrawal, remaining bivouacked in remote mountain retreats and only venturing forth to undertake the occasional assault on police posts sited in Ichocán, San Marcos and neighbouring districts, or rare ambushes launched against combined army–police patrols. Under pressure from capture or surrender, the initial response from local commanders was to consolidate armed groups into one column that would be better placed to defend itself. When a modicum of stability had been attained by mid-1996, however, two *Fuerza Principal* units were re-established, one operating in highland La Libertad, the other in Cajabamba–San Marcos. Intelligence information noted that both consisted of approximately twenty members, all armed with modern weaponry; the military commissar appointed to each contingent was a woman, the political commissar a man.[103] Nevertheless, conducting military actions was not the central concern, for rebuilding the Party's political wing held top priority.

In order to restrict damage to the political structure, contact with the civilian population was minimised during 1994 and became far more secretive in localities where key cadres had been captured or surrendered, providing high-grade intelligence to the security services. A reorganisation of branches was implemented, the apparatus being strengthened by the drafting in of experienced members from jungle areas and the coast. Importantly, the Party's former practices were subject to critical appraisal, and a major policy change emerged on the thorny question of relations between 'river' and 'fish': now the goal was to be less sanguinary, pay greater attention to grass-roots complaints and become more 'peasant-friendly'. Having decided the new line, the PCP–SL moved to re-engage with the populace. By mid-1996, *escuelas populares* were again being held after nightfall in former areas of influence, such as Sitacocha and Cachachi. The impact of these measures signified that between 1994 and 1996 the zone was: 'living an apparent calm … the terrorist organisation is taking advantage of the situation in order to evaluate its activities, restructure its cells, along with its method of acquiring arms, ammunition, medicines and food'.[104]

Although regional Party leaders successfully restructured the political apparatus, in the process preventing its complete collapse, they still had to cope with serious reversals. Between 1 January 1995 and September 1996, the security services in Cajamarca detained 127 *senderistas* – not all necessarily PCP–SL cadres. Perhaps the most important loss to occur during this period took place on 5 June 1995, when several members of the Northern Regional Committee were detained in Trujillo. The following year (16 August 1996), a police squad combing the Condebamba Valley seized fifty-year-old Santos Alberca ('Pablo'), the *mando político* for Cajabamba–San Marcos. This was followed by the detention of a further fifty '*senderistas*' in Cajabamba–Huamachuco during the first half of 1997.[105]

In the face of renewed PCP–SL activity, efforts were made from mid-1996 to reactivate the CDCs, but given past problems, little enthusiasm existed among the populace for this initiative. Mobilising the population became more difficult, since the guerrillas happened to be conducting few armed actions. Physical attacks against civilians had also declined significantly. Against this backdrop, Cachachi was one among the minority of localities where a CDC continued to function, leading to a clash between the militia and a fifteen-strong rebel detachment in the hamlet of Rodiobamba on 6 November 1997. The encounter was not pursued with vigour on either side and no casualties occurred. The inconclusive outcome of this incident neatly epitomised the contemporary situation. Insurgent forces were much reduced compared to 1992, yet although they no longer represented *una opción de poder,* they had managed to survive. The state, for its part, had decisively shifted the correlation of forces in its favour, without being able to eradicate the guerrillas. Meanwhile, the mass of the population, fearful and distrustful, stood watching on the sidelines, hoping to be left in peace.

Conclusion

In broad terms, the trajectory of the civil war in the northern highlands during the early 1990s mirrored that found elsewhere in Peru. Most people failed to cross the divide between 'passive' and 'active' support. While insurgent forces might receive backing for armed land occupations and a clampdown on what was viewed as unacceptable behaviour, points of rupture developed in peasant–guerrilla relations across a wide range of issues as the Party strove to push through the second phase of its *batir el campo* strategy. Here, the Party mindset, in which 'the peasant world seemed flat, two-dimensional, without historical density or social complexity' proved a fundamental problem.[106] A particular area of tension in both Cajabamba–Huamachuco and Ayacucho surrounded the proclivity of PCP–SL cadres to engage in excessive violence. This inability to achieve a judicious calibration between decisiveness and lightness was viewed negatively by the populace, creating a chain of aggrieved relatives and friends who, when the opportune moment presented itself, were in a position to exact revenge through providing information to the authorities and participating in anti-guerrilla actions.

A related point of convergence between the north and Ayacucho concerns the quality and behaviour of PCP–SL cadres. In both locations, inexperienced individuals possessing low levels of political education, who rose to fill middle-ranking positions within the insurgent organisation, turned out to be adventurers who fastened on to the insurrection as a means of making their way in life. By using their power to abuse the population and settle personal feuds, these combatants not only discredited the Party and spawned hostility, their actions also gave the state a potent propaganda weapon with which to attack the guerrillas. The negative impact for the PCP–SL was compounded by: (i) a reluctance to sanction their activities; and (ii) the tendency for these 'social climbers' to desert and collaborate with the army when the situation facing the rebels deteriorated.

Regarding contrasts between events in the north and theatres of conflict further south, several aspects of the insurgency merit mention here (others will be addressed in the following chapter). First, the influence of religion stands out. Whereas in the Apurímac river valley and adjacent areas in Ayacucho, members of evangelical churches played a prominent role in establishing CDCs and led the fight against the PCP–SL 'antichrist', in Cajabamba–Huamachuco such sects did not possess a strong foothold. Regarding the socio-economic dimension of peasant–guerrilla interaction, the local Party organisation made no rigorous attempts to impose a ban on market contact in villages under its influence. Equally, it did not engage in forced recruitment in a consistent fashion. Perhaps the most important difference between the trajectory of the civil war in Cajabamba–Huamachuco with that of Ayacucho and its environs concerns the impact of PCP–SL activities on peasant mobilisation. Armed rebellion in the Ayacucho region commenced in a social environment characterised by low levels of organisation and produced social breakdown along with political paralysis in the countryside. During the latter half of the 1980s, however, the rural population mobilised spontaneously against the PCP–SL through the formation of grass-roots self-defence militias, which, once they had proved their effectiveness, received backing from the state. Playing a key role in the front-line struggle against the PCP–SL caused peasant self-esteem to rocket, as did levels of social organisation and solidarity at village level. The outcome, it is argued, has been greater social cohesion, capacity to mobilise and ability to pressurise the state for additional resources, with CDCs expanding their activities to assume community development initiatives.

The sequel in Cajabamba–Huamachuco stands in stark contrast: from being in a stronger position during the early 1980s, peasant unions and the *rondas campesinas* collapsed in the late 1980s, to the degree that by 1997 the rural population was extremely atomised and its capacity for mobilisation very low. In the north, the existence of peasant unions and anti-theft committees gave the state (which, in the 1980s lacked an efficient intelligence service) a readily identifiable target to attack, whether motivated by suspicion of complicity with the guerrilla (as in the case of the army and police), or greed (as in the case of judges and lawyers). As a result, leaders and activists in the peasant federations and *rondas campesinas* suffered harassment, imprisonment and beatings. They also came under pressure from the PCP–SL. Faced with this harrowing situation, some opted to flee their farms; others decided to maintain a low profile. Whatever the individual response, the spreading fear throughout the countryside produced declining participation in any activity that might be interpreted as 'political'. Neither could the creation of military-driven Comités de Autodefensa fill the vacuum. Not only did a *conciencia rondera* result in the militias being viewed with circumspection but it also ensured that they became associated with abuse and blackmail through the immoral behaviour of leading figures within their ranks. Paradoxically then, the presence of *rondas campesinas* and peasant unions in this region of the Andes reduced the ability of smallholders to confront the PCP–SL on a scale comparable to that found in Huanta and the Apurímac river valley. It also made it more difficult for them to defend their interests in relation to agricultural and other matters.

References

1   *Caretas* 1008, 30 May 1988, pp. 31–32. The interview with Nunja (as well as the implications of Morote's capture) was analysed in *Quehacer* 53, July–August 1988,

pp. 16–22.

2   On 'strategic equilibrium' see D. Poole and G. Rénique, *Peru: Time of Fear*, London, Latin American Bureau, 1992, pp. 95–96; and more generally, R. Taber, *The War of the Flea: Guerrilla Warfare Theory and Practice*, St Albans, Paladin, 1974, pp. 52–55.

3   The relevant literature is detailed in Chapter One, notes 89–102.

4   See the interview with Raúl González, *Idéele* 36, April 1992, pp. 15–20; and 'Sendero: duro desgaste y crisis estratégica', *Quehacer* 64, May–June 1990, pp. 8–15.

5   Berg, 'Peasant Responses', p. 96. A summary of Berg's argument is provided in Chapter One (notes 70 to 72).

6   Interview # 5, 26 March 1997.

7   Interview # 9, 30 March 1997.

8   Interview # 24, 14 April 1997. Regarding the Church, important differences between Cajabamba–San Marcos and the highland provinces of La Libertad deserve mention. In Huamachuco the clergy was dominated by conservative Spanish priests trained in the Francoist school, who proffered a 'pie in the sky when you die' brand of Christianity. Alternatively, the former provinces fell under the jurisdiction of the diocese of Cajamarca, which was headed, until his retirement in December 1992, by the progressive 'liberationist' bishop, José Dammert. Clergy in San Marcos and Cajabamba adopted a policy of evangelisation among the rural poor, enabling them to develop close ties with sectors of the peasantry. This activity, allied to Dammert's public criticism of human rights abuses and his refusal to attend the weekly raising of the national flag ceremony in the *plaza* of Cajamarca, bred suspicion within the security services. These attitudes are evinced in the following extract from an intelligence appraisal: 'It cannot be discounted that in previous years links existed in the provinces of … and … between the PCP–SL, priests and catechists, both nationals and foreigners'. It was also asserted that local human rights committees, which were only able to function because of Church financial and moral support, comprised 'guerrilla front organisations'. Indeed, early February 1984 saw a French ex-nun, Anne Marie Gavarret, arrested at her home in the *caserío* of Carrizales, near Cajabamba. She was accused of 'terrorism' but was later released due to a lack of evidence. The charges were far-fetched – anybody even faintly acquainted with the sister would realise that her 'other worldliness' made her a liability for any clandestine organisation. Comments from the security services appear in PNP, 'Apreciación de la situación subversiva en …', mimeo 1996.

9   Interview # 23, 14 April 1997.

10   In the 1990 congressional election, Fujimori's Cambio-90 group did not return a single deputy for the department of Cajamarca (which had ten seats in the lower house) and won only one representative for La Libertad (out of eleven seats). Fujimori received just 5.6 and 9.8 per cent respectively in the first round of the presidential ballot, compared to 45.5 and 60.1 per cent for APRA's candidate.

11   Interview # 12, 4 April 1997. Pedro Huillca, a member of the pro-Moscow Communist Party and General Secretary of the General Confederation of Peruvian Workers (CGTP), was assassinated on 18 December 1992.

12   Interview # 27, 20 January 2000. Political rivalries notwithstanding, *campesinos* with a history of supporting the left also drew a distinction between on the one hand 'the rich', resident in Lima, and provincial-level *gamonalillos,* and on the other, their *aprista* neighbours who filled government posts at district or parish level. Differentiation along these lines can be garnered from the following testimony: 'Although we have our disagreements, our brother peasants who back APRA are essentially like us. They are not our real opponents. They do not exploit us and it is not their fault that we live in poverty. If we want to change things for the better,

we need to get them on our side and work with them – and you can't achieve that by killing them.' Interview # 5, 26 March 1997.

13 Interview # 2, 22 March 1997.

14 Interview # 4, 26 March 1997.

15 Interview # 11, 3 April 1997.

16 Interview # 9, 30 March 1997.

17 These events in Ayacucho are detailed in Coronel, 'Violencia política', pp. 47, 69; del Pino, 'Tiempos de guerra', pp. 135–38; and Fumerton, *From Victims to Heroes*, pp. 79–81. On Junín, see Manrique, 'La década de la violencia', pp. 147, 166–69.

18 'We have our own leaders that we chose to follow. Often they don't act correctly, so we remove them, or everyone ignores them until others who are suitable come along. The *senderistas* descended on the area like wolves and wanted to change and dominate everything ... But we peasants are egotistical and like to do things our own way. For this reason the actions of the *senderistas* were not well looked upon. We wanted to continue making our own decisions and not be bossed around like naughty children.' Interview # 21, 12 April 1997.

19 For an insightful exploration of these aspects of village life in the southern Andes, see Paul Gelles, *Water and Power in Highland Peru: the Cultural Politics of Irrigation and Development*, New Jersey, Rutgers University Press, 2000.

20 Favre was among the first to highlight these issues. See, 'Perú: Sendero Luminoso y horizontes oscuros', pp. 29–30.

21 Often such acts of sabotage would be coordinated as part of a province-wide '*paro armado*'. For example, on 14 July 1989, an 'armed strike' was declared, aimed at shutting down the town of Huamachuco. At dawn, local banks, public buildings and utilities, including the electricity generator, fell target to dynamite attacks, while logs and boulders were used to block traffic moving between the town and jungle, the main coast road and the route linking Huamachuco with Cajabamba.

22 Interview # 7, 27 March 1997.

23 Interview # 1, 21 March 1997.

24 Interview # 5, 26 March 1997.

25 Mao Tse-tung (Zedong), 'On Protracted War', p. 186.

26 Ibid.

27 Interview # 24, 14 April 1997.

28 Interview # 27, 20 January 2000.

29 Interview # 9, 30 March 1997.

30 Interview, # 22, 14 April 1997.

31 For an insightful analysis of the problems emerging in the region's cooperatives prior to the PCP–SL's appearance in Cajabamba–Huamachuco, see José María Caballero and Jesús Foronda, 'Algunos aportes para el conocimiento de los problemas post reforma agraria en ciertas zonas de Cajamarca y La Libertad', mimeo, Lima 1976.

32 This was a common refrain voiced by cooperative members in conversation with me during the early 1990s.

33 Interview with Oscar Saénz, Huacraruco, 8 August 1994.

34 Interview # 21, 12 April 1997.

35 Interview # 8, 30 March 1997.

36 Interview # 26, 20 January 2000. '*El chino*' was the affectionate nickname given to Juan Velasco, who was of Chinese extraction. The slogan that landowners would no longer eat at the peasants' expense was pronounced frequently by military officers and high-ranking Ministry of Agriculture bureaucrats during the agrarian reform period.

37 Interview # 15, 5 April 1997.

38 Interview # 24, 14 April 1997.

39 *Expreso*, 20 March 1986.

40 On 'punish but don't kill', see Degregori, 'Dwarf Star', p. 14. Fumerton, however, makes a valid observation on this issue: 'more than a few peasants showed themselves to be rather less adherent to the supposed Andean ethic of "punish but don't kill" than Degregori would have us believe ... In practice, "kill the rich and share out their possessions" seems to have been the more common motivation of many Ayacuchano peasants embroiled in the political turmoil, at least before the escalating violence became more random and arbitrary.' *From Victims to Heroes*, p. 301.

41 *La Industria*, 5 April 1988.

42 Vicaria de Solidaridad [hereafter, VS], testimony dated 27–29 May 1993. Identities from this source have not been disclosed, as many of the individuals concerned are still engaged in legal proceedings.

43 Billie Jean Isbell, 'Shining Path and Peasant Responses in Rural Ayacucho', in D. S. Palmer (ed.), *Shining Path of Peru*, London, Hurst and Company, 1992, p. 78.

44 VS, testimony dated 20 March 1995.

45 Interview # 23, 14 April 1997.

46 Interview, # 6, 27 March 1997.

47 Interview # 2, 22 March 1997.

48 Ibid.

49 VS, testimony dated 19 July 1995.

50 Ranajit Guha, 'Domination Without Hegemony and its Historiography', in Ranajit Guha (ed.), *Subaltern Studies VI*, New Delhi, Oxford University Press, 2003, pp. 231–32. Employing less academic terms, an intelligence analyst working for the security services in the conflict zone reached a similar conclusion. As part of a wider assessment of PCP–SL 'vulnerabilities', the operative noted that the insurgents 'are open to Psychological Operations because they have not become embedded in the belief system of the population. They have not become integrated into its traditional ingrained customs and culture and have not won them over totally', for which reason, s/he calculated, the insurgents 'do not enjoy the support of the inhabitants'. PNP, 'Apreciación de la situación de inteligencia en ...', mimeo 1993.

51 Nor was this the only case. The *senderista* detachment that killed Alipio Arroyo in September 1992 contained individuals who had earlier been released by the courts in Chiclayo.

52 According to the Peruvian legal code, minors under eighteen years of age could not be given jail sentences and were consequently referred to young offenders institutions, where the security regime was usually very lax and escape a formality. After a series of incidents in which adolescent *senderista* combatants committed serious offences (including homicides and bombings), demands increased among the judiciary, the media and the political class for the age of immunity from incarceration to be lowered to sixteen, along with normal sentencing for grave crimes. See *Caretas* 996, 7 March 1988, pp. 36–39; 997, 14 March 1988, pp. 30–34.

53 Taylor, 'Counter-insurgency strategy', p. 51.

54 On changing military practices, see Carlos Iván Degregori, 'Ayacucho después de la violencia', in C. I. Degregori (ed.), *Las rondas campesinas y la derrota de Sendero Luminoso*, Lima, Instituto de Estudios Peruanos/Universidad Nacional San Cristóbal de Huamanga, 1996, pp. 25–28; and del Pino, 'Tiempos de guerra', pp. 151–52, 176.

55 These figures are most probably inflated and by no means all CDCs were active. According to other figures released by the Peruvian army, some 916 rifles had been distributed to CDCs in Cajamarca and a further 858 supplied to their sister organ-

isations in La Libertad. Committee formation continued over the following year –
official sources declared that by August 1996 La Libertad housed 520 units, which
mobilised around 35,000 people. See *El Peruano*, 21 October 1994; *El Comercio*, 4
November 1994; *La Industria*, 1 November 1995; 10 August 1996. Unlike the *ceja
de selva* zones of Ayacucho, the use of cocaine money to purchase weapons for the
CDCs does not appear to have been common practice in Cajabamba–Huamachuco
(localities adjacent to the Marañón excepted).

56 Interview # 10, 3 April 1997.

57 Interview with counter-insurgency operative, Cajamarca, 12 April 1997.

58 Fujimori's efforts to restructure the state during his first period in office are detailed
in Philip Mauceri, *State Under Siege: Development and Policy Making in Peru*,
Boulder, CO, Westview Press, 1996. The negative impact of official behaviour was
recognised by the security services. Under the sub-heading 'Predisposition to collaborate with the authorities', one intelligence analyst opined that: 'This depends on
the authorities. The civilian population is susceptible to how the authorities act. If
government officials are competent and respect the population's rights, the people
will respond positively. When the opposite occurs, which is the norm, the populace
intuitively knows that its rights are not being respected, causing them to become
indifferent and to distance themselves'. PNP, 'Apreciación de la situación de
inteligencia en ...', mimeo 1993.

59 In Cajabamba, for example, the army upgraded the local airstrip – an investment
obviously designed with counter-insurgency considerations in mind. Construction
also began on a new road to link the province directly to the Chicama Valley. With
its dense population, the Chicama Valley was a source of significant demand for
locally produced agricultural commodities and the opening of a direct link had been
the subject of frequent petitions by *cajabambinos* since at least the 1960s. In addition to its military usefulness (troops could be moved up from the coast more
quickly), this project would consequently benefit local farmers.

60 To help spread defeatism inside the PCP–SL, the security services not only utilised
psychological ploys such as parading Guzmán in a cage wearing risible convict attire,
they also engaged in 'black propaganda'. According to an intelligence document,
this was employed to 'suggest the existence of dissident and disloyal elements within
the ranks of SL and the MRTA. It specifically aims to spread confusion and complicate their activities.' Quoted from PNP, 'Apreciación de la situación de inteligencia
en ...', mimeo 1993. It is not surprising, therefore, that shortly after Guzmán's arrest
it was reported that twenty-five *senderistas* had stopped a bus travelling through the
mountains from Huamachuco to Trujillo and demanded money from the passengers because 'everything has come to an end and is lost'. The cash was needed so
the rebels could 'return to their villages in (the department of) San Martín. The
guerrillas stated that the capture of Abimael Guzmán was the reason for ending the
struggle.' *El Comercio*, 19 September 1992. Doubts exist about the truthfulness of
this article. First, most PCP–SL cadres in the Cajabamba–Huamachuco region originated from the Andes and the coast (the MRTA possessed a higher proportion of
members from the jungle areas in San Martín). Second, it would have been far safer
for anyone opting out of the armed struggle to travel home by foot, vehicle transport being monitored closely by the forces of law and order.

61 Figures taken from PNP, 'Apreciación de la situación subversiva en ...', mimeo
1996. An unknown number of individuals located in the PCP–SL's support base
simply curtailed active involvement and continued undertaking their normal activities.

62 Robles' life story was summarised in *Panorama Cajamarquino*, 1 September 1997.

Sometimes he adopted the name of Gilberto. Two other *arrepentidos* who caused numerous arrests were Santos Dorito Rodríguez, a *campesino* from the hamlet of Igosbamba in Cajabamba, and Pedro Jacinto Soto. Rodríguez was captured following information from a girl with whom he maintained a romantic connection. She informed her mother about his activities, who went to the police. In reprisal, Rodríguez denounced the girl's father, a community health worker who made a modest living travelling around Lluchubamba, Marcamachay and neighbouring hamlets selling medicines. Adding a further twist to the plot, members of the Cauday police station attempted to take advantage of the situation, demanding 500 *nuevos soles* to 'cross off his name' from the list of suspected terrorists. Soto, a smallholder from Chillacauday (Cajabamba), joined the PCP–SL in April 1989 and, before his capture in 1993, conducted Party business under the alias of 'Rene'.

63   VS, testimony dated 30 March 1995.

64   Ibid., testimony dated 15 January 1996. Mistreatment of prisoners was, unsurprisingly, standard fare. The experience of a young smallholder from the *caserío* of Migma was typical in this regard: 'I was captured on 17 January 1995 in the sector of Cachur Bajo, where I had gone to sow my wheat. There I happened upon the police from Cajabamba, who asked my name and after looking through some papers, arrested me and escorted me to the DINCOTE in Cajabamba. After five days they transferred me to a secret house and locked me up. Afterwards they brought me out, put a hood over my head and beat me. They ordered me to declare if I had collaborated with the terrorists. I did not reply because I know nothing. One of them said I had been involved. At the time these individuals interrogated me, I was 16 years old.' Ibid., testimony no date.

65   Ibid., testimony dated 15 January 1996. Also see the petition dated 2 January 1995. Denunciation, violence and extortion also occurred within families. One particularly traumatic case involved a woman from the *caserío* of La Laimina (Cajabamba), whose husband was assassinated by his own brother with the assistance of two accomplices. A labourer employed on the farm also lost his life. Then, with the collaboration of Judge Damasen in San Marcos, the assailant arranged his sister-in-law's arrest on charges of terrorism and seized her property. Ibid., testimony dated 16 December 1994. Damasen's scandalous role in this affair met with widespread repudiation and anger among the citizenry. Shortly afterwards he was transferred to the court in Trujillo.

66   In Giuseppe di Lampedusa's classic novel, *The Leopard*, the Prince of Salina's nephew, Tancredi, assessed the threat posed to the family's aristocratic position by the *garibaldini* and with appropriate *raffinatezza* considered that: 'If we want things to stay as they are, things will have to change'.

67   See Instituto Nacional de Cooperativas, 'Informe técnico sobre la Cooperativa Agraria de Trabajadores José Santos Chocano', 22 March 1994. On 18 April 1986, the then Director of the Ministry of Agriculture in Cajamarca, Jorge Chiclayo, had declared the partition of the cooperative illegal, as 'it was practised in a discriminatory fashion, favouring some individuals more than others, in contravention of the equality laid down in law'. Given the interest of PCP–SL activists such as Salvatierra, this ruling may have played a part in the assassination of Chiclayo on 30 September 1987.

68   VS, testimony dated 31 October 1994. DINCOTE is the acronym for Dirección Contra el Terrorismo, then the main counter-insurgency section within the security apparatus.

69   VS, petition dated 2 May 1995. [Capitals as in original document.] In this uncertain environment, widows found themselves in especially vulnerable circumstances.

According to a woman who had been allocated 1 hectare of land in the 24 September 1987 redistribution: 'During the last months I have been threatened by señor Pedro Cruz, resident in the *caserío* of Chingol, who says that if I do not hand over the plot where I live, he will denounce me as a "subversive" with the backing of repentant terrorist Isabel Salvatierra'. Ibid., testimony dated 29 September 1994.

70   Interestingly, these 'golden' informants possessed a common profile: they were mostly local, male, aged between twenty and thirty-five years and possessed a rural background. Women proved far less likely to adopt this path and tended to be harder to break down under interrogation. Interview with counter-insurgency operative, Cajamarca, 12 April 1997.

71   On 'localism' it was noted that: 'the unit of social organization everywhere is the clan, consisting of people having the same family name. In the Party organizations in the villages, it often happens that a branch meeting virtually becomes a clan meeting, since branches consist of members bearing the same family name and living close together.' Under these circumstances, party-building 'is very hard indeed'. On the issue of defections, where CPC membership had increased rapidly and 'the leaders of the branches and district committees were mostly new members, good inner-Party education was out of the question. As soon as the White terror struck, the careerists defected and acted as guides for the counter-revolutionaries in rounding up our comrades, and the Party organizations in the White areas mostly collapsed'. This could only be rectified through dissolution of the Party's grass-roots organs and a re-registration of cadres following the principle of 'better fewer, but better'. Mao Tse-tung (Zedong), 'The Struggle in the Chingkang Mountains', pp. 93-95.

72   Mao Tse-tung (Zedong), 'Report on an Investigation of the Peasant Movement in Hunan', pp. 28-29, 38.

73   Mao Tse-tung (Zedong), 'Problems of Strategy in China's Revolutionary War', p. 211.

74   Mao Tse-tung (Zedong), 'On Policy', *Selected Works*, Vol. 2, pp. 411, 446-47.

75   VS, testimony no date (September 1994?).

76   Taber captures the interconnections here: ' ... what is indispensable is ideological armour. Above all, the revolutionary activist must stand on solid moral ground, if he is to be more than a political bandit ... To be successful, the guerrilla must be loved and admired. To attract followers, he must represent not merely success, but absolute virtue, so that his enemy will represent absolute evil.' Furthermore, 'There are judicious uses of terror, no doubt, but no guerrilla can afford to use it against the people on whose support and confidence he depends for his life as well as for his political existence. People are quick to detect the difference between opportunism and dedication, and it is the latter that they respect and follow.' *The War of the Flea*, pp. 147-48. James Scott detected similar tendencies towards 'localism' and an over-reliance on personal relations to that encountered in the PCP-SL within the PKI (Indonesian Communist Party). See *The Moral Economy of the Peasant*, pp. 222-24.

77   Mao Tse-tung (Zedong), 'The Struggle in the Chingkang Mountains', pp. 81-82; 'Problems of Strategy', pp. 185-87.

78   Gorriti, *Sendero*, p. 140.

79   PCP-SL, 'Analisis de nuestra guerra en la región comprendida entre los años desde 1980 hasta 1985', mimeo 1995. Orin Starn kindly supplied me with this document.

80   Ibid.

81   Ibid.

82   Degregori, 'Ayacucho después de la violencia'; Fumerton, *From Victims to Heroes*.

83 VS, testimony January 1994 (no day). According to this detainee, his accusers had been forced into making a false statement by police stationed in Cajabamba, who were keen to whip all opponents of the CDCs into line.

84 On Protestantism, see del Pino, 'Tiempos de guerra', pp. 118–19, 130–38.

85 Although rumours concerning mass graves continue to circulate freely throughout the country districts of Cajabamba and highland La Libertad, no full-blown massacres on the scale of Ccayara, Accomarca and other villages in Ayacucho were reported, nor have remains been discovered. Rather, smaller-scale human rights violations involving one or two extra-judicial killings and disappearances were the norm. One of the most striking incidents occurred during late 1993 in the northern province of the department of Cajamarca, Jaén. A 'repentant' member of the MRTA named Rómulo Silva (alias 'camarada Mono') was compelled by an army officer to shoot five reputed members of the organisation in order to prove that he had 'truly repented'. A lieutenant operating under the pseudonym 'Tigre' then ordered the villagers of San Patricio de Potrero to bury the corpses, which were later exhumed by judicial order in August 1996. Overall, however, progress around questions of truth, reconciliation and justice in Cajabamba–Huamachuco remains far less advanced that in Ayacucho and many issues still need to be resolved. Senderista militants who formed part of the regional Party apparatus, which gave them an intimate knowledge of events in the districts where they operated, and who are currently imprisoned in the Huacariz jail, claim a series of extra-judicial killings. They petitioned president Paniagua to investigate an array of incidents: 'During 1988 at the hamlet of Totorillo (Cajabamba), the police detained a female student from the local technical college. She was raped and tortured before they cut off her hand and killed her. In the Huacariz jail, officer Castillo boasts openly about having participated in this inhumane act … At San Marcos in 1991 (caserío Venta), the worker Lorenzo Liñán Burgos was assassinated; as were six young students in March 1992. At Pimentel, department of Lambayeque, on 17 June 1991 the PNP and army arrested four youths, among them Tito Montalvo Fernandez and his wife, who was pregnant. Both were tortured and executed. She received the worst treatment: they raped her before putting a rifle into her mouth and shooting her. In La Libertad department, the army, led by General Cornejo Chávez and accompanied by the police, committed genocide against more than thirty campesinos in Santiago de Chuco province (August 1992), principally in Angasmarca. Among those murdered figured the schoolteacher from the hamlet of Casablanca. Over the following months, a succession of extra-judicial assassinations occurred. One involved the seventy-five-year-old widow Rosenda Sarc from Inca Corral. She was tortured with burns and cut with a bayonet before being murdered with dynamite. Her corpse was encountered buried in the grounds of the Angasmarca counter-insurgency base. The son of peasant Gregorio Tumbajulca Tumbajulca (of Inca Corral) was also assassinated. A similar fate befell campesino Teodoro Sarc (Huacas Corral), as well as another peasant from Tambillo and his two-month-old son … In Cajabamba (hamlet of Suro Grande), ronderos following orders from the army based at Huamachuco used an axe to dismember Felipe Burgos Liñán, a student from the local technical college in Cajabamba … On 13 August 1993 in the hamlet of Espinal (Sayapullo district), the army executed the campesino Desiderio Calderón and his young 12-year-old son, Lenin Contreras. Two other youngsters from the parish were also killed. Their bodies have still not been found. In 1994 in Sunchubamba, a combined force of police and ronderos killed the district health worker …' These cases await investigation and judicial process. Letter to president Valentín Paniagua from PCP–SL 'Political Prisoners and Prisoners of War', Huacariz penitentiary, 11

July 2001.

86 VS, testimony dated 4 November 1993.

87 VS, testimony dated 9 January 1996. The woman was arrested, but was released in December 1995. Her partner remained imprisoned in Cajamarca but protested that: 'At night they took me from my cell and administered physical and psychological torture. The torture was unbearable and lasted night after night. They made me sign blank papers and continued asking for the whereabouts of my brother, stating that if I told them they would release me. They also demanded to know how many guerrilla actions I have participated in.'

88 *Panorama Cajamarquino*, 27 November 1996.

89 *Panorama Cajamarquino*, 25 November 1996; 5 December 1996.

90 VS, testimony dated 7 April 1994.

91 VS, testimony dated 4 November 1993.

92 VS, petition dated 9 September 1994.

93 Ibid.

94 VS, testimony dated 18 January 1993.

95 VS, testimony dated 30 May 1994. Torture became standard procedure as soon as the Chaquicocha facility opened. In 1987, after enduring severe mistreatment, schoolteacher Alberto Paredes was killed by the novel method of having a police vehicle driven over his body.

96 *La Industria*, 6 January 1996.

97 *Panorama Cajamarquino*, 26 June 1996. A similar situation regarding abuses committed by Comités de Autodefensa in the central highlands appears to have arisen, such incidents being mentioned briefly in the Truth and Reconciliation Commission Report, Volume II, sub-section 1.5. See http://www.derechos.org /nizkor/peru/libros/cv/ii/92.html

98 Interview #7, 27 March 1997.

99 PNP, 'Apreciación de la situación de inteligencia en ...', mimeo 1993.

100 Ibid. Local smallholder Mario Ponce was arrested in the vicinity, the police suspecting that he had been ordered to guard the material pending an ambush against a military convoy.

101 PNP, 'Apreciación de la situación de inteligencia en ...', mimeo 1993. In this zone, *senderista* detachments entered territory that was being colonised by the MRTA. After the capture of Wilfredo Saavedra in 1989, MRTA activity diminished, to later expand in Cajamarca's northern provinces of Jaén and San Ignacio during late 1992 and early 1993; the areas of greatest presence were Celendín (Cajamarca) and Bolívar (La Libertad). This was achieved by drafting into these provinces well-equipped columns from the neighbouring department of San Martín. On 1 March 1993, MRTA guerrillas attacked the district police post of Miguel Iglesias. Security sources estimated that eighty guerrillas participated in the assault – the seven columns of around a dozen members each combined to carry out the action. Despite possessing modern weaponry, the MRTA was never able to put down roots in Celendín. Their dilemma was described by intelligence officers in the following terms: 'The absence of long-term political work of an ideological nature hinders their attempts to recruit cadres for their armed wing'. Ibid. Following the capture of leading cadres in 1993 and 1994, the MRTA's organisation in Celendín and surrounding provinces collapsed.

102 Further details on these developments and the subsequent split in the PCP–SL are forthcoming in Manrique, *El tiempo de miedo*, pp. 245–61. Durand was in turn captured on 14 July 1999.

103 PNP, 'Apreciación de la situación subversiva en ...', mimeo 1996

104 Ibid.
105 Interestingly, the occupational background and age profile of those arrested did not conform to the standard *senderista* stereotype, e.g. young, student and 'outsider'. Of the nineteen suspects detained by the security forces in February 1997, the youngest was in his mid-twenties, fourteen of the nineteen were aged between thirty-three and forty-nine and the three women involved were forty-one, forty-two and forty-nine. All came from local peasant stock. This issue is discussed further in the following chapter.
106 Carlos I. Degregori, 'Reaping the Whirlwind: the *Rondas Campesinas* and the Defeat of Sendero Luminoso in Ayacucho', in Kees Koonings and Dirk Kruijt (eds.), *Societies of Fear: the Legacy of Civil War and Terror in Latin America*, London, Zed Books, 1999, p. 67.

CHAPTER SIX

Peasants and Revolution

This concluding chapter addresses an array of wider questions in the light of the PCP–SL's insurrection in Cajabamba–Huamachuco, structuring the argument around issues raised by some of the most interesting work published recently on Peru's civil war. A first conundrum concerns the social background of PCP–SL cadres and supporters. One common theme advanced in the literature examining the insurgency in Ayacucho department is the claim that there is no link between rural pauperisation and backing for guerrilla forces. José Coronel, for example, holds that 'a direct correlation between poverty and support for political violence does not exist'; among cottagers in the Huanta Valley 'more sustained collaboration came from those peasants who had relatively better living conditions' and, to a somewhat lesser extent, from small-scale merchants. Furthermore, 'the first *senderistas* who arrived at the province's communities and hamlets during 1980–82 were young university and secondary school students from Ayacucho town and smaller urban centres scattered throughout the region'.[1] For his part, Mario Fumerton echoes Coronel's assessment:

> ... hardly any of Shining Path militants (not to mention its leadership), were peasants, and not one of its senior or middle-level leadership was even of peasant origin. In terms of its social complexion, Shining Path was still very much an organisation of predominantly urban-based students and educators, and a few middle-class professionals. It was this sector that would continue to be its principal source of recruits in decades to come ... the majority of them were young, single and childless, often members of the Andean, provincial urban 'elite,' though they often came from among the nation's poorest and most underdeveloped provinces.[2]

Although the class extraction of PCP–SL cadres operating in the Cajabamba–Huamachuco sector is a complex phenomenon that in many respects defies definition, given the populace's high level of occupational multiplicity, to view the guerrilla organisation in the region as a party composed primarily of kulaks, schoolteachers and adolescent students would be a gross simplification. Indeed, while schoolteachers and students could be found at various levels within the regional apparatus, a significant proportion of local militants operating on the northern front came from the most deprived peasant strata.

To supplement information forthcoming in interviews, pointers to the occupational profile and family background of Party members can be gleaned from data collated on detainees held in Cajamarca's jail. Of the 243 inmates charged with terrorism housed in the penitentiary during September 1996, some fifty – including seven women – had been arrested in the vicinity of Cajabamba and the Andean provinces of La Libertad (it was normal prison-service practice to move people away from their place of activism). All but a few of those captured in the northern *sierra* had at this time admitted participating in the insurgency and by 1996 *senderista* organisational discipline within Huacariz was as strong as in the Lima jails. Most of these inmates had surmounted the intense psychological ferment that invariably accompanies the initial period of arrest and been integrated into the Party's effective mutual support system, which helped cadres cope with a harsh prison regime. Regarding the white-collar/middle-class/student dimension commonly advanced to describe the 'typical' *senderista* cadre in Ayacucho, among the fifty prisoners figured one lawyer and three students. Schoolteachers were better represented, five having been incarcerated for 'terrorism'. Counterbalancing this 'middle class' component, however, three detainees gave their main occupation as 'labourer', three earned a living as informal-sector proletarians (*ambulantes*), while an additional four worked as skilled artisans and wage labourers (two carpenters, a bricklayer and a motor mechanic).[3] Clearly, teachers, students and other 'middle-class' elements enrolled in the PCP–SL, but the Party apparatus proved far more diverse in terms of the membership's class profile than is usually acknowledged.

Reflecting this situation, '*campesino*' ('peasant') comprised by far the largest occupational group, accounting for twenty-five out of the fifty imprisoned *senderistas* who had been captured in Cajamarca and highland La Libertad. Interestingly, of the twenty-five, six were illiterate and eight had not completed primary school; a further ten had gone through primary school. Only one detainee had commenced secondary school – a nineteen-year-old youth from the rural hinterland of Chiclayo, who had been arrested in Huamachuco – and even he had not finished this basic level of education. That such an overwhelming proportion were illiterate or had failed to advance beyond primary school suggests that these individuals originated from resource-scarce peasant households whose parents lacked the wherewithal (but not necessarily the ambition) to provide a decent education for their offspring.

Apart from casting doubt on the assertion that 'hardly any of Shining Path militants … were peasants', the prisoners' age profile and personal circumstances also failed to conform to the popular picture of the mainly 'young, single and childless' *senderista* militant described by Fumerton. First, they did not form a particularly youthful group: only fifteen of the fifty were aged below twenty-five years. Nor had the youngest *senderistas* attained many educational qualifications, as was to be expected if one was dealing with an organisation staffed heavily by students – a mere two of the fifteen had advanced beyond primary school; two of this cohort could not read or write. Nearly half (twenty-four) of the detainees were aged thirty years or more. Thirty had children, twenty of whom possessed considerable family responsibilities, with three or more offspring to support. Indeed, three smallholders who threw in their lot with the PCP–SL had, over time, acquired extremely heavy personal commit-ments, each having produced nine living children.

Rather than emphasising the 'young, single and childless' stereotype, quali-ties that conjure up an image of footloose, unattached individuals having the freedom to dedicate their lives full-time to the revolution, *senderista* member-ship can be more profitably comprehended by focusing on kinship networks. Binding *Gemeinschaft* attributes explain as much, if not more, as notions of a pool of highly atomised cadres detached from their social roots. Just as in decades past the kernel of bandit gangs and political factions in the northern highlands was structured around extended family and close friends, the local PCP–SL apparatus also depended to a significant degree on blood ties and *compadrazgo*. Once it is understood that maturity, larger family size and density of local connections were all advantages, one can appreciate why approximately one-third of inmates held for subversion in Cajamarca had a close family member in jail elsewhere in Peru or on the run from the security services. An extreme example of this phenomenon involved a thirty-three-year-old *ambu-lante* arrested in Cajabamba, whose sister was also in prison for PCP–SL membership, while two of his brothers were still at large and being hunted by the police.

Nor is the assertion that peasants did not occupy 'senior or middle-level' leadership positions straightforward when one considers the Party organisation in the northern *sierra*. Although 'imported' cadres such as the *ayacuchano* Osmán Morote may have led the regional political apparatus and EGP units throughout the period of rapid expansion that occurred between 1985 and 1992, during the insurrection's crucial first phase a number of activists from poor peasant backgrounds filled positions of responsibility. Individuals such as Félix Calderón, Roberto Barrios and Sixto Nicasio provided much of the early impetus that enabled the PCP–SL to establish a foothold in the countryside during 1980 and 1985. Moreover, during the late 1980s and early 1990s, small-holders were appointed to *'mando'* positions within province-wide Comité Zonal and the district-level Fuerza Local, a situation verified in intelligence service reports.

As has been noted on various occasions in preceding chapters, contrasts between the position encountered in Cajabamba–Huamachuco and in Ayacucho can in part be explained by the areas' different historical legacy. Especially relevant are the rural populations' strong sense of political identifi-cation and a more developed tradition of unionism dating from APRA's appearance on the local scene during the 1930s. Over many years, considerable numbers of the rural population of Cajabamba–Huamachuco had undergone exposure to ideological discourse and schism as a result of working in highland mining camps or through migration to seek employment in sugar, rice and cotton enterprises on the littoral. Here, trade union membership in Casa Grande, Laredo and similar coastal enterprises proved a normal part of everyday life, with competition between APRA and Peru's plethora of left groups becoming especially intense during the 1970s and early 1980s. Compared to Ayacucho, regional affiliates of the CNA and CCP in Cajamarca and the Andean provinces of La Libertad had exercised greater influence in the years immediately preceding the launch of armed struggle in 1980. The rural population in Cajabamba–Huamachuco, therefore, did not approximate a lump of inert 'clay that could be moulded in the service of the revolution'; instead, significant numbers of country people possessed sufficient political skills to enable them to reach considered decisions on complicated issues.[4]

Aside from the question of political experience, another dissimilarity with Ayacucho concerns Coronel's link between support for the PCP–SL and kulak status. No evidence has been unearthed to sustain a *coq de village–senderista* connection in Cajabamba–Huamachuco. Two principal reasons can be advanced to account for this. One factor that helps explain the relatively low propensity for the offspring of prosperous peasant and small-scale merchant families to join the rebels stems from the aforementioned weight of traditional party loyalties. In the northern highlands, this component of the petty bourgeoisie formed the backbone of APRA and had been imbued with a deep-rooted *aprista* political culture that spanned several generations and contained a large dose of anti-communism. The presence of a '*mística aprista*' or '*aprismo popular*' made this influential sector of local youth more resistant to the overtures of PCP–SL recruiters, especially when APRA formed the national government (1985–90). As chance would have it, Alan García's administration coincided with a period of rapid guerrilla expansion; if an overtly rightist 'oligarchic' party had been in office at this juncture, the PCP–SL might have proved more attractive to some disgruntled *apristas*. On the other hand, party attachments in Ayacucho were weaker, which, when combined with the longer period of activism and greater strength of the Party in its birthplace, allowed the rebel organisation to proselytise more successfully among this particular category of rural youth.

In addition, an important group within the strata of better-off smallholders had expanded their assets through occupying positions of power in the region's cooperatives. According to Party doctrine, these individuals comprised newly emergent *gamonalillos*, who epitomised continued exploitation in a purportedly 'semi-feudal' Andean Peru. Counter to Mao's admonishment to handle the more prosperous elements of the petty bourgeoisie 'sincerely and kindly', in order to avoid driving 'the sparrows into the thickets', *senderista* doctrine held that they had to be eliminated as part of the overall drive to 'churn up the countryside'. A key component of kulak households, whose ranks had been expanding since the accelerated dissolution of haciendas after 1960, became, in consequence, a target for attack. Under these circumstances, they were unlikely to provide backing for the guerrilla. On the contrary, in 1992–93 they could be found occupying leadership positions within CDCs.

Regarding the opposite pole of the *campesinado*, the particular configuration of post-agrarian reform rural social structure in this sector of the northern Andes can also be advanced to explain the comparatively high percentage of *senderista* detainees who possessed peasant roots. In Ayacucho, a relatively weak presence of the hacienda and the resultant near-absence of cooperatives signified that insurgent forces had few fixed assets to offer pauperised *campesinos*. By contrast, in Cajabamba–Huamachuco considerable areas of land and large numbers of pedigree livestock remained concentrated in the hands of a few enterprises established during the Velasco government. Greater opportunity correspondingly existed to satisfy the aspirations of the most resource-starved sector of the farming community through pursuing 'the agrarian revolutionary war' and, in turn, gain adherents. For this reason, the claim that following land redistribution and the restoration of elected government in 1980, the PCP–SL was operating 'in the wrong nation at the wrong time', might hold water for Ayacucho, but is difficult to sustain for Cajabamba–Huamachuco. Paradoxically, this is because the reform had had a greater impact in the northern *sierra*, while the 'open' polity bred mass alienation.[5] Land reform did not put an end to agrarian conflict in the region, it simply made its contours more labyrinthine, or, as Mao would label it, 'tangled'.

The issues touched upon in the preceding paragraphs necessarily call into play questions about the structure of rural society, the trajectory of social change and the motivational factors that produced support for *senderista* guerrillas. In this regard, one of the more laudably ambitious contemporary studies is the comparative analysis of insurgent movements in El Salvador and Peru undertaken by Cynthia McClintock. In opposition to Coronel's position that there existed no 'direct correlation between poverty and support for political violence' in the *ayacuchano* countryside, McClintock builds on her frequently cited 1984 article to place peasant 'subsistence crisis' at the heart of her model aimed at explaining PCP–SL expansion. Following James Scott's arguments in *The Moral Economy of the Peasant*, it is posited that demographic increase, land fragmentation and negative town–country terms of trade coalesced to produce 'a threat to peasants' subsistence' in the 1970s that even the enactment of a thoroughgoing agrarian reform failed to redress. No more than 25 per cent of rural households benefited from redistribution, while coastal farmers did better than their Andean counterparts. The outcome was that 'in Peru hunger was an intense concern by the early 1980s in the rural highlands'.[6]

Another dimension of the crisis that engulfed Peru in the late 1970s and 1980s, highlighted by McClintock, included an economic meltdown that produced plummeting living standards across the urban population: 'the sine qua non in Peru's revolutionary experience was the nation's economic debacle'.[7] Mass unemployment not only embraced its usual working-class victims but middle-class families also suffered from falling incomes allied to an dearth of suitable job opportunities, which frustrated their aspirations. When coupled with state atrophy owing to recession, bringing decreasing tax revenues and a haemorrhaging of funds available for social investment, in addition to growing corruption, the political system underwent a debilitating legitimation crisis. This *mélange*, posits McClintock, stoked popular alienation, propelling individuals from various walks of life into the arms of the PCP–SL: 'Peru's economic plunge was a spark igniting dry political timbers'.[8] Based on this assessment, it is argued that the 'misery matters most' school in the academic literature on the origins of revolution, associated with authors such as Gurr and Goldstone, best explains why rebel groups like the PCP–SL could prosper. Heavily state-centred analyses that 'deride' socio-economic causes and focus on regime type, which became popular during the 1980s under the influence of Skocpol's seminal work ('closed authoritarian regimes provoke revolutionary challenge'), are regarded as inappropriate. For McClintock, as the PCP–SL's insurrection underwent a period of uninterrupted and rapid expansion within a democratic political system during 1980–92 (albeit one that suffered a legitimation crisis), 'the Peruvian experience contradicts the prevailing scholarly wisdom that the ballot box is the coffin of guerrilla movements'.[9] Contrary to the arguments of the 'state matters most' school, 'economic misery' rather than political exclusion spread discontent and led people to sympathise with the rebels, providing a steady flow of recruits for PCP–SL cells.[10]

McClintock's emphasis on the interplay between economic and political factors when accounting for PCP–SL growth between 1980 and 1992 broadly concurs with the account of the civil war presented in preceding chapters. On the matter of 'subsistence crisis', widespread rural poverty in Cajabamba–Huamachuco created a pool of 'sympathy' for the *senderistas* and induced a minority of smallholders to proffer full 'support'. It is difficult to erase declining rural living standards from the insurgency equation. The present author remembers an occasion in July 1982 when he was sitting on a sunlit patio conversing with Roberto Barrios, who, the following year would enter the ranks of *senderismo* and occupy a pivotal position within the organisation's Cajabamba operation. Replying to the banal comment that his village (Chorobamba) was located in an idyllic position, Barrios responded laconically: 'Unfortunately, you can't eat the scenery!' A couple of months later, on this occasion observing the impressive Andean landscape from the hills above the town of San Marcos in the company of a union activist in the ranks of the CCP, this friend surveyed the surroundings and exclaimed: 'Do you see Lucho? That's what it's all about! So much natural beauty. So much human misery!' Exhibiting typical forthrightness, Félix Calderón gave a sharper edge to the matter in a FEDECC editorial penned in 1979: 'You cannot have social peace when you kill people through hunger'.[11] Such comments proved wholly intelligible. With three-quarters of the farming community operating *minifundios* too small to meet household needs, resulting in generalised malnourishment, it would have been surprising if discontent was not widespread, especially as the reordering of land tenure under the military had not only raised expectations but also stimulated debate and reflection throughout the countryside. Having bypassed the overwhelming majority, the agrarian reform engendered disappointment. Taber's

observation that 'the hope of social change stimulated by even a little education produces a new social phenomenon' neatly captured the contemporary
socio-political milieux.[12] For too many *campesinos* who farmed in the northern
highlands, life remained 'nasty, brutish and short', but the extensive brouhaha
that accompanied land redistribution heightened an awareness among the
populace that their misery had a human agency.

The second variable advanced by McClintock to explain PCP–SL growth –
the impact of the 1980s debt crisis and economic mismanagement, which
limited employment opportunities for ever-expanding numbers of young people
completing tertiary education – also resonates with the situation found in
Cajabamba–Huamachuco. Over the previous chapters, examples are to be
found of schoolteachers – such as the *cajabambino* Alberto Paredes and students
from local colleges of further education (viz. the infamous *'camarada* Patty') –
who joined the ranks of *senderismo*. Even though they by no means dominated
the guerrilla apparatus to the extent suggested in the literature detailing events
in Ayacucho, they had an important role to play in the bloody drama
surrounding guerrilla activity on Sendero's 'northern front'.[13]

Equally relevant is McClintock's focus on the progressive erosion of state
legitimacy, which advanced year-on-year throughout the 1980s. After Velasco's
ousting in 1975, the perception spread steadily that government bureaucracies
held scant concerned for the citizenry's well-being. Anger on this score was
fuelled during the late 1980s and early 1990s by systemic official corruption. In
Cajabamba–Huamachuco, the nefarious activities of crooked judges,
policemen, mayors, minor officials and the greed-driven persecution of the
rondas campesinas, when allied to gross failings on the part of the political class
at national level, combined to produce a significant erosion of state ideological
hegemony. Over these years, thousands of the region's inhabitants (as
throughout Peru) would echo the Digger Gerrard Winstanley's observation that
the state was 'a government of highwaymen'. As secret service documents and
popular accounts from the study area testify, unscrupulousness combined with
incompetence made substantial numbers of citizens less disposed to collaborate with the authorities, while simultaneously increasing the likelihood that the
disaffected would proffer 'support' for the PCP–SL in all its various degrees.

Noting the shortcomings of Skocpol's strong rejection of 'voluntarist' interpretations that place emphasis on the role of insurgent apparatuses within
revolutionary situations, McClintock sympathises with Selbin's call to 'bring
the people back in' to the analysis of revolutionary situations, while recognising
the difficulties inherent in such an endeavour:

> There is no set of criteria for an 'effective' revolutionary organization that
> can be determined by social scientists. Rather the effective organization is
> one that is appropriate to its context …what matters is not the organization,
> but the fit between the organization and its context. Revolutionary organi-
> zation is a necessary but never sufficient variable in a revolutionary
> situation.[14]

Proceeding on the grounds that 'revolutionary organizations and leadership matter', even though 'rigorous analysis' of this type of apparatus 'is difficult, if not impossible', it is argued that the PCP–SL's rigid hierarchy, discipline, the personality cult surrounding Guzmán and a proclivity to employ excessive violence, all comprised strengths that became liabilities: 'on 12 September 1992, when Guzmán was captured, all the assets of authoritarianism suddenly appeared as deficiencies'.[15] Guzmán's detention 'was devastating to the organization', which, when allied to the state's improved counter-insurgency effort and new anti-terrorist legislation, 'decimated' the Party.[16] Although the discussion remains restricted to a general level, McClintock is surely right to address the issue of the PCP–SL's apparatus and the conclusions drawn generally hold true when one assesses the civil war's trajectory in the northern highlands.

Indeed, rather than minimising the impact of revolutionary organisations in the manner of Skocpol, leading scholars on the question of rural revolt and revolution have emphasised the importance of outside forces in channelling discontent. Some even go as far as Marx in arguing that peasants are 'incapable of enforcing their class interests in their own name … They cannot represent themselves, they must be represented'.[17] Jenkins, for example, holds that 'the political role of the peasantry depends on the actions of other groups. Peasant rebellion might provide the "dynamite", but other groups must provide the organizational basis.'[18] A similar position is advanced by Popkin when constructing his critique of 'moral economy' approaches to the study of unrest in the Vietnamese countryside. Arguing from a 'political economy' perspective, he posits that 'rational' peasants make 'cost-benefit calculations' and will only engage in collective mobilisation when competent 'political entrepreneurs' offer clearly discernible 'incentives'. Given that individual agriculturalists 'make the choice which they believe will maximize their expected utility', the key to mounting effective rebellion lies in the ability of outside organisations to deliver the right carrots in sufficient quantities.[19]

Such a narrow, utilitarian view of peasant political action that minimises factors such as ethnicity, political tradition and notions of what is 'right' and 'wrong' (i.e. village-based 'moral economies') cannot provide a holistic explanation of the complex relationship between PCP–SL 'fish' and peasant 'river' in Cajabamba–Huamachuco. Would *campesinos* participate in a high-risk 'prolonged people's war' of indeterminate duration, whose likely outcome was either death or torture followed by twenty years' incarceration, solely on the calculation that they might attain an extra 3 hectares of land? Rather, a complex amalgam of non-individualistic and non-economic considerations also influenced their decision-making. Popkin, like Taber before him, does nevertheless hone in on certain aspects of revolutionary organisation that have relevance to the historiography of the civil war in the northern highlands. It is argued that the 'self-abnegation of the leadership' is of crucial import if an insurgent group is to register success.[20] Rightly or wrongly, rumours spread around the region's villages that *senderista* cadres did not always act in a just manner and practise 'the self-denial of Communist organizers', as occurred in Vietnam, producing uncertainty about the motives of combatants: were they 'actually going to use the resources' acquired during the pursuit of agrarian revolutionary war 'for common rather than selfish purposes'?[21] Apart from the quality of cadres, a number of other areas were pinpointed in the previous chapter that illustrate the PCP–SL's imperfect grasp of the complexities of social life in the post-agrarian-reform countryside, all of which indicates that insufficient calibration existed, to employ McClintock's terminology, between 'the organization and the context'.

The question of 'context' and 'fit' immediately brings to mind Jeffery Paige's thought-provoking analysis on the roots of collective mobilisation. In contrast to 'moral economy' interpretations, he builds a class-based theory that sees the stimulant for rural revolt not in subsistence crisis per se, but in the nature and intensity of direct-producer exploitation within commercial agricultural systems. Particular combinations of 'cultivator' and 'noncultivator' socio-economic relations allow predictions to be made regarding the nature of unrest in the countryside. It is postulated that a certain rural social structure engenders a given type of grass-roots activity, two key determinants being the resources available to the elite and the organisational capacity of the poor. Four patterns are indentified. First, where a non-modernising elite, wholly dependent on land for its income, confronts smallholders who are also land-dependent ('the commercial hacienda system'), Paige maintains that agrarian revolt will result – 'a short, intense movement aimed at seizing land, but lacking long-run political objectives'.[22] The second scenario is a situation in which a 'modern' elite in possession of mercantile capital enters into commercial relations with direct producers. Here, a reformist farmers' movement is likely to develop around questions of prices and markets. Third, when agribusiness corporations and 'modern' plantation owners employ wage labourers, the ability of the employers to grant concessions brings a flexibility to class relations, producing a reformist labour movement primarily concerned with piecemeal improvements in wages and working conditions. Fourth, where a non-modern elite that derives its income from land employs sharecroppers or migratory semi-proletarians, the likely outcome is, respectively, a socialist or a nationalist revolutionary movement – because landowners find it difficult to grant concessions, while direct producers having little attachment to the land are endowed with powerful organisational capabilities:

> The homogeneous poorly paid, concentrated mass of workers that Marx saw as the vanguard of the revolution are found not in industrial societies, but in commercial export agriculture in the underdeveloped world. It is in such societies that the greatest incentives for class-based organization and class conflict exist.[23]

With Peru as one of the three case studies, the nation's rural economy is examined at some length and within the overall theoretical schema, the situation found in the Andes is placed in Paige's first scenario, 'the commercial hacienda system'. A striking feature of the analysis is the very stereotyped image of rural society that is presented. Following a dualistic interpretation, whereby the coast is 'modern' and the highlands 'backward', it is claimed that:

> The sierran population, cut off from outside influences by the cordillera of the Andes, remained until the 1960s a separate society with little or no participation in national life ... The agricultural export sector is almost entirely concentrated on the coast, while the subsistence sector is confined to the sierra. Coastal agriculture is capital and land intensive, orientated towards outside markets, and based on irrigation and mechanization, while sierran agriculture is land extensive, poorly capitalized, and based on an agricultural technology little changed from the time of the Incas. The manorial economy of the sierra is based on forced labor by dependent serfs and expands through the acquisition of additional landholdings rather than through technical improvements. Investment by either internal or external capital is limited to a few modern ranches.[24]

Additionally, it is claimed that 'sierran agriculture remains at subsistence level'; 'in almost all the sierra the hacienda was a purely subsistence enterprise', which operated at a technological level akin to that employed by peasant smallholders.[25] Given this degree of primitiveness, the agricultural cake is supposedly fixed ('either the peasant expanded production at the expense of the estate or the estate expanded production at the expense of the peasant'), producing a 'zero-sum' struggle over resources, chiefly land, in which the landowners strove to maintain their position through the imposition of 'serfdom' and a 'rigid, often brutal opposition to workers' organizations'.[26] In this struggle, *hacendados* could not 'concede anything because they had nothing to concede'.[27] The outcome of this situation was short-lived agrarian revolts (labour strikes by estate workers reputedly did not take place in the Andes) over land characterised by limited goals, for peasant 'interest was solely in gaining and defending land, and once this objective had been attained, they showed no interest in continued political action'.[28] Sustained mobilisation and organisation proved difficult because of smallholder 'political conservatism' and 'weak class solidarity'; once they had seized land 'they relapsed into conservatism and indifference'.[29]

This caricature of the Andean countryside, which was widely accepted in the 1970s, fails to appreciate the complexity of agricultural change and social relations in Cajabamba–Huamachuco during the twentieth century. Furthermore, it is remarkably similar to the vision of an unchanging, 'semi-feudal' Peru held by the PCP–SL: Sendero also subscribed to the myth of a subsistence-farming system cut off from the national economy, and placed an exaggerated emphasis on forced labour and 'serfdom'. As demonstrated in Chapter Two, all sectors of rural society in the northern highlands possessed a long history of involvement in commodity and labour exchange. Extensive migration had occurred since the late nineteenth century. Acceleration in agrarian capitalist development took place after 1920, with technical improvement introduced over significant areas of land on a number of substantial *latifundia*. Modernisation also arose through an intensification of production targeted at areas favourable to husbandry and crop cultivation on smaller estates and medium-scale properties, broadly along the lines predicated by Karl Kautsky in *The Agrarian Question*. In Cajabamba–Huamachuco, there was not a 'fixed agricultural product' due to an absence of productivity gains and, in consequence, a straightforward 'zero sum' situation did not arise.[30] On the other hand, a subsistence crisis did afflict the peasantry, but that is another matter.

On the social front, rural unionism had been advancing steadily within and without the hacienda sector since the 1930s, accompanied by labour and rent strikes in addition to the usual 'hidden' forms of direct-producer resistance. The claim that Andean country people are imbued with 'political conservatism, weak organization, and weak class solidarity, and as a result political mobilization is usually low', with estate workers exhibiting 'almost pathological conservatism', paints a one-sided picture that ignores the multifarious life experiences and the impact of mass migration on the consciousness of the denizens of Cajabamba–Huamachuco.[31]

Amid the erroneous historical analysis, however, Paige does pinpoint a difficulty that confronted PCP–SL cadres active in the northern highlands – how to sustain *minifundista* support for 'prolonged people's war' after land had been seized through *senderista* backing. Once successful smallholder invasions led to the acquisition of property, Paige maintained that peasants 'relapsed into the conservatism and indifference characteristic of cultivators drawing their income from the land'.[32] This conclusion smacks of an 'end of history' position that needlessly forecloses unforeseen eventualities. Given the harsh living conditions endured by the majority, 'indifference' is not an option and the current downturn in open political activity does not necessarily signify apathy or inherent 'conservatism'.

What, then, does the future hold? Did the defeat of the PCP–SL in 1994–95 signify the end of a story, or merely the conclusion to a particular chapter? Opinions on this question differ. McClintock notes that 'the decimation of the revolutionary movement did not address what was widely believed to be the root causes of the guerrilla challenge', namely widespread deprivation; as it is posited that in post-Cold War Latin America 'democracy is not enough to doom revolution' and 'economic problems are a likely catalyst of post-Cold War revolutionary movements', the implication is that insurgency has not been removed fully from Peru's political agenda.[33] Fumerton takes a different tack, arguing that although poverty and the conditions for armed rebellion persist, 'citizenship incorporation and enlarged democratic participation mean that peasants today have a greater stake in preserving and defending the system more than ever before'.[34] A more practical explanation for present-day demobilisation can be gleaned from Scott, who argues that: 'The tangible and painful memories of repression must have a chilling effect on peasants who contemplate even minor acts of resistance. It may well be that the experience of defeat for one generation of peasants precludes another rebellion until a new generation has replaced it'.[35] Given continued misery (epitomised by a cholera epidemic that swept Cajabamba in November 1997) and the multiple shortcomings of Peruvian 'democracy' in regard to its treatment of Andean countrymen and women, claims that 'peasants today have a greater stake in preserving and defending the system' are highly debatable. Since 1997 there has existed an apparent political calm in Cajabamba–Huamachuco, but this does not indicate contentment. For the moment, hunger and alienation find an expression in crime: April 1998 witnessed the mayor of Cachachi gunned down in a settling of accounts, a fate that also befell the mayor of Santiago de Chuco in December 2004. Indicatively, suspicion of being the 'intellectual author' behind the latter homicide fell upon Manuel Sánchez, burgomaster of the district capital of Mollebamba and brother of deceased '*uomo di panza*' of the region's largest drug-trafficking clan, Perciles Sánchez.

To paraphrase Guha, there exists a situation of 'domination based on minimal consent'. Large-scale disgruntlement simmers below the surface on which the ship of state floats, while clandestine *senderista* cadres continue navigating among the currents. It is as well to remember Emperor Tang Taizong's caution: 'The water can make the boat float, but it can sink it too'. All, then, appears peaceful in much the same fashion as that described to Henry Mayhew by a London costermonger during the decade following the high point of Chartist agitation: 'People fancy that when all's quiet that all's stagnating. Propagandism is going on for all that. It's when all's quiet that the seed's a-growing. Republicans and Socialists are pressing their doctrines.'[36] One hundred and fifty years later, a similar sentiment happened to be expressed more colourfully by a *senderista* prisoner held in Cajamarca's Huacariz jail, who, on 24 September 2001 penned a birthday greeting to Abimael Guzmán in his Lima cell. Clearly not having given up the struggle and promising 'to work to construct a better future for humanity', the letter to 'Presidente Gonzalo' ended on an optimistic note: 'We are the planters of beautiful seeds in fertile soil, which will put down roots and cover the fields with pretty flowers. The present weeds (*maleza*) will only remain a bad memory'.[37]

References

1   Coronel, 'Violencia política', pp. 43–45, 104–5.
2   Fumerton, *From Victims to Heroes*, pp. 58–59. His assessment is based on Dennis Chávez de Paz, *Juventud y terrorismo. Características sociales de los condenados por terrorismo y otros delitos*, Lima, Instituto de Estudios Peruanos, 1989.
3   Figures in this and following paragraphs are taken from the census of inmates undertaken by human rights lawyers working for the Vicaria de Solidaridad, Cajamarca, September 1996.
4   Isbell, 'Shining Path and Peasant Responses', p. 73.
5   Timothy Wickham-Crowley, *Guerrillas and Revolution in Latin America: a Comparative Study of Insurgents and Regimes Since 1956*, Princeton, NJ, Princeton University Press, 1992, p. 298. Quoted in Fumerton, *From Victims to Heroes*, p. 302. On the supposedly 'tranquilising' impact of land reform, see Wickham-Crowley, *Guerrillas and Revolution in Latin America*, p. 119.
6   Cynthia McClintock, *Revolutionary Movements in Latin America*, Washington, DC, United States Institute of Peace Press, 1998, pp. 14–15, 31, 168–84.

7   Ibid., p. 14.
8   Ibid., p. 161.
9   Ibid., pp. 93–94.
10 Nearly two decades earlier, Taber anticipated many of McClintock's arguments: 'Poverty does not itself engender revolution. But poverty side by side with progress creates a new amalgam; the hope of social change stimulated by even a little education produces a new social phenomenon: the ambitious poor, the rebellious poor, the cadres of the revolution, who have nothing to lose, and see much to gain around them. Without a clearly articulated cause, without forceful and persuasive leaders, without political organization, generations of slum dwellers have lived and died in misery, generations of peasants have scratched the soil, and there have been few real revolutions. What has changed in Latin America? First of all, the poor have become *poorer*, more numerous and desperate. There has been an unprecedented growth of population everywhere, a population explosion that has brought with it a corresponding *decline* in *per capita* income ... With every passing day, there are more hungry mouths to feed in Latin America and there is proportionately less food to feed them. And yet, strangely enough, their wants are not less, but greater than formerly. For while the poor have been getting poorer, they have also become increasingly aware of the wealth around them, the *potential* in which they might share ... Awareness creates, if not a revolutionary class, then a revolutionary base ... spreading misery creates a powerful revolutionary base.' *The War of the Flea*, pp. 157–58 [italics as in the original]. A fine survey of theories of revolution can be accessed in Michael Kimmel, *Revolution: a Sociological Interpretation*, Philadelphia: Temple University Press, 1990. Also see Jack Goldstone (ed.), *Revolutions, Theoretical, Comparative, and Historical Studies*, New York, Harcourt, Brace, Jovanovich, 1986; and Jack Goldstone, Ted Gurr and Farrokh Moshiri, *Revolutions of the Late Twentieth Century*, Boulder, CO, Westview Press, 1991. A particularly 'hard' version of the 'state matters most' approach is argued in Jeff Goodwin and Theda Skocpol, 'Explaining Revolutions in the Contemporary Third World', *Politics and Society* 17: 4, 1989, pp. 489–509.
11 See Chapter Three, note 8.
12 Taber, *The War of the Flea*, pp. 157–58.
13 Based on an estimate by ex-Minister of Education, Gloria Helfer, McClintock suggests that: 'By the early 1990s, perhaps thirty thousand teachers – or 15 per cent of all Peru's teachers – were Senderistas'. *Revolutionary Movements*, p. 273. This is surely an exaggeration. Ministers of Education tend to rarely leave their Lima offices and have little idea of what is happening in remote Andean provinces.
14 McClintock, *Revolutionary Movements*, p. 16, and for the argument restated, pp. 34–35, 45. Also see Eric Selbin, *Modern Latin American Revolutions*, Boulder, CO, Westview Press, 1993. Writing in 1928, César Vallejo placed equal emphasis on human agency: 'The revolutionary feeling, created by Marx, proves precisely that history is always in a balance in which each side is controlled by the apathy or the activity of men, and not by some secret or mysterious force, alien to human will'. César Vallejo, 'El espíritu polémico', *Obras completas: artículos y crónicas (1919–1939) desde Europa*, Lima, Editorial DESA, 1997, pp. 450–52.
15 McClintock, *Revolutionary Movements*, pp. 45, 91, 293.
16 Ibid., pp. 91, 140.
17 Karl Marx, 'The Eighteenth Brumaire of Louis Bonaparte', in Karl Marx and Frederick Engels, *Selected Works in One Volume*, London, Lawrence and Wishart, 1973, p. 171.
18 Craig Jenkins, 'Why do Peasants Rebel? Structural and Historical Theories of

Modern Peasant Rebellions', *American Journal of Sociology* 88: 3, 1982, p. 512.

19 Popkin, *The Rational Peasant*, p. 31.

20 Ibid., p. 261.

21 Ibid.

22 Jeffery Paige, *Agrarian Revolution: Social Movements and Export Agriculture in the Underdeveloped World*, New York, The Free Press, 1975, p. 43. Also see Margaret Somers and Walter Goldfrank, 'The Limits of Agronomic Determinism: a Critique of Paige's Agrarian Revolution', *Comparative Studies of Society and History* 21, 1979, pp. 443–58. In response to the charge of 'agronomic determinism', Paige has undertaken a number of valuable case studies (mainly on Central America) that attempt to incorporate a political dimension to the original analysis that focused heavily on rural class relations. This has led to an examination of issues such as competing factions within the agrarian elite, their respective economic strength, differences in ideological outlook and positioning vis-à-vis respective nation states. See Jeffery Paige, 'Social Theory and Peasant Revolution in Vietnam and Guatemala', *Theory and Society* 12: 6, 1983, pp. 699–737; 'Cotton and Revolution in Nicaragua', in Peter Evans et al., *States versus Markets in the World System*, London, Sage Publications, 1985, pp. 91–116; 'Coffee and Politics in Central America', in Richard Tardanico (ed.), *Crises in the Caribbean Basin*, London, Sage Publications, 1987, pp. 141–90; and *Coffee and Power: Revolution and the Rise of Democracy in Central America*, Cambridge, MA, Harvard University Press, 1997.

23 Paige, *Agrarian Revolution*, p. 34.

24 Ibid., p. 127. Paige's analysis of Andean society reflected the state of academic research in the 1970s. He used few Spanish sources and those published in English included Solomon Miller's doctoral dissertation on estates in the *sierra* of La Libertad. Two of his case studies – the Vicos Project run by Cornell University and the peasant movement that arose in La Convención – are also atypical, which adds further distortions to his interpretation of Andean society.

25 Ibid., pp. 164, 167, 339.

26 Ibid., pp. 127, 166, 341, 347.

27 Ibid., pp. 340–41.

28 Ibid., pp.131, 338, 341.

29 Ibid., pp. 342, 348.

30 Ibid., p. 341.

31 Ibid., pp. 168, 342.

32 Ibid., p. 348.

33 McClintock, *Revolutionary Movements*, pp. 139, 301, 312.

34 Fumerton, *From Victims to Heroes*, p. 333.

35 Scott, *The Moral Economy of the Peasant*, p. 226.

36 Quoted in Edward P. Thompson, *The Making of the English Working Class*, Harmondsworth, Penguin Books, 1977, p. 781.

37 Guzmán's well-wisher employed *maleza* to convey two meanings. In addition to 'weeds', it connotes '*malestar*'– 'malaise' or 'bad times'.

Bibliography

Acosta, V., 'Historia de la comunidad de Licliconga', mimeo, San Marcos, 1988.

Anon., 'Banco Agrario y violencia terrorista en Cajabamba', mimeo, Cajabamba, 1990.

Anon., 'Plan Verde: apreciación de inteligencia', mimeo, Lima, 1990.

Arce, L. (ed.), *Guerra popular en el Perú: el pensamiento Gonzalo*, Brussels, no publisher, 1989.

Becker, M., 'Mariátegui y el problema de las razas en la América Latina', *Revista Andina* 35, 2002, pp. 191–220.

Berg, R., 'Peasant Responses to Shining Path in Andahuaylas', in D. S. Palmer (ed.), *Shining Path of Peru*, London, Hurst and Company, 1992, pp. 83–104.

Berg, R., '"Sendero Luminoso" and the Peasantry of Andahuaylas', *Journal of Inter-American Studies and World Affairs* 28: 4, 1986, pp. 165–96.

Bonifaz, N., 'Las rondas campesinas, el estado y la política', mimeo, 1985.

Caballero, J. M. and J. Foronda, 'Algunos aportes para el conocimiento de los problemas post reforma agraria en ciertas zonas de Cajamarca y La Libertad', mimeo, Lima, 1976.

Cameron, M. and P. Mauceri, (eds.), *The Peruvian Labyrinth: Polity, Society, Economy*, Pennsylvania, Pennsylvania University Press, 1997.

Chavarría, J., *José Carlos Mariátegui and the Rise of Modern Peru*, Albuquerque, University of New Mexico Press, 1979.

Chávez, D., *Juventud y terrorismo. Características sociales de los condenados por terrorismo y otros delitos*, Lima, Instituto de Estudios Peruanos, 1989.

Chen Yung-fa, 'The Blooming Poppy Under the Red Sun: the Ya'an Way and the Opium Trade', in T. Saich and H. van de Ven (eds.), *New Perspectives on the Chinese Communist Revolution*, New York, M.E. Sharpe, 1994.

Claudin, F., *The Communist Movement: from Comintern to Cominform*, Harmondsworth, Penguin Books, 1975.

Clutterbuck, R., 'Peru: How to Defeat SL?', *Army Quarterly and Defence Journal*, 1992.

Congreso Nacional del Perú, *Congreso Ordinario de 1925. Diario de los Debates del Senado*, Lima, Casa Editora E. Rávago, 1925.

Coronel, J., 'Violencia política y repuestas campesinas en Huanta', in C. I. Degregori (ed.), *Las rondas campesinas y la derrota de Sendero Luminoso*, Lima, Instituto de Estudios Peruanos/Universidad Nacional San Cristóbal de Huamanga, 1996, pp. 29–116.

Cortegana, J., *Sendero en Cajabamba: Cachachi*, Trujillo, Artes Gráficas Richard Burgos, 2001.

Crabtree, J., *Peru Under García: an Opportunity Lost*, Basingstoke, Macmillan, 1992.

Deere, C. D., *Households and Class Relations: Peasants and Landlords in Northern Peru*, Berkeley, CA, University of California Press, 1990.

Degregori, C. I., *Ayacucho 1969–1979, El surgimiento de Sendero Luminoso: del movimiento por la gratuidad de la enseñanza al inicio de la lucha armada*, Lima, Instituto de Estudios Peruanos, 1990.

Degregori, C. I., 'Ayacucho después de la violencia', in C. I. Degregori (ed.), *Las rondas campesinas y la derrota de Sendero Luminoso*, Lima, Instituto de Estudios Peruanos/Universidad Nacional San Cristóbal de Huamanga, 1996, pp. 15–28.

Degregori, C. I., 'A Dwarf Star', *NACLA Report on the Americas* 24: 4, 1990–91, pp. 10–19.

Degregori, C. I., 'Reaping the Whirlwind: the *Rondas Campesinas* and the Defeat of Sendero Luminoso in Ayacucho', in K. Koonings and D. Kruijt (eds.), *Societies of Fear: the Legacy of Civil War and Terror in Latin America*, London, Zed Books, 1999, pp. 63–87.

Degregori, C. I., *'Sendero Luminoso', Parte I: Los hondos y mortales desencuentros, Parte II: Lucha armada y utopia autoritaria*, Working Papers Nos. 4 and 6, Lima, Instituto de Estudios Peruanos, 1986.

Espinoza, W., 'Geografía histórica de Huamachuco', *Historia y Cultura* 5, 1971, pp. 5–96.

Favre, H., 'Sendero Luminoso y horizontes oscuros', *Quehacer* 31, 1984, pp. 25–34.

FEDECC (Federación Departamental de Campesinos de Cajamarca), 'Acuerdos de la IV Convención Campesina de la FEDECC', mimeo, Cajamarca, February, 1974.

FEDECC, 'Acuerdos del Primer Congreso departamental de la FEDECC', mimeo, Huacataz, August, 1978.

FEDECC, *Luchas campesinas en Cajamarca*, Cajamarca, no publisher, 1975.

Federación de Rondas Campesinas de Huanico, 'Primer Congreso Interdistrital de rondas campesinas de Huanico', mimeo, Cajamarca, 1989.

Federación Provincial de Campesinos de San Marcos, 'Encuentro provinical de rondas campesinas de San Marcos', mimeo, San Marcos, 1987.

Flores Galindo, A., *La agonía de Mariátegui: la polémica con la Komintern*, Lima, DESCO, 1982.

Fournier, E., *"Feliciano": captura de un senderista rojo*, Lima, NRC Corporación Gráfica, 2002.

Fumerton, M., *From Victims to Heroes: Peasant Counter-rebellion and Civil War in Ayacucho, Peru, 1980–2000*, Amsterdam, Rozenberg Publishers, 2002.

García Sayán, D., *Tomas de tierras en el Perú*, Lima, DESCO, 1982.

Gelles, P., *Water and Power in Highland Peru: the Cultural Politics of Irrigation and Development*, New Jersey, Rutgers University Press, 2000.

Giesecke, M., 'The Trujillo Insurrection, the APRA Party and the Making of Modern Peruvian Politics', PhD thesis, University of London, 1993.

Gitlitz, J. and T. Rojas, 'Peasant Vigilante Committees in Northern Peru', *Journal of Latin American Studies* 15: 1, 1983, pp. 163–97.

Goldenberg, S., 'Los montoneros de Huanta: una jornada en las alturas navalizadas', *Debate* 28, 1984, pp. 40–45.

Goldstone, J. (ed.), *Revolutions, Theoretical, Comparative, and Historical Studies*, New

York, Harcourt, Brace, Jovanovich, 1986.

Goldstone, J., T. Gurr and F. Moshiri, *Revolutions of the Late Twentieth Century*, Boulder, CO, Westview Press, 1991.

González, R., '"Desexorcizando" a Sendero: una entrevista con Henri Favre', *Quehacer* 42, 1986, pp. 44–48.

González, R., 'Puno: el corridor senderista', *Quehacer* 39, 1986, pp. 49–58.

González, R., 'Sendero: duro desgaste y crisis estratégica', *Quehacer* 64, 1990, pp. 8–15.

Goodwin, J. and T. Skocpol, 'Explaining Revolutions in the Contemporary Third World', *Politics and Society* 17: 4, 1989, pp. 489–509.

Gorriti, G., *Sendero: historia de la guerra milenaria en el Perú*, Lima, Editorial Apoyo, 1991.

Gorriti, G. and A. Arroyo, 'La guerra de Sivia', *Caretas* 838, 18 February 1985, pp. 36–38, 72.

Graham, C., *Peru's APRA: Parties, Politics and the Elusive Quest for Democracy*, Boulder, CO, Lynne Rienner, 1992.

Guha, R., 'Domination Without Hegemony and its Historiography', in R. Guha (ed.), *Subaltern Studies VI*, New Delhi, Oxford University Press, 2003, pp. 210–309.

Hancco, C., 'Lauramarca y el movimiento democrático revolucionario del campesinado por la tierra y contra la semifeudalidad', *Crítica Andina* 3, 1979, pp. 157–73.

Haya de la Torre, A., *El retorno de la barbarie: la matanza en los penales de Lima de 1986*, Lima, Bahia Ediciones, 1988.

Hertoghe, A. and A. Labrousse, *Le Sentier Lumineux de Pérou: un nouvel intégrisme dans la tiers monde*, Paris, Editions la Découverte, 1989.

Huber, L., *'Después de Dios y la Virgen está la ronda': las rondas campesinas de Piura*, Lima, Instituto de Estudios Peruanos, 1995.

Idrogo, D., 'Informe sobre la masacre de la Guardia Civil a los ronderos de la ex-hacienda Santa Clara', mimeo, Lima, 1987.

Instituto Nacional de Cooperativas, 'Informe técnico sobre la Cooperativa Agraria de Trabajadores José Santos Chocano', mimeo, Lima, 1994.

Isbell, B. J., 'Shining Path and Peasant Responses in Rural Ayacucho', in D. S. Palmer (ed.), *Shining Path of Peru*, London, Hurst and Company, 1992, pp. 59–81.

Jenkins, C., 'Why do Peasants Rebel? Structural and Historical Theories of Modern Peasant Rebellions', *American Journal of Sociology* 88: 3, 1982, pp. 487–514.

Kimmel, M., *Revolution: a Sociological Interpretation*, Philadelphia, Temple University Press, 1990.

Kirk, R., *Grabado en piedra: las mujeres de Sendero Luminoso*, Lima, Instituto de Estudios Peruanos, 1993.

Klarén, P., *Formación de las haciendas azucareras y orígenes del APRA*, Lima, Instituto de Estudios Peruanos, 1976.

Kruijt, D., *Entre Sendero y los militares: seguridad y relaciones cívico-militares, 1950–1990*, Barcelona, Editorial Robles, 1991.

Lenin, V. I., 'Better Fewer, But Better', in *Collected Works* Vol. 33, Moscow, Progress Publishers, 1966, pp. 487–502.

Lenin, V. I., 'One Step Forward, Two Steps Back', in *Collected Works* Vol. 7, Moscow, Foreign Languages Publishing House, 1961, pp. 203–415.

Lenin, V. I., 'An Urgent Question', in *Collected Works* Vol. 4, Moscow, Foreign Languages Publishing House, 1960, pp. 221–26.

Lenin, V. I., 'What is to be Done?', in *Collected Works* Vol. 5, Moscow, Foreign Languages Publishing House, 1961, pp. 347–527.

Letts, R., *La izquierda peruana: organizaciones y tendencias*, Lima, Mosca Azul Editores, 1981.

Manrique, N., 'La década de la violencia', *Márgenes* 3: 5–6, 1989, pp. 137–82.

Manrique, N., *El tiempo de miedo: la violencia política en el Perú, 1980–1996*, Lima, Fondo Editorial del Congreso del Perú, 2002.

Manrique, N., 'The War for the Central Sierra', in S. J. Stern (ed.), *Shining and Other Paths: War and Society in Peru, 1980–1995*, Durham, NC, Duke University Press, 1998, pp. 193–223.

Mao Tse-tung (Zedong), 'Analysis of Classes in Chinese Society', in *Selected Works* Vol. 1, Beijing, Foreign Languages Press, 1967, pp. 13–21.

Mao Tse-tung (Zedong), 'The Chinese Revolution and the Chinese Communist Party', in *Selected Works* Vol. 2, Beijing, Foreign Languages Press, 1967, pp. 309–14.

Mao Tse-tung (Zedong), 'Introducing The Communist', in *Selected Works* Vol. 2, Beijing, Foreign Languages Press, 1967, pp. 289–90.

Mao Tse-tung (Zedong), 'On Protracted War', in *Selected Works* Vol. 2, Beijing, Foreign Languages Press, 1967, pp. 113–94.

Mao Tse-tung (Zedong), 'Problems of Strategy in China's Revolutionary War', in *Selected Works* Vol. 1, Beijing, Foreign Languages Press, 1967, pp. 179–254.

Mao Tse-tung (Zedong), 'Problems of Strategy in Guerrilla War Against Japan', in *Selected Works* Vol. 2, Beijing, Foreign Languages Press, 1967, pp. 79–112.

Mao Tse-tung (Zedong), 'Problems of War and Strategy', in *Selected Works* Vol. 2, Beijing, Foreign Languages Press, 1967, pp. 219–35.

Mao Tse-tung (Zedong), 'Report on an Investigation of the Peasant Movement in Hunan', in *Selected Works* Vol. 1, Beijing, Foreign Languages Press, 1967, pp. 23–59.

Mao Tse-tung (Zedong), 'The Struggle in the Chingkang Mountains', in *Selected Works* Vol. 1, Beijing, Foreign Languages Press, 1967, pp. 73–104.

Mao Tse-tung (Zedong), 'Why is it that Red Political Power can Exist in China?', in *Selected Works* Vol. 1, Beijing, Foreign Languages Press, 1967, pp. 63–72.

Mariátegui, J. C., *Ideología y política*, Lima, Empresa Editora Amauta, 1971.

Mariátegui, J. C., *Seven Interpretive Essays on Peruvian Reality*, Austin, TX, University of Texas Press, 1974.

Marx, K., 'The Eighteenth Brumaire of Louis Bonaparte', in K. Marx and F. Engels, *Selected Works in One Volume*, London, Lawrence and Wishart, 1973.

Mauceri, P., *Militares: insurgencia y democratización en el Perú, 1980–1988*, Lima, Instituto de Estudios Peruanos, 1989.

Mauceri, P., *State Under Siege: Development and Policy Making in Peru*, Boulder, CO, Westview Press, 1996.

McClintock, C., *Revolutionary Movements in Latin America*, Washington, DC, United States Institute of Peace Press, 1998.

McClintock, C., 'Why Peasants Rebel: the Case of Peru's Sendero Luminoso', *World Politics* 37: 1, 1984, pp. 48–84.

Méndez-Gastelumendi, C., 'The Power of Naming, or the Construction of Ethnic and National Identities in Peru: Myth, History and Iquichanos', *Past and Present*

171, 2001, pp. 127–60.

Mercado, R., *El Partido Comunista del Perú 'Sendero Luminoso'*, Lima, Editorial Cultura Popular, 1982.

Meseguer, D., *José Carlos Mariátegui y su pensamiento revolucionario*, Lima, Instituto de Estudios Peruanos, 1974.

Miller, S., 'Hacienda to Plantation in Northern Peru: the Processes of Proletarianization', in J. H. Steward (ed.), *Contemporary Change in Traditional Societies. Volume III: Mexican and Peruvian Communities*, Urbana, IL, University of Illinois Press, 1970, pp. 134–225.

Nagl, J., *Counterinsurgency Lessons from Malaya and Vietnam: Learning to Eat Soup with a Knife*, London, Praeger Publishers, 2002.

Nugent, D., *Modernity at the Edge of Empire: State, Individual and Nation in the Northern Peruvian Andes, 1885–1935*, Stanford, CA, Stanford University Press, 1997.

Obando, E., 'Diez años de guerra antisubversiva: una pequeña historia', *Quehacer* 72, 1991, pp. 46–53.

Ortega, V., *Un episodio de la revolución de 1898*, Lima, Imprenta Luz, 1947.

Paige, J., *Agrarian Revolution: Social Movements and Export Agriculture in the Underdeveloped World*, New York, The Free Press, 1975.

Paige, J., 'Coffee and Politics in Central America', in R. Tardanico (ed.), *Crises in the Caribbean Basin*, London, Sage Publications, 1987, pp. 141–90.

Paige, J., *Coffee and Power: Revolution and the Rise of Democracy in Central America*, Cambridge, MA, Harvard University Press, 1997.

Paige, J., 'Cotton and Revolution in Nicaragua', in P. Evans et al., *States versus Markets in the World System*, London, Sage Publications, 1985, pp. 91–116.

Paige, J., 'Social Theory and Peasant Revolution in Vietnam and Guatemala', *Theory and Society* 12: 6, 1983, pp. 699–737.

PCP–SL (Partido Comunista del Perú–Sendero Luminoso), 'Analisis de nuestra guerra en la región comprendida entre los años desde 1980 hasta 1985', mimeo, 1995.

PCP–SL, 'Contra las ilusiones constitucionales y por el estado de nueva democracia', in L. Arce (ed.), *Guerra popular en el Perú: el pensamiento Gonzalo*, Brussels, no publisher, 1989, pp. 93–111.

PCP–SL, 'Desarrollar la guerra popular sirviendo a la revolución mundial', in L. Arce (ed.), *Guerra popular en el Perú: el pensamiento Gonzalo*, Brussels, no publisher, 1989, pp. 217–304.

PCP–SL, 'Desarrollemos la guerra de guerrillas', in L. Arce (ed.), *Guerra popular en el Perú: el pensamiento Gonzalo*, Brussels, no publisher, 1989, pp. 179–204.

PCP–SL, '¡Gloria al día de la heroicidad!', mimeo, Lima, 1987.

PCP–SL, 'Programa general de la revolución democrática', in L. Arce. (ed.), *Guerra popular en el Perú: el pensamiento Gonzalo*, Brussels, no publisher, 1989, pp. 412–13.

PCP–SL, 'Retomemos a Mariátegui y recontituyamos su partido', in L. Arce (ed.), *Guerra popular en el Perú: el pensamiento Gonzalo*, Brussels, no publisher, 1989, pp. 59–91.

Pino del, P., 'Tiempos de Guerra y de dioses: ronderos, evangélicos y senderistas en el valle del río Apurímac', in C. I. Degregori (ed.), *Las rondas campesinas y la derrota de Sendero Luminoso*, Lima, Instituto de Estudios Peruanos/Universidad Nacional San Cristóbal de Huamanga, 1996, pp. 117–88.

PNP *see* Policia Nacional del Perú

Policía Nacional del Perú (PNP), 'Apreciación de la situación de inteligencia en …', mimeo, 1993.

Policía Nacional del Perú (PNP), 'Apreciación de la situación subversiva en …', mimeo, 1996.

Poole, D. and G. Rénique, 'The New Chroniclers of Peru: US Scholars and their "Shining Path" of Peasant Rebellion', *Bulletin of Latin American Research* 10: 2, 1991, pp. 133–91.

Poole, D. and G. Rénique, *Peru: Time of Fear*, London, Latin American Bureau, 1992.

Popkin, S., *The Rational Peasant: the Political Economy of Rural Society in Vietnam*, Berkeley, CA, University of California Press, 1979.

Reid, M., *Peru: Paths to Poverty*, London, Latin American Bureau, 1985.

Rénique, G., 'Apogee and Crisis of a "Third Path": *Mariateguismo*, "People's War" and Counterinsurgency in Puno, 1987–1994', in S. J. Stern (ed.), *Shining and Other Paths: War and Society in Peru, 1980–1995*, Durham, NC, Duke University Press, 1998, pp. 307–38.

Salcedo, J. M., 'Puno: ¿esperando a Sendero?', *Quehacer* 36, 1985, pp. 51–64.

Scott, J., *The Moral Economy of the Peasant: Rebellion and Subsistence in Southeast Asia*, New Haven, CT, Yale University Press, 1976.

Selbin, E., *Modern Latin American Revolutions*, Boulder, CO, Westview Press, 1993.

Somers, M. and W. Goldfrank, 'The Limits of Agronomic Determinism: a Critique of Paige's *Agrarian Revolution*', *Comparative Studies of Society and History* 21, 1979, pp. 443–58.

Starn, O., *'Con los llanques todo barro': reflexiones sobre rondas campesinas, protesta rural y nuevos movimientos sociales*, Lima, Instituto de Estudios Peruanos, 1991.

Starn, O., '"I Dreamed of Foxes and Hawks": Reflections on Peasant Protest, New Social Movements and the Rondas Campesinas of Northern Peru', in A. Escobar and S. Alvarez (eds.), *The Making of Social Movements in Latin America: Identity, Strategy and Democracy*, Boulder, CO, Westview Press, 1992, pp. 89–111.

Starn, O., *Nightwatch: the Politics of Protest in the Andes*, Durham, NC, Duke University Press, 1999.

Starn, O., 'La resistencia de Huanta', *Quehacer* 84, 1993, pp. 34–41.

Starn, O., 'Sendero, soldados y ronderos en el Mantaro', *Quehacer* 74, 1991, pp. 60–68.

Taber, R., *The War of the Flea: Guerrilla Warfare Theory and Practice*, St Albans, Paladin, 1974.

Tapia, C., *Las fuerzas armadas y Sendero Luminoso: dos estrategias y un final*, Lima, Instituto de Estudios Peruanos, 1997.

Taylor, L., 'Agrarian Unrest and Political Conflict in Puno, 1985–1987', *Bulletin of Latin American Research* 6: 2, 1987, pp. 135–62.

Taylor, L., *Bandits and Politics in Peru: Landlord and Peasant Violence in Hualgayoc, 1900–1930*, Cambridge, Centre of Latin American Studies, 1986.

Taylor, L., 'Counter-insurgency Strategy, the PCP–Sendero Luminoso and the Civil War in Peru, 1980–1996', *Bulletin of Latin American Research* 17: 1, 1998, pp. 35–58.

Taylor, L., 'Main Trends in Agrarian Capitalist Development, Cajamarca, Peru, 1880–1976', PhD thesis, University of Liverpool, 1979.

Taylor, L., *Maoism in the Andes: Sendero Luminoso and the Contemporary Guerrilla*

Movement in Peru, Working Paper No. 2, Liverpool, Centre for Latin American Studies, 1983.

Taylor, L., 'The Origins of APRA in Cajamarca, 1928–1935', *Bulletin of Latin American Research* 19: 4, 2000, pp. 437–59.

Taylor, L., 'Sociedad y política en Contumazá, 1876–1900', in L. Taylor, *Estructuras agrarias y cambios sociales en Cajamarca, siglos xix–xx*, Cajamarca, Asociación Obispo Martínez Compañón, 1994, pp. 45–104.

Thompson, E. P., *The Making of the English Working Class*, Harmondsworth, Penguin Books, 1977.

Thompson, R., *Defeating Communist Insurgency*, London, Chatto & Windus, 1966.

Thorndike, G., *El año de la barbarie: Perú 1932*, Lima, Mosca Azul Editores, 1973.

Uceda, R., *Muerte en el Pentagonito: los cementerios secretos del Ejército Peruano*, Bogotá, Editorial Planeta, 2004.

Vallejo, C., 'El espíritu polémico', in *Obras completas: artículos y crónicas (1919–1939), desde Europa*, Lima, Editorial DESA, 1997.

Vargas Llosa, M. et al., *Informe de la Comisión Investigadora de los sucesos de Uchuraccay*, Lima, Editora Perú, 1983.

Vanden, H., *National Marxism in Latin America: José Carlos Mariátegui's Thought and Politics*, Boulder, CO, Lynne Rienner, 1986.

Vásquez, F., 'Las alturas de Sendero: informe de Puno', *Debate* 40, 1986, pp. 29–38.

Wickham-Crowley, T., *Guerrillas and Revolution in Latin America: a Comparative Study of Insurgents and Regimes Since 1956*, Princeton, NJ, Princeton University Press, 1992.

Wolf, E., *Peasant Wars of the Twentieth Century*, London, Faber & Faber, 1971.

Zaugg, M., 'Textile Production and Structural Crises: the Case of Late Colonial Peru', PhD thesis, University of Liverpool, 1993.

Index